THE
STRENGTH
OF A NATION

THE
STRENGTH
OF A NATION

Six years of Australians fighting for the nation and
defending the homefront in WWII

MICHAEL McKERNAN

ALLEN&UNWIN

First published in Australia in 2006

Allen & Unwin
83 Alexander Street
Crows Nest NSW 2065
Australia
Phone: (61 2) 8425 0100
Fax: (61 2) 9906 2218
Email: info@allenandunwin.com
Web: www.allenandunwin.com

National Library of Australia
Cataloguing-in-Publication entry:

McKernan, Michael, 1945-.
The strength of a nation : six years of Australians fighting for the nation
and defending the homefront in WWII

Includes Index.
ISBN 978 1 74114 714 8.

ISBN 1 74114 714 X.

1. World War, 1939 - 1945 - Participation, Australian. 2. Australia -
History, Military - 20th century. I. Title.

940.540 994

Maps by Map Graphics
Index by Russell Brooks
Set in 12/14.5 pt Goudy Old Style by Midland Typesetters, Australia
Printed in Australia by McPherson's Printing Group

10 9 8 7 6 5 4 3 2 1

CONTENTS

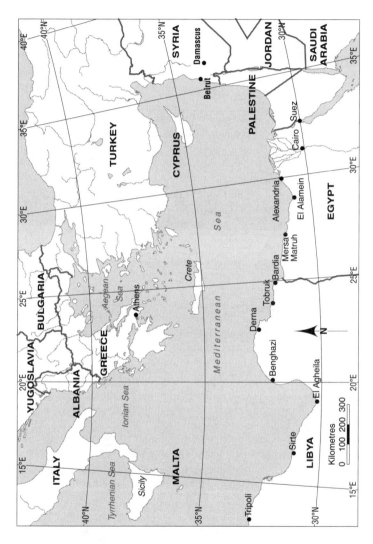

The Eastern Mediterranean, 1940–41

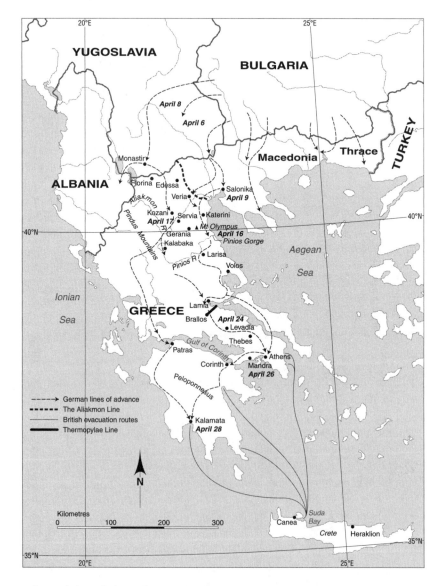

The withdrawal through Greece, 1941

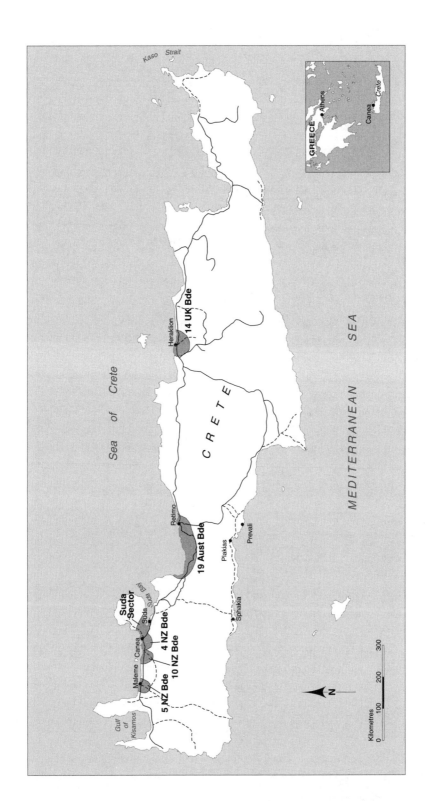

Crete, May 1941

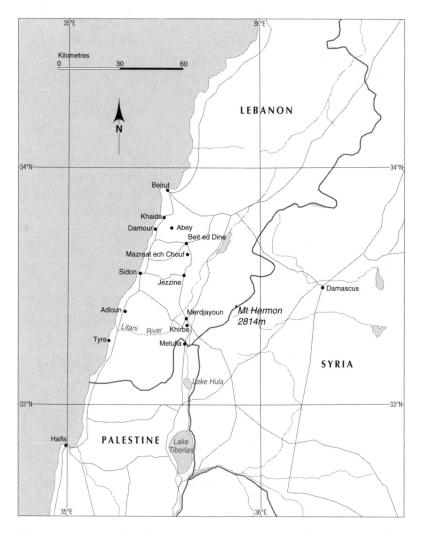

The 7th Division field of operations, 1941

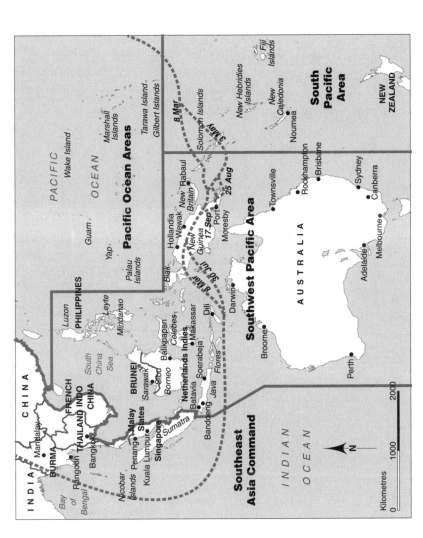

South-West Pacific area and the extent of the Japanese advance

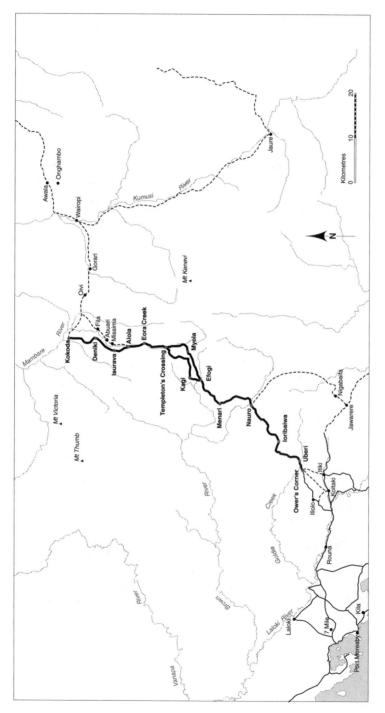

The Kokoda Track, Papua New Guinea

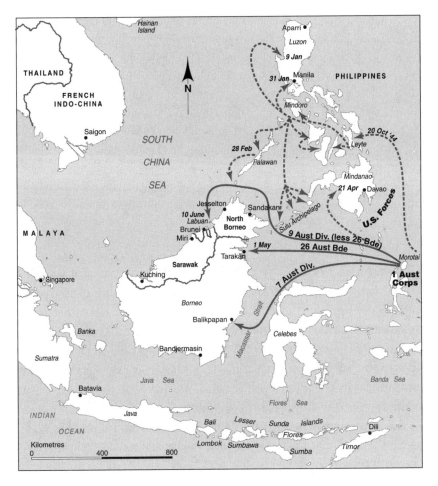

Allied political campaigns, 1945

ACKNOWLEDGMENTS

For me this book is the culmination of many years of working in the field of Australian military history. I have enjoyed a happy working life first teaching courses in Australian history as an academic, then working as a museum administrator and historian at the Australian War Memorial, and also as a historical adviser to three successive ministers for Veterans' Affairs taking veterans from the First and Second World Wars on return visits to the battlesites they had made famous.

So I have had the enormous privilege of walking on First and Second World War battlefields with Australians who fought there. I have listened to their stories and seen battle and war through their eyes.

I also worked with those making the Keith Murdoch Sound Archive of Australia in the War of 1939–1945 for the Australian War Memorial, and listened to a part, at least, of every tape to certify its place in the archive. As a reviewer and broadcaster I have read a great number of the books published in Australia in the past decade that deal with the Second World War.

In shaping and writing this book I know how much I am indebted to the people with whom I shared all these experiences. The veterans with whom I travelled; colleagues with whom I worked at the Australian War Memorial from 1981–1996; historians and writers whose books I have read with admiration and interest; friends for whom the issues and questions of Australia in the war of 1939–1945 are still lively and engrossing.

To assist with the research and writing of this book I was delighted to be appointed Adjunct Professor in the John Curtin Institute of Public Policy at the Curtin University of Technology, Perth, Western Australia. I thank those who arranged the appointment and I am, of course, honoured by it.

Though my debts are many, this book is not footnoted as is normal for history. To have footnoted it adequately would have involved a note at the end of almost every sentence, seriously placing at risk the reader's potential enjoyment of the book. But I do say to any reader who wishes to track down a source, contact me through my publishers and I will be only too happy to provide references and further evidence.

Those who know this field well will recognise how much I have depended upon the following writers: John Coates for his remarkable *The Atlas of Australia's Wars*; David Horner, our finest current military historian; Peter Brune; the editors of *The Oxford Companion to Australian Military History* and the editors of *The Oxford Companion to the Second World War*; the editors of *The Australian Dictionary of Biography*; Peter Dornan; Barney Roberts; Bill Edgar; Neil McDonald; Harry Gordon; Alan Warren; Phillip Bradley; Tom Frame; Mark Johnston; Peter Stanley; Joan Beaumont; Alan Stephens; the official Australian historians of the Second World War; and dozens of others.

I thank particularly Stephen Yorke and Paul Macpherson for their careful reading of the manuscript, and where I rejected their advice I know I did so at my own peril. I thank, too, Geoffrey Pryor for his lively interest, expansive knowledge and stimulating conversation. I thank Ros Casey for technical assistance and moral support, and Alex Casey for his generosity of spirit.

I thank my publishers Allen & Unwin for support and encouragement, particularly Ian Bowring; and my editors, Alexandra Nahlous and Joanne Holliman.

My last thanks, as always, are to my wife Michalina Stawyskyj and my daughters Katherine McKernan and Jane McKernan. They are my inspiration and my guides without whom the whole enterprise would be pointless.

'The strength of a nation is determined by the character of its people.'

John Curtin
Prime Minister of Australia
3 September 1942

PROLOGUE

The first Sunday in September 1939 was Father's Day. Seen as something of an American notion, Father's Day in Australia was not as overtly commercial as it is today; it was really a family day. Many fathers that day might have been in a reflective mood, more perhaps than was usual for Australian men; they could probably sniff the danger in the air.

To be a father in 1939 meant you would not have been born much later than 1920. It also meant that you would have been born into one of the most taxing times in Australian history. Older fathers on that day of 3 September 1939 might have remembered the years they had spent at the Great War—those born in 1890 or the decade earlier must have faced the dilemma of whether or not to go to war. Some would now have sons and daughters in their late teens and early twenties and were perhaps pondering whether their young would soon be facing the same prospect. Cruel timing. To be turning thoughts to war just as a man might have been looking to the future with a little more confidence than he would have had during previous decades.

Australians had looked to the future with optimism in the first decade and a half of the twentieth century, but life became grim with the war from 1914 to 1918 and all its suffering, and then the grief and uncertainty that followed throughout most of the twenties. In the 1920s Australia had become a disputatious society with people, it seemed, forever at each other's throats. There was revolution—Bolshevism—in the air, industrial turmoil and a society that seemed to have lost its way. And to top it off, the Great Depression.

The Great Depression, born in America, savaged most of the world, and it had been particularly tough in Australia which suffered from high debt and too great a dependence on fragile rural industries. Fathers might have only just got back to work in the last 12 months or so after years of enforced idleness. Some of their sons might still have been looking for work as they probably had been since leaving school. If there was a time *not* to be born in Australia, 1890 was about it.

Is this version of Australia from 1914 to the 1930s what today's conservatives call black armband history: the idea that historians always seek out the negative and the bad? I do not think so. To me it feels like the reality experienced by many Australians back then. So Father's Day in 1939 would have been a good chance for a long quiet think: 'Thank God we at least survived it all', many might have thought. 'But, my God, where is the world heading now? Not war again, don't tell me that.'

In Kew, one of Melbourne's more affluent suburbs, one family had gathered around the fireplace in the living room, toasting crumpets as they finished off a quietly pleasant day. A father, his wife, their two daughters and the father's unmarried aunt, Ethel. The earlier war had personally touched only Aunt Ethel. The father had not enlisted, he was just a bit too young his people had said—they were determined to keep him at home. His decision not to go to war had rankled and unsettled him for years; moreover, he had felt forever left out of the fellowship of the Australian male. Even so, his wife and daughters loved him no less, and although the Great Depression had seen cutbacks and shortages—recycled clothes and few, if any, luxuries—most of Melbourne would have considered them pretty well-off. And anyway their factory was busier now in 1939, and Bedggood shoes were selling well again, all around Australia. What was there to be troubled about?

The radio in this warm and pleasant room was playing in the background—Sunday night music, respectful of the day, relaxing. Then an announcer interrupted: 'Here is the Prime Minister of Australia.' This family knew Prime Minister Menzies personally, his wife and his children. The Bedggoods shared a back fence with the Menzies and had been neighbours for years, yarning in the streets when pushing the babies in their prams, that sort of thing. Pleasant agreeable conversations about the cricket and the football, the children's schools, the way the world was.

Australians of a certain generation can still probably make a fair fist of most of the prime minister's words that night. When Robert Menzies came across the airwaves he was on every radio station in the country, national and commercial—the first time such a hook-up had been achieved. Menzies' words became etched into the memories of that generation. 'Fellow Australians,' he began, 'It is my melancholy duty to inform you officially . . . that Australia is also at war.' There was nothing in the prime minister's presentation, or in his words, that was joyous, boastful or excited. Quite the reverse; his tone was sombre, his words measured. Indeed he concluded in a way that showed his deep concern for the events he was anticipating: 'May God, in His mercy and compassion, grant that the world may soon be delivered from this agony.'

After the prime minister had finished speaking the station resumed its program of music. In those days there were no experts to leap in headfirst after a politician had spoken. No hastily summoned commentators ready in an instant to dissect and debate, to put a spin on what it all might mean. Experts back then—and there were few of them—were largely university men, who wrote out in longhand their thoughtful summaries of world news, their judicious explanations of what was happening and why. These experts were given days, often weeks, to prepare their

opinions from the peace of their studies, scripts to be read out on
the radio that would be densely argued, almost footnoted. Not
instant and excited debates and point-scoring between a man of
the left and a man of the right. The only people able to interpret
for listeners what the future might hold and what Australia might
expect from the war were the editorial writers in the newspapers
that would be delivered over the coming days. Unsigned pieces,
though measured, thoughtful, with nothing brash or shrill.

Beryl Bedggood, just 16 years old, sat still during the broadcast,
trying to take in all that the prime minister, her neighbour, had just
said and what it would mean for them and their country. It was a
significant moment in this young woman's life and she remembered
it with precision and clarity even 50 years later. These people, like
others in living rooms across the country, had seen it coming of
course; indeed there had been an official warning of the likelihood
of war from the prime minister only a few days earlier. But he had
had to make that broadcast in the dead of night—the timing
dictated by the announcement from London—even with the likelihood that very few people were listening, in order to start the
motions that the Commonwealth War Book laid down. Over
the Father's Day weekend people had kept the radio on, even in the
foyer of cinemas and in dance halls on the Saturday night, just in
case there was something to be said. While they had expected the
news, when it came it was still shocking.

No one spoke for a few minutes and the house in Kew was
quiet. What would it mean for the family, for friends? Would the
boys at Scotch, with whom Beryl was just now becoming friendly,
be caught up in it? And the boys in all the other schools. Tennis
partners, dance lesson survivors, talkers and walkers, would they
all be going to war? And would there be a place, too, for girls in this
war? You would think about those things if you were 16 and your
prime minister told you, officially, that Australia was at war. Beryl
remembered looking around the room, at her mother and father,
absorbed, and then at her great aunt, and she was shocked to see
aunt Ethel in tears.

'You girls don't understand it,' the older woman said. 'The loss
of loved ones, the waiting for news, the casualty lists.' Her 'best
boy' was killed in the Great War and she was never to marry—that

was the cost to this one Australian woman. There were tears in many households that Father's Day. Worried men everywhere damped down the fire, put out the cat and went to bed, perhaps not to sleep.

Worried men, men not sleeping. How do I know that; how can I write that? Alright, I'm guessing. World War II was as vast in its involvement of the peoples of the world as any event in human history. We cannot possibly know the story of each person that the war touched and shaped, but we can try to enter their lives imaginatively to see how this vast and awful event involved so many of them. We can look at the lives of some individual Australians and find they might be representative of the wider body of people. We can try, and yes, that might involve a bit of guesswork.

Even in Australia—a small country in terms of population, just some seven million people—nearly one million men and women eventually ended up in uniform. But that only scratches at the surface of Australia's involvement. Do not forget the mothers and the fathers of those one million, their brothers and sisters and their friends. Do not forget, either, the millions in war industries, factories and farms, that would keep that million uniformed people fed, clothed and equipped—and other nations' troops too, for Australia would have a vital role in feeding and supplying them. Do not forget for a second, either, the boys and girls too young to fight but doing what they could to help Mum and Dad. Earnest little boys learning aircraft identification, or taking one of the world maps that the newspapers loved to print, sticking it on a wall in the bedroom or kitchen and then moving Australian troops and airmen and ships around the globe. Just to be seen to be doing something.

All sorts of Australians were involved in some way. Am I going to tell you each one's story? Of course not. But I will tell you some of the stories that have come to me in such a variety of ways over time. And then I will ask you to believe that it was like that, too, for others. A man bailed me up in a car park years ago, after a talk I'd given about war, to tell me his story. He had been at school for all the war years but his father and his older brother had served. He was at home in South Melbourne with his mother and his older sister. They saw a lot of his older brother's wife, his sister-in-law, though she lived a few suburbs away. His brother had become a prisoner of war when Singapore fell; they had a few letter-cards to let them know that he was alive. Nothing more. The agony of not knowing was his mother's and his sister-in-law's war. One Saturday morning—he remembered the day so well, it was after the peace had come on 15 August 1945 and he was in bed having a bit of a lie-in, relaxing—he heard his mother scream, a sound he will never forget. He rushed to the kitchen: what was wrong? His mother looked awful; his sister was in tears. Barry was ordered back to his room. Later, he's not sure how long really, his sister-in-law arrived and the terrible sobbing started again. His own sister then told him that they'd got a telegram to say his brother had died in captivity at the hands of the Japanese many months before. Hopes deferred were now hopes denied. The joyous and much-anticipated homecoming would never be. This is what happened in that one family. I can't tell you that it was like that for all the families of the 8000 Australians in the Japanese prison camps who died in captivity, but I have no reason to believe that it was not like that for most.

I am asking you to accept as you read this book that the lives we encounter here stand in some way for many other lives, too. That what happened in Kew on that momentous Father's Day happened elsewhere and was a part of the Australian experience of war. That what happened at South Melbourne after the end of the war was a part, also, of the Australian experience of war. That in knowing something of the individual experience we can know something of the general experience too.

1. LEGACY

In 1923, in Hobart, one of the better leaders of the First Australian Imperial Force (AIF), Major General Sir John Gellibrand, founded what he called the Remembrance Club. It was designed for the mutual support and to foster the business interests of Tasmanian survivors of the First World War. Initially, when the soldiers had come home from France or Palestine, they had wanted to forget all about war, to get away from it, from orders, from discipline, from their own memories. So in the early years after the war, instead of coming together in fellowship and memory, the old soldiers tended to go their own separate ways.

But it did not work for many. Indeed, as many of them found, they definitely needed one another. They discovered that those who had not served in the war simply could not understand them. Many of the returned soldiers were in and out of jobs, unsettled, looking for something, but they did not know what. Even General Gellibrand felt like that, filling top jobs as befitting one of his rank—public service commissioner in Tasmania, police commissioner in Victoria, member of the federal parliament—but never really sticking at one thing during the 1920s.

The Remembrance Club was initially designed to look after the interests of ex-servicemen, to help those who needed the companionship of their mates, who needed help to cope with civilian life, for whom the bonds forged in war were still the strongest bonds of all. It inspired a similar club in Melbourne. But what were they to call it? One of the earliest members, Frank Selleck, wrote: 'We have got to remember that in a way we survivors have received a legacy to see that the ideals our comrades died fighting for are maintained in Australia.' So they named it the Legacy Club. Perhaps they were right to think that they were the special possessors of this legacy of remembrance, but other Australians could feel, and decidedly did feel, that they were also the inheritors of it. There are two streams, then, in the legacy that was bequeathed by the men of 1914–18: to the survivors of the war themselves, and to all other Australians.

If the men who had been to war were doing it tough, as many were, how hard was it for the widows and fatherless children of the men who did not return? The survivors, the men of the old AIF, felt a special responsibility for the dependants of their mates. In some senses caring for these dependants was a means for the returned men to cope with the thought that surfaced too often: I survived while he is gone. 'Why me, why did I survive,' a Second World War veteran asked me in a far-off war cemetery in Borneo in 1995, 50 years after the end of his war, 'while better men than me and men with families, too, died?' It was a question that veterans of both world wars so often asked themselves.

To ease, in part, the pain of what some have called 'survivor guilt' the veterans of the First World War took on a measure of responsibility for the forlorn families of their mates who had been killed. There were war widow pensions paid in Australia, but they were pretty miserable really. In 1926 Melbourne Legacy directed its attention, its reason for being, to the children of the men who had died at war, or had died in Australia afterwards from the effects of war. But Legacy was not just about money, though even a little bit helped, Legacy was a presence in the home, a friend that a woman could turn to for advice, for a steady hand when needed, a source of help for the kids in their schooling, in their life choices, for a bit of a boot up the backside when needed, just as Dad would have done. Legacy Clubs handed on the torch that was their symbol with the slogan: 'They know, after the war comes the battle.'

But the legacy of the 'Great War'—the soldiers' name for the most awful war the world had yet seen—extended way beyond these clubs. The Great War permeated every part of Australian life during what we now term the 'inter-war years'. Let a kaleidoscopic picture try to capture something of that legacy before we settle down to detailed aspects of the Great War experience which would severely impact on Australia in the Second World War, for it is my argument that you simply cannot come to the Second World War without a clear understanding of how much of it is shaped by the war that had ended just 21 years earlier.

George Johnston makes up the first pieces of this picture in his novel set during the inter-war and Second World War years, *My Brother Jack*. Both Johnston's parents served overseas in World War I: she as a nurse, he as a soldier. Perhaps they came back with their fair share of survivor guilt. In any case, in the novel the nurse–mother continues her work at the Caulfield Repatriation Hospital in Melbourne and her sons, Jack and Davey Meredith, visit the wards every Sunday for the sake of the veterans.

Turn the kaleidoscope ever so slightly to the men in hospital—some for months, some for years, some forever—another legacy of that war. The 'man in the bath', having lost his outer skin cover in France in a gas attack, was sentenced to spend the rest of his life immersed in a bath of some liquid to hold off immediate and fatal infection. 'G'day, digger,' people would greet him as they went about the vast repatriation hospital. 'I nursed him at Concord,' someone said to me when I told this story in public one time. 'He was cheerful enough and died in the late 1940s, I think.' It is shocking, truly shocking, even to think about the life this man lived.

Then there were the amputees, bravely carving out a new life for themselves. There were the men who would die too young with gas in their lungs, living, they knew—even as they struggled to provide for their families—on borrowed time. A wheat farmer in Victoria's Mallee—a soldier–settler granted his patch of land on returning from the war—first arrived in Australia in 1912, aged 20, and enlisted in 1915. Returning decorated with the Military Medal and Bar, he married a local farmer's daughter in 1925 and had five children—four daughters and a son. This man died in 1943, aged 51; the result of gas, they said. At first, in compiling records in the 1920s for the Australian War Memorial's Roll of Honour, which would record the name of every Australian killed by war, they tried to keep track of those who died after returning to Australia, just as much war casualties as those blown up in France. But they soon gave up the effort; there were too many.

But these men had at least come home. Davey Meredith, the central character around whom *My Brother Jack* revolves, is just a little kid in an early grade at school, walking in a street near the Elsternwick shops in Melbourne, stopping outside a long-abandoned photographer's studio. They'd done well in the years of the Great War, the photographers; every soldier needed a portrait of himself for his mum, and probably for his girlfriend or his wife. Young Davey is looking at a collection of these portraits in the shopfront window, the portraits curling up a little, fading in the sunlight, dust-covered, but recognisably the faces of men— strong, Australian men. An older boy comes down the street, kicking a tennis ball as boys do. Davey knows him by sight from school. This boy stops to look in at the portraits, too. They both stand there, not saying anything. Eventually the older boy speaks, to no one in particular: 'All of them blokes in there is dead, you know.' Davey runs home, trying not to cry because, as he says, 'I didn't know what it was I wanted to cry about.'

Robert and Isabella Fothergill, though, knew what their tears were for. I first came across them and their surviving children in the 'In Memoriam' columns of the Melbourne *Argus*. I was writing a history about the Australian War Memorial and I wanted something that would capture, with force, the strength of the grief so many Australian mothers and fathers, wives, brothers and sisters had lived with in all the years since the Great War. I knew of it first hand. My own grandfather had lost two brothers in that war, their deaths a month apart in mid-1918, with the war so very nearly over. Jack Fothergill, second son of Robert and Isabella of Euroa, died much earlier than my great-uncles, on 25 April 1915, the first

Anzac Day. I was looking in the paper at the 'In Memoriam' notices for another Anzac Day, dated some seven years after 1915. Would the terrible grief still be there, I wondered. I read the Fothergill's prose poem in memory of their son:

> ... plucked like a flower in bloom, so bright, so young, so loving. It's sad but true the best are first to die. Darling Jack, if only I could see your grave I would die happy.

That was enough for me, I had the quote I needed to describe that widespread, post-war grief: 'if only I could see your grave I would die happy'.

Years later, though, looking for stories that would help explain the cemeteries at Gallipoli and on the Western Front that I visited when I was taking Australians on battlefield tours, I thought of those words. I wondered if there were more. And so I returned to the newspaper. There was an 'In Memoriam' notice in 1916, on the first anniversary of Jack Fothergill's death, from his 'sorrowing parents, brother and sisters', and an eight-line poem. There was nothing in 1917, but in 1918 the notice was inserted by 'R. and I. Fothergill, late of Euroa', and I wondered if they had missed inserting a poem in 1917 in the mess of moving from Euroa to Melbourne. And I wondered, too, if they had moved because the little town of Euroa held too many memories for them of their much-loved son. There was an 'In Memoriam' notice thereafter in the *Argus* on 25 April each year from 1918 to 1948. For 30 years they had recalled and written about their grief. It never died; it never went away. And each year a freshly minted poem, not recycled, original each year, stood testament to that. Robert Fothergill died on 19 August 1939; Isabella died sometime in 1945–46. 'However long our lives may last', they had written in 1925:

> Whatever land we view,
> Whatever joys or grief be ours
> We will think of you, Jack
> And think of how you died, darling
> You gave your long life for others
> And we are left behind to grieve.

I don't believe every bereaved family in Australia went to such efforts to publicly record their grief, but I do think thousands upon thousands of Australians knew and understood the grief that the Fothergills wrote about. It is the backdrop to the war that comes next in the Australian story.

Turn the kaleidoscope again and see how the Great War is recalled during one part of inter-war Australia. Boys and girls at their desks in their classrooms, learning to read and then strengthening their understanding of the world by reading 'good writing'. In Victoria they did this with the help of the *Victorian School Readers* series—a book for students each year from years 1 to 8. (The other states had similar aids, too, it is just that I have the Victorian series on my shelves.) Working backwards from the eighth book, which includes: 'The Departure of the Anzacs from Mudros' by John Masefield; 'At Anzac' by Leon Gellert; 'Greater Than We Knew' by Mildred Huxley; 'To the Fallen' by Laurence Binyon; 'The Legacy' by C.E.W. Bean; with pictures of the beach cemetery at Anzac, and maps too. The seventh book: 'The Landing of the Anzacs' by John Masefield; 'Leaving Anzac' by John Masefield; 'Anzac Day' by Capel Boake. Even the fourth book: 'Simpson and His Donkey' (with drawings)—'thus died one of England's noblest sons, and deeply did the Anzacs mourn for him. Though his voice is now silent, he has left us an example that will never die.' Teachers would have turned to these stories and poems in April each year to tell and retell the story of Anzac, and the *School Paper*, distributed monthly to senior primary school students, would have reinforced the message. As would headmasters, closer to the day, and ministers and priests in church, and civic leaders at the memorials being built in every suburb and town.

The historian of war memorials in Australia, K.S. Inglis, made as complete a survey of these memorials as possible. According to the survey, First World War memorials standing in public places—that is, not in churches, halls, schools, offices or businesses—numbered 1453—516 in New South Wales, 360 in Victoria, 239 in South Australia, 197 in Queensland, 80 in Western Australia, 61 in Tasmania and two in the Northern Territory. Each of these had funds raised, largely by public subscription, was designed and built, and was unveiled with significant civic ceremony. For the Fothergills and all the others like them, they were places of deep meaning, not just a feature in the urban landscape. Then there were the church memorials, more common in Anglican and Protestant churches than in Catholic, and the memorial halls and other commemorative devices. Each one would have several stories to tell.

Take one such hall at Briagolong, via Maffra, in Victoria's Gippsland district. The Mechanics Institute there has an honour roll to the men and women from the district who served in the First World War. Most such halls do. Among the names on the roll are those of six boys from the one family—six brothers, who all went away to war. Three of the brothers died overseas, one came home and died quite soon after from the terrible injuries he had received, and the other two survived. Such was the mother's grief that the local people felt that she should not be confronted with the remembrance of her family's sacrifice every time she came into the hall for musical evenings and so on, and so they erected a holland blind above the Roll of Honour, the fittings still clearly evident today, that could be drawn down whenever she might come to the hall. It was a forlorn gesture, but at least other folk were trying.

This is such a personal story, about that community and about that mother and her remaining family. It is a story that tells us about local people, about grief, about the importance of the detail in seeking to make a general case. As historians we see glimpses of the real lives of people only too infrequently, but perhaps we have seen enough here to know that the impact of the First World War was present everywhere in Australia in the late 1930s. In grief and suffering, and in pride, too, they had done their bit, had fought, as they believed it, to make Australia and the world a better place. But to celebrate a new war now in 1939? Hardly.

What was it that Charles Bean, the official historian of the First World War had written at the conclusion of his monumental history?

The Old Force passed down the road to history. The dust of its march settled. The sound of its arms died.

Having written that, he must have paused, for a few paragraphs later on he seems to contradict himself:

> the Australian Imperial Force is not dead. That famous army of generous men marches still down the long lane of its country's history.

Indeed it had been marching, in a sense, as soon as it returned home. The AIF was one of the great constants of the time, a permanent presence in Australia during the inter-war years. It was what Australians were measured by. Its former members were accorded a special place in society. Particularly, the Old Force was important when Australians thought about how they might fight another war, if it ever came. It had been established, had it not, that the Australian soldier plucked from factory or field, trained little enough at home then in Egypt or Britain, was 'good' at war. As D.C. McGrath, a federal Labor parliamentarian, put it in 1920:

> If the war proved anything, it proved that young Australians, many of whom had not previously known one end of a rifle from another, were, after training for a month or two, equal to, if not superior to any other troops.

Foolish man, fatal doctrine: 'training for a month or two'. What this parliamentarian was saying was that if war came again the shearer and the brickie, the factory hand, all of them, would simply once more roll up their sleeves, take up their rifles and convert themselves into efficient and deadly soldiers.

Australia, unique among all the nations of the world, held the doctrine that there was no need for a professional army, for money to be spent on training over the years, for an officer class, for a profession of arms. Australians had shown at Gallipoli, at Pozieres, and in the great victories of 1918 that they could endure and would ultimately prevail—it was all too simple. This was, actually, the stuff of myth, but it was a dominant myth. It was a legacy from the Great War, that thinking, and it nearly proved fatal.

If such a view was common in Australia in the 1920s, and there was no reason to think that it was not, what kind of a man would seek to make a career in the army? Despised professions rarely attract the best candidates; they might attract the man for whom there is no clear or better alternative, the time-server, the misfit. Though, to be fair, they might just also attract the man who is farsighted, single-minded and prepared to be at odds with most of his fellow human beings because he can see the importance of the despised profession or job. Such a man was Henry Douglas Wynter, born near Bundaberg in Queensland in 1886.

Wynter had only finished elementary schooling before helping out on the family's dairy farm; later he worked in a butter factory. He joined the part-time militia, probably just for something to do, found he liked what the military had to offer or, perhaps, found the thought of a military career more congenial than working in a butter factory. So he joined the permanent Australian military forces in 1911. War service from 1916 saw rapid promotion for him as a staff officer with General Birdwood, who commanded the Australians. Wynter was mentioned in despatches four times. He had abilities and aptitudes that perhaps even he had not suspected were within him.

However, the development of Wynter's military career after the war was terribly slow. He remained in the tiny permanent forces, attended Staff College at Camberley in 1921–22 and the Imperial Defence College in 1930. By 1935 he had only just been promoted to temporary colonel as director of military training. But the 'war to end all wars' had rendered the need for officers and training redundant, and the profession of arms was by then on the nose. In 1921, for example, the number of applications for places at the Royal Military College, Duntroon, did not equal the number of vacancies. Talk about taking the best men; they'd have been forced to take almost anyone who had applied. The pay was low, too, another measure of the lack of regard for the military and the unattractiveness of the job. It was about 60 per cent of what an officer of equivalent rank would have received in Britain, and much less again than what was on offer in the Indian army. No wonder, then, that Australian officers found prospects in India brighter and many transferred there in the 1920s and 1930s.

Gavin Long, the official Australian historian of the Second World War, pointed out one important impact the salary on offer to military officers had: 'The low pay helped to prevent [officers] from taking their proper place in social life outside the army.' Long's point was that these officers became insular and isolated from broader society. They were unused to, perhaps, vigorous debate and the questioning of ideas—a bit, well, slow. And remember, none of this is theoretical. Later we will examine the performance of the 8th Australian Division in Malaya and in Singapore when the greatest number of Australians ever marched into captivity. One of the most important points that must be made about that episode is the very low level of efficiency and suitability of the officers commanding the division's brigades and battalions. Good officers require good training. They need to be men of experience, maturity and first-rate judgement. Qualities which were lacking in Malaya and at Singapore, with disastrous consequences.

Instead of developing a culture and an organisation where such officers might thrive, successive Australian governments cut and slashed as if they truly believed there would be no more war. And perhaps governments everywhere believed that—subsequent to the Washington Treaty of 1922, which saw the nations of the world reduce their naval and military forces. Australia reduced its permanent army by 467 men, including 100 officers and 188 warrant officers, the latter the backbone of any force. Australia also reduced the part-time force (its establishment anyway), the militia, from 3256 officers and 85 568 men to 2332 officers and 35 228 men. Annual camps were cancelled, training centres in rural Australia closed; compulsory service in effect applied to urban Australia only. And if that wasn't bad enough, what happened during the Great Depression was even worse. As Jeffery Grey, an historian of the Australian Army, concluded: 'In 1939, war found the Australian Army less militarily capable than it had been in 1919.'

It was not only about saving money and some starry-eyed response to the naive idea that the world had abolished war; there was also an accepted notion that Australia could get by without substantial military forces. This idea can be summed up in one word—Singapore. It is really hard to explain to a more sceptical age what an article of faith the Singapore strategy had become in Australia. Was it wishful thinking? Blind faith in the Empire? A refusal to face facts? Part of all of these and possibly more besides. But make no mistake, Australian governments believed they did not have to take defence issues seriously. Essentially, Australia's security would be guaranteed by the inability of any enemy in Asia to mount an attack on Australia because of the naval superiority of the British at Singapore. Menace Australia and capital ships from Singapore would carve you up: your troops, your navy, your home ports, your supplies. Singapore, Australian politicians liked to intone, was Australia's Maginot line. A defence which could not imaginably be breached.

There were certainly military men in Australia prepared to point out that this particular emperor had no clothes. And there were naval men in England with the same message. There were several problems with the theory. In the first place, because of the Treaty of Washington the Royal Navy was declining in size and could not be increased. Too few warships could be based permanently at Singapore as there were not enough ships to go around. The Singapore strategy also depended on two assumptions. That if war broke out in the Pacific, or anywhere in the Australian region, war would not have simultaneously broken out in Europe—if Britain was fighting on two fronts there would certainly not be enough ships available to send a sufficient fleet to Singapore. And second, if war broke out in Asia or the Pacific, Singapore could be defended militarily for as long as it would take to send a sufficient fleet to the island fortress. The flaw in this latter assumption was that, in reality, the strength of the Japanese navy was such that to even meet the Japanese on level terms the Royal Navy would need to send almost all of its capital ships to Singapore. If those ships were needed anywhere else, or could not reach Singapore in time, the fortress would become a figment of Australian imaginations. And the interesting thing is that any serious thinker in the British Admiralty could easily make, and were making, this very sensible and realistic strategic assessment. In London, among those in the know, very few took Singapore seriously.

There were also thinkers in Australia reaching the same conclusion. Poorly paid though they may have been, some senior Australian military officers had not simply retired their brains in a sulk. Douglas Wynter, for one, was telling anyone who cared to listen that Australia's defences needed urgent attention. Identifying weaknesses in Australian defence preparations that historians would pounce on with the glee of discovery long after the Second World War, Douglas Wynter argued in the 1930s that Australian defence was not automatically secured simply because promises and pledges had been made in Britain. In lectures to the United Services Institutes in Melbourne and Sydney, Wynter suggested that the naval base in Singapore might be subject to successful attack and that Britain and Australia's defence interests might diverge if, simultaneously, Britain was at war in Europe and Australia was at war in the Pacific.

Gavin Long, writing after the war, described Wynter as 'perhaps the clearest and most profound thinker the Australian Army of his generation had produced'. Little good it did Douglas Wynter at the time. Alarmed that Opposition Leader John Curtin was using Colonel Wynter's arguments to condemn the government's defence unpreparedness, Minister for Defence Archdale Parkhill had Wynter posted to a relatively junior position in Queensland, at reduced rank and pay. An action designed, no doubt, to discourage anyone else from expressing such views. Who would now dare to speak up? Yet the strategic and theoretical flaws in Australian defence were all too glaringly obvious, at least to those who bothered to think about it. Militarily, Australia had become a fool's paradise.

Or had it? How can we now know how deeply the carnage of the Great War was playing on the Australian mind. Might it not be that the thought of another war was just too horrible to contemplate? All those men lost, all those lives ruined, all that grief. Take H.V. 'Bert' Evatt, born in 1894, appointed to the High Court of Australia in 1930, widely acknowledged as one of the very brightest of his generation. Evatt would soon be a senior and influential minister in John Curtin's wartime government. He had wanted to go to the war in 1914 but his weak eyesight kept him in Australia—he wore the rejected soldier's badge throughout the war years, either to show that he had wanted to go or to ward off white feathers. Two of his brothers, Ray and Frank, had enlisted. Ray served on Gallipoli, in the Middle East, in France and in Belgium, was a lieutenant and was awarded the Military Cross in March 1917. He died at Passchendaele in September 1917.

Frank died of wounds almost exactly a year later in 1918, taking part in the final Australian advance of the war. When Evatt's mother Jeanie was given the news of the death of her second son at war, she fell to the floor in a faint and it is said that she never fully recovered. She died on her 59th birthday in 1922.

Again this is the story of just one family. But Bert Evatt might have legitimately believed that the war had robbed him of the core of his family—two of his brothers and his mother (his father had died when Bert was seven). He might also have thought that the war had robbed Australia of two men who might have made a substantial contribution to its development, just as Evatt himself was to do. As we bemoan the second-rate politicians and leaders that seem too numerous in Australia in the inter-war years, should we not reflect that the very best of our young manhood lay buried in the thousands of cemeteries on the Western Front and Gallipoli? Who would readily, willingly, go to war again? So the thought of war was pushed to one side with a breezy, 'She'll be right', and faith was placed in Singapore. It had to be the answer. No more war.

Bob Menzies, too, was born in 1894, but in rural Australia; his father was a storekeeper at Jeparit. His two older brothers, Frank and Jim, like Evatt's brothers, had gone to war, but as there were just three boys in the Menzies' family they had sat down with their younger brother Bob before they had enlisted. In effect, they said that they would go so long as Bob promised to remain at home. It was a sensible arrangement and thousands of Australian families were entering into similar pacts in 1914 and 1915. There had to be someone to remain behind to look after the old folk in their declining years; for sons then bore responsibility for their parents. Yet Bob Menzies was of an age for war and when war broke out was already in the militia, in the Melbourne University Rifles. Was it hard for him not to join the fellowship of Anzac; was it tough to keep his family pledge? Bob Menzies never told us, so let us turn instead to the testimony of one of the most honoured historians Australia has produced, Sir Keith Hancock.

Historians, I assume, have a special regard for correct facts, correct dates, and especially for telling the truth. Keith Hancock became a meticulous historian yet for many years he could not tell the truth about his own age. 'I developed a furtive streak about the war', he wrote:

> even when I was becoming a middle-aged man I used some-
> times to find myself lying about my age—giving out that I
> was thirty instead of thirty-two, for fear that people would
> work the sum backwards to 1918 and ask me: 'I suppose you
> were in France.'

Keith Hancock had two older brothers in the war, you see. Jim, who was obliterated by a shell on the Somme—although posted as 'missing', 'prolonging and poisoning my mother's grief' as Keith Hancock put it—and Justin. His parents simply refused Keith permission to enlist. Two boys at the front was enough, they said. Keith would stay at home. 'What could I say to my classmates when they asked me whether we should all go along to the recruiting office at the end of term?' Is there any reason to think that Bob Menzies, four years older too, was any less sensitive than Keith Hancock to the fact that he had not been in France?

Frank and Jim Menzies both came home from the war and would watch in great delight the wondrous and burgeoning career of younger brother Bob. As Bert Evatt shone in the law in Sydney, so did Bob Menzies shine at the law in Melbourne. He was a King's Counsel at 34—a rapid promotion. Menzies turned to politics earlier than Evatt, entering the Victorian Parliament in 1928, becoming a minister in 1932. He joined the federal parliament in 1934 as the member for Kooyong. Prime Minister Lyons immediately appointed him a minister, attorney-general and, soon enough, heir apparent.

Poor old Joe Lyons, father of ten, prime minister in the Depression years when the conservatives simply could not find one of their own number with sufficient appeal to the public to force the distasteful economic medicine down. Lyons, a Labor man through and through, seemed avuncular enough, honest enough for Australians to trust him in their time of economic trial. He was 52 years of age when he became prime minister and approaching 60 when he died unexpectedly while still in office, unless you took into account the cares of office and the sadness of what he had thought he had needed to do.

When Lyons died Bob Menzies was no longer a minister in the Lyons government. He had resigned on a matter of principle only a few weeks earlier. Some said the turbulent cabinet meetings and the evident disunity had hastened the prime minister's end. Regardless, it was certain that the United Australia Party, in coalition with the Country Party, would elect Menzies their leader, making him prime minister. But it seemed the death of the prime minister had intensified the disunity in Canberra. Leader of the Country Party, a medical man and a returned soldier, Earle Page, declared he would take his party out of the coalition if the UAP dared to elect Menzies as its leader. Why? Because he was a treacherous man, said Page, not fit to lead his country.

These were not sentiments muttered behind closed doors or to a few conspirators in the corridors of power. Earle Page stood up in parliament to say what he thought of Menzies. He stood at the despatch box in the House of Representatives as prime minister that day, former deputy to Lyons, as of Country Party right. Has an Australian prime minister ever spoken, before or since, as Page did on that day? One of the vilest speeches ever heard in that place, people claimed. With compelling symmetry Page mentioned three incidents which, to his way of thinking, meant that Menzies was unfit for the high office. 'Twenty-four days previously,' Page reminded the House, Menzies had walked out of the Lyons government. Disloyal and destabilising in a time of national emergency. 'Twenty-four weeks ago,' Page continued, Menzies had seemed to question Lyons's capacity for leadership. Disloyal and destabilising again. And then came the clincher:

> Some twenty-four years ago the right honourable member for Kooyong was a member of the Australian Military Forces and held the King's Commission. In 1915, after having been in the military forces for some years, he resigned his commission and did not go overseas.

At this point from the opposition benches a Labor member, Rowley James, a miner from Newcastle, interjected, 'That is dirt,' he said. But not to have served in the Great War and not be eligible for a rejected soldier's badge, that still counted in Australia in 1939. Mightily. Just ask Keith Hancock. Menzies replied in a dignified fashion but how the attack must have hurt him.

Look at Menzies, sworn into office on 26 April 1939, then aged 44, distinguished with greying hair, a large man, somewhat chubby, with curiously soft and youthful skin. A brilliant speaker, with a quick wit, a lover of company, widely respected but not, however, widely liked, at least not among his political colleagues. What did the future hold for a 44-year-old who had become prime minister? In the joy and excitement of the moment it may not have been a question to which Menzies gave much thought. He was appropriately proud and possibly quite confident as he took on the top job. Menzies was a romantic—an 'extraordinary romantic' according to his biographer, Allan Martin, 'and, as that often means, somewhat naive'.

On his first trip to Britain in 1936 Menzies, then 42, gave almost unbridled expression to this romanticism, but he was not alone in doing so. The Australian historian of the federal movement of the 1890s, John La Nauze, had lost his father in the Gallipoli campaign, and his own reputation among his professional colleagues was that of a hard man. His early interest had been in economics. La Nauze made his first trip to Britain, arriving there in December 1931 as a 20-year-old, half the age Menzies was when he made a similar voyage five years later. Approaching England for the first time, La Nauze remembered, 'I recalled a lot of English literature as we drew near—it was dark, at night, and I could see lights. I felt like crying.' There was a sense, La Nauze believed, that he had come home. Knowing John La Nauze as I did, I can appreciate Menzies' romanticism better. The views they both eloquently expressed on arrival in England found echoes, perhaps less beautifully written, in the letters and diaries of Australian soldiers arriving in Britain for the first time from 1916 onwards.

But it is at this point that I have difficulty in understanding Menzies. When he reached England he was a minister in the Australian government. He represented not only the people of Kooyong but the people of Australia in a broader sense. A sensitive man, he would have been aware, as well as any, of the burden of grief still current in Australian society as a result of the Great War. 'If only I could see your grave', Robert and Isabella Fothergill had written, a sentiment echoed, surely, by thousands of Australians still in 1936. And yet Robert Menzies, who travelled extensively in Britain and who had crossed France by train in order to catch a ferry across the English Channel to Dover, never thought to stop in France to visit even a few of the war graves where some 40 000 Australians lay. Denial again?

The legacy of the Great War in Australia in 1939 was complex and conflicted. Grief was a constant for many Australians, while appeal to a golden age when Australia showed its mettle attracted others. Younger men yearned, some of them anyway, for the opportunity to do what their fathers had done and to show that they could do it better. Other men turned away from war, hiding illnesses from those who loved them, knowing that they lived on borrowed time. Still others turned from war because it bored them, all this talk of heroes; look at them now, physical wrecks, were they ever any good, really? Whatever the legacy of the Great War was for individual Australians one thing is crystal clear: it would shape and determine, in great measure, the story of Australia between 1939 and 1945.

2. AUSTRALIA IS ALSO AT WAR

What was it that Bob Menzies had said? 'In consequence of the persistence by Germany in her invasion of Poland, Great Britain has declared war upon her, and that, as a result, Australia is also at war.'

Britain was at war; that was the central point. And what was it that Douglas Wynter had been saying before he was effectively cashiered? That Britain and Australia's defence interests might diverge if, simultaneously, Britain was at war in Europe and Australia was at war in the Pacific. That Singapore might not be the secure fortress it was hoped to be, unless it could be reinforced with almost every capital ship at Britain's disposal. And what was it that Earle Page had said back in April after Joe Lyons had died? That Bob Menzies was not the man to lead the country 'in a time of national emergency'.

The world had been lurching to war for many months now. Everyone could see it coming. Manning Clark, an Australian historian, then a student at Oxford with a fiancée in Bonn, had arrived on a visit to Germany on 8 November 1938. It was the morning after 'Kristallnacht', the night when Hitler's storm-troopers looted and burned Jewish shops and homes. Ninety-one Jews were murdered across Germany. It had seemed shocking. 'Glass was everywhere on the footpath', Manning Clark remembered, 'the windows of Jewish shops had been broken, and their goods scattered over the pavement and the road. There were trucks with men in uniform standing in the tray'. The evil of Nazism was revealed so starkly yet British Prime Minister Neville Chamberlain and German Chancellor Adolf Hitler had signed their 'peace in our time' agreement in Munich just five weeks earlier.

Keith Hancock, now a professor of history, had been in Birmingham since 1934 and had watched at first hand the refusal of his colleagues, the British thinking classes and the politicians to face up to Hitler. He reflected on 'the British gift for being only just in time', but began to fear in 1938 and 1939 that this time they were 'cutting it too fine'. Hancock believed that had the British confronted Hitler four or five years earlier they may have saved the peace. Even on the day that Hitler invaded Poland, Hancock in Birmingham feared the British government might back off again.

Bob Menzies would have disagreed with Keith Hancock. He found Neville Chamberlain 'a man of clear-headedness and determination', who brought to the existing international tensions 'such a degree of horse sense that real trouble may be avoided'. This was in 1938 when Menzies was in London, able to look at the situation for himself. He was there with two other Australian ministers, attempting to negotiate a better trade deal for Australia with the British government. And there was test cricket too: 'To be in England in the summer when a Test series was on was for [Menzies] veritable heaven and one of his first engagements was a dinner given at Lord's to the Australian XI', Allan Martin wrote.

Menzies also took the opportunity of visiting Germany for a few days. His main contact was the British ambassador to Germany, Sir Nevile Henderson, 'an extremely clear-headed and sensible fellow' in Menzies' view, but described later by the historian Robert Rhodes James as 'a persistent, able and lamentable advocate of an Anglo–German settlement on any terms'. Menzies left Germany not, he said, 'an uncritical admirer' but an admirer of Germany nevertheless. Hitler, he thought, was 'a dreamer, a man of ideas, many of them good ones. He propounds the idea, Goering gets it carried out, and Goebbels tells the German people how marvellous it is.' Bob Menzies left for home on 9 August 1938. Three months later, almost to the day, Manning Clark was stepping around the glass and all the looted Jewish goods in Bonn.

While he was in Germany Bob Menzies had a senior member of the German Foreign Office at his disposal. Senior public officials gave him lunch or dinner. While it was not an official mission, a dominion's minister could not merit that, Menzies met some of the people who mattered. Manning Clark sat drinking wine in the front room of his fiancée's boarding house in Bonn with an art historian from the university. The art historian told Manning Clark, 'in a menacing voice', that unless the British accepted Hitler's demands for the Polish corridor, the return of the German colonies and German living space in eastern Europe, then the German army would reduce London to rubble. And what about Australia, Manning Clark said he asked timidly. 'Australia doesn't matter,' the art historian muttered.

Ken Clift was in the shower at his parents' home at Bondi on that Sunday evening in 1939 when Bob Menzies started talking on the radio. His father rapped on the bathroom door and shouted the news of war across the noise of the shower. Clift was 22 years of age and he later recalled that the news caused a powerful thrill of excitement to run through his body. There and then he knew that he would be at the recruiting depot first thing the next morning. For men like him this war, hardly unexpected, was an adventure and a chance to show that he and his mates were just as good as the 'old man' and all his mates' fathers. They had grown up with war—grown up, that is, with their fathers' stories of war; with their teachers' telling and re-telling of the Anzac legend; with forced attendances at a variety of services and war memorial unveilings across the inter-war years. If young men will almost unconsciously measure themselves against their fathers to show that they are men then this business of war was beginning to get them down. They could contest their fathers' memories of their achievements at sport, at work, with the girls, but they could not meet them on the one playing field that between 1918 and 1939 was the only real test of Australian manhood: the battlefield. But now they could. 'To be young was very heaven.'

For some. By no means did every young Australian male feel like this. John Kingsmill turned 19 on 1 September 1939, the worst time to be coming into his manhood. He was not swept away with the slogans, the one-in-all-in nonsense, as he called it. He would take his time about this war and he would think carefully. He remembers that he asked himself endlessly, in the deepest level of his being: 'What is the reason which can justify my laying down my life, what do I owe them that makes this sacrifice rational and proper?' But he knew he would go eventually: 'I knew there was no escaping that.' And that was the grim reality for most young men. In their own minds, in their own individuality, they could respond with an excited sense of adventure, or with a proper sense of caution. But with Australia at war, and at 19 or 22 years of age, there was no way the war would pass over them, leaving them unscathed. One way or another it would touch every Australian man in that age group, and very many women too. That is what war is like; that is what war does.

John Kingsmill was the eldest of six children—five boys and a girl. He had left school at 15 for what he described as a miserable 'clerking' job. Shades of Charles Dickens's blacking factory enter his account of this part of his life. John was at work because his family needed him to be, needed the meagre wage—25 shillings a week—that he would bring in. It is convenient that John Kingsmill was born in 1920, so easy for our calculations. He was nine when stockbrokers started jumping out of windows on New York's Wall Street, heralding an economic collapse that would hurt Australia at least as badly as any other 'rich' nation, and worse than most. Australia had borrowed heavily for the First World War and in an attempt to kick-start a sluggish economy in the 1920s. Australia was too dependent on wheat and wool to pay for these borrowings, and when the prices for these staples collapsed Australia's debt threatened to suffocate the entire nation. With six children to feed and little money coming in, his father bankrupt, the Kingsmills and thousands of families like them were reduced to serious poverty. That word is not an exaggeration; back then you couldn't take it for granted that the state would support a man who could not feed his family. Boys and girls and their mothers and fathers went hungry during the Great Depression in Australia; they were cold, and many could hardly dress themselves decently. That is the way it was. 'I'd rather do ten years at the war,' one man who had fought in France in the horror of 1916 and 1917 told a journalist, 'than one year in the Mallee [in drought and depression].' The grinding poverty of the farmer was ten times worse than the fear and awfulness of the soldier? It must have been bad.

What then would a boy brought up in such circumstances think that he might owe his country? Why should we assume that the call of war automatically wiped away the months and years of cold and hunger from every young man's mind? Why should we assume that a young man might feel patriotic love for a country that had forced him from school and life's opportunities as soon as he could legally earn a wage, to watch in envy the schoolboys and varsity fellows playing their games and learning to take their expected place in society? 'Me, give my life for a country that despised and degraded my parents, that wouldn't mention the word "opportunity" within my hearing. A country that was happy to have me go to work at 15 to help to put food on our table when I might have been exploring the world of learning, playing my games, being a boy. What duty did I owe such a country?' If the historian is ever to offer a glimpse of the people behind the generalisations we trade in, we must, at least, suggest that such questions might have occurred to some of the young men of Australia whom war would scoop up.

Ken Clift was at the gates of Victoria Barracks in Paddington, Sydney, bright and early the next morning, 4 September 1939. He had decided to enrol in the air force. Too many of those who had been at war the first time had said that the infantry was 'for mugs'—poor, bloody infantry. The horror and misery of the trenches, the mud, the constant shelling from both sides across no man's land. These were the embedded images from World War I. But now Australia had an air force and surely that would be a better place to be, away from the mud and the rats. Many young men were thinking that way and their fathers were encouraging them. But there was a shock in store for Ken Clift and the other like-minded young Australians—a profound shock. Nobody wanted them. There were no plans to enlist anyone; not a recruiting sergeant to be seen anywhere. The young men were insistent. Would somebody please take their names down? Eventually someone in the office at the barracks produced some hastily roneoed forms—name, age, occupation, address—just in case these blokes might be needed. Then they all went home, perplexed. 'Flocking to the colours' had never been like this.

Geoffrey Street was the minister for Defence in the first Menzies government. Born in Sydney in 1894, Street was a blue blood, his great-grandfather had arrived in New South Wales in 1822 and the family's wealth came, initially at least, from the land. He had joined the Australian forces in August 1914, immediately after war was declared. He knew all about 'flocking to the colours'. Street was wounded at Gallipoli but then survived the Western Front unscathed, until he was shot through the right wrist in September 1918. He had served under the legendary 'Pompey' Elliott in the 15th Infantry Brigade and emerged from the war with a Military Cross. Street entered federal parliament in 1934 as a Victorian Country Party member. He was one of those returned service members who pushed hard for defence awareness and for a new army for Australia, particularly from 1938 onwards as the world situation deteriorated. He became Minister for Defence in November 1938 and oversaw the final preparations of the Commonwealth War Book, which would establish Australia's response in the last days of peace and the first days of war. There would be no Australian expeditionary force, Street had said almost as soon as his prime minister had announced that Australia was at war. No recruiting, no clamouring at the barracks' gates, no 'flocking to the colours'. This is not 1914, Geoffrey Street said, things are different now.

But he could not say how they were different; common sense and the language of diplomacy tied his tongue. What the minister might have said if he had been free to speak openly would have started and ended with Japan. He might have told his audience how our expeditionary force, leaving Australian shores on 1 November 1914, was escorted by the Japanese cruiser *Ibuki*, among others. Australians at Gallipoli, and I was one of them, he might have continued, experimented with a Japanese trench mortar. If not formally allies, we were then very good friends. But now? Geoffrey Street knew better than most the good sense that Douglas Wynter had been speaking when he warned of the real difficulty for Australia if Britain was at war in Europe at the same time that Australia was at war in the Pacific. We will have to wait, Street might have told his audience, to see what Japan will do before we can make any plans for an Australian role in Europe. We simply cannot yet risk sending our troops abroad, Geoffrey Street might have said. But of course he said no such thing. The idea central to the survival of Australia, from the moment Great Britain went to war, was to keep Japan out of any war, anywhere. And not to in any way provoke this most frightening potential enemy.

Also helping to keep Australia out of the European war was the intense calm that had settled over Europe since the British had declared war. Nothing happened. Certainly people, and children particularly, flooded out of London and the other big British cities because of the widespread and firm belief that war would mean an immediate and appalling reign of terror from the skies. All the predictions had warned people to forget all they knew about war from earlier times. Everyone's vision had been of soldiers in trenches facing each other across a narrow belt of contested land, with shells the terrible means of killing opponents. This new war would see war in the sky. The bomber would be the agent, indiscriminately killing soldiers and civilians, seeking out factories as eagerly as military establishments, bombing to submission whole nations, stopping cities in their tracks, creating havoc and starvation. That was the expectation for the first hours and days of a new war and yet so far nothing had happened. 'The Bore War', the British press called it, 'The Twilight War', in Winston Churchill's words. It was almost as if the British and the French believed, still, that war could be negotiated away. Leo Amery, a British member of parliament and later a wartime minister, asked why munitions factories in Essen were not being bombed. They were private property, he was told. It was not until December 1939 that the British suffered their first service casualty in France, and not until March 1940 that the first British civilian was killed as a result of an air raid. By comparison, in the first three months of World War I the British had lost 50 000 soldiers killed.

So, said Prime Minister Menzies, echoing his British counterpart, it was 'business as usual', a singularly inept expression that would come back to haunt the government. The show went on as usual in Melbourne, people flocked to the Spring racing carnivals in Melbourne and Sydney, the cinemas and dance halls were full; if anything there was a little more confidence in the air, the belief that now, at last, the economy might be on the mend. Somewhere, people might once more need wool and wheat. Perhaps Australians would all have jobs again soon. Business, possibly, even better than usual.

Yet the memory of 1914 hung heavily. This was not what war was like. 'In my day,' hundreds of returned men started off saying wherever they were, at home, in pubs, at work, 'in my day' there was a rush to enlist. Australia had then wanted to show her support for the 'Mother Country' and stood squarely with her in raising an expeditionary force within days of the declaration of war. Just like that, 20 000 men; 50 000 within a few months. That's what they did 'in my day'. The newspapers chimed in alongside the returned men, raiding that special room in the newspaper offices where wartime clichés were apparently stored. It was journalists who wrote about the colours, the rush to enlist, the honour of the nation. Why? Informed journalists knew better than most the danger that Australia faced from a Pacific war; most of them could have written an excellent version of that speech the Defence minister simply could not yet give. Instead the newspapers seemed to want to whip up agitation for an Australian expeditionary force. The *Sydney Morning Herald* led the way. 'This Commonwealth', the editor thundered, 'was the first of the Dominions to range itself with Britain in war against Germany. The action was surely meant, as it was accepted, to be an offer of military help'.

A section of the people kicked the newspaper campaign along. There were letters in the newspapers, public meetings, petitions and claims that thousands of men were eager to enlist, virtually camped at the barracks' gates. It all went back to Anzac in the end. 'We used to be told', someone wrote, 'that Australia found her soul at Anzac. It may be well to remember that a soul can be lost, and that there is no profit in gaining the whole world and losing one's soul'. Was this Anzac legend such an insecure, ephemeral thing that an Australia standing out of a European war could trash the legend and the memory of all those who had previously served? Was Anzac forever to be an excuse for Australia to rush to wars, when national interest and national security might dictate sitting it out on the sidelines? Three or four months more of the phoney war in Australia might have answered some of these questions. We will never know the answer now because, in the face of all the protests from his government's traditional supporters, the prime minister began to give way.

The *Sydney Morning Herald* had shown him the best way out of his dilemma. Open recruiting to two forces, the newspaper had suggested—one for service at home, the other for service abroad. Then the people can make up their own minds. Of course, the government had been pushing on with national service training of the militia to create an Australian force for defence at home. That was ongoing. A force of some 80 000 trained men. But it was an expeditionary force, an overseas force, that the urgers wanted.

In a national broadcast on 15 September 1939 the prime minister announced that the government had indeed decided to create a 'special force' of 20 000 men, distinct from the militia, for service at home or abroad 'as circumstances permit'. Defence Minister Street emphasised that no name had been given to the infantry division of 20 000 men, which would be officially known as the 'Proposed Special Force'. The uncertainty surrounding the eventual destination of the force prevented it being named an Australian Imperial Force, the minister ruled: 'No man could say at this juncture whether the new force would go abroad or not.' Nor was the special force to be allowed to interfere with the recruitment and training of the militia, yet finding recruits for the special force might be difficult if the young men could not be certain that they would serve in the war overseas. But they might.

Young men of the Ken Clift variety again threw their hats in the air and rushed to the recruiting depots, determined to grab a spot among the elite 20 000, only to have their hopes dashed again. Steady, counselled Defence Minister Street to these enthusiasts, recruiting for the special force cannot commence before 9 October, we won't be ready until then. In Melbourne alone, just two days after the prime minister's grudging concession that a new force would be recruited for service somewhere or other, 5300 men had wanted in. All were turned away and told to cool their heels until October.

In Western Australia, one of those waiting for the chance to join the special force was Ralph Honner, born in August 1904. Ralph's had been a curious childhood, lonely and disconnected. At the age of just 13 he was sent by his parents to school in Perth some 300 kilometres south of the family home. Ralph Honner was effectively on his own thereafter. His father, a police constable and farmer, could not afford for the boy to return home for each of the school holidays so he visited his son instead, perhaps three or four times a year, at his lodgings. Lonely? Ralph Honner had read the complete works of William Shakespeare by the time he was 15. Ralph had moved to Perth in 1917 when the Australians were in the worst of their fighting around Ypres in the mud of Flanders. Naturally a lonely 13- to 14-year-old boy would follow the fighting with a passionate intensity, might invest war with more meaning than would a boy with parents and siblings around him to deflect him from its close scrutiny. At the age of 18 Ralph Honner embarked on a career as a teacher, graduating from university and teachers' college in 1925, unofficially engaged but unable to contemplate marriage for another eight years as money was too tight. His intended was a teacher, too, who would have to resign from teaching on her marriage. Ralph and Marjory simply could not afford that. It was that Depression, again. Married in 1934, there were two sons (born in 1936 and 1938) by the time war broke out in 1939. Ralph Honner was then 35 years of age.

Why would such a man enlist, immediately too, in October 1939, for this 'proposed special force'? A married man, father of two, an older man. What was driving him? Here the historian needs to pause and really ponder what we can know about human motivation. Why people do the things they do is at the heart of every historical inquiry and might seem to us, at times, simply unknowable. Every one of the eventual near one million Australian men and women in uniform in the Second World War would have had an individual and unique answer to the question of why he or she had joined up. Ralph Honner had been preparing himself for war since 1936, the year of the birth of his first son. Seeing war coming, he said, he had joined the militia. He had also started brushing up his French, German, Spanish and Italian, to be of a little more use to the military, to convince them that they should let him in. But why? 'If I hadn't made strenuous efforts to get in, I could hardly have held my head up again,' he said. Go back to that lonely and impressionable boy, far from his family, pouring over newspaper accounts of the fighting at Passchendaele, at Villers-Bretonneux, of the Australian victories of 1918. The men he was reading about then defined for Ralph Honner what it meant to be an Australian. It was as if he had been programmed for war. And what a war leader he would become. But first for him it was Northam Camp, outside Perth, as a lieutenant—a modest rank— in charge of C Company, 2/11th Battalion.

Bob Menzies was contemplating war leadership, too, but way beyond the likes of Ralph Honner commanding men at the company level. Bob Menzies, instead, had to find the overall commander of his 'proposed special force'. Think of the men, Douglas Wynter was one of them, who had kept the faith in the military during the dreary years after the Great War. Reduced in number, reduced in pay and reduced in rank, they had needed to be true believers of a special kind to have kept that faith. The profession of arms, they had insisted, was an honourable profession, yet the rest of Australia had almost laughed in their faces. Gavin Long, journalist and historian, had been right: insular, isolated and downright poor, forced to the Indian army for work and experience, these soldiers had indeed been putting up with a great deal just to serve their country. The politicians had even closed the Royal Military College at Duntroon at one stage, so little did they seem to value the profession. And now the greatest indignity of them all was coming to these men, just as the tiny professional officer class thought that they might at last be seeing the light at the end of the tunnel.

The prime minister ruled that the commander of the proposed special force would come from the ranks of the militia, not from the ranks of the regulars. Leap-frogged, overlooked, spurned, read it any way you will; it was a brutal message to send to the officer group who had kept the faith. What was in the prime minister's mind? There were two main contenders for the top job from the ranks of the regular officers: Gordon Bennett, of whom subsequently almost no one could say a good word, and John Laverack, of whom Menzies was particularly and unnecessarily wary. To avoid either of these two, Menzies, acting unilaterally, turned to the militia officers. Geoffrey Street disagreed, but what could he do? Menzies was insistent when it came to choosing his senior military people.

The leading contender in the militia was Thomas Albert Blamey, the eighth child of a butcher from Wagga Wagga in New South Wales. Blamey had served with distinction at Gallipoli and with great credit as an officer on General Monash's staff in France. His 'battle orders were the nearest to perfection I have ever seen,' said Major General Iven Mackay. And his letters home to his mother from Gallipoli, anyway, are light-hearted, readable, admirable: 'I've bottomed on the simple life and I'm really enjoying it, absolutely, being a primitive savage suits me. I love my job, it's absolutely A1. It gives me a little adventure, a little excitement and a lot of fun.' He also wrote honestly to his mother: 'Our landing perforce broke up organisation and I saw what I never hope to see again—the beginning of a defeat.' And towards the end of this five-page letter the future field-marshal wrote: 'It is marvellous how the strain does for some men while others have the resilience to buck up again.'

If there is one word that might describe Tom Blamey's character, it is resilience. 'Short of stature, rugged in appearance', a bar-room scrapper you might think, certainly he pushed the limits for most of his life. Only to bounce back. His biographer, David Horner, on the whole was sympathetic, but nevertheless conceded that Blamey:

> was probably not Australia's most accomplished battlefield commander. He was not a great innovator or reformer. He did not reshape the Australian Army and leave a new organisation as his legacy. He was not loved or even admired as an effective leader of men. He was not respected for his honesty and upright character.

And that, from an admiring biographer. Decent, intelligent men like the journalist and war correspondent, Chester Wilmot, could not stand Blamey, who would eventually brawl with most of his senior commanders during the war, wrecking careers as he ruthlessly set his own course. Chosen to take command of the 'proposed special force' in October 1939, Blamey was there on the USS *Missouri* in Tokyo Bay in September 1945 for the Japanese surrender. Of all the leaders and followers we will meet in our journey through Australia during World War II, Blamey alone will survive at the top the entire war. Resilience.

Did Bob Menzies see that when he selected Blamey? It was a risky appointment if only for the peculiar manner in which Blamey had trashed his own reputation. Appointed chief commissioner of police in Victoria in 1925, it was only a matter of weeks before Blamey's own badge was found in the possession of another man during a police raid on a Melbourne brothel. I lent my key ring, with my badge attached, Blamey said improbably in his defence. To the public at large he said his badge had been stolen—equally improbable. Melbourne gossiped and never quite believed Tom Blamey again. But Bob Menzies did. Menzies never seemed comfortable with military types; he might have worried that they looked down on him, a deserter, in Earle Page's terms, from the fellowship of Anzac. Perhaps Menzies believed that Tom Blamey was the one military leader in no position to look down his nose at the prime minister. And perhaps also there was a side to Menzies that truly liked the knockabout, larrikin type, and enjoyed a deep-throated laugh with a drink in hand. For that, Tom Blamey was your man. Yet there was something more. Edmund Herring, that model of Melbourne respectability, the general and the chief justice, a man of high public virtue and impeccable morality who was not afraid to tell the world what was the right thing to do, had made Blamey his mentor and guide, possibly even his friend. It is well to be alert to the complexity of Tom Blamey's character from the moment we meet him, otherwise we too risk having the wool pulled over our eyes.

Surely the first question that Tom Blamey must have asked his prime minister when the command of the special force was offered to him would have been: 'Where are we to serve?' For weeks now

Menzies had been fighting the urgers who wanted to take Australia straightaway, right now, to the European war. In February 1940, Menzies would privately lament to the Australian High Commissioner in London, Stanley Bruce, 'that if only a kindly Providence would remove from the active political scene here a few minds which are heavily indoctrinated by the old soldiers' point of view my task would be easier.' Menzies wanted to keep his special force in Australia at least until he could be sure of Japanese intentions. He was confident that he could bat off his Australian critics, who were demanding an instant commitment to the Empire in 'her hour of need', but he was coming under intense pressure from London to send some Australian troops 'to France' to demonstrate Empire solidarity.

Menzies may have been determined that Australian security must come first, but in London, Dominions Secretary Anthony Eden was not so sure. Eden believed that 'the psychological effect on our French friends and on Germany of the knowledge that these troops will be in the field in France, probably in time for a spring campaign, will be most salutary'. These troops being from Canada, New Zealand, South Africa and Australia. Canada would not be much bothered about Japanese intentions, nor South Africa, but New Zealand might be. It was to the 'Shaky Isles' that Bob Menzies turned his attention. He cabled New Zealand Prime Minister Michael Savage, inviting him to look closely at the Australian objections to sending troops overseas. But before Savage received this cable he had already agreed to an overseas commitment of his small New Zealand force.

Menzies had also cabled his minister in London, Richard Casey, sent there in response to a British request for a meeting of dominion ministers, outlining again the case against troops leaving Australia, the case for the primacy, as Menzies saw it, of Australian security. And anyway, Menzies asked Casey, what of the woeful lack of British shipping that would prevent the early despatch of an Australian contingent? There is not much point in promising what we cannot deliver, Menzies was saying. But when he learned that the Canadians and New Zealanders were sending troops to Europe, Menzies recognised that the game was up; 'Australia would be there', too.

What really infuriated Bob Menzies in the unfolding of this argument about retaining or sending the Australian force to Europe was that the British had already 'miraculously' found the required shipping for the Australian contingent before the Australian government had agreed to their departure from Australia. In a breathtaking display of arrogance and intimidation, they had already sent those ships on their way to Australia. A gun to the head of the Australian prime minister? No less than that, and not for the last time, either. We know that you will do our bidding, Bob, and won't you look a clown if our troop ships turn up in your harbours before you have decided to commit Australian troops to our war?

'We feel that in this matter', Menzies cabled Casey:

We have been in effect forced into a course of action which we would not otherwise have adopted . . . we resent being told that shipping is already on its way for the purpose of collecting our troops . . . when we were not consulted before the departure of the vessels.

Menzies might well have remembered this episode when he came to consider the British request for Australian troops for the doomed Greece campaign, and might have drawn John Curtin's attention to these October 1939 cables when Curtin had his own battle about the return of Australian troops to Australia for the defence of their homeland in early 1942. It is no trivial thing to send your troops to war. It must be one of the gravest and heaviest decisions a politician can ever be called upon to make. We do Menzies an injustice if we see him merely as a 'knee-jerk' Empire man. Rather he was trying desperately hard to balance the competing interests of Australian security and traditional ties to Britain. 'We have been . . . forced into a course of action', Menzies had written, acknowledging that the British had just assumed the right to use Australians as best suited British interests. Menzies had every right to feel let down.

On 8 October 1939, the day before recruiting began, Defence Minister Street had announced that the special force would indeed be known as the 2nd Australian Imperial Force. To encourage pride and a sense of military tradition the old battalion numbers would also be used again, only with a 2 in front of them to show that they were different, but the same. The First World War 14th Battalion, AIF, for example, was forever known as Jacka's Mob, named after the first Australian to be awarded a Victoria Cross at Gallipoli, Albert Jacka, its most famous member. The 2/14th Battalion, the military hoped, would embrace the spirit and the legends of the originals and be a better outfit for that. Bert Jacka, though, had died in January 1932, one of the thousands of men of the 1st AIF not to make old bones, a victim of the Depression. What a pity he would not be there to see the new men take up the traditions he and his mates had created.

Battalions are organised into brigades and then into divisions. As there had been five divisions of the AIF in France by 1918, people assumed that by numbering the first division of the 2nd AIF the 6th Division, the military were forging another link with the past. It was not so. The militia in Australia, the home defence, was organised into five divisions; the new special force division auto-matically became the 6th. Whether those flocking to the colours in October 1939 would make better soldiers because of the links to the force of their fathers remained to be seen, but the numbering and the name made the point about the weight of history on this force. Some objected to giving the new force an old name: 'The title was won in 1915–18 . . . leave the AIF to the boys who earned it', wrote one. 'Membership of the AIF in 1914–18 was won in the crucible of blood and fire', wrote another, 'and its members . . . are entitled, even at this late stage, to something better than the diminutive appellation of "the old AIF"'. 'Good luck to them', wrote a third, '[they] are entitled to the initials AIF as they are facing a bigger problem than we did'.

It was not until 29 November 1939, however, that the prime minister announced that the new force would serve overseas after all. The full cabinet had met the day before, finally authorising the decision: 'The 6th Division, which was raised for service at home or abroad as occasion required, can be permitted to proceed overseas when it has reached a suitable stage in its training, which it is anticipated will be early in the new year.' The men in the camps were delighted, reported the *Sydney Morning Herald* a day later. 'There was considerable excitement and cheers were heard from many huts. An army officer expected the news to give a definite stimulus to recruitment.'

The truth was that men of the Ken Clift or Ralph Honner type were not apparently all that thick on the ground. Delayed and debated as the new force was, quaintly named to begin with and then embracing the full burden of history, raised during the 'Bore War' in Europe, the 2nd AIF was not proving an attractive destination for most young men. A week before the announcement of the decision to send the AIF abroad the military released recruiting figures. Only Queensland had exceeded its target of 2453 men, but only by less than 100. New South Wales was 2.63 per cent below its target of 6352 men; Victoria was a whopping 21.4 per cent behind its target of 5729 men. The other states were variously behind, but not as badly, in percentage terms, as Victoria.

There were a couple of reasons for this. In the first place the government had reserved half the places in the AIF for militia men, already partially trained at least and presumably fit. But the militia was not showing any marked inclination to move over to the AIF. Second, the government had published a list of what were termed 'reserved occupations' from which a man was not permitted to resign in order to enlist for service overseas. The move made planning sense. Unlike the unfettered enlistment of men from all walks of life in 1914 to 1918, it seemed sensible to ensure that industry and domestic life were not unduly affected by the war. Australia needed farmers and factory workers, and the creation of the reserved occupations was intended to ensure the orderly use of manpower. There was an expectation among some, anyway, in the earlier war that every fit man should go. There was no such expectation in government in 1939. Fit men would be needed in all walks of life.

There was an easy way to start a fight in Australia up until only a few years ago: mutter the words 'economic conscripts' to men of fighting age in 1939. These men deeply and permanently resented the notion that early recruits came from the ranks of the unemployed. There is evidence, however, to support this contention. One man wrote to the *Sydney Morning Herald* to complain about reserving so many places in the AIF for the militia: 'Today I am unemployed', he wrote, 'and when the war broke out, like many another man in a similar position, hoped that a chance of enlistment would arise and take me off food relief, and give me a chance to become a useful citizen again'. Then there was the man, reported in the *Age*, coming into the pay office for his first week's pay as a new member of the 2nd AIF. Called to receive his money, the man threw out his arm in the Nazi salute and shouted, 'Heil Hitler.' Asked what on earth he thought he was doing the man replied, 'I've been out of a job for two blinkin' years. This is the first blinkin' pay I've had in two blinkin' years.' The officer dismissed the man with a caution, but the story could only give credence to the notion that most of the first recruits were in the same boat, that they were, indeed, 'economic conscripts'.

It was the reserved occupations, said the men of the 6th Division. If you wanted to get in you had to be sure that when you listed your trade or job the officer wouldn't consult his list and then tell you he could not accept you. Best to pretend you came from the ranks of the unemployed to ensure you did win a spot in the AIF, which all these potential recruits so dearly wanted. The truth about economic conscription as a major motivator for recruitment to the 2nd AIF would lie in both directions; after all, there was a disastrous drought in Australia in 1914 to 1915 that might have forced more than quite a few farmers' sons and farm labourers into the original AIF and no one then thought to call those recruits 'drought conscripts'.

By the end of December 1939 there were some 20 000 Australians in camp, training hard and now certain that sometime soon they would be on their way to war. Perhaps the process had been a little slower and a little more difficult this time than in 1914. Then war had broken out in August and the first Australians were on their troopships in October. Now war had broken out in September and the 2nd AIF could sense a January 1940 departure from home shores. It was their mothers and wives and, most particularly, their fathers, who worried about it on their behalf because they knew about war. At Briagolong in Victoria's Gippsland, did they still lower the holland blind over the town's honour roll in the local hall when the mother with four sons dead from the first war came in for a fundraiser for the men of the Second World War? There would be tears and much putting on of a brave face when this force sailed to war. Much less of the bands and the streamers, and the shouts of, we hope you see some action.

3. THE AIR WAR

The Great Depression meant that Frank Austin had to leave school at 15 to work as a jackaroo on his family's property, Goonambil, near Urana in the Riverina district of New South Wales. In 1936, realising that war was a distinct possibility, Frank joined the local unit of the Light Horse. He enjoyed being a part-time soldier; a Sunday of drill and training every so often, a camp once a year. Then in October 1939, with the war already underway, training intensified. The Light Horse would be working at it for a full month. Frank was given charge of the unit's Hotchkiss machine gun, a cumbersome thing to lug about on a horse. After a fair bit of this type of training the unit was drawn up before the colonel for some of the inspirational stuff. 'Look,' the colonel said, 'you fellows are lucky. You are on horses and a horse would be able to outflank a tank any day.'

To Frank Austin, and almost certainly to most of his mates, this was simply arrant nonsense. And no doubt dangerous, too. Frank had no hesitation in chucking in the Light Horse there and then, and made up his mind to join the air force. He figured they might have a slightly more sophisticated take on modern warfare. Such are the reasons that propelled men to war.

There is no doubt that the Royal Australian Air Force was the glamour service in 1939. Young men in any period seem peculiarly attracted to motors and to speed. The possession of a motor car in 1939 might have been well beyond the reasonable aspiration of most young men, but all of them seemed fascinated by the car and the freedom it offered. To fly in an aircraft was even further beyond the reasonable aspirations of most Australians, but the RAAF showed young men that there was a route to such a dream.

Well, in a manner of speaking. At the outbreak of war the permanent air force in Australia consisted of 310 officers, 3179 airmen and 246 aircraft, of which only 164 were operational. To put that in context, the men of Australia's air force, all of them, could just about fit into a decent-sized concert hall or cathedral in one of Australia's capital cities, allowing for the use of a bit of standing room. For such a small, popular force it *was* possible to keep standards sky high and to make sure they were recruiting only the right men—in the pre-war days every applicant for the RAAF was interviewed by a seven-person committee. That would now have to go. In November 1939, two months into this new war, the RAAF came up with the sensible but pretty obvious idea that there should be a recruiting depot in each of the state capital cities and in 12 provincial centres as well. They were opening up membership of the club, just a bit.

Yet everyone was saying that the war in the air would make the difference. Trench warfare becomes impossible once aircraft technology allows for the accurate despatch of bombs and bullets. So the standard idea of war, the Western Front, was now obsolete. And as we will see in Greece and Malaya—but it was true everywhere else too—troops lacking comprehensive and continuous air support were troops simply awaiting defeat. Ships without air support were vulnerable as well from the bombs and torpedoes of enemy aircraft, in a way that had never occurred before. Aircraft would indeed be the deciding factor in this new war. The air war would also allow for the incapacitation of the enemy's sources of war—its factories, its bases, its military installations and camps, its transport, its shipping, its supply of civilian workers. Bob Menzies knew this—anybody who thought about war knew this—yet Australia went to war with a rudimentary air force. If Australian troops were to go into action the British would have to supply the aircraft to protect them, and the British, surely, must have an air force; that was the way people were thinking.

Even so, while people were pondering the extent and destructive nature of air power, it still remained the great unknown of this war; it was unproven. Some envisaged a fiery, intense and destructive bombing campaign once war was declared—short and sharp. Three weeks into the war Menzies told the people: 'In our hours of greatest difficulty the Mother Country [might be] asking more insistently for help in the air than for help on the land or the sea.' 'Victory in this war,' said J.V. Fairbairn, soon to become Australia's first ever Air [Force] minister, 'will depend on mastery in the air.' No wonder young men flocked to the RAAF; it was glamorous and it would be where the action was. Added to this, the men of World War I told their sons to keep out of the infantry—all that mud, all that horror, all that squalor. And if the young men sought reinforcement of their fathers' message they only had to read any war novel published during the inter-war years. Even the most mundane of them emphasised the utter awfulness of trench warfare.

Australia started its wartime air force virtually from scratch. Just imagine the complexity of this. Perhaps you did need only a few months to turn the average farmer's son or factory worker into a soldier. As a Labor member in the federal parliament, D.C. McGrath, said in the early 1920s: 'If the [first world] war proved anything, it proved that young Australians, many of whom had not previously known one end of a rifle from another, were, after training for a month or two, equal, if not superior, to any other troops.' Clearly such thinking was disastrous for any type of defence preparedness, but it was simply ludicrous when thinking of the requirements of an air force. Recruits to an air force had first to be taught to fly, or to equip themselves with other highly technical skills, such as air navigation, engineering, ground crew tasks of all types. Acquiring these skills could not be rushed. Indeed in the first place the need was for the training of instructors who might then pass on the specialised training to those who would be on the frontline. So in the early days of the war the RAAF scoured Australian flying clubs and appealed to commercial and other experienced pilots to become instructors, not with much initial success.

It was all such a painfully slow process which, if rushed, could lead to an unacceptably high level of training accidents—the RAAF had already been under great pressure in pre-war days for exactly this reason. So slow it all down was the cry, and be careful. By 30 March 1940, 11 500 men had applied for enlistment as aircrew. Of these, 4617 had been interviewed and 1973 selected. But only 184 of them had actually begun training; 1789 were on a waiting list. The situation was just as dire for ground crew—56 777 had applied to the RAAF, 7894 had been selected, but only 5346 were enlisted and in training. To put it at its worst, this war could certainly have been lost before Australia had put even a slightly credible air force into the skies.

The politicians were having a tough time of it. Bob Menzies had been talking a very good air war from the beginning. But the men attracted to enlistment by his dramatic speeches were the same frustrated men cooling their heels in their civilian jobs, just knowing that they were on some air force waiting list somewhere. On 13 November 1939 Menzies announced the appointment of Australia's first minister for Air, James Valentine Fairbairn—one of Australia's blue bloods, from a prominent grazing family in Victoria's western district. Fairbairn had served in the Royal Flying Corps in the First World War and had probably survived that service by spending the last 14 months of the war as a prisoner of the Germans. Elected to federal parliament for the seat of Flinders in 1933, Fairbairn regularly flew his own aircraft from his property to Canberra. By 1939 Fairbairn had flown himself around Australia and from England to Australia. In the first Menzies government he was minister for Civil Aviation, and then from November for Air. When appointed to the new Air ministry Fairbairn was in Canada negotiating a crucial cooperative air force agreement between the dominions and Britain. So complex were the issues under discussion in Ottawa that Fairbairn was in regular cable and radio telegram contact with the prime minister in Australia. In an unusual twist Fairbairn was sworn into the Australian ministerial office as minister for Air by the governor-general of Canada, Lord Tweedsmuir, the novelist and writer John Buchan. Sadly, both men taking part in that unique ceremony were to die in 1940. As the only Australian minister to take the oath of office from a 'foreign' governor-general, the action shows how keen Bob Menzies was to have Australian ministerial representation at the important Ottawa conference.

When Jim Fairbairn left Ottawa for London he found himself in another long and difficult debate with Menzies in Canberra. After his death, tragically in an air accident in Canberra in August 1940 which also took the life of Army Minister Geoffrey Street among others, Bob Menzies said of Fairbairn, 'he was gifted in exposition and resolute in advocacy of what he believed to be true.' Perhaps Menzies was thinking of those days in London and Canberra just seven months earlier when Fairbairn and Menzies had clashed over who was to lead the air force.

Leadership of Australia's infant air force in the inter-war years had fallen to those who had distinguished themselves in what air war there was during World War I. Those, that is, who were prepared to gamble on a career in a permanent air force in a country as apparently defence illiterate as Australia in the years after the Great War. One of these men was Richard Williams, who ultimately became air marshal. But his long administration of the RAAF from the 1920s onwards was severely criticised in a report commissioned in mid-1938 from Marshal of the RAF Sir Edward Ellington. Such was the shallowness of Ellington's month-long study, the Englishman did not find it necessary to consult with or interview Chief of the Air Staff Williams; and the Air Board, the RAAF's peak decision-making body, learned of Ellington's appointment from the newspapers, not from an official communication from the Defence minister. Ellington went about his work, wrote air force historian Alan Stephens, 'in a boorish and patronising manner'. But the report meant that Dicky Williams was banished to London just when the RAAF was putting itself on a war footing.

By late 1939 the leadership of the RAAF was again in dispute. The obvious course was to bring Dicky Williams back home from

England, and Jim Fairbairn, the new minister, was urging his prime minister to do so. But Bob Menzies had decided that only an Englishman would do. He had already appointed an Englishman, Lieutenant General E.K. Squires, to head the army as chief of the general staff, and there had never yet been an Australian in charge of the Royal Australian Navy. Currently its head was Admiral Sir Ragnar Colvin. Why not, then, complete the trifecta and give the air force an Englishman too, even though he would know little about Australia, its people and their traditions.

'British to the bootstraps', they said of Bob Menzies and, although he had sought to stand up to the British over the destination of the 'proposed special force', he was now operating a leadership policy for the services that effectively said 'no Australian need apply'. Was this mindset what Australia really needed from its national leader in time of war? Would not Australian military leaders have helped Australians to think independently about the issues and problems that the war would throw up? When would Australians realise that it might be possible for British and Australian interests to diverge? You can see why Jim Fairbairn would have fought so intensely for his corner in his cable war with Menzies; but he lost. In any case, was it likely, Fairbairn might have argued, that the 'Mother Country', acutely alert to the possible peril from the air war soon to come, would happily release one of its best and brightest to take over the tiny Australian air force. Indeed not. The British put forward only two men for Jim Fairbairn to run the ruler over: Air Chief Marshal Sir John Steel and Air Marshal Sir Charles Burnett. Steel was 62 years of age and two years on the retired list; Burnett was 57, with, as Dicky Williams bitterly pointed out in his autobiography, less combat experience and less wartime leadership experience than the Australian. And eight years older. Fairbairn fought hard for what he thought was right, and kept Dicky Williams informed about what he was saying to Menzies and what the prime minister was replying. Williams believed that Fairbairn was 'very annoyed' at what was being done, but he told Williams that Menzies simply must have an Englishman in the job. Menzies would not budge and secured a cabinet decision; there was nothing that Jim Fairbairn could do. Having interviewed both Englishmen in London and having chosen Burnett as the lesser of two evils, but only for a year as the Air minister forthrightly insisted, Fairbairn then asked Williams to return to Australia to act as a member of the Air Board. Menzies even objected to this, but Fairbairn told the prime minister it was too late and that he had given a definite commitment to Williams. In the event, Burnett would be on the job in Australia until May 1942.

Few have had much good to say about Sir Charles Burnett. To Alan Stephens he was an 'uninspiring' and 'undistinguished' leader 'who seemed to regard the RAAF solely as a source of manpower for the war in Europe'. Even the official history, a series not known for overt criticism of either individuals or government decisions, reported the widespread disquiet at senior levels in the service and in parliament at the appointment of Burnett. Archie Cameron, the leader of the Country Party, complained about the appointment of Englishmen to the top Australian service positions: 'The present policy is tending to the belief that Australians are incapable of occupying some of the most important positions in the armed forces. This is in direct contradiction to the experience of 1914–18.'

Even worse was in store for the RAAF. It had become apparent in Whitehall that the United Kingdom was simply incapable of producing the number of pilots, observers and other aircrew who would be needed for the coming air war. So defence planners in London looked without hesitation to the dominions—Canada, South Africa, New Zealand and Australia. Looked with envy to the large numbers of educated, adventurous and possibly idealistic young men who might make aircrew. They summoned to Ottawa ministers from each of the dominions and hammered out an agreement where each of them would kick-start the training of potential aircrew at home; those who survived the initial orientation would travel to Canada for higher level training; those who survived that would be sent to Britain for a little more training, before being posted to an operational squadron. A South African squadron for the South Africans? An Australian squadron for the Australians? Possibly, if it could all be arranged, but in the meantime, no. Those who finished their training would be posted to wherever the need was greatest.

They called it the Empire Air Training Scheme. It was designed to supply 50 000 aircrew annually. In the agreement signed on 17 December 1939, Britain would recruit and train four-ninths of the RAF's annual aircrew requirement, and the dominions would recruit and train the rest. Of the rest, Canada would supply 56 per cent and Australia 36 per cent. Eventually, the RAAF was to contribute 27 899 men to the scheme. Australia signed up to the Empire Air Training Scheme (they called it, revealingly, the Commonwealth Air Training Scheme in Canada) when there were, all up, just 3500 in the Australian air force, ground crew included.

If the Australians had been kept together in Australian squadrons they might have been able to fight for their own country in its time of greatest need. But dispersed as they were throughout RAF squadrons in Britain, Australian aircrew were effectively lost to their own country for the duration. And unlike Canada, Australia did not insist on Australian command of Australian lives. The fate of an airman was intimately affected by his posting. To send a pilot to bomber command in the early years of the war was virtually a sentence of death as survival was linked inexorably to the number of missions flown; too many missions reduced the chance of survival to nil. Australia might have asserted the right to make these decisions about its young men. Surrendering that power, writes the air force historian, Alan Stephens, 'reduced the RAAF's contribution to cannon fodder'. Surrendering national authority, Stephens continued, 'allowed the RAF to allocate roles and deploy units with a disdain for national sensibilities which bordered on contempt'.

All these decisions were made and the agreement signed at the same time that Bob Menzies was complaining to the Australian High Commissioner in London about British high-handedness in assuming, by providing shipping in advance of the decision, that the 2nd AIF would serve Britain overseas. That formidable power, of which no one in Australia was prepared to speak publicly—Japan— forced the Australian government to think long and hard before committing troops to lands far from the homeland. 'We might need them here', Bob Menzies was telling the people in his coded way. But not airmen? Was there not something odd in the way that Menzies would fight for Australian troops on the one hand and meekly surrender control of Australian airmen on the other? Did Japan not possess an air force of skill and sophistication? Or could a Japanese air force not conceivably reach Australian shores? That was part of the reasoning. The Australian decision to hand over such a significant proportion of its air force to Britain depended, to some extent, on an outdated notion that the Japanese simply could not reach Australian shores by air; that Australia was simply too far away. But there was also the sense that Menzies understood the absolute vulnerability, nakedness if you like, of Britain in the skies. Flying time from Germany to England was easily within the range of the aircraft pouring from the German factories, and the United Kingdom might simply be pulverised before the war had really even got under way. Menzies had said within three weeks of the outbreak of war that the Mother Country might ask for help more insistently in the air than on the land or sea. They asked and Bob Menzies emphatically answered their call.

Robert ('Bob') Brazenor was born in Ballarat in 1922, the son of a man who had reached the rank of colonel in World War I, commanding the 23rd Battalion in France from 1916 to 1918—and awarded the Distinguished Service Order. Bob's father did not talk about his war very much within the family when he came home, but he was a severe disciplinarian—he once told Bob's older brother, Geoff, 'I've had thousands of men under me that were frightened of me. I'm not going to put up with a whipper-snapper like you.' Though he kept the war close to himself, he had been gassed in France and that had affected him. He died in 1945, aged only 57.

Despite all this, Bob Brazenor was happy enough to go to war. After school he had joined the bank in Ballarat as a 'bank boy', the lowest rung on the ladder. Though he worked in the bank for 18 months Bob hated the work and the life indoors. One of his first jobs each morning was to collect the bank's mail from the Post Office. Arriving one morning at the letterboxes Bob saw a new poster: 'Be a Pilot in the RAAF.' He said that he could not get his application in quickly enough. He had his interview in either late 1939 or very early 1940, and a medical examination a month later. Bob passed all of this with flying colours, but it was not until 18 August 1940 that he actually entered the service. For a young man, taking himself to the innermost parts of his being, debating with himself what he owed to his country and what he owed to his family and himself, and then finally screwing up all his courage and taking the momentous decision to offer, potentially, his life for his country, to then sit out his time in a bank or an office for more than a year while the air force, apparently, dithers about his offer. The young man and others would struggle to believe that the authorities were taking all this seriously. Bob Brazenor offered in December, was interviewed in February, and by August still hadn't heard. Was this war, or what? It was slow going, as we have seen, and despite the urgency of the Ottawa agreement Bob Brazenor was one of the very first Australians to follow the route the Empire Air Training Scheme proscribed.

First it was to Sydney, to Lindfield, for the Initial Training School. Number Two, he thought it was. 'We were there for six weeks doing drills and physical exercises, different classes, gunnery, meteorology, everything in general.' Then he was sent to Narrandera in the Riverina to the Elementary Flying Training School, 'where they taught us to fly Tiger Moths.' There is a theory that a person can either fly or not; that there is something innate in the skill, beyond teaching. Everyone points to champion Melbourne footballer 'Bluey' Truscott. No one could doubt Truscott's physical coordination, his balance, his fitness and his bravery. But he was no natural flyer, and if it hadn't been for his high reputation as a footballer and the massive public interest in his progress, it is doubtful that Bluey Truscott would have survived the EFTS. He did pass out to become a highly visible, well decorated and, apparently, skilled pilot shooting down eleven German aircraft over Europe and later serving at Milne Bay only to be killed in a training accident in 1943.

Bob Brazenor, on the other hand, seemed a natural at flying and within weeks was on his way, by ship, to Canada for advanced training. Airmen identified as pilots, like Bob, travelled in first-class cabins; observers—later known as navigators—travelled in second-class cabins; the remaining aircrew, the gunners, were down in the bowels of the ship with the crew. They resented, as you might expect, this class snobbery that seemed rife in the RAAF. 'It was just the RAAF,' said Bob Brazenor; many thought the RAAF had been a sort of men's club before the war, and now it was in the hands of an Englishman. Training at Fort McLeod in

Alberta at the foot of the Rocky Mountains, Bob Brazenor was now in a class of 34 Australians and 14 Canadians. Bob was just 19 years of age and you would think, as the real war was rapidly approaching, perhaps a little apprehensive. He says not; he was simply enjoying the experience 'all at government expense.' The 'Battle of Britain', as Churchill called it, is generally accepted to have run from mid-June 1940 to mid-September, although the main German assault began on 13 August. The attacks on London, which so dominate our thinking of this terrifying air war, began in earnest on 7 September and would merge into the Blitz after the Luftwaffe called off the battle. Best estimates are that the RAF lost 788 aircraft during the Battle of Britain and the Luftwaffe lost 1294. Bob Brazenor had every reason to be concerned for his future as he watched it unfold from afar, but anxiety was possibly not part of the make-up of 19-year-old pilots then.

With one other pilot, a Canadian, and four other Canadian aircrew, Brazenor sailed in a tiny Swedish ship in what he thought was the first ever Atlantic convoy. The remaining 33 Australians in training with Bob Brazenor went their separate ways; Bob was now entirely on his own. 'I never heard from the other chaps at all.' He was at the disposal of the British Air Ministry—entirely in their hands. At first he was sent to Uxbridge, near London, for a couple of days and then to an Operational Training Unit at Church Fenton near York, in the north of England. He was there for two or three weeks, getting the hang of operational aircraft. As it was now May 1941 and Hitler was engaged in Russia, the British skies were eerily quiet. Bob was to be in Britain for about ten months.

After his operational training on the night fighter, the Beau-fighter, Bob Brazenor was posted to No. 29 Squadron, RAF, with the legendary Guy Gibson as his commanding officer. 'G'day, digger,' said Gibson when they met. 'G'day, Sir,' said Bob Brazenor, the only Australian in the squadron. They welcomed him, alright, as they knew how much they needed him. At full strength the squadron would have 24 pilots; there were just eight when Bob Brazenor arrived, he made the ninth. And of the other Australians on his training course at Fort McLeod? Four of them stayed in Canada, joining coastal command and flying out of Prince Edward Island, and all of them lived to come home to Australia after the war. The other 29 Australian pilots were assigned to bomber command and none of them, not one of them, survived the war. For Bob Brazenor it was luck or, as he believed, someone looking after him.

The RAAF had certainly taken a couple of big hits in the early days of the war, losing control of a considerable proportion of its people for most, if not all, of the war, and having a leadership imposed upon it that was certainly not the best that could have been found among the ranks of the senior Australian officers. But for the man eagerly awaiting news about when he could start his training, the major failure seemed to be the glacial pace at which the RAAF went about its business. People might have considered more carefully how difficult it must be to start up an air force virtually from scratch. The tiny size of the pre-war service hardly justified the title that it so proudly carried. The point about the perception of the leisurely pace that seemed to infect the RAAF was that it reinforced the emerging public view that this war need not be taken too seriously. In fact, the RAAF could point to considerable achievement by way of putting into place the infra-structure that would eventually create a functioning air force.

By 1942, the RAAF was running five initial training schools, ten elementary flying training schools, five service flying training schools, two bombing and gunnery schools, four air-observer schools, and two wireless operator—air gunner—schools. Every month from 1942 onwards the schools were turning out 800 oper-ational pilots, fully capable of fighting with resourcefulness and skill the air war in which Australia was involved. All of these new pilots had no previous flying experience at all when they began their RAAF training. With hindsight we could argue that the air force infrastructure should have been established from 1936 onwards, but the legacy of the Great War, as we have seen, stood in the way of that. Without infrastructure, the RAAF had to start at the very bottom—initially, and with difficulty, training the trainers. While officers could explain why things had gone so slowly, to the public the lack of urgency seemed, well, indicative of the whole war.

At the end of 1939, as the 2nd AIF was preparing for embarka-tion for a war that had really not yet started, the RAAF seemed quite indifferent to the war and appeared to be going about its business at a terrifyingly slow pace. Observers on the homefront could be forgiven for losing interest in a war that seemed, at best, far away and of little direct relevance to Australia. A small enough force, grudgingly conceded, was off to war but with nothing like the hype and excitement of last time. It was all too confusing. 'In my day,' the men with their pots of beer were saying. In my day the war was on, right from the very start.

Walk along the Roll of Honour at the Australian War Memorial in Canberra looking at the names of all those killed in World War I. Each battalion will list upwards of a thousand men, sometimes many more. It is an appalling demonstration of the terrible cost of that war. 'Fortunately,' I would say to those I guided through the memorial, 'the lists on the Roll of Honour for the Second World War demonstrate no such numbers in the lives lost. Battalions suffered nothing like these losses, except for No. 460 Squadron, RAAF, that is. Bomber Command.' 460 Squadron suffered higher casualties than any other unit in either of the three Australian services during the war. The figures are staggering: 51 per cent of 460 Squadron aircrew were killed in action; only 24 per cent survived service with the squadron uninjured in action. One thousand and eighteen airmen died on active service with 460 Squadron on 368 raids; 169 aircraft were lost on operations. Formed in early 1942, the squadron flew its first mission on 12 March 1942 to the German city, Emden—the city which had given its name to the ship which, 'beached and done for' in the Indian Ocean in November 1914, gave Australians their first moment of cheer in World War I. That connection was not likely to be uppermost in the minds of Australian aircrew of 460 Squadron as they made the first of their 368 raids over Germany and occupied Europe. The squadron served from Britain until the European war ended, and was disbanded in October 1945.

Flying the Lancasters for which they were particularly known, but also Mosquitoes, Wellingtons, Halifaxes and a number of other lesser known aircraft, Bomber Command was specifically tasked with taking the fight to Germany, attacking bases, factories, and all manner of installations. It was extraordinarily taxing work, a test on each mission of the courage, skill, endurance and team work of every member of the command. Look at the faces of aircrew in Bomber Command in photographs of the time. You know them to be young men—that is what the records tell you—and yet the faces seem to be those of much older men. It is the strain of their service that has so aged them. Take these men out of Bomber Command and they are young men again.

Coming to 460 Squadron, as commanding officer of its home base, RAF Binbrook, in February 1943, was Hughie Edwards—one of the most decorated airmen of the Second World War, with a Victoria Cross, Distinguished Service Order and Distinguished Flying Cross. And he was Australian; born in 1914 in Western Australia, educated at the delightfully named White Gum Valley School, near Fremantle, and Fremantle Boys' School. Edwards made his career in the air force after a brief stint behind a desk as a shipping office clerk. Described by a crewmate as a 'tall, taciturn Australian with a very severe limp'—the result of an air accident in 1938 that might easily have taken his life—Edwards was one of those Australia surrendered to the service of the Empire. He was never an Australian flyer.

Hughie Edwards, as he was universally known, was awarded the Victoria Cross for leading a daylight raid on Bremen on 4 July 1941. Observed by German shipping on their journey to their target, Edwards knew that the twelve aircraft in his force would now attract heavy enemy fire. He determined that his aircraft would go low into their target, at 15 metres, under the high-tension electricity cables and the barrage balloons. The anti-aircraft defences were waiting but still Edwards pushed on; every aircraft in the flight was hit and four were destroyed, but the mission was accomplished. 460 Squadron had a man they could look up to.

It is hard to imagine how aircrew in Bomber Command could have returned again and again to fly the operations that they were given. To have flown at all strikes those who now look back on this aspect of the war simply as remarkable bravery. To do it again and again, night after night, seems almost beyond bravery. But the men themselves were more matter-of-fact.

We were driving some years ago on a battlefield tour to the northern French town of Bullecourt, where the Australians suffered terribly in April 1917. We passed, as you inevitably do in that part of France, a number of war cemeteries. 'If we come back this way we could stop at that cemetery,' one of the tourists said, 'It means a bit to me.'

It was the HAC British War Cemetery (the Honourable Artillery Company). Like all the others, there were headstones, a Cross of Sacrifice, and a table of stone, or an altar, with the words, 'Their name liveth for evermore'. As a cemetery created while the battle for the Hindenburg line raged, there were originally only about 120 graves in the HAC Cemetery, but after the war it grew substantially as smaller cemeteries were consolidated there. Now the HAC Cemetery commemorates about 2000 soldiers killed in the region in World War I and perhaps contains about 1000 graves. There is a pleasant brick building at the rear of the cemetery, a place of rest for visitors, and behind that a place to store the gardening equipment used to maintain the gardens. It was to this building that the battlefield tourist led us.

Born in Western Australia in July 1923, this man enlisted in the RAAF in June 1942, just before his nineteenth birthday. He was posted to England and to Bomber Command. He was a rear-gunner on a Lancaster, possibly the most dangerous position on the aircraft. One of the other gunners, John Beede, wrote a novel based on his experiences, called *They Hosed Them Out*; it was a common enough way of describing the fate of the rear-gunners.

'We'd agreed to group up over northern France,' our traveller told us as we stood by the garden shed. 'In our aircraft we were circling and waiting for the others to join us when the searchlights locked on us, we were in 'the cone'; knowing that, almost inevitably, the aircraft was now doomed, the skipper told us to get out as quickly as we could, we were just like a rabbit in the headlights. Fortunately, that field behind us,' he said, pointing to the field on the other side of the little cemetery stone wall, 'was heavy with wheat, just waiting for the harvest. My parachute opened once I was clear of the aircraft and I drifted to the ground. I scrambled in among the wheat and lay there; I knew the Germans would come looking. They did, but not too thoroughly, and I bided my time. After a long wait I stood up and looked about. There was this solid brick building that I could hide in while I worked out what to do next. I stayed there for a couple of days and the French people came to me with provisions. They had seen what had happened and were waiting so as not to draw attention to my hide-out. I told them that the next day was my twenty-first birthday and they came back again with half a bottle of gin. It was as much as they had. Like a fool, I drank it in one sitting.'

The local people told the Australian airman to stay where he was as the area was overrun with Germans, but the airman believed he had a duty to return to his squadron so that he could fly again and he set off along the escapers' route. It was July 1944; the Allies were already in France, he might have waited. There were still adventures too; cycling into a village early in the morning, the airman saw a German checkpoint ahead. But just as he passed the village church parishioners emerged from an early morning Mass. One of them sized up the airman's predicament, flipped his beret to the cyclist who promptly put it on and was waved through by the Germans as a Frenchman, naturally.

At length, our co-traveller told us, he made his way back to his squadron in England. They were delighted and surprised to see him. He was the first and the only member of his crew to return. And then anger entered this man's voice as he finished his tale. They wouldn't let him fly on operations again; you've done enough, they said, and they shipped him back to Australia. But he had enlisted to serve for the duration, he told us, and the job was not yet done. And we, who had gone to pay tribute to the Australians vainly assaulting the Hindenburg line at Bullecourt in 1917, had been transported immediately to the Second World War, as if the one were but a continuation of the other. That garden shed and First World War cemetery probably saved this Australian airman's life.

4. AT HOME

W ar was, they said with numbing frequency, the great test of the worth of a nation. A test of a nation's capacity for sacrifice, a test of the strength of the idea of placing the nation above the individual, of giving one's life for one's fellow man. It was also the one great Christian mission, they soon added, because this war will redeem and regenerate a nation that had become flabby, selfish, sinful. Christian ministers and priests of all denominations spouted this nonsense throughout the Great War, and too few people pointed at them and said the emperor had no clothes. Oblivious to the horror and complete human degradation of the trenches, the mud, the rats, the body parts scattered randomly about, the preachers said, perversely, that war would ennoble us, would reaffirm our human dignity. It was an utterly mad doctrine.

On that account war was a test of individual and national worth. But this second time around, this was an ideology that would be much more difficult to sell. Who would try to sell it? Well, first, churchmen, perversely again, but in a gentler way, perhaps, were still banging on about giving one's life for one's friends, and the greater good of sacrifice and the denial of self. Then politicians, as well, perhaps because they had to say something and they wanted their war to be popular and they needed the Empire to hold together. The military, too, probably, to make sense of what they were doing, to help raise recruits, to justify the killing that might start at any time. But there were so many problems with the 'war is good for you' mantra. Obviously, it wasn't.

The nation had not been transformed and made holy as a result of the terrible and immense Australian sacrifice the last time. Depending upon who you listened to, the nation was still at the mercy of the self-interest of big business or big unions; was hopelessly divided by poverty and the Depression; was divided along class lines, too, and by religion; was still sinful and unregenerate, as churchmen were too happy still to spout. Then there were the old soldiers still in the repatriation hospitals, the men who had lost their minds or their limbs and would spend their remaining days in the care of nurses and doctors—they were living testament to the horror and evil of war at the individual level. And I have already discussed the grief that still consumed thousands of Australian families. War good for you? Few in Australia in 1939 would have thought so.

This war, though, was far away and nothing was happening. Why would Australians become excited by it; what was in it for us, they would ask? But the moral-worth brigade were already out in force. Closely scrutinising the enlistment figures. Disappointing for the army, quite encouraging for the air force. How was the national moral temperature on this reading. So-so, maybe at best a little lukewarm.

Turn to the civilians. Were they making sacrifices for the war? Joining volunteer organisations to make, well, camouflage nets, or to knit socks, or to provide 'comforts' (cakes and the like) for the fighting men? Were they going to church in greater numbers, manifesting a seriousness in their personal lives that showed there was a war on? Or were they hell-bent on pleasure—down at the beach, at the races with some money in their pockets for the first time in years, having a beer with their mates, or talking about the cricket and the nags, rather than the war? The newspapers sold their product on the basis of the footy, the cricket, the gallops and all the rest of what people perceived as a decent Australian life, and then they filled up the front part of their papers with moans about the indifference of Australians to the war.

Tom Blamey, hitting his stride as the AIF's commander, was at it from the start. The mood of the nation was all wrong, he would say over and over again until, mercifully, they shipped him off to the war that was yet to get going. People need to know that we could be at risk, he would say, that they need to become serious about what was happening to the world. As if anyone would take seriously a lecture on morals from Tom Blamey. It was not leadership he was offering, it was nagging.

Over in England there was a young West Australian, Paul Royle. He had been in the military from an earlier age, entering the Naval College at Jervis Bay in 1928. To enter the permanent air force in the 1930s he was prepared to go to England for training, and that is where he was when war broke out. At RAF Hullavington, to be precise, near Chippenham in Wiltshire. Paul missed his home and the company of other Australians—there were only a very few of them in training at Hullavington—so he kept sending home a steady stream of letters, although to be frank the routine of training gave him very little to write about.

From about August 1939 Paul Royle began to take the prospect of war seriously, but not in the way the war-is-good-for-you brigade might have expected. 'If war does break out', he wrote, 'don't let Gun [his brother Gordon] come over here in a moment of intense patriotism; there is nothing really worth fighting for, as far as you people are concerned . . . it is all so stupid and ridiculous.' Perhaps that wasn't clear enough, for a couple of weeks later he was at it again: 'So Gun wants to come to war? Try to make him forget all about it; gone are the days when it was a glorious adventure, now it is just subterfuge, cunning and murder.'

Did Paul Royle's letters pass around his mates in Perth? You'd have to wonder. Were others thinking and writing like this? It would be good to know. Paul's dad had been in World War I and may have had a pretty rough time of it, at least that's the impression he'd left with his son. 'You are well out of it this time, Dad', Paul wrote when war had finally been declared. 'I have stepped into your shoes with a vengeance, but hope to escape more lightly than you did. At any rate, I will be living with much less discomfort than you were.'

If indifference or even downright opposition to the war was widespread as 1939 edged into 1940, it would be leadership that would make the difference. Australia needed a leader who would present the issues clearly to the people, telling them openly of the evil ideology of the enemy, of the importance of making a stand against the doctrine of Aryan supremacy; a stand against racism as bad as the world had ever known. Not the leadership of the nagging Tom Blamey nature, or of the war-is-good-for-you brigade, but of sensible reasoning from the highest political levels about the risks to national security from the German quest for domination, and of the importance of Australia, among the nations, taking a strong stand against evil in the world. It would be Bob Menzies who would need to awaken the nation, to issue the instructions that would rouse the people from their slumber. Could he do it?

It might require a fair prime ministerial sleight of hand for there were many in the community who saw Menzies, like Chamberlain in Britain, as an appeaser, blinkered, if you like, to the true evil of Nazism and Hitler. This was what Bob Menzies was saying on Melbourne Cup Day in 1938:

> The peace [he was referring to Chamberlain's 'peace in our time'] had brought about a better understanding between Great Britain and Germany, and, to some degree, Italy . . . In the ordinary course of events it was unlikely that Australia would be attacked by a European nation but Europe was not the only continent in the world . . . Australia had many friends and at least one potential enemy.

Not designed really to encourage young men to fight in another European war or to send the nation into overdrive when a European war broke out.

Two weeks later, still in 1938, Bob Menzies was a guest at a lunch for Old Melburnians (old boys of Melbourne Grammar School). A reporter from the Melbourne *Argus* wrote that Menzies said that 'from [his] talks with leaders in Great Britain and Germany [Menzies] had concluded that Germany had some real grievances with Czechoslovakia'. But when he said this publicly, Menzies confided to the old boys, people said he was pro-German. 'People who thought that France was always right and Germany always wrong,' Menzies told his audience, 'were the type who perpetuated international trouble.' On a recent visit to Germany, Menzies continued, he had been much impressed by German industrial efficiency and, while democracy suited Australia, that did not mean it suited every country and circumstance. The majority of the German people, he said, were satisfied with their government and the young were particularly enthusiastic support- ers of Herr Hitler. Those very same young people, perhaps, whom the Melbourne papers had reported just four days before Menzies gave this speech to the old boys, had burned down synagogues across Germany, had looted Jewish shops and murdered Jewish shopkeepers. Bands of Nazis had been armed with crowbars, the *Argus* had reported. Surely Bob Menzies had not missed reading that report of Kristallnacht? Yet even after this atrocity Menzies could still speak as if accommodation with Germany was desirable and good.

Perhaps people in late 1939 had forgotten what Bob Menzies had been saying less than a year earlier, but you have to think that he might now have a struggle on his hands to convince people that the war with Germany was suddenly worth the loss of Australian life. Was that one potential but unspoken enemy still lurking out there? Was Europe still not the only continent in the world? Was the satis- faction of the German people with their government, despite the problems about which Australians had been reading, guarantee enough that they should be allowed to make their own way in the world? Of course, circumstances had changed, but a war leader needs conviction and consistency if he is to encourage his people to genuine hardship and sacrifice. We should not necessarily blame the people if they were only half-listening to Bob Menzies as Christmas began to make its pleasant reappearance in Australia in 1939.

Paul Royle was still thinking of home as atrocious weather conditions in England denied him much in the way of flying time. 'I'd give a lot to be in the air force at home', he wrote, 'the dust and the heat of Kalgoorlie is quite appealing'. But there were aspects of home life, as reported by his parents, that Paul found mighty hard to understand. 'Fancy having a black-out in Perth', he wrote in late September 1939. 'Surely they don't expect a German air-raid. Still it might give you an idea of the conditions here, where every night is absolutely black.' It must have seemed odd reading of blackouts in the Empire's most remote city when war was potentially on your doorstep.

Yet some Australians had taken terror from the skies seriously. On 4 September 1939, 2000 potential air-raid wardens had jammed into the Sydney Town Hall to learn how to protect city buildings. At Brighton, a seaside suburb some 15 kilometres from the centre of Melbourne, wardens established a first-aid post and decontamination squad. Why? In Sydney the education department was advising teachers that community singing might be a good idea to assist in preventing panic if children had to be evacuated from their schools. It was almost inevitable, you would have to think, that the department fell back on World War I songs for the calm-inducing community sing-song; tunes such as 'It's a Long Way to Tipperary' and 'Pack Up Your Troubles in Your Old Kitbag'. There were also practise school evacuations in Sydney, and at one large school of 1200 pupils it took 13 minutes to disperse the school at the first attempt but only seven minutes at the third.

Was there any real danger at all in the Australian skies in September 1939? It would be very hard to think so. There is nothing wrong, of course, in planning and preparing for a community to respond to an emergency. There was nothing to say that Australia might not come under attack from an unspecified enemy at some later date. But if the Germans were unable even to cross the English Channel in 1939, and schoolchildren in Britain were returning home after the early mass evacuations of the first days of the war, was it even remotely likely that German bombers might find their way to Perth, or even to Sydney for that matter. Excited and slightly hysterical responses in the first days of the war ran the risk of confirming the population in its complacency. People are not easily sucked in by the ridiculous and many regarded the largely self-appointed air-raids precautions' people as pompous and somewhat ridiculous. People could sniff out the phoney.

Perhaps Bob Menzies understood the danger of a confected war. Perhaps he recognised that silly and hysterical responses when there was no realistic threat to Australia might sound too much like 'the boy who cried wolf'. If there was no real danger now, then the trouble was that when danger did eventuate the people might just shrug their shoulders indifferently and talk about being conned once before. So Menzies tried to shut down the hysteria. 'Australians,' he said, 'must not become victims of obsession, or give themselves up to any form of hysteria, however popular . . . Thank God there is plenty of room in our life for laughter and games, as well as for serious things.' And he still portrayed an optimistic view of where the world might be heading when speaking at the East Kew Bowling Club's season opening in late 1939: 'I hope you will carry on with great success. I trust that when we meet at the opening of the 1940–41 season we may be able to have our celebrations in a more pleasant and hopeful atmosphere.'

People took Bob Menzies at his word as he preached 'business as usual'. 'Who said depression, recession or gloom', asked one journalist in Sydney, after noting that 63 000 racegoers had trooped to Randwick in October to watch Feminist win the Metropolitan, while 67 500 Melburnians had watched the running of the 1939 Caulfield Cup and 95 000 were at the Melbourne Cup. Menzies asked people, as if it were necessary, to preserve the Christmas traditions of gift-giving and feasting. He was looking to the unemployment figures, fearing that too much war fever might make people cautious about Christmas. The secretary of Victoria's central unemployment committee estimated that there were still 30 000 to 40 000 unemployed men in that state, although the official figure stood at 12 000. Throwing more people out of work was the last thing the government would have wanted. 'Buy Australian-made gifts wherever possible,' Menzies urged.

He need not have worried about Christmas spending. For the first time in years there was an air of prosperity all around the country, as if the war was the last thing on people's minds. In Sydney, large department stores and small specialist shops alike were so jammed with customers that a reporter said it was almost impossible to move. Someone estimated there was something like 400 000 people in the centre of Sydney on the last shopping day before Christmas. Sales were well above the norm of recent years, and it wasn't the practical or the war-related items that were selling but the frivolous and the luxurious: 'The lightheartedness of the crowds was more noticeable than for many previous years', a reporter observed. What were people doing? Having a last, final fling before the war became serious; or looking with hope and expectation to the fuller employment and modest prosperity that war might at last bring? Or, in reaction to a war that was utterly unlike what they remembered or had been told about, were people merely relaxing in relief that the expected gloom and sadness had not engulfed them?

With Christmas over and initial training completed, Paul Royle was now awaiting his first posting. He was sorry to be leaving his mates at Hullavington, 'as we were all good friends'. Of the 45 pilots and navigators with whom he had trained only six of them, Paul included, were sent to an army school where they would learn to fly in support of the British Expeditionary Force (BEF), which was expected to see the bulk of its fighting in France. Of these six, three were Australians. Paul Royle had written home a little earlier that the 'war has a perpetual depressing effect on me'. It was the boredom of training and waiting. 'I can understand why so many people take to drink', he wrote, '[but] when we get into action I expect it will be different'. And so a posting to the army on Salisbury Plain promised some excitement; action seemed, at last, around the corner. It failed to materialise. In three letters home from early January 1940 to mid-February Paul Royle showed that he was nearly expiring from boredom: 'The war is very dull'; 'We are all waiting for something to happen. This cannot keep up for ever'; 'The war seems to have petered out entirely with no air or land activity at all. Wonder when it will start, if ever.' If such were the views of a man in uniform, in the glamour service, and near enough to the centre of it all, how can we possibly expect Australians, throwing off at last the constraints of the Depression and enjoying their traditional summer holidays with no sniff of danger to arouse them, to do anything but follow the government's injunction for business as usual?

The 'outer' at the Melbourne Cricket Ground, the 'temple down the road', is as good a place as any to spend a few idle days in summer reverie. In the first days of 1940 Bradman would be batting for South Australia in a Sheffield Shield clash with Victoria, and that was a mouthwatering prospect. 'Who cares who wins the shield?' said one man as he was taking his seat, 'I want to see Bradman get going.' And the greatest cricketer of them all did not disappoint. The Don scored his 90th century and 34th double-century in first-class cricket, thus helping South Australia to a massive first innings total of 610 runs, for a first innings lead over the Victorians who had scored a creditable 475 in the first day and a half of the match. Cricket can hardly ever have seemed so exciting. Later, two prisoners of war in the hands of the Japanese made their captivity at least slightly more bearable by recalling to each other in great detail notable games they had seen at the SCG and the MCG respectively. Was this Victoria–South Australia clash one of the games they talked about? It is lucky that we cannot see into the future because you would have to think that, of the thousands of innocent and happy holidaymakers watching Bradman on those glorious first days of 1940, some of them at least would later be trudging the Kokoda Track, or on Bomber Command in Europe, or at HellFire Pass on the Burma–Thailand Railway. Enjoy the cricket while you can.

One of those who was probably not at the cricket was Beryl Bedggood's father, Ted. Like his two older brothers and one younger, Ted Bedggood had been destined to work in the family's shoe-making firm since birth. That was the way it was, even if the youngest son, Bruce, would have much preferred to have been a jazz musician. But when war broke out Ted Bedggood immediately sought release from the firm for service in the air force. Not as a pilot or other aircrew—he was too old for that—but in some capacity. As an equipment officer at Victoria Barracks, as it turned out, entering the service in the first days of 1940. Neither of his older brothers had served in World War I, though they were of an age to do so, and there was a feeling in the family that Ted was enlisting to make up, in some part, for the family's earlier lack of service.

Beryl was still at school, in her last year, when her father joined up, and she was very proud of him but aware, too, of the pressures on the boys with whom she played and partied, aware that they were thinking about enlistment when their school year ended in

December. Boys from 'good' schools like Scotch in Melbourne, brother school to Beryl's Fintona, had been brought up on the notion of sacrifice and service as exemplified by Old boys who had fought in the Great War. All 1207 of them—including ten of the 1st XVIII football team of 1914, every captain of the school from 1904 to 1916, every dux, and every captain of cricket and football for the same period—enlisted or was rejected. The most famous of them was John D. Burns, prefect, first-class scholar and, as it turned out, poet—his 'Bugles of England' became a rallying cry for recruiters throughout the land:

> The bugles of England were blowing o'er the sea
> As they had called a thousand years calling now to me
> They woke me from dreaming in the dawning of the day
> The bugles of England and how could I stay?

John Burns was killed at Gallipoli in August 1915 after only three weeks in the trenches.

No one was writing like that in 1940, but that does not mean that the pressures were less intense on those who now prepared themselves to take their final school exams, just as John Burns had once done. Boys at Scotch, boys at just about every school in their senior years, talked about the war and talked about enlisting when their school days were over. Less intently, perhaps, as they came back to school after the holidays of 1939–1940, but more earnestly as the school year unfolded, as the war warmed up.

While Melbourne was basking at the cricket, the Sydney summer on the harbour was also in full swing. Into that harbour in early January had come a flotilla of British cruise liners, as they would have been called then. How can the British suddenly find the shipping for an Australian contingent, Bob Menzies must have mused, when shipping for Australian wool and wheat and all the other items of Australian trade could not be got? It was simple really. Passenger liners circled the globe as the only affordable means of international travel, even for the well-off. With holidays in the colonies now out of the question, and with powers of requisition, the British government simply converted the passenger fleet into troopship carriers. The ships in Sydney Harbour in early

January, the *Ortranto*, the *Orcades*, the *Orford* and the *Strathnaver*, had, in all the haste, undergone minimal transformation and would carry about the same numbers of troops as they had of paying passengers. This was the way to go to war, in some luxury.

Troops in training since November realised soon enough that something was up. At the big holding camp at Ingleburn outside Sydney, men were closing the first chapter of the book of their life in the army, stuffing their allowed possessions into kitbags ready for embarkation. Where would they be going? Their dads had gone to Egypt first, but now there were other possibilities. Singapore to shore up the British defences there, should the unthinkable happen and the Japanese enter the war. India for garrison duty and further training. Egypt for training and for quick movement to battlefields in either direction, east or west. England, perhaps, for movement to France to fight alongside the BEF in what everyone assumed would be, again, a battlefield of years. The Germans would hammer the Maginot line and British and French resistance would again keep the enemy tied down and frustrated, near enough to Paris but with no success in taking the capital, as before. That was how it would be, people thought, just like last time. So they talked, the men at Ingleburn, endlessly discussing the possibilities and opportunities, listening to rumours and supposed inside knowledge, knowing now, at least, one thing: their destination was entirely at the decision of others. They had surrendered, they now realised, their liberty and independence until this war was over.

In homes across Australia there were similar debates about where these men would be going. Please God, women would pray, to somewhere safe, not in the thick of the fighting. Please, said men in their pubs, not to the trenches of France, not that again. It would be too cruel if the Somme became a killing field again, if our sons would go to their war passing the cemeteries in which our mates lie. To fight outside of Flers, for example, around the AIF Burial Ground Cemetery. No, they prayed, that would be too cruel. So they steadied themselves for the farewell. These men who had already known war told one another that their sons must not see that we grieve for them, that we worry for them. We will send them off, they vowed, with a hearty handshake and a steady gaze. There will be no tears, the wives and mothers said, at least until the ships are well out into the harbour. Is there a harder thing for a mother or father to do than to send a boy to war? Why? their minds would keep screaming. Why my boy, why again? What does it have to do with Australia? they'd asked. Was it Dad's example that sent him to enlist, is it my fault that he has gone? When will we see him again? Oh, why?

The military would have liked to have kept the news of the departure of the first contingent of the 2nd AIF something of a secret but all of Sydney knew the boys were going, and all of Sydney, it seemed, turned out to say goodbye—as if for the start of a Sydney to Hobart yacht racing classic, as people would know it later in the harbour's history. All Australians now can visualise the scene at the start of that race—the sunshine, the sparkling harbour, the deepest blue, and white, too, from the churn of hundreds of boats, the noise of a thousand hooters and whistles. So it was at the height of the summer in January 1940. The men excited and impressed by the send-off. The crowds had even formed along the railway line from Ingleburn, waving like mad and cheering. 'Good luck,' they yelled, and as the trains slowed for stations and street crossings the bystanders could even make out the faces of some of the boys. Proud and excited, to be sure, but was there a hint of apprehension there, too?

Those who boarded their troopships at Woolloomooloo Wharf would have marched past a drinking fountain at the entrance gates to the wharf. How many even gave it a second thought. It was raining in Sydney back on Anzac Day 1922, but even so a large number of women gathered at these gates, as they had done every year since 1916. The women started arriving at about 1.30 in the afternoon. When they came they began to hang wreaths made of laurel or rosemary, or flowers picked from home, on the gates. They had been doing that, every year since 1916. But this day was special. At 2 p.m. Governor-General Lord Forster and Lady Forster arrived.

Typical of the type then: Eton, New College Oxford, captained Hampshire in the county cricket, represented the Gentlemen against the Players, and Sevenoaks and then Bromley in the House of Commons from 1892 to 1919—on the Conservative side, of course. Henry Forster was sworn in as Governor-General of

Australia on 7 October 1919. He stayed until 1925 although it annoyed him that he had to draw down 2000 pounds of his own money every year just to keep the office working as he wanted it. Lord Forster died in 1936. He had said being governor-general was just like looking after a big constituency.

When the Governor-General arrived at Woolloomooloo on that day the Salvation Army band played the national anthem. A commemorative service was held, led by the Reverend W. Price and a former army chaplain, Reverend John Cope, gave an address. Cope had enlisted when he was 48 years old as a chaplain in the AIF in September 1915, so he missed Gallipoli. He served with the 14th Battalion, Jacka's Mob, in France so he may have been at Pozieres and Bullecourt. If he was he would have seen some of the worst fighting the AIF endured. I do not know what he said in his address to the crowd of mainly women and children at the wharf gates in 1922. Something about his experiences with their husbands, their sons, their brothers, you would expect.

We do know a bit of what the governor-general said: 'I have just unveiled the memorial fountain erected by the women of New South Wales to commemorate those touching scenes of farewell to the brave men who passed through those gates out into the Great War.' He spoke of heroic deeds done for country and Empire and, on a personal note, added an 'understanding sympathy' for those dressed in mourning at the ceremony. He and Lady Forster had lost two sons at the war: 'Let this fountain be held in high honour in memory of the brave men who went and the brave women who sent them.'

Did he slip up there in his expression? The women who sent them sounds a bit strong. These women had come to the gates every Anzac Day during the war and kept up the tradition ever since. They came to remember that, for many of them, this was the last spot from which they had glimpsed their beloved son or husband going off to war. Most of those who enlisted in New South Wales during the First World War passed through the gates at Woolloomooloo on their way. Did hands clutch out to grab their tunics as they marched onto the wooden wharf? Family and friends were allowed access to the wharf when the troops were safely on board their troopships. They would have thrown streamers as a link between those on the land and those on the ship pulling out into the harbour. How they must have yearned for those streamers never to break. No wonder Woolloomooloo had such an important place in their memories. No wonder they returned each year for their own unique remembrance. That place may have meant little to returning soldiers. It was just one of dozens of places they passed through: Woolloomooloo, Cairo, Southampton, Marseilles perhaps, Boulogne, Etaples. But to the women and children it was a natural place of pilgrimage.

The first Australian contingent in 1940 sailed out of Sydney Harbour on 10 January to the cheers and encouragement of a huge crowd of people on the water and lining every possible vantage point on the land on both sides of the harbour. The departure date was supposed to be a secret, but when on 9 January the Sydney *Sun* had published a cartoon farewelling the troops, people took the hint and the harbour was packed the next day. And where were they going? German radio announced that they were on their way to Suez and that seemed as good a bet as any.

Historians will not do their readers any favours if they do not try to look behind what was happening to attempt to discover its meaning. I can tell you that in both Melbourne and Sydney in early January 1940, there were big city parades as the new AIF made its first appearance in public. I can also tell you that citizens turned out in huge numbers to cheer on the marching troops. In Sydney people waited for hours to see the soldiers, and newspapers suggested there were more than half a million people along the route. There was confetti and streamers and Union Jacks everywhere. How did the soldiers look? Again we turn to the newspapers: 'They came by in sixes, every face browned by camp life, every body trained and fit . . . young, bronzed, clear-eyed, and so obviously conscious in their demeanour of their high responsibility.' Take all that with a grain of salt, I'd say. Do you remember an airman, Paul Royle, describing war as 'subterfuge, cunning and murder'?

One of my heroes in this second AIF is Salvationist Albert Moore. I met him in the last years of his life when he came to the Australian War Memorial to donate his letters and diaries from his time at war. Albert Moore had served in the war first as a 'comforts' man, trying to make the military bearable for the troops with hot coffee and cocoa, writing materials in Salvation Army clubrooms, that type of thing. Later he served as a Salvation Army chaplain on the Kokoda Track. He is the man lighting the injured digger's cigarette in that iconic picture, one of the best known from that war. I stood with Albert Moore in front of the photograph on display in large format in the gallery at the War Memorial. It is a very famous photograph but Albert Moore did not think that the incident was anything special. After he had left the memorial that day I looked into the diaries he had just donated. The next day I rang him—he was still in Canberra. 'There is so much that is deeply personal in your diaries, Albert,' I said. 'You might wish to consider closing them for a period of years if you think they might embarrass you or your family.' 'That is why I donated them,' was this good man's honest reply. 'I wanted people to know what war is really like. Let people see what I have written, then they might understand.'

I well remember opening up the parcel of diaries just a few minutes after Albert Moore had left the memorial. Historians are trained to make judgements early about documents like these. Can the writer tell a story? Alert us to place and people? Paint a picture? Reflect? Give us his world and some characters? Reading the first words in Albert Moore's diaries, I doubted it. The language was humdrum; verbs shaky. His world was that of hundreds of other soldiers. He was at camp in Geelong in late 1939. He wrote of training drills and marches, of stew and tea, of his 'comforts' hut with its 'Hop In' sign of a big kangaroo. And of trips up to Melbourne on his days off to see his family—his wife, Violet, and his son Kelvin. Albert always seemed to sleep-in while in Geelong, missing the early train. That was annoying—perhaps the only emotion I'd been experiencing while reading this stuff; I would have bought an alarm clock to make the early train on time. Routine really. I must have read hundreds of diaries like this. I turned the pages, a page for each day; handwriting good, that makes it easier. Nothing here, though, let's get him overseas.

It was the entry for 14 December 1940 that shocked me: 'It was the last night at home with Vi and Kelvin perhaps for a long time.' Albert was going to Sydney the next day with the troops, to the troopships and to war. 'So [the] three of us slept together. Could

feel Kelvin cling to my arm whilst in bed. He's a great boy.' The
next entry, the next day, was of a terrible pain:

> This is the day I have dreaded for many months in fact ever
> since war started. Today I leave those whom I love . . . Most
> trying experience of my life, and loved ones clung to me and
> refused to let go. Finally farewelled Vi and my bonnie boy
> who to my surprise clung to me like a leech & cried bitterly,
> this the last straw, God alone knows my love for this child,
> the sacrifice is great, almost too much to bear. The whistle
> goes and still he is clinging, the train moves out and I have
> to tear him away. My God be Thou our sufficiency. I sunk
> into carriage seat feeling that the bottom had fallen out of
> my world. Vi, Boy, gone.

In Sydney Albert learned that the troops would not be sailing
at least until after Christmas. He called his wife in Melbourne;
it took ages to get through, not until 10.20 p.m., in fact. 'Kelvin
broke down whilst talking to me, this made the evening a very
distressing one.' Albert suggested to Vi that Kelvin might come
over to Sydney by train to spend a few days with his dad, but she
thought this might distress the boy even more. Violet relented
though and Kelvin arrived in Sydney on 21 December. Naturally
his dad was there to meet him at the train: 'Wonderful to see him,
had cherished fond hope that my Vi might be with him, but this
was not so.' They went to the zoo together, father and son, spent
Christmas Day at a Salvationist young persons' camp at Collaroy,
where Kelvin went swimming. They went to Manly twice, doing all
the things that tourists in Sydney do. And then at 8 o'clock on
Christmas night Kelvin was gone, back to Melbourne:

> My boy has gone. I shall never forget this night. This is an
> enormous sacrifice. God make me equal to it. Hasten the
> peace and our reunion with Vi, Kelvin and loved ones.

Marching off to war, these light-hearted happy warriors, the
papers had said. Not every one of them, not by any means.

5. ACTION STATIONS

People simply could not tell where this war was going. The troops who had sailed so grandly out through the Sydney Heads in early January reached Ismailia on the Suez Canal on 12 February 1940. To show a deep gratitude the British had sent out to Egypt the secretary of state for the dominions, Anthony Eden, to greet the Australians. The point of the welcome was to let the Germans know that 'we are all in this together; one race, one destiny'—that sort of thing. Then the troops went by train to Gaza and on to a camp at Julis in Palestine. The officers divided the camp into five sections and named them after First World War Australian military leaders: Monash, Hobbs, Leane, Goddard and Gellibrand. The force was then largely lost sight of in Australia as the soldiers went into general and specialised training. While the war correspondents tried to file copy back home that would interest and arouse readers, it was tough going. There was nothing doing.

On 17 April Governor-General Lord Gowrie opened the second session of the fifteenth federal parliament in Canberra.

Gowrie was a good man, a military officer who had served in Egypt before World War I and had become the first militia officer to be awarded the Victoria Cross. Married in 1908, his wife's family thought of Alexander Hore-Ruthven, as he then was, as 'the impecunious son of an impoverished family'. He fought at Gallipoli and was severely wounded at Suvla, and he also served in France. Retiring from the army in 1928 Gowrie became Governor of South Australia, and then of New South Wales in 1935. In 1936 he replaced Sir Isaac Isaacs, the first Australian governor-general. Gowrie was due to return home in September 1939—he had been governing for 11 years—but the war meant that he was asked to stay on for another year. He would officially handover to the Duke of Gloucester in January 1945, although Gowrie left Australia in September 1944. He remains Australia's longest-serving governor-general. Gowrie's only surviving son, Patrick, would be killed in action in 1942. But now, in April 1940, this man of military bearing was seated in the Senate reading the 'address from the throne' to open the parliament. Germany had invaded Norway, the first sign of an actual war on the ground. The situation was grave, the Governor-General told the parliament, but there was no reason, at this stage, for additional defence or security arrangements. Steady as she goes. Seven months into the war and still nothing doing. And then, suddenly, it all changed.

Beryl Bedggood took French as one of her subjects in her last year at school and needed to do well as she was hoping to go on to university. There was a weekly period of one-on-one French conversation to prepare her for the oral examination. Beryl vividly recalls one class when she and her French-born teacher simply sat through the lesson in tears, unable to converse, as they tried to come to terms with the news of the fall of Paris. It somehow seemed personal to Beryl and frightening to large numbers of Australians. In the few weeks since Lord Gowrie had spoken in parliament, the war had suddenly become hot and the world had changed dramatically. After such a long period of inactivity and business as usual, almost all of Europe had fallen to the Germans, and here was Hitler walking down the Champs Élysées in triumph. Germany had invaded Denmark and Norway on 9 April 1940; a day later the Danish king had ordered a ceasefire. The Norwegian king was evacuated from his capital on 30 April and Norway surrendered on 9 June.

At dawn on 10 May 1940 the German army had simultaneously invaded Luxembourg, Belgium and the Netherlands. The prize, of course, was France; the symbol, Paris. In the First World War the Germans had come close enough to Paris, and it was the Australians at Villers-Bretonneux in April 1918 who had barred their way to Amiens, preventing the possibility of the German army reaching Paris. In this new war, now in full blaze, with a combination of skill and some luck the Germans spearheaded with panzer (tank) attacks that threw away all the certainties and hesitations of war as the planners had remembered it from the Western Front. In their rush to the channel ports, in which the Germans deployed about the same number of divisions as the French and British, but with a vastly better air force, the Germans seemed to take on a cloak of invincibility. They were, it seemed, unstoppable. On 23 June Hitler was in Paris and French resistance was over. The British were hurriedly evacuating their troops across the channel in whatever ships and boats could be found. Dunkirk, they called it—one of those British disasters that could be turned into heroism and eventual triumph. The stark fact was that the British had been booted out of Europe.

Paul Royle, in action at last with the RAF's No. 53 Squadron attached to the British ground forces, took off on his first flight over enemy territory on 18 May 1940—a reconnaissance flight between Poix, where he was based, and Vitry in northern France, near territory over which his father might have fought 24 years earlier. Having taken off, as far as his squadron was concerned, that was the end of Paul Royle. A telegram from Defence in Melbourne, wrongly written to Mrs Royal but fortunately giving the right address, informed Paul's mother, as his next of kin, that he was missing in action. Later, the commanding officer of 53 Squadron would write a personal letter stating that Paul had 'promised to become a most valuable member of the squadron', although he had been with the squadron and on active service for only a couple of days. Eventually, the family would discover that Paul Royle was a prisoner of war in the hands of the Germans. The telegram announcing that Paul was missing in action was one of the very

first of its kind sent out from Defence in Melbourne. There would
be many, many more.

The scale and speed of the German victories in France was
stunning. Was it a question of a will to fight? Winston Churchill
thought so. Becoming prime minister only on 10 May 1940, the
day the war really started, Churchill made a quick visit to Paris on
16 May to try to find out for himself what was going on with the
French army. Churchill returned to London a deeply worried man.
Was there among the French, he wondered, a real sense of determination, a real desperation for the defence of their homeland?
Where was the man, Churchill asked, who would rouse the French
to the determined patriotism that alone could resist aggression?

The French had suffered dreadful losses during World War I.
Go to any French village, no matter how small, and inspect the war
memorial, found often at the town hall or otherwise most likely
at the village church. Name after name after name, even for the
tiniest village; too often listing several men with the same
surname—brothers most likely, cousins at least. Stand with the
French people at a commemorative service—and there are several
throughout the year—and hear the name of each man on the
memorial called out aloud. *Mort pour la France*—'he died for
France'—the people say as each name is read out. Something of
France died with these millions of young men in that most awful
first war. Was any war, any tyranny, worth this scale of sacrifice, the
French wondered and debated throughout the 1920s and 1930s?
And here, just a generation later, war comes again. Who can blame
the French if the will to fight was just not there? But into the
explanation for the collapse of an entire nation in little over a
month must also go poor planning, overconfidence (the Maginot
line), and the misuse of the troops that were available to fight. On
14 June Paris fell, undefended, and on 22 June the French signed
an armistice in the same railway carriage that had been used for
the armistice to end the Great War on 11 November 1918. During
six weeks of fighting the French had lost 90 000 dead, 200 000
wounded and possibly 1.9 million troops taken prisoner. The
Germans had lost under 30 000 dead, with a total casualty figure
of 163 000. With France utterly crushed, the outlook for Britain
was grim indeed. The battle for Britain could not be far off.

Bob Menzies was in Canberra when he heard the news that the German army was on the move into Western Europe. By 21 May he was in War Cabinet with a range of proposals that indicated that he was alert to how quickly the situation had changed. There was a real prospect, Menzies now believed, that Britain might be invaded and, unthinkably, defeated. Australia, therefore, could no longer rely on Britain for its security and national integrity. A simple sentence to write or to read but, for any Australian of Menzies' generation, absolutely devastating to contemplate. Britain was the key to Australian defence. Now the Germans had taken that key and seemingly hurled it into the nearest dam. And the Australian government needed to respond.

Men and equipment, it was as simple as that. An army for Australia, more men for an expeditionary force that might hold up or delay Hitler in the Middle East, for example. Australia would need its own munitions industry to arm the men, the situation now required. Menzies recommended to cabinet the appointment of manufacturing giant Essington Lewis as director-general of munitions with supremo powers. And a fourth division of the AIF, should the British agree and should enough arms be found for them.

Two of the existing three divisions of the AIF were largely still paper plans in military offices, but the terrible news from Europe so stimulated Australian recruiting that by late July 1940 there were 82 000 new recruits in the expeditionary force and a further 13 000 others awaiting medical examination. There were enough men, in other words, to fill the two paper divisions with enough left over for a fourth. Even so, everyone was calling on the government to 'do something'. Australians, enough of them anyway, were deeply engaged in the disaster unfolding in Europe.

On 19 May, Captain Ralph Honner's C Company, with the other three companies of the 2/11th Battalion, moved to Kilo 89 Camp in Palestine, which would be their home for the next six months. The battalion was training for war and watching in horror as the war for Britain disintegrated in Europe. Honner was developing into a rare war leader; at the bottom of the chain of military command, certainly, but at the place where military leadership could make a real difference. His biographer, Peter Brune, wrote that 'as a matter of pride (and astute leadership) C Company was required to march further, march faster'. Honner, 35 years of age, 'could march all day and at top pace—he was at the top of his form'. Honner and his boys were doing something, he would have thought, but few Australians were paying much attention to their troops training in Palestine. The real war was in France and, possibly—almost unbelievably—in England.

With the loss of France and the entry of Italy into the war as part of the Axis powers, the war at sea became vastly more complex. If the British were to maintain a naval presence in the Mediterranean, adequate reinforcement in the Far East would be impossible. It is what Colonel Wynter had been saying several years before: Britain could not be at war in two places at once—not adequately, that is. Even so, in May the Australian government offered *Australia* and *Canberra* to the British for service in either British or Mediterranean waters, to join *Sydney* and several other Australian warships for service with the Royal Navy. The British decided to make a stand in the Mediterranean. The Australian Navy, too, would be 'doing something' but, again, not too many in Australia knew of it.

If there was to be a German invasion of Britain, as seemed increasingly likely, there would at least be some Australians there to meet Hitler's forces. While most of the AIF had settled down to training in Palestine, two battalions of Australians—the 2/9th and 2/10th of the 9th Division, departing Sydney on 5 May 1940—were destined for Britain. With them was the Australian official war correspondent, Kenneth Slessor. The troops arrived in the Firth of Clyde on 16 June 1940, lined up on the deck in full marching kit from seven in the morning for their first glimpse of the Scottish countryside, but not actually to disembark until the evening of the next day. The Australians were welcomed to Britain with a personal message from the King, read to them by the officer commanding troops in Scotland. The King visited the Australians in their camp on the Salisbury Plain on 4 July 1940. Slessor began his account of this visit with great drama: 'For the first time in his reign, the King of Britain, which means the King of Australia, inspected an Australian fighting force.' Walking along the Australian lines the King paused occasionally 'to talk casually with equally casual privates ... face to face with these men who had travelled so far to fight for his kingdom'. After a march past, the King lunched with their commander, Lieutenant General Wynter, the same man who had been campaigning, as strongly as the rules would allow, for increased focus and expenditure on defence in Australia in the 1930s. The man who had said that Australia could not expect protection from Britain if there was a war, simultaneously, in Europe and the Pacific.

The Australians in Britain would see no fighting there; instead they used their time in Britain for extensive training, as did their mates in Palestine. Army camps on the Salisbury Plain would be bombed from time to time and all the troops were turned out one dramatic night when it was rumoured that the Germans had landed on the south coast in force. Even so, Kenneth Slessor's despatches made reasonably dull reading for there was little drama in a steady account of six months' training. Slessor wrote that he was glad when he left Britain 'for a chance to get real work at last'. Slessor's value, as far as his Australian readers were concerned, was that he had a front-row seat to the war in the air that was fought across British skies from mid-June 1940 onwards. There were other Australian journalists in London, of course, and elsewhere in Britain, but Slessor could look at the Blitz through the eyes of the Australian soldiers there.

On 2 July 1940 Hitler ordered the invasion of Britain, code-named 'Operation Sealion'. To soften up the population for the intended invasion the German air force, the Luftwaffe, commenced an aerial assault on British airfields, and then on London, other principal cities, docks and munitions factories, military bases and prominent civilian targets. As mentioned, the Battle of Britain ran from mid-June until mid-September, the major assault starting on 13 August. The Luftwaffe relied on a core of 750 long-range bombers, 250 dive-bombers, more than 600 single-engined fighter aircraft and 150 twin-engined fighters. It took only six minutes for these aircraft to cross the English Channel to Dover from bases in France, and ten minutes for the bombers to be over London. What had been feared throughout the 1930s—full-scale aerial warfare—had now become a reality.

The Battle of Britain, effectively lost by the Germans in mid-September 1940, transformed horribly then into the Blitz with seemingly ceaseless air attacks on British cities from August 1940 to mid-May 1941. This gave us some of our most enduring images of the war. The world had never seen anything like it. From August until mid-November 1940, an average of 200 bombers attacked London every single night, but one. The terror that lies behind that statement is almost impossible for an Australian of any generation to comprehend. Every night of every week for nearly 100 days London was pounded, and then the bombers turned their attention to Coventry, Southampton, Birmingham, Liverpool, Bristol and Plymouth, with only occasional raids on London. In 1941 the Germans found other targets, including, with enormous ferocity, Clydeside, to destroy its ship-building capacity. At least 43 000 British civilian lives were lost in the campaign and another 139 000 civilians were injured, for the loss of about 600 German bombers; a considerable number of the German losses due more to landing accidents in bad weather than to the action of British gunners or aircraft. Australians looked to Britain with great sorrow and sympathy during this terrifying ordeal but there was very little from afar that they could do about it.

Kenneth Slessor's own batman, Henry Murray, was in the thick of several bombardments in London, helping to carry away two survivors of one blast by stretcher and, when returning for a third, finding that another bomb had fallen and obliterated the man. On another occasion Murray came across the 'macabre sight' of a taxi with two corpses in it—the driver and his fare. Slessor himself reported a London cabbie of 'a noticeably taciturn breed' nearly in tears at the sight of the ruined churches and other ancient buildings: 'They're worse than cannibals them that did this,' the driver said. The official correspondent also reported on the first Australian soldier to be wounded in action in Britain in this war. He was Lance Corporal Albert Webb of South Australia. 'After all the training we've had against an imaginary enemy,' Webb said from his hospital bed, 'it gives you a shock to find a real one having a go at you.'

Yet those in Australia reading these accounts still felt remarkably remote from it. While some people complained that life should now be very different, there was not, in fact, very much that

Australians could do. Aircrew were moving to Canada in steady numbers for training, and the training of the army at home and abroad continued. What else was there that Australia might do? The simple and unglamorous fact was that work in the factories and on the farms to provide goods for Britain or to replace such goods as Britain had once provided Australia, was about the best the nation might offer. So work, hard work and plenty of it, was what the nation could offer, so from this point onwards many people would have two jobs—the work they did by day and the voluntary work they did at night. Bob Menzies said that the watchword was now an 'all-in' effort, and there were hundreds of stories in the papers of people doing things and making sacrifices. While these stories made everyone feel a bit better, in reality there was not much real help that Australians could provide.

Kenneth Slessor might have been one of those trying to give Australians a realistic understanding of what was happening at the war, but it is hard, he found, so very hard, to keep those so remote from war fully abreast of what is happening. There are two associated questions here: how much can those at home be allowed to know, and how much can they truly comprehend? Not too much, either way, probably, which I now believe diminishes in importance all those studies in recent times of the homefront at war. Look at what the Australian people were being fed at this time of Britain's greatest-ever crisis.

Minister for Air Jim Fairbairn, in Canada and London for the inauguration of the Empire Air Training Scheme in December 1939, had taken the opportunity of visiting the Maginot line— the key to the defence of France—in early January 1940, well before the German assault had begun. Fairbairn reported that he was very impressed with the fortifications and had found that men would be able to live underground for 12 months; 'They shall not pass,' he had said. Just before Anzac Day 1940, a Melbourne weekly newspaper, the *Australasian*, reported that Hitler's war against Norway must be seen as a 'colossal blunder' from which Germany would emerge 'greatly weakened'. A week later, the same paper announced that the fate of the Germans in Norway was beyond doubt: 'Either extermination wherever they are caught or ignominious expulsion.' The minister for External

Affairs, John McEwen, agreed, telling the House of Representatives on 3 May that the Allies would hold northern Norway,
despite the British withdrawing from the south: 'German forces
isolated at Narvik will now be quickly dealt with.' With the crisis
in France deepening, the Allies, in fact, abandoned the campaign
in the north and Norway capitulated to the Germans on 7 June.

On 19 May in a broadcast to the nation, with the crisis in
Europe engulfing the France that he had enlisted to fight for in the
First World War—although the war had ended before he could
reach the frontline—McEwen reviewed for his listeners the events
of the past ten days. Germany's effort, he said, represented a
'colossal gamble. What is happening is an attempt by Germany to
shoot her way out of a deadly predicament, and she is doing it
without scruple and without quarter.' Speaking in Melbourne at an
Empire rally two days after France had signed an armistice with
Germany, but before news of this had become available in
Australia, Bob Menzies had said: 'No-one should believe that the
great French armies could be brushed aside in a week or two . . .
we should not have to wait very long for a counter-stroke by
France.' And writing, perhaps, the greatest nonsense of all, the
Sydney Morning Herald turned the evacuation of British troops
from Dunkirk from a disaster to a triumph: 'The British have been
driven into the sea, it is true, but the sea is the natural element of
our race and in the shallow waters of the French coast the Navy
was able to redress the balance.'

These examples of half-truths, wishful thinking and sheer
ignorance are not given here to enable us to have a good laugh at
the immaturity and naivety of Australia's foreign minister, or
the ill-informed nature of the press. They are to show, rather, the
difficulty in obtaining a clear picture of what was happening so far
away, and to show, too, a cultural assertion among Australians, a
habit of mind if you like, that said that Britain would always prevail
and that bad things simply could not be happening. Germany had
failed in 1914 to 1918, and it was very difficult for Australians to
accept that the German people would not fail again. This is why
these middle months of 1940 are so important in developing our
understanding of how Australians responded to a war that they
sincerely believed was distant and would be won. If 1942, when the

war came to Australia, was a profound shock for the people, part of the reason was the unexpectedly slow start to the war in 1939, and then the difficulty of accepting in 1940 that Britain was on its knees, facing a real prospect of defeat. Bob Menzies was telling people even as late as April 1940 that it would be wrong to pin their faith on a negotiation between Britain and Germany that might lead to peace, indicating that there were still many in the community who believed that the war could be called off by peaceful means.

But other people were searching for things to do themselves and demanding that the government, too, do something. There were public meetings all over the country to assert that the Empire would survive, and to do what could be done for the war's victims. There was a large crowd in Melbourne in June to inaugurate the Lord Mayor's British Bombing Victim's Fund, which subscribed more than £80 000 before the meeting closed. This was a staggering sum of money and clearly indicated the public's determination to 'do something'. Similar meetings, for a variety of causes, were held all around Australia,

It was intensely frustrating, said Bob Menzies, this national determination to be involved. 'I work fifteen hours a day, seven days a week,' Menzies lamented, 'and I have to devote at least one third of my time to warding off blows aimed at me, not from the front, but from those who are supposed to be my supporters.' Why not a national government, the urgers suggested? Bob Menzies floated the idea of a government of all the parties to produce a unified national effort but Labor would not be in it. Why not do something about the disloyalists on the coalfields with their strikes at this time in the nation's history? Menzies bravely faced strikers in April 1940 on the Hunter Valley coalfields to argue for industrial peace, but since the contentious and acrimonious strikes and lock-outs of the 1920s, and the appalling depressed conditions of the 1930s, workers were not in a very forgiving mood. Even in wartime, therefore, strikes remained a part, often a prominent part, of Australian life. Why not suspend the constitution, people suggested, to ensure that there would be no contentious and time-wasting general elections while there was still a war to be won? But this, like a national government or the outlawing of strikes, proved impossible to

arrange. Australia was, instead, heading for the first general
election of the war, and you would think that the odds would
heavily favour the incumbent government. Why make a change in
such unpropitious circumstances? Even so, an election might prove
a distraction for both those governing and being governed.

Yet, strangely, the tide seemed to be flowing to Labor. There
was a by-election in February 1940 for the seat of Corio, centred
on Geelong in Victoria, vacated when the dashing potential rival
to Bob Menzies, R.G. Casey, took up an appointment in Washington. Labor's John Dedman easily won the election and people took
it as an omen; in a general election the government might well
have a fight on its hands. Menzies set the date for an election—
21 September 1940—but just as he was ready to announce it his
government suffered a terrible, and possibly a terminal, blow. It
would be unfair not to recognise that the disaster of 13 August
1940 must have unsettled and unnerved, for a time at least, the
prime minister and his cabinet, increasing the pressure on all of
them just as the people were clamouring more intensely that they
'do something' about the dreadful war in Europe.

Until the 1960s, really, Australia was administered from two
capitals: Melbourne and Canberra. Melbourne was the seat of the
administration, Canberra was the home of parliament. In May
1940 the Melbourne *Age*, reflecting on the difficulty for ministers
and for the orderly administration of government of the split
between the two cities, suggested that urgent consideration be
given to the transfer of parliament to Melbourne for the duration
of the war: 'The arrangement is as feasible as it is desirable.' As it
was, ministers were forever shuffling between Canberra and
Melbourne, and back again. Here was something practical that
they could do, they could bring parliament back to Melbourne.

Bob Menzies might have agreed with the *Age* privately, but he
well understood that Australians outside Victoria would never
accept the return of federal parliament to Melbourne. Menzies was
a Melbourne man, after all, but he might have liked the parliament
in Melbourne for more substantial reasons than that. The second
session of parliament opened in mid-April and, even though the
House of Representatives had sat for only 30 days by mid-August,
the sittings dragged the prime minister and his ministers from

Melbourne to Canberra. The second weekend in August 1940, for example, saw Menzies in Canberra during the week, then on the night train to Melbourne on Friday 9 August, sitting up all the way. He was at War Cabinet meetings on both Saturday and Sunday in Melbourne, and was then planning to leave for Canberra, again on the night train, on Sunday night because parliament was sitting from Tuesday onwards. Why did War Cabinet have to meet in Melbourne? Because all of the government's senior military and civilian advisers were in Melbourne, at their offices in Victoria Barracks or scattered around the city. There was simply not enough office accommodation, or domestic accommodation for that matter, to house all these people in Canberra. What a chore and what a waste of the prime minister's time to be travelling between Canberra and Melbourne so frequently. And it was like this for the ministers as well, week in and week out. Back and forth, back and forth, with occasional trips to Sydney, just to wave the flag there.

Menzies' private secretary heard that three ministers were planning to fly up to Canberra on Tuesday morning, 13 August 1940, for the resumption of parliament. He urged the prime minister to join them on the plane—it would be one less long and tiresome train trip and would save the prime minister's time. It would leave him, perhaps, a little more refreshed for the last sitting week of parliament before the election. But Menzies declined to change his plans and was on the Sunday night train out of Melbourne, as usual. Perhaps he enjoyed it and read a little more widely on the train than merely among the government files and cabinet papers that always accompanied him; a hawk-eyed journal-ist had seen him buy a couple of books for a late July trip from Melbourne, Georgette Heyer's *They Found Him Dead* and John Buchan's *The Free Fishers*.

Menzies was back at work in his Parliament House office on that Tuesday morning when someone came in to tell him that an aircraft had crashed into the low hills to the east of the Canberra airport, within sight of Parliament House. The prime minister might almost have heard the noise of the crash; certainly he could have seen the smoke from his office window. And then it became known that the crashed plane was an RAAF Lockheed Hudson bomber carrying the three cabinet ministers, the chief of the general staff (Sir Brudenall White) and six others. Bob Menzies might easily have been killed with them. Providentially, he took the train.

Soon enough the facts of the accident were known. The plane had made an approach to the airport but had aborted the landing, possibly because the pilot had seen something on the runway. The pilot had then gone around over Queanbeyan to the east and, making a second approach, the aircraft had stalled and slammed into the hill, in daylight and in good conditions.

Killed instantly were Minister for Air Jim Fairbairn, who often flew his own aircraft to Canberra; Minister for the Army Geoffrey Street, and Vice-President of the Executive Council Sir Henry Gullett. Gullett was 62 when he died, Fairbairn 43, Street 46. Menzies was devastated and his government was gutted. Not personally close to many in politics, he described these three as 'close and loyal friends'. When Earle Page had made his scurrilous personal attack on Menzies as he came to the prime ministership in April 1939, Menzies' wife, Pattie, had quietly left the visitor's gallery, unable to listen to the bilious speech any longer. Jim Fairbairn had seen her leave and had left his own seat in the House to find and to comfort her. A man would never forget such kindness shown to his wife, and Menzies spoke with genuine affection of Jim Fairbairn, and his colleagues, in the condolence motions in parliament the next day.

Nevertheless, cruel and distressing as the tragedy undoubtedly was, the business of government had to continue and Bob Menzies had to push on. Effectively, the election campaign hinged on one relatively straightforward issue: which man, Bob Menzies or John Curtin, was best fitted to lead the country in time of war and great national danger, and which party would best support the leader in doing that? In the event, the voters said, we don't know. In the old parliament Menzies had enjoyed a majority of ten: 42 seats on his side to 32 on the Labor side. In the new parliament Menzies would have 36 seats, as would Labor, and there would be two independents. After providing a Speaker, Menzies would have a majority of one seat, assuming that both independents always voted with the government. Labor had made its gains in New South Wales, while the Coalition had more or less held its own elsewhere. Some suspected that voters in New South Wales were responding unhappily to the Victorian-centred flavour of the Menzies administration. Everything happened in Melbourne, the prime minister was always going there, was the way it was put around Sydney. A correspondent to the *Sydney Morning Herald* wrote: 'Victoria is getting everything, and Sydney is being deprived. Even the BBC announcers have, while giving items of news, stressed Victorian achievements. Why Sydney-siders have put up with it for so long, I cannot understand.'

Heavens no, had it come to this? At a time of real danger for the country, genuinely a time of national crisis, had the federal election been decided on petty state jealousies and anxieties? It would seem so. Labor, it is true, had fielded some very strong candidates in the 1940 election in New South Wales: a former justice of the High Court of Australia with a reputation for great intelligence and learning, Bert Evatt; and a former politician, Ben Chifley, with a high reputation for adherence to the best possible Labor values. Both men had won their seats easily. Which is more than could be said for John Curtin in Fremantle. Possibly voters there were miffed at the amount of time that Curtin was spending in the eastern states, another indication of petty regional jealousies, and his opponent, F.R. Lee had run a very good campaign. On election night and for days thereafter it appeared that Curtin had, indeed, lost his seat. While Labor members were queueing up to stand down for their leader to ensure that he would have some place in parliament, Curtin said that he would abide by the decision of the voters. F.R. Lee might have gone down in history as the man who deprived the nation of its greatest ever prime minister, although no one could have known Curtin's claim to that title in September 1940. The soldiers overseas saved John Curtin, possibly recognising only his name on the ballot paper and so, in their vote, they contributed far more than they could possibly have known to winning the war for Australia.

If the terrible air disaster had unsettled Menzies, the election result compounded the problem. This was his first election as prime minister, the first chance for the people to have their say on his leadership. It was hardly a ringing endorsement. There was a sense throughout the campaign that Menzies was a loner with a decent capacity to feel sorry for himself. Voters derived little sense of a team of capable and enthusiastic ministers, supporting a confident and dedicated leader. The remark that he worked 'fifteen hours a day, seven days a week' was just one of a number during the election campaign of a prime minister slightly miffed by the way the people had treated him. Here he is writing in a draft letter, probably and wisely never sent, to Hugh McClure Smith, editor of the *Sydney Morning Herald*:

> I tell you quite honestly that my own defeat would, as such, leave me cheerful. As Prime Minister I have sweated day and night under recurrent difficulties and disappointments . . . I have gone on despite it all, doing my indifferent best, sniped at and loftily admonished . . . For many months I have done all that any man could do . . . to avoid bitterness . . . Do you wonder that men of intelligence prefer to keep out of politics and cultivate their own garden?

Anyone is entitled to moments of self-pity, but when one is leading his country in time of war?

Too often, there was a note of self-pity and self-mockery in Menzies' speeches that the electorate picked up on and pondered. Menzies was still a relatively young man, only ten years older than Ralph Honner who was then driving his battalion hard across the plains and hills of Palestine. Menzies had lost three of his ministers in tragic circumstances, two others at the election, and was inclined to be dismissive of the capacities of most of his remaining colleagues. One of those he did admire more than most was the opposition leader, John Curtin, for whom party politics were almost anathema at this time of national crisis. Curtin understood the burden that Menzies carried and seemed eager not to do anything that would add to it. He believed Australia deserved no less. Speaking before the parliament was to be dissolved for the election, Curtin had said:

> Whatever government is in power should be given the respect and support of the people of Australia . . . I feel

that the Prime Minister, as head of the Government during the war, is entitled to special respect and support, and I have attempted, without abating my opinions . . . to ensure that he was not unnecessarily hampered, thus adding to his difficulties which are already heavy enough . . . I have greatly valued the association that has developed between us.

When Menzies turned, after the election, to reconstructing his government, with the numbers so evenly balanced between the parties and with Menzies having lost some of his better people, it is not surprising that he turned again to the idea of a national government. Curtin would not agree, believing that the freedom for Labor to speak out in the national interest was something all Australians cherished. But Curtin would agree to an advisory war council, on which government and opposition would have equal representation as a means of ensuring the greatest possible harmony in the prosecution of the war.

Historians have tended to be somewhat dismissive of the Advisory War Council because it was not a decision-making body. Its importance lies, however, in this first phase of its work at least, in bringing Labor into a full and informed understanding of the detail of the issues confronting Australia. Opposition can be heartbreaking for political parties, not least because oppositions have no access to the detailed information that governments have at their disposal. Oppositions most often have to rely on whatever the government doles out, or on informed observers, such as journalists, on leaks, and on what their own research can discover. All of this can be frustrating and can send oppositions down dead-ends and byways, much to the government's delight. The Advisory War Council brought Labor in from that oppositional cold, making John Curtin and his colleagues not partners in government, but deeply and appropriately aware of the issues now confronting Australia.

6. WAR

IN THE

DESERT

We left the 6th Division of the 2nd AIF in Palestine, in training. Tom Blamey had arrived to join his troops on 20 June 1940, just as the French were preparing to surrender in Europe, and not long before Hitler would order Operation Sealion, the intended invasion of Britain. The Australian force in the Middle East was growing in numbers and would soon form the largest individual contingent of fighting troops in a force that included soldiers from Britain, India, South Africa and New Zealand. The Commander-in-Chief in the Middle East was General Sir Archibald Wavell, born in 1883 at Winchester, Hampshire, and destined for the army from an early age. Wavell served in World War I and had lost an eye. The British government had appointed him Commander-in-Chief in the Middle East in July 1939; significantly, Wavell was not one of Winston Churchill's appointments. Indeed, when he clashed with the new prime minister in August 1940, Wavell cabled to Churchill that a big butcher's bill was not necessarily evidence of good tactics. The two of them loathed each other from that point on, until Wavell's death in 1950.

Wavell was a commander who spoke his mind. When he first addressed the Australians under his command, in this case the 16th Brigade at Gaza in February 1940, memories of the 'colonials' he had encountered during World War I may have been uppermost in his thinking. In his opening words the Commander-in-Chief referred to the Australian reputation for lack of discipline and returned to the subject later in his speech. 'I look to you,' he said, 'to show [the local people] that their notions of Australians as rough, wild, undisciplined people given to strong drink are incorrect.' Was this the best introduction the Australians troops could have gained from their most senior commander? Later, when those men who had gone on to England and then come to the desert to join their mates were receiving their welcoming speech from General Wavell, he complained about the lack of discipline of the 6th Division—'a subject on which he had been wrongly informed', wrote official historian Gavin Long.

Wavell's insensitivity to the Australians, which may have been shared broadly by many British officers—the colonial as uncouth and undisciplined—was in strong contrast with what the Australians had actually been achieving in training, although with woefully inadequate equipment. A year is a long time to train and certainly no other Australian division in either world war was better prepared for battle than the 6th, but efficiency and skill may be only two of the objectives of such intensive training. More important is the development of a spirit and a unity within the battalion, a sentiment nicely captured by the soldier–son of one of the cabinet ministers killed in the Canberra air disaster. 'At that time', Henry ('Jo') Gullett wrote in his book, *Not As Duty Only*:

> an infantry battalion at battle strength was made up of about six hundred men. But six hundred men do not make a battalion. The six hundred men have to learn the soldiers' trades and disciplines. Even then they are not a battalion. An effective battalion in being, ready to fight, implies a state of mind . . . it implies doing a hundred things together—marching to the band, marching all night long,

being hungry, thirsty, exhausted, filthy; being near but never quite mutinous. It involves not the weakening but the deferment of other bonds and interests; the acceptance that life and home are now with the battalion.

A sharper eye than Archibald Wavell's might have noticed that during that year in their training in Palestine the Australians had achieved these things.

It was now time for battle, but why in the desert of North Africa? Could any worse conditions have been found for the fighting that would go on there for at least the next two years? In Gavin Long's view:

> the discomforts the desert imposed were greater than those inflicted by the enemy. In that stony area it was a laborious task to dig even shallow ditches to give protection against artillery fire, bombs, wind and dust . . . the water ration was half a gallon a man a day for all purposes; in practice this generally meant one bottle of unpleasantly saline water . . . for drinking and washing. If a man shaved he could not wash his body.

Long also wrote of the dust-storms; of:

> dust, fine as talcum powder, [that] would penetrate every-thing that was not tightly wrapped. The faces of men who had been working or sleeping in it would be powdered yellow-grey. It would sift into packs and food and choke the mechanisms of weapons.

Walking over that desert these days confirms what Long wrote 50 years ago; it is a brutal landscape, more rocky than sandy, hard under the foot, uncomfortable to walk on, with surprisingly steep ravines and gullies—a bad place for men and, except for a few roads, a bad place for vehicles too. A place that would very quickly tire you—physically and spiritually.

Was it simply a display of masochism that placed the troops there? Hitler had intended to march through Spain and then take

North Africa to restrict British influence in the Mediterranean, to close off the Suez Canal, in effect to confine the British to their home island. Effectively to strangle them. But Mussolini, the Italian dictator, jumped the gun. With a huge number of troops already stationed in North Africa he ordered an invasion of Egypt on 13 September 1940. Suez would be his prize. The Italians, hundreds of kilometres to the west of Cairo in country known then as Cyrenaica, a part of Libya, would push east; the British forces, protecting the Nile delta, and Cairo, would push west to meet them. It is important to understand that this desert campaign was mobile warfare at its fastest. What was witnessed in this fighting, first with the Italians, then later with the Germans under Rommel, was the fast movement of troops around the curve of the coastline of North Africa, across hundreds and hundreds of kilometres. War as Australians, indeed anybody, had very rarely experienced it.

The Italians had advanced as far as Sidi Barrani, across the Egyptian border, some 400 kilometres from Alexandria, within three days then stopped to await supplies—a constant, pressing problem in this desert warfare. In their own territory, in Libya, the Italian defence was based on two fortress towns: Bardia 25 kilometres from the Egyptian border, and Tobruk a further 100 kilometres to the west. Tobruk had a very good harbour and port, and thus could be readily supplied. Hence its importance later in the story. But for the moment the Italians were not thinking of defence; they were on the attack, and if they were forced to fall back it would be to their heavily defended fortress at Bardia first.

It would be too easy to dismiss the Italian armies in the desert as something of a joke; in truth, they suffered a series of crushing defeats and lost a staggering number of troops, mainly captured. There is no doubt the Italian soldiers were dispirited, that they lacked confidence in their commanders, that they were poorly equipped with limited air support. This was not a promising position for any army at war. Even so, the Italians had the advantage of prior occupation. At Bardia and Tobruk they had constructed strong defences, consisting of anti-tank ditches, wire, a multitude of defended posts across their perimeter, backed with further redoubts and strong artillery emplacements. Both fortresses were well supplied and had ample water.

The first task for Wavell's troops was to expel the Italians from Sidi Barrani. He ordered two of his divisions, a British Armoured Division and the 4th Indian Division, to attack at Sidi Barrani on 9 December. By the night of 10 December the battle was effectively over, the Italians routed and forced back to their strong post along the coast at Bardia. For his assault on Bardia, Wavell withdrew the Indian division and replaced it with the 6th Australian Division, commanded by Major General I.G. Mackay, who had taken command of the division when, with other Australian divisions being formed, Tom Blamey had been promoted to corps commander. Australian soldiers would go into action for the first time in this war in early 1941, led by a general they much respected.

Iven Mackay was born at Grafton in New South Wales in 1882, the son of a Presbyterian minister from Scotland. Destined either to be a teacher or possibly an academic, Mackay had also had a good career in the militia—first in the school cadets and later at university. He enlisted in the AIF immediately after the Great War had broken out. Mackay landed in Gallipoli on 8 May 1915 and was so badly wounded at Lone Pine in August that he was evacuated to England. He did not rejoin his battalion, the 4th, until it was in Egypt in early 1916. Given command of the battalion in France, Mackay was in action at Pozieres, Mouquet Farm and Bullecourt, places forever associated with some of the toughest fighting the Australians saw on the Western Front. Returning to Australia after the war Mackay became a university lecturer in physics, a university administrator, and headmaster of Cranbrook School, a Sydney Anglican school, in 1933. When he joined the 2nd AIF in April 1940 at the age of 58 and was given command of the 6th Division, Mackay was known to the troops, obviously enough from the movies, as 'Mr Chips'. School masters might make good military leaders with their emphasises on training, planning and preparation. At least Mackay did. But was he ruthless enough for battle? Time would tell, but as we have seen, no Australian division ever went into battle better prepared than Mackay's 6th. And with strong preparation came great confidence.

You might think I am labouring the point about the linkages between the two world wars, but it is remarkable how the

Australians, consciously as they prepared for battle, reminded themselves of the deeds and spirit of their fathers on the Western Front. But it was more than that. They had even adopted their tactics, for most of the Australian commanders in 1941 had learned the business of war on the Western Front. 'Peaceful penetration', they had called it then, developing an idea by 1918 that the enemy must never feel comfortable, must never feel 'in possession' of no man's land. Australian patrols in France, containing only a very few men, were constantly out from their own lines, under cover of darkness and without artillery support, crawling across the wasteland between the trenches to deliver powerful blows to the enemy's frontline trenches. And then they had to crawl back 'home' again. This aggression put the enemy on edge and cost few Australian lives. The Australians by 1918 had learned that they must wage war with the minimal loss of life. There were simply too few others back home to replace them.

The Australians of the 2nd AIF put these tactics into operation as soon as they entered the war in the desert on 21 December 1940. Small parties of men would move out towards the Italian defences to reconnoitre the land over which they would later fight, and to stir up the enemy with grenades and rifle fire. If detected they would lie still for up to a couple of hours. Because the desert is a cold place at night they went out well rugged up—greatcoats and sweaters. They also wore steel helmets, of course, and looking at pictures of these men, or of them charging to battle a few days later, you could almost think them to be at Hamel or Mont St Quentin in 1918. Indeed, looking at the black and white photographs of the two sets of troops, the similarities are uncanny.

The ease with which the Allied troops had driven the Italians from Sidi Barrani and the numbers of prisoners they had taken led some to believe that the war in Libya was virtually over before it began. That the Italians would almost refuse to fight. The Australians, with their 'peaceful penetration', began to draw another conclusion altogether. The land in front of them at Bardia was skilfully defended with a substantial anti-tank ditch, a great deal of wire, heavily fortified and well-manned defensive posts right along the perimeter, and well-massed artillery. What was not known with any certainty was how many Italians Wavell's troops would face or what the spirit of these Italians would be. The Australians would soon discover that many of the Italians would not throw in the towel readily.

Iven Mackay moved among his soldiers on 2 January 1941, the day before the battle would commence. In his careful planning Mackay had been anxious to ensure minimal loss of Australian life. He had learned the lessons of 1918 well. The general found his troops excited, for the most part, and conscious too of the heavy weight of tradition on their shoulders for they were the first Australian soldiers to be engaged in battle since October 1918. The diarist of the 16th Brigade wrote, 'everyone is happy, expectant, eager. Old timers say the spirit is the same as in the last war. Each truck-load was singing as we drove to the assembly point.' But he would write that, wouldn't he? Remember, the diarist, a younger officer in all likelihood, was writing after the battle, after the victory, and in a manner that he might have thought was expected of him. Most men, looking back now, when speaking, for example, for the oral history archives that have been created over the past 20 years or so, will speak of being 'scared' of finding the fury and intensity of the enemy's artillery 'scary'. That is not to say that they did not do their job, of course they did, but we treat them with less respect than they deserve if we believe that they went into battle, even in this the first battle they faced in the Second World War, with some sort of jolly indifference to the worth and value of their own lives.

Each of the Italian defensive posts ringing the Bardia perimeter had been numbered to allow commanders to identify the path and progress of the attack. Soldiers do that; there is no point ordering them to 'attack that hill over there'; it must be clearly identified so that everyone knows that everyone else is talking about the same hill. Lone Pine, Hill 971, are easily identified once named or numbered. Mackay had set his battle plan to concentrate on the western side of the perimeter and in the centre. The attack would commence at 5.30 a.m. on 3 January 1941 with a massive artillery barrage designed to keep the enemy below ground or inside their posts and to encourage an early surrender of troops whose spirit was suspected as not being strong. At the same time, Mackay ordered a diversionary attack, a feint, on the southern end of the perimeter to keep the Italians there tied down and possibly to confuse the others, but the southern part of the battlefield was not intended to be an attack in force.

This is where we can see the negative side of the legacy of the Great War. The 2/6th Battalion was to make this feint in the south against Posts 9 to 11; its commander was Colonel Arthur Godfrey, born in 1896 in Camberwell, Melbourne. Godfrey had commanded troops on the Western Front, first into action himself when he took a raiding party out into no man's land at Petillon, near Fromelles in northern France in September 1916. So aggressive was he in this raid, the last out and bringing back a wounded Australian with him, that he was awarded the Military Cross. Gassed in France, Godfrey eventually returned to Australia and was an auctioneer in Geelong, Victoria, when war called him a second time. One of his soldiers in the 2/6th Battalion was Jo Gullett, about to go into action for the first time. Gullett looked to his battalion commander with some awe, he thought of him as an old man who knew battle; Godfrey was 44, Gullett was 26.

What is a 'feint attack', Gullett wanted to know. 'How far do you press it home? When do you call it a day and how do you judge that moment in the fury of the battle?' They called Fromelles, when the first Australians went into battle on the Western Front in July 1916, a feint, ludicrously intended to draw Germans from the fury of the Somme battles; Fromelles cost Australia 5500 men killed or injured overnight. A feint, right, where Arthur Godfrey would win his Military Cross a few months later. Colonel Godfrey did not believe in feint attacks. Addressing his company and platoon commanders before the attacks on the southern perimeter on 3 January 1941, Godfrey had said: 'No matter what happens to us, when we go forward we shall give the enemy such a thrashing that they will never willingly stand up to an assault by Australian infantry again.' Later, just to make the position perfectly clear, Gullett's company commander, Captain Max Little, said to his platoon commanders: 'I will see you then in Post 11 tomorrow morning, or I shall not see you at all.' This is not what General Mackay believed was the prudent use of men. A feint would not be given the artillery and tank support of the main attack; it was not the main attack.

Gullett described the fighting around Post 11 in compelling detail. There were two platoons in the attack—Gullett's and that of Lieutenant John Bowen, with whom Gullett had gone to school—each platoon consisting of about 30 men. They were facing possibly 400 men. These Australians had a fair amount of ground to traverse before they got into an attacking position, including going down into the Wadi Muatred, a typical desert dry watercourse, although this one was particularly deep, then scaling the other side. After that they would need to cut gaps in the wire to make a passage, to take out the machine-gun post defending Post 11, and then wait in position. When all this had been done, in the increasing tension, the men were to await John Bowen's order to proceed. 'I'm ready, John,' Gullett shouted to his mate. 'Up! D Company! Up! Up!' Bowen shouted 'and every man got up and we raced forward shouting'. To be met by a hail of machine-gun and rifle fire, artillery and grenades. It was a suicidal attack, and in a short time D Company 2/6th Battalion was a remnant with very few men left, Jo Gullett one of them, though he was badly wounded. In total the battalion lost 38 men killed or missing and 26 men wounded in the attack on posts 9 to 11. The action, however, did tie down the Italians in that sector and gave us a fine battle picture, Ivor Hele's *2/6th Battalion Attack on Post 11 at Bardia*. Elsewhere, but with substantial artillery and tank support, although much the same tactics on the ground, the battle had gone very much better for Iven Mackay.

Captain Ralph Honner, company commander of C Company, 2/11th Battalion, 19th Brigade, was disappointed that Mackay had designated his brigade, of the three in the battle, the reserve. Honner, in his frustration, did extract a promise from his battalion commander, Lieutenant Colonel Louch, that when they did finally go into battle C Company would be one of the attacking companies. The battalion waited in reserve on 3 January, but when it seemed that the 17th Brigade had become stalled Mackay called up the 19th Brigade. With the attack for Honner's men to start at 9.15 a.m. on 5 January, the company commander with his platoon leaders, early in the morning, went to reconnoitre the land over which they would soon fight. It was nearly a tragi-comedy, really. Honner went too far into the battlefield in the truck, found himself in Italian-held territory, picked up four prisoners as protection, and made a dash back to the Australian line. Honner then found that he had left the timing a bit tight and needed to rush his men to the start line, five kilometres or so away—and all of this with only half an hour to go. Imagine being late for the start of your war. C Company did make it in time and immediately set about rushing the enemy.

Ralph Honner does not come across as a big-noter yet it was a luxury for his biographer and a treat for all of us that he sent detailed accounts of his fighting in the desert to his wife, Marjory, back home in Perth. Whether she understood all that he described is open to question; who can really understand battle if they have not experienced it? Possibly Honner was using these letters as a means of getting down on paper what he had gone through so that after the war he could return to the story in quiet and meditative reflection. Unfortunately, what he does not describe in his account of the fighting around Bardia is the mood that he and his men took into battle. But a man cool enough to be inspecting the lie of the land just hours before he would fight over it, is a man clearly in control of himself as he faced one of life's most exacting challenges.

From Honner's accounts, and from what others have recalled, we know that this company commander led from the front and he was at all times clearly visible to his men. He had decided that leadership at his level required just that. To be first in doing what he required his men to do, and to let them see that he was doing it too. He was, after all, a company commander. Yet Ralph Honner had a terrible moment on this battlefield. When advancing under cover of artillery fire, at a certain point your own artillery must stop to allow your men to rush forward to attack the defended post; they would be supported at this juncture by tanks only. This was classic Western Front doctrine. 'Our barrage ceased', Honner wrote:

> and left us in full view of the enemy posts ahead, their artillery opened up with such accuracy that we were sure they had previously registered on the line we were crossing. The shells dropped across the two leading platoons and my small command party between them. I was buffeted by the

blast but kept my feet. I could not see through the dust to my left, but to my right, where the three sections of 15 Platoon were moving in their wide arrowhead formation, I was horrified to see first two sections and then the third blown over. As nothing moved in the dust I thought 'This is it—one platoon gone—how long will the rest last?' But after a moment the dazed sections scrambled to their feet and hurried forward.

Honner, in fact, had thought that he had lost a considerable number of his men. When the machine-gun fire then swept the ground over which C Company was advancing Honner stayed on his feet while his men dived to the ground. His coolness steadied them and they rose again to rush forward. The tanks came on too and suddenly the enemy started to surrender in large numbers. 'The only thing that held us up was dealing with prisoners', Honner wrote. He had gained his objectives with, apparently, only one casualty. As his biographer, Peter Brune, wrote: 'It was a dream start by Honner to an illustrious career.'

The battle for Bardia raged for two days before the fortress surrendered on 5 January. British intelligence had estimated that there were around 20 000 to 25 000 Italians defending Bardia. In fact, 40 000 finally surrendered in addition to the more than 1000 Italian soldiers killed or wounded in the fighting. The Australians lost 130 killed or died of wounds and 326 wounded. 'In almost every platoon', Gavin Long wrote, '[there] were men whose fathers had served in the old AIF and who were resolved to prove themselves as formidable as their fathers. The success at Bardia', Long concluded, 'demonstrated that there is no fortress so strong in its engineering that men of determination and cunning, with weapons in their hands, cannot take it'.

There was little time for self-congratulation though. The Italian commanders were seen leaving Bardia on foot, heading for their next strong post at Tobruk, and in this war of movement Wavell's troops would follow them, almost as if they already had the enemy on the run. Wavell decided that he needed to take Tobruk because, with its excellent harbour, it would make the increasing problem of supplying his troops just that much easier. So even as troops were still mopping up at Bardia on 6 January, the British Armoured Division and some of the Australians were already on their way to Tobruk. For rapidly moving troops, supply would always be a problem; it was a constant sight in this war in the desert to see abandoned vehicles, and armaments were quickly taken up and used by the captors against the fleeing vanquished as stocks diminished. And this was on both sides. The Italians might find their own weapons used against them; later the British troops would have the same experience. And this applied to their opponent's food and water, too. After Bardia the Australians had been searching desperately for water. One fortunate man in Ralph Honner's C Company came across a 50-gallon keg of wine. Well it was liquid; it would just have to do.

Tobruk will be a name to figure prominently later in the story of Australians at war, but for the moment, in January 1941, it was but a way station on the road through Derna to Benghazi, after which Churchill thought it best that his troops rest a while. He would allow them three months to reach Benghazi, he thought. The Australians, with solid British armoured support, reached the Tobruk perimeter within days of their victory at Bardia. Here the defences were just as well prepared, but on a bigger scale. There were 128 defensive posts on the Tobruk perimeter, along a 50-kilometre front. This sounds impressive, but in fact concentration of the Italian force might have provided a better defence. Such an extended front required a large number of troops and, with the number of prisoners already captured, troop numbers for the Italians were becoming a problem. The attackers might hit at any number of places, with the defenders stretched too thinly to successfully oppose them.

The battle at Tobruk might have commenced almost immediately, so swiftly were the attacking troops in place, but they had outstripped their supply of ammunition and the battle would have to be delayed until supplies could be built up. Iven Mackay worried that his Australians were in danger of becoming overconfident and certainly they had lost a large measure of respect for the Italians whom they had captured in such large numbers. 'Civilianism is beginning to break out', Mackay wrote to his troops. But to be fair, while the troops awaited the arrival of supplies, they were probing the territory in front of them, reconnoitring and unsettling their enemy with their aggressive tactics.

The battle plan at Tobruk was similar to that at Bardia: an intense artillery barrage, a dawn attack against selected posts and tanks in support to subdue opposition. The battle was timed to commence on 21 January 1941. As at Bardia, the Italian resistance was patchy: in some areas of the perimeter defence the Italians defended with spirit and skill; elsewhere, it was clear, the soldiers' hearts were not in the fight. From dawn onwards on the second day of the battle, reports came from all along the front that the Italians were intent on surrender. An Italian general was affronted that he was expected to surrender to a relatively junior Australian officer. While he squabbled over whether he might, with dignity, surrender at least to an Australian major, his protests were over-taken by a procession of several thousand of his officers and men delivering themselves into the hands of the Australians anyway. They were destined, some of them at least, to work as prisoners of war on Australian farms and orchards for the remainder of the war. Of the 12 Italian divisions that went into war when the Italians crossed the Egyptian border and captured Sidi Barrani, only five divisions now survived. This was a shocking rout in a very short period of time. In the battle for Tobruk, 49 Australians were killed or died of wounds and 306 were wounded.

It would be wrong to give the impression that this desert warfare was something of a cakewalk for at times the Australians did encounter stiff resistance. Tom Louch, Honner's battalion commander, writing to his brigade commander, Horace Robertson ('Red Robbie'), about the fighting around Derna, beyond Tobruk, emphasised the capacity of the Italian artillery: 'The shelling, judged by 1918 European standards, is really heavy. He has more guns and far more shells than we have and his guns are skilfully placed and well-served.' Even so, Wavell's troops (Robertson's 19th AIF Brigade, in fact) had reached Benghazi by 7 February 1941, whereas Churchill had anticipated reaching the destination sometime in March. In two months, for an overall cost of 475 killed, 1225 wounded and 43 missing or taken prisoner, the British force had travelled over 800 kilometres, taken something like 130 000 prisoners, and captured a huge amount of enemy weapons, ammunition and supplies. The 6th Australian Division had been given a very instructive introduction to warfare and had acquitted itself well. The men of the 6th Division may well have felt that they had the 'old AIF' monkey off their backs.

The division's sense of a job well done, though the troops realised it was far from finished, was reinforced when Bob Menzies, the Australian prime minister, arrived to spend time with them on the former battlefield at Tobruk and elsewhere in the desert, to thank them and congratulate them on their success. It would certainly have boosted the morale of the Australians to see their prime minister among them; with photographs and newsreel footage, it would have done Menzies no harm, either, boosting his status at home as a wartime leader. It would not do to be too cynical about this, though. There is a 'down home' charm about Menzies' time with the Australians in the desert that speaks to us of a different age. One of his great strengths was his skill in working a crowd. In fact, while a stopover in Cairo and in the desert seemed sensible and necessary, Menzies was on his way to London to argue, at a time still of the greatest peril for Britain, for better defence preparedness at Singapore.

Despite the contribution the Australians were making in the desert, a small power cannot assume that its friends and allies will constantly have its needs at the forefront of its strategic and alliance thinking. Like an annoying younger brother, the small power must, with shrill voice, constantly push its interests just to be remembered. Menzies was going to London, frankly, with cap in hand, despite all that the Australians had achieved in the desert for Wavell, Churchill and British morale. For Singapore remained the great Australian concern. Taking pride in the achievements of their troops in the desert, nevertheless, the Australian War Cabinet, the Advisory War Council, and some few commentators, continued to watch the position at Singapore anxiously. Could it be defended? Were there enough troops on the island? Was the navy strong enough, and could reinforcements arrive quickly enough? Could more be done? Fortunately for homefront morale and peace of mind, the Australian public seemed blissfully unaware that anything was amiss with Australia's Maginot line. But Menzies felt he needed to keep London minds focused on 'the East'.

The prime minister left Australia by flying boat on 24 January 1941 and would not return until 24 May 1941. It was far too long an absence from his country during a time of war, as the Australian high commissioner in London, Stanley Bruce, himself a former prime minister, perceptively warned. For Menzies, being away was a matter of months; for the troops he was visiting, it would be a matter of years and we do well to recall the impact of these absences on the troops themselves and on those they left at home. Think of the agony of mind that Albert Moore endured, saying goodbye to his wife and boy, and think, too, of their evident grief in seeing Albert leave. Think of Marjory Honner in Perth, with her two small boys, desperately missing, you would think, her husband, his comfort and his love. Honner's letters, though quaintly technical in describing the war and his company's part in it for his wife, are full, too, of his tender love and aching homesickness. It was no less so for Bob Menzies' family, seeing Bob off to the war and London. And why would the families of politicians miss their husbands and fathers on war duty elsewhere any less? 'We miss you very much', Patti Menzies wrote, just days after Bob had left, 'and somehow the heart has gone out of these holidays . . . [she and her children were at the Menzies' holiday home at Mt Macedon, outside Melbourne] it is very disturbing to know you are reaching Australia's first battle-line. If wishes had power and strength ours would turn your flying boat and bring you back to us.'

Only Tom Blamey found a way of escaping such a heartfelt letter as this. After badgering the government for months from his headquarters in Cairo, ministers finally relented and granted Tom's relatively new wife, Lady Olga Blamey, a passport to travel to Egypt to be with her husband. Just imagine how this played with the troops. Australians strongly resent those in power who use that power to cut special deals and privileges for themselves. Homesick and lovesick as most of the soldiers were, but prepared to make the sacrifice because this is what soldiers had always done, how it stuck in their craw that the corps commander had brought his wife out to be in Egypt with him. 'I miss you, Vi', Albert Moore might have written, 'but at least Tom Blamey will be content tonight'. 'What a fool the little man has been over her', wrote Colonel George

Vasey, one of the officers working most closely with Blamey, 'he can't afford to fight everyone all the time'.

Menzies went first to Palestine and on 3 February 1941 had his first contact with Australian troops on active service, at the Scottish Hospital, close to Bethlehem, where he visited Australian casualties from the fighting at Bardia. He found them 'all in good heart, and we exchange badinage'. At Gaza there was a cocktail party and dinner in the Officers' Mess; 'a splendid day', wrote Menzies in his diary. The next day the prime minister visited Julis Camp where the 21st Brigade of the 7th Australian Division was in training, taking over the facilities the 6th Division had used when it had trained so extensively there. There was spick-and-span and military precision everywhere for Menzies' benefit; marching troops and slick salutes. And there were also the 'old and bold', as Menzies described those exercising the perennial Australian right to drop a bloke down a peg or two: 'How are you, Bob,' they shouted.

Menzies stood up to speak to the soldiers, even those who were chiacking him, delivering a message of support from Australia and a message from them of support 'to the gallant people of Great Britain'. 'No cheap promises', he wrote of his talk, and he told them that at home Australians would try to work for them so as to be worthy of them. It would be tough, though, standing before men over whom, ultimately, you had the power of life and death, to speak at ease and with good humour to them. The 'mask of command' it has been called, the ability to appear relaxed and at ease, supremely confident, knowing that those standing under a desert sun in front of you, almost certainly, will be shelled and bombed and machine-gunned by an enemy intent on killing every single one of them. Let the mask of command slip, let the human emotions of anxiety and concern show through and you do them no favours because they think they are invincible, that death might come to the other fellow, and you don't want to do anything that would take that confidence from them. No easy thing, even for an experienced politician. 'It is a moving thing', Menzies wrote, 'to speak to thousands of young men, mere boys, in the flower of their youth, many of whom will never see Australia again'.

On 8 February Menzies flew over Sidi Barrani and Bardia before landing at Tobruk. He was astonished by what he saw; the strong fortifications at both Bardia and Tobruk, the awful country over which the Australians fought, hundreds and hundreds of abandoned Italian vehicles and guns. At Tobruk, 'the vast perimeter of the defences, about 20 miles, could be seen, tank-traps and all, as if drawn on paper. Abandoned guns, tanks and lorries.' Menzies addressed two battalions of Brigadier Arthur Allen's 16th Brigade. Allen, described as 'choleric yet kindly', has been unlucky in history; he is known universally to historians, readers and veterans alike as 'Tubby'. Even Menzies called him that in his diary: 'Tubby Allen seems solid, with some good battalion commanders.' No one dared call Tom Blamey 'Tubby', although it might have knocked some of the pomposity out of him. Another officer Menzies met at Tobruk was Acting-Brigadier Arthur Godfrey: '. . . fit, cheerful [who] has, I am told, done well.' He was speaking of that feint at Bardia, when the weight of the 'old AIF' hung heavily on him, that lead to casualties that were unnecessarily and unacceptably high. Done well? Menzies again spoke to the troops, although he does not say what he said except that they 'were boyishly pleased when I pointed out the world significance of the campaign they have been winning'. Later, Menzies wandered the streets of Tobruk, almost alone it seems, having a look for himself and chatting to 'various groups of AIF'. It is an intriguing picture, the Australian prime minister wandering about this smashed-up port town, seeing for himself and mingling with his men. 'A dash of humour is the right solvent', he found, 'and they are friendly boys, wise now in terrible things'.

After a couple of days in Cairo Menzies was back out among the Australian troops at Benghazi, travelling this time with Tom Blamey. He hears good things of Iven Mackay, but writes that Mackay looks 'as gently ineffectual as ever. The face is not the index of the man'. He visited the artillery, again speaking to the men: '. . . good interjections and good reception.' You would almost think that Menzies is writing of a political rally, but he was a man of quick wit who relished the way Australians 'called no man lord or sir, or tipped their hat to no man'. It is a good Australian scene this, battle-hardened troops taking the piss out of their prime minister, all in good fun.

Later, Menzies met General 'Jumbo' Wilson, the Commander-in-Chief of the British Forces in Egypt, and was quite underwhelmed: '... tall, fat and cunning.' What riled him about this particular Englishman was that he could only complain about the Australians and their 'irregular conduct' on guard duties and in training. He said nothing, Menzies wrote 'about their great fighting'. What a stupid, insensitive way to speak to a prime minister who has just spent several days in the company of his own troops, fresh from significant first victories in battle. Mightn't Wilson at least have been more tactful? Did Englishmen like him really understand the way Australians thought and behaved, or did they regard Menzies as a colonial leader of little account and his troops merely as soldiers at Wilson's disposal, expected to act as nearly as they could to what British soldiers would do? Bob Menzies might have taken pause at this point. He had got on well with General Sir Richard O'Connor, the man on the ground under Wavell who had probably done more than any other military leader to ensure victory in the desert. For Menzies, O'Connor stood out as 'the only one of the whole bunch [of British generals] who intelligently understands' the Australians. But Menzies would have done well to take care, for those he was meeting may play a part, greater than you might think, in his own fate.

As well as glad-handing the troops, Menzies was also in top-level discussions about the future deployment of the Australians. The problem was Greece. The Italians had invaded Greece from Albania on 28 October 1940, but the opposition of the Greek troops had been so effective, particularly in the mountains, that the Italians had been driven back to Albania with relative ease. This success may have induced some confidence in the capacity of the Greeks to contribute to their own security, but a German invasion of Greece would be a much tougher proposition.

Tom Blamey had first become aware that the British government might wish to use Australian troops in Greece in mid-November 1940, and he was very wary of becoming involved in a Balkans campaign. Indeed just the mention of the Balkans seemed to worry military planners and thinkers; confused, divided, tumultuous, impenetrable might all be words that leapt into the minds of the generals when the politicians mentioned the Balkans.

Keep well out of it, most Australian military men would have been saying to one another; and certainly Tom Blamey would have been saying the same thing to his government at home. With Menzies on his patch, Blamey could well have been saying that to him face to face. It seems, though, that the two Australian leaders did not sit down to a long and forthright discussion about Greece. Perhaps Blamey thought that Menzies had already made up his mind. Although for Menzies, it would seem, Greece was not yet firmly in his sights. The failure by Menzies and Blamey to speak about Greece is one of the great missed opportunities of Australia in the Second World War.

It should have taken a lot to convince the Australian government to release its troops for service in Greece. In the first place there was a war in North Africa still to win, and it could now be won by the troops pressing on with determination and sufficient resources. Instead Wavell spoke to Menzies of the desirability of a 'certain latitude' in the use of the Australian forces, without necessary reference back to Canberra.

The national force should always have been at the absolute control of the national government, but this was an idea that was stronger in Canberra than in London. As ever, it was a problem for a small power. In London there was a tendency to see the Australian troops, and those of the other dominions, at the discretionary use, ultimately, of Winston Churchill. It was a courtesy, this view ran, to consult the Australians about deployments, but they were running the war in London. They saw the big picture; they understood the broader alliance issues. Australians, ultimately, should do as they were told. In their conversations in Cairo, Blamey had told Menzies of his strong belief that the Australian government, and its military leaders, must control the destiny of the Australian troops. Menzies left the battlefield convinced that Australia had the right man in the job. A man who would stand up for and protect Australian interests. Menzies flew off to London on 14 February 1941, almost blissfully unaware of the problems in front of him. The 6th Division rested for a moment in the desert, confident that they would soon be in Tripoli.

7. A
FORLORN
HOPE

A party of Australian veterans was returning to Athens to commemorate the 50th anniversary of the end of the war. There was to be a city tour and they were in the hands of an experienced Greek tour guide—a woman, perhaps approaching 60 years of age. 'It is the proudest moment of my life,' she said to them, 'to welcome you Australian soldiers, sailors and nurses back to Athens. The proudest moment of my life. I remember,' she continued, 'when you were last here and how we thanked you and blessed you for coming to help us in our time of greatest need.' And then she cried in front of the veterans, genuine, heartfelt tears of remembrance and gratitude. Later, at the Phaleron War Cemetery in Athens, one of the veterans wanted to see, for the first time, the grave of a mate who had died in Greece in 1941. We went looking for it, found the headstone, and the veteran knelt reverently before it. Then he burst into uncontrolled sobbing. Tears that had been welling up for 50 years.

The decision of the British War Cabinet to go to Greece would have been made in minutes, Bob Menzies believed, if he had not been in the room. Despite the fact that Menzies would spend several weekends at Chequers, the country home of the British prime minister, and was considered by Churchill as one of those men with whom 'it was agreeable to dine', Menzies quickly developed reservations about Churchill's way of running the War Cabinet. When the possible despatch of troops to Greece came up for discussion at Menzies' first British War Cabinet meeting on 24 February 1941, Churchill was quickly out of the blocks: '"You have read your file gentlemen, the report of the Chiefs of Staff Commitee. The arguments are clear on each side. I favour the project." And then around the table', continued Menzies, 'Nobody [said] more than three or four sentences. Does this denote great clarity and directness of mind in *all* these Ministers or has Winston taken *charge* of them as the one man whom the public regard as indispensable'.

Menzies asked some questions as was his right; after all, if the British government was to support the Greeks against a German invasion 60 per cent of the troops for the campaign would consist of Australians and New Zealanders. Was the shipping adequate to transport the troops and all the equipment, weaponry and ammunition that they would need, Menzies asked the cabinet? Could the troops be evacuated if the enterprise failed? Was the campaign anything more than a 'forlorn hope'? At this question Churchill snapped back that that was 'something the Australian Cabinet must assess for themselves on Mr Menzies' advice.' Bob Menzies' questioning, though, had drawn the matter out to 45 minutes of discussion with the only decision taken being that Menzies would return to the cabinet with the response to the proposal from the Australian War Cabinet. He had managed to buy time to consider the matter more closely.

Menzies might have been in a stronger position if he had taken the opportunity to discuss Greece with Tom Blamey in Cairo and with Archibald Wavell just a few days earlier. But Menzies' biographer, Allan Martin—not a man ever to have rushed his judgements on men and events—uses uncharacteristically strong language when writing about Wavell's briefings to the Australian prime minister on Greece. He says Wavell was 'dissembling'; he suggests he was 'misleading' of both Menzies and Blamey; and that Wavell was 'dishonest' when he informed the British and Australian governments that Blamey was in favour of the campaign. The last thing that Wavell wanted was for Menzies and Blamey to sit down together and openly discuss the strengths and weaknesses of an incursion into Greece. He wanted Menzies to gain the view that Blamey was in favour of sending his troops to Greece; he wanted Blamey to form the view that Menzies wanted the Australians to be in Greece. So the last thing Wavell wanted was the two men to openly air their considerable doubts and hesitancies. If the decision had been a matter of cable traffic between the Australian government and General Blamey, on the one hand, and the Australian government and the British government, on the other, it is likely that the misunderstanding between Menzies and Blamey would never have arisen; their views would have been carefully thought out and articulated with precision in the writing of the cables. Face to face, and later communicating with each other through British channels, neither man ever seemed to understand what the other man was actually thinking. Yet Tom Blamey had a clear obligation to tell the Australian government of his reservations and concerns about the Greek campaign, regardless of whether this might appear that he was going behind Wavell's back, or even his prime minister's back.

Country Party leader Arthur Fadden was acting prime minister in Australia, with full authority, and the Australian War Cabinet had the ultimate authority for the disposition and use of Australian troops. Fadden cabled the Australian War Cabinet's 'resentment' that it appeared to have been by-passed on the Greek decision and suggested to Menzies that this 'deeply affects the question of Empire relationship'. The small power at home was squirming in the recognition of its relative powerlessness, Bob Menzies was glowing at being in the inner circle in London, and Tom Blamey was simply not doing his job for the Australian government at home.

Would a more informed discussion in Canberra and the assertion of Australian rights have made much difference to the outcome in London? Probably not, unless you can envisage Menzies and this Australian government defying Winston Churchill after the British prime minister had set his heart on the adventure. Churchill wanted to go to the assistance of the Greeks, even though he knew that the campaign would, in near certainty, fail. He believed a tough contest in Greece might alter the situation in the Balkans, and possibly even bring the Turks into the war, on the side of the Allies. That would have pleased Churchill, but it must be said that during all this debate about what to do with the Greeks, Churchill's firm gaze was not on the Balkans, but on America. The freedom of the Greeks from oppression and any possible developments in the Balkans were of secondary consideration behind America, in Churchill's view. The British prime minister had one settled conviction: only when the Americans came into the war would Hitler be defeated. The American entry into the war in 1917 had swung the balance so decisively in terms of numbers of troops and might of equipment that victory became almost inevitable. That would be the way it would happen again.

Even in April 1941 the Americans remained hesitant about another European war, and would certainly stand out if it seemed that England was on the brink of defeat. If the British would not even fight in Greece, were they not in fact on the canvas with the count at nine? Why then should the Americans enter a war that was apparently already lost? That, in Churchill's view, was the way the Americans would see a refusal to help the Greeks; an admission of defeat, or near defeat; that the game was up. So to Greece the British must go to keep the pressure on the Americans, to show them that the British were still a viable proposition in this war. Thus Churchill had no time to waste and, without letting Menzies know, he had already put the wheels in motion for a Greek campaign. He would take the victorious troops from the desert, deferring their ultimate destruction of the Italian army and passing up the opportunity for the capture of the major port of Tripoli, and move the only troops available to him at short notice to Greece. While Bob Menzies was carefully answering Australian concerns from home, putting the pros and cons of the Greek campaign before his Australian cabinet colleagues and then finally recommending that the Australians actually do take part, the first Australians had already been ordered to embark for Greece three days before that recommendation.

And who was to lead them into battle this time? Lieutenant General Sir Henry Maitland Wilson, 'Jumbo', that's who: 'tall, fat and cunning', in Menzies' words, who little understood Australians, in his estimation. Military historians will tell you that Wilson was somewhat unlucky in his career, that he handled the evacuation from Greece with skill, and that subsequent postings did not allow him to display, to the full, his strategic leadership abilities. Or maybe Bob Menzies was right.

The German invasion of Greece began on 6 April 1941 and, unlike the Italians six months earlier, the Germans had a substantial air force, giving them complete air dominance to support their troops on the ground. It would be an unequal contest. The simple fact is that the Australians, who had begun making their way to Greece on 3 April, would take part in an evacuation that would begin on the night of 24–25 April, with the final evacuation of troops taking place on the night of 30 April–1 May. In less than a month, therefore, it would all be over. The campaign, in its entirety, was a fighting withdrawal; a debacle. It was Churchill's worst miscalculation of the war and, without Menzies, his War Cabinet would have approved it with less than ten minutes' conversation. If it wasn't so tragic the words of the children's nursery rhyme might seem appropriate: 'The grand old duke of York, who had ten thousand men, he marched them up to the top of the hill and marched them down again.' Except that in the marching up and down, the troops were subjected to hell from the skies and to very great danger from all around them. The campaign in continental Greece and then on Crete virtually destroyed the 6th Australian Division, which had fought so well in the desert. On the mainland, of a force of 17 125 the Australians lost 320 men killed, 494 wounded and 2030 captured to become prisoners of war. On Crete, of a force of 6500 men the Australians lost 274 killed, 507 wounded and 3102 captured. The total Australian losses in the campaign were 6727 men, or nearly 40 per cent of the force despatched from North Africa. All within a matter of weeks. And all, it seems, utterly predictable.

Simply in terms of numbers, the campaign was doomed before it began. In the area of British operations, the northeastern part of the country, the Greeks could muster four divisions, and the British forces possibly two, although moving them by rail and road from Athens was remarkably difficult with only one rail line and just a few rudimentary roads. Even driving the route today is not at all easy. Against these six divisions the Germans could muster potentially 29 divisions; in fact they only ever needed ten, reducing to seven given the early successes. The British could put up 80 aircraft; the Germans ten times that number. The Germans could stream into Greece at a number of points; the defenders struggled in the narrow valleys and passes of almost impossible territory.

General Blamey took personal charge of the Australians and New Zealanders, gaining Wavell's permission to name his corps the Anzac Corps. Arriving in Greece on 19 March, Tom Blamey had made a thorough inspection of the land over which his troops would be fighting and thought the mountains and narrow passes would greatly assist the Anzac Corps in resisting the invasion. But Blamey also visited the southern beaches, even before the Germans crossed the border, because he believed that evacuation would be inevitable. With the Australian force arriving in Greece from early April, Blamey was quick to draw the geographic links for his soldiers. Recalling that it was just 26 years since the Australians had landed at Gallipoli, Blamey said: 'We have now landed again in these regions to fight alongside the Greek army to overthrow once more a German effort to enslave the world.' Writing on 11 April to announce the formation of the Anzac Corps Blamey noted: 'The reunion of the Australian and New Zealand divisions gives all ranks the greatest uplift. The task ahead though difficult is not really so desperate as that which our Fathers faced in April twenty-six years ago. We go to it together with stout hearts and certainty of success.'

For Ralph Honner the true nature of the campaign became clear when his battalion was forced to disembark on 12 April onto private yachts and small boats in Piraeus Harbour for the trip to shore because the wharves and docks had been destroyed by German bombing. Already. The beauty of Greece deeply impressed itself upon men who had grown used to the desert. Honner told his wife of 'the sight and scent of green and flowering things'; of driving through the suburbs of Athens to the cheers of the Athenians, still clinging desperately to a notion that the Germans could be turned back. But by then, battalions of Brigadier Vasey's

19th Brigade were already fighting a rearguard action, and one of Vasey's battalions, the 2/8th, had reported that it was down to 18 officers and 290 soldiers. A third of its strength.

Greece, to repeat, is a mountainous country, with thin valleys and narrow passes, funnelling men into positions of the greatest danger from the air and from artillery. Any military planner would attempt to disperse his force to limit the impact of an enemy's attack. In Greece this proved almost impossible. Crossing points at rivers and passes through the mountains were few. Men were congregating, slowing each other up, falling on top of each other, really. And becoming target practice for the all-dominant German air force. Vehicles in a slow procession were slow-moving targets, and were abandoned each time an air raid threatened. Nor were the roads wide enough and strong enough for the extent of the traffic.

I spent years in meetings at my workplace, the Australian War Memorial, gazing at Sir William Dargie's painting, *Brallos Pass, Greece*, which hung on the wall opposite me. High mountains rear up on both sides of the painting, with a narrow valley in the centre. In the foreground two figures are dwarfed by the mountains. Exaggerated, I suspected; how on earth could men be expected to protect themselves and hold up their pursuers in such country? Surely Dargie must have misrepresented the narrowness of the pass, truncated the width of the valley. How could you defend such a place, I've often wondered. Driving along the route of the Australian withdrawal in 1998, my car suddenly swung around a corner into view of the pass. What I was seeing was precisely what Bill Dargie had painted. The place was impossible for fleeing soldiers. Good to defend, you would have thought, except the Germans were coming from both sides of the country, and the fear was that the Australians might soon find themselves fighting an enemy in front of them and behind as well. The Greek army on the western side of the country had collapsed. The Anzac Corps had no option but to retreat.

And this is what it had come to by 24 April: the order to withdraw and evacuate had been given, and men who could hold the advancing Germans at Brallos would mightily assist their mates somewhat closer to the evacuation points, who might just get out in something like good order. The navy could muster seven cruisers, 20 destroyers, two infantry assault ships and 19 medium-sized troopships. It sounded impressive, but the men had to first reach the beaches that Tom Blamey had so thoughtfully inspected three weeks earlier. The fighting was intense; the planning crucial; ensuring that men were fighting into the ground with section slipping through section, fresher men at the enemy, delaying, harassing, holding. It was the same at Thermopylae, further east. That is what it had come to so soon, a fighting withdrawal.

Few had time to write down their impressions of all this, they were too busy fleeing and surviving. But the official Australian war correspondent, Kenneth Slessor, was with them in Greece to let the people at home know what was happening. In his diary, before the fighting had really begun, Slessor recorded travelling the entire route over which the Australians would retreat. He had gone up to the front with other correspondents and then needed to go back to Athens. This was on 7 April; the day after the Germans had begun their invasion: '. . . our route through Larisa, Pharsala, Lamia, Thermopylae, Levadia, Thebes and Eleusis. In all these towns streets of waving, shouting Greeks, very patriotic and excited by German war news.' Slessor was back in contact with Australian soldiers near the front on 11 April and already understood that this was by then a withdrawal. Indeed he wondered how the convoys carrying the troops could possibly get through along the narrow roads, packed with refugees fleeing from the mountains, in the dark. Already the Australians were mining roads and blowing bridges to slow the German advance, which meant, of course, that they had given up any chance of counterattacking. The Greek army, Slessor found, was using horse-drawn carts for their soldiers.

Slessor witnessed several bombing raids; in one case there were 18 Dornier aircraft in flights of three, escorted by 'swarms' of fighter aircraft higher up, but not needed, as there was no resistance to the bombers. The bombers would form up, circle and then dive towards their targets; Slessor could see sticks of bombs actually falling. There were 'screamers' attached to their planes to make the noise of the bombing more intense and more terrifying. Soon the bombers were being supported by Heinkels, which flew very low and slow, looking for troops to machine-gun. The air dominance was fatal to the British cause. As he slowly made his way back to Athens Slessor passed along roads littered with Greek and Australian vehicles, these trucks now greatly impeding progress. Some of the trucks had been bombed, many others had slithered in the mud on the narrow and dangerous roads and had simply crashed, left where they had stopped. On 22 April Slessor was told of the decision to evacuate. The intelligence officer briefing him said, 'The fact of the matter is we seem to have been left with a job which is too big for us. The wisest course is for us to get out now before we get into it any deeper ... it is mostly a matter of promises which were not kept.' Slessor evacuated on a ship crowded with refugees who were crying and weeping as they left Piraeus. This was 22 April. Some of the Anzac Corps would have another eight days to endure in Greece.

At Megara, northwest of Piraeus, on 27 April, Barney Roberts was dreaming of a boat. Hope, he knew, lay in the sea: 'The sea and beyond to Crete; beyond Crete to Alexandria; and beyond to Cairo ... an ordered withdrawal.' The day before had been a shambles: 'Pull out. Retreat. Prepare for evacuation—embarkation. German bombers flying low, not bombing, machine-gunning anything that moved—a small black dog in full gallop on the road with bullets spitting dust all around it and surprisingly not being hit.' There was nothing that Barney Roberts could do. By day he and his mates would hide under the cover of the branches of the olive trees, watching the German aircraft patrolling the sky for any sign of movement; by night, they were milling around at the water's edge, hoping for a boat. Barney and his mates had no drinking water whatsoever, and it was driving them mad; Roberts wrote of 'a wooden wedge for a tongue'.

The Australians around Megara had heard of a boat and, yes, it was true: 'Our commanding officer and a few of his cronies had left us.' The men decided then to go back the way they had come for water: they must have water. At a German airfield they surrendered to a lone officer, who spoke with an American drawl. 'I'll probably get an Iron Cross for this,' the officer had said, 'taking all you guys prisoner, single-handed.' Barney Roberts was born in 1920 on a farm in north-western Tasmania, left school at 15 to work on his father's farm before going into the bank as farm work was too hard on his asthma, then joined the AIF in 1940 to gain release from the boredom of the bank. Greece was the first of Barney's fighting, and the last. At Megara, along with 180 others, Barney became a prisoner of war. He would get home to Flowerdale after the war, to become a dairy farmer with a renewed and passionate love of the land he had left for war. The land gave Barney Roberts wisdom, and he would write one of the great Australian memoirs of captivity: *A Kind of Cattle*, he called it. Less than 20 days in the war and four years a prisoner, all to impress the Americans—that is what you had been doing in Greece, Barney. Drawing them into the world war. Ironic then, Barney, that you and your mates had surrendered to an American serving in the Luftwaffe.

Barney Roberts's commanding officer was not the only one to leave his men to fend for themselves. Tom Blamey had quit Greece at 5 a.m. on 24 April. He had been ordered to Athens at midnight, was shown the order recalling him to Cairo and when he opened his mouth to speak, 'Jumbo' Wilson, his boss, cut him off: 'It's an order Blamey. You have to obey.' And you can see the sense of it. You could not run the risk of having Australia's most senior officer captured by the enemy. But, as usual, Tom Blamey gave his critics reason to complain because he ordered his son, also Tom Blamey, a major in intelligence, onto the plane with him. As Tom Blamey senior wrote to his wife when he arrived in Alexandria: 'I brought young Tom out with me. As liaison [at] HQ he had information I needed for immediate use.' Well, possibly, but it was the look of the thing. If I'd only been born a Blamey, Barney Roberts might have thought if he had known the story, I would have escaped four years in a prisoner-of-war camp.

Back in Australia the debacle in Greece came as something of a shock. The government recalled parliament to discuss the position in Greece and to explain why the Australian troops had been sent there in the first place. To be announcing and explaining the reason for being in Greece even as the reports of failure and departure were also becoming public knowledge was to risk confusing and depressing the public. There simply was not time for people to come to terms with Australian troops in Greece before they had to come to terms, too, with the fact that they were being booted out.

The Labor Party, some of its members anyway, was far from pleased. Bert Evatt, a Labor member of the Advisory War Council, said that 'it was not right to give a small force a task which was impossible', and complained that the Greek adventure had never even been discussed by the council. There had been no consultation about Greece whatsoever, he said. Acting Prime Minister Fadden could hardly have said, although he might have wanted to, that the failure to consult the Advisory War Council on Greece was on Bob Menzies' explicit instructions. To Labor and to those many Australians wary of Churchill since the Gallipoli adventure 26 years earlier, the whole thing looked like another of Winston's madcap ideas. People were suggesting, too, that Menzies had been duchessed in Britain and had not stood up to Churchill in a forthright manner to assert Australia's national interests. So strong was this criticism that it was reported in America that Australia was about 'to pull out of the war' and Japanese newspapers reported that the 'Empire was crumbling'. This was far from helpful. With Churchill urging him on, Menzies made a radio broadcast from London to Australia 'to stop the rot' as he put it in his diary.

Menzies' broadcast address reads well from the newspaper but I assume that coming from London it was heard in Australia with a fair amount of the wheezes and whirls common to short-wave broadcasting then. Would that have given the address greater authenticity? Clearly Menzies believed he had to dress it up a little because at the top of the talk he announced the appointment of General Blamey as Deputy Commander-in-Chief in the Middle East under Wavell. As the *Sydney Morning Herald* rather gleefully noted, this announcement was clearly inserted in the speech at the very last moment—an early example of 'spin' designed to hand out some good news before coming to the truly lamentable part of the talk, perhaps. Blamey's new job, Menzies said, 'will assure to us an effective voice, that of our own leader in the making of decisions which are of such moment to Australia'. About time, his listeners might have been thinking.

'Meanwhile,' Menzies continued, 'the battle ebbs and flows,' He could not keep off his main message for too long; he was there to make sense of the disaster in Greece. We thought, he royally announced, that fighting in Greece would be 'hazardous', but we also believed that there was a real prospect of military success. To have abandoned the Greeks as the Germans attacked, no doubt 'we' thought again, 'would have been one of the infamies of history,' Menzies said. 'We should have been subjected to a storm of criticism all over the world [in America, possibly?] and would have lost our own self-respect. We cannot win this war without losses,' Menzies observed. Look, he said, how the British have been battered yet their resolve is undiminished: 'We Australians are of the same stuff . . . we may have to draw heavily upon our accumulated reserves of patience and courage and good cheer. But we shall come through.' So for heaven's sake, Menzies might have said if he were speaking more directly, buck up and stop complaining.

'I have told [the British people] in your name that we are with them to the full, in foul weather and fair, in temporary danger as in victory.' Careful there, an adviser might have cautioned, do not get anywhere near the 'last man and last shilling' stuff of the previous war; remember our interests are now closer to home. Menzies had gone to London in the first place to remind the British War Cabinet of the need to strengthen the fortress at Singapore. In March he had said that war in the Pacific was far from inevitable, a type of appeasement, the Sydney Morning Herald had labelled the statement. Speaking from London, all his attention focused on the European war, Menzies might have given some Australian listeners the impression that he had almost forgotten the original purpose of his mission.

There were those in Australia who found it odd that their prime minister would be explaining the war to them from London by short-wave radio broadcast when he might have been in Canberra, working hard, 15 hours a day, seven days a week, as he had earlier put it, for the Australian war effort. 'He owes it to his high office to return with all possible speed', the Age had declared on 16 April; 'his clear duty is to supply in his own person that authoritative leadership which Australia meantime lacks . . . he should not therefore indulge in any extensive detours and delays on his way home.'

In times of crisis in war—and if Greece was not seen as a crisis in Australia it was certainly seen as a major setback—it had been the case in the past that recruitment would surge. During the First

World War, when the Australians had absorbed the news from the Dardanelles, July 1915 was the month that saw the greatest number of men enlisting; August 1915 was the second highest month for enlistment for the war. It was as if men were saying, 'Hang on, this is serious, I'd better go.' Nothing like that happened after April 1941. On 10 April, with the campaign in Greece only just beginning, Minister for the Army Percy Spender appealed for an extra 8000 men for the AIF per month: 'Every blow the AIF strikes at Hitler,' he said, 'and at his men in the Balkans, or the Middle East, or elsewhere, is a blow struck in defence of every quiet home in Australia.' They set up a recruiting depot in Martin Place in Sydney just before Anzac Day 1941, but it was hardly rushed. On the first day 136 men joined the AIF and 40 joined the RAAF. About 600 men enlisted in the first four days the booth was in operation, but officials were disappointed that the average age of recruits was so high. The war was not yet attracting the younger men. The June recruiting quota for Australia was 10 000 men; the actual total of 7094 men fell well short. Was it national leadership that was wanting, or did this war seem just too remote?

If Greece was a mystery to most Australians, then Crete only deepened the puzzle. Those Australians with war maps on a kitchen or bedroom wall—and the newspapers had been keen to publish them at first—would have been hunting hard for information about it. Crete is the largest of the Greek islands, about 240 kilometres south of Athens, and it is long and narrow—260 kilometres by 60 kilometres at its widest, 12 at its narrowest. The southern part of the country was barely habitable; the three main towns were clustered in the north. The roads were rudimentary; a high mountain range separated the north from the south of the island. Crete would have, armchair strategists might have thought, little significance for the world war.

The soldiers who had been fighting the retreat in Greece were exhausted and shocked; the campaign there had been such an obvious fiasco. They were looking for rest and renewal, mourning mates now dead or captured. Look at Ivor Hele's masterful painting, *Australian troops disembarking at Alexandria after the evacuation of Greece*, and study the faces of the soldiers in the foreground of the canvas: these are men at the end of their endurance. And now, back in Egypt, they faced one of the most unpalatable facts about the Greek adventure: the savage weakening of the forces in the desert. The territory of North Africa and Egypt, which they fought for with such success just four months earlier, was now lost and would have to be retaken. The 7th Australian Division, and others of course, were even now in deadly conflict at Tobruk, where only a few weeks ago, it seems, Bob Menzies had been wandering around before dinner, congratulating his troops on their victory. Lost, all lost, for Greece.

Barney Roberts had been dreaming of a boat, dreaming too of Crete, then Alexandria, possibly Cairo, and some leave, rest and respite from the bombing and the guns. For Barney those dreams would have to wait; for some of those evacuated, Crete was not just a passing point on the way to Alexandria. It was the stopping off point, the next stage in the Greek campaign. 'Why?', the soldiers disembarking at Heraklion or Suda Bay would have been asking—why?

There was nothing much in it for the British; prestige and credibility had already been destroyed on the mainland, so waving the flag was a hollow gesture now. But for the Germans, to deny the British Crete would be to deny their aircraft access to the Romanian oilfields and to weaken their grip on the eastern Mediterranean. You could see from your war map why the Germans might want to be in Crete. It is hard to make a case for why the British would want to put up a fight there. A chance cabled remark from Wavell to Churchill? No, surely, it was more than that.

Advising Churchill in mid-April that Greece would probably have to be evacuated, Wavell had added that he assumed Crete would be held. Churchill assured him that indeed it would. If Crete was ever discussed at the British War Cabinet in Menzies' time in London, Bob Menzies makes no mention of it in his diary, but then he was gone from Britain on 3 May, moving his King in a final audience with his departing words: 'Farewell and good fortune from seven million Australians.' Blamey told the Australian government that the navy had advised that it was 'vital' to hold Crete, and cabled his minister, Percy Spender, that 'it should not be given up without [the] sternest struggle to retain it as our whole position in Eastern Mediterranean would be seriously affected.'

Fine words and, doubtless, strategically correct. But where would the British find the troops to defend the island and where was the equipment? The troops would come from among some of those fleeing the mainland. But their trucks and their guns, in large numbers, were lying abandoned on the mountain tracks and roads of mainland Greece, or had been left to rot at the harbours and beaches of southern Greece as the troops stole away at night. There had been little hope of boarding even a small number of them. The troops transferring to Crete, therefore, were camping in the olive groves around the pleasant beaches of the northern part of the island; soldiers in name, but lacking even the rudimentary equipment that would make them soldiers in fact. And once again, of course, without any form of protection from the German dominance of the air. Churchill knew from Ultra—the British penetration of secret German codes—that Crete would be attacked in force. When was it time to cut and run? To fight on Crete would put at risk of death, incapacity or imprisonment men who might be useful in the increasingly massive fight in the desert.

Ralph Honner liked what he saw of Crete on arrival:

Late in the morning we reached this island and marched eight miles in the afternoon up into the hills laden with weapons, ammunition and rations. That's all we carried . . . I arrived with only the clothes I wore and my battle equipment—pistol, binoculars, respirator, compass, ammunition, about a week's rations and a Bren gun.

'Lord Haw Haw'—the Anglo-American, William Joyce, 'Hitler's Englishman', who broadcast Nazi propaganda to British troops and other listeners—described Crete as 'an island of doomed men'. Honner told his wife, 'It's a very pleasant doom so far'. He continued, 'these mountains and hills and groves and streams form a sunlit paradise by day'. The best time to visit Crete? Spring or autumn, the travel people advise; well, the Australians were there at the best of Spring.

While Lieutenant General Bernard Freyberg, the New Zealander given command on Crete, worked on the disposition of his troops to defend the island, the troops themselves were busy marching about to retain condition and to better understand the terrain over which they would fight. Long marches, as Ralph Honner described them, and hard too. Without formed camps, the men must carry most of all that they possessed, but that wasn't much—rations ran short, so the soldiers spent some time every day in the villages trying to buy food. The Cretan people embraced these Australians, as the people of mainland Greece had done, but with the much smaller numbers involved this was more personal. It was as if the soldiers became part of the extended Cretan family, and that would be important to many of them later.

Returning 50 years later for anniversary celebrations, the Australian veterans received an extraordinarily warm and whole-hearted welcome, not merely from an individual, as with the tour guide on the bus in Athens, but from the whole people who still remembered that these 'doomed men' had come to live among them as the German invasion threatened. No Australian or New Zealander of a certain age will ever be other than an honoured member of the family among Cretans of a certain age. The bond seems indissoluble.

Men awaiting their fate can still, however, enjoy themselves and the Australians did. Mixing with the villagers, eating with them, talking together somehow across the gulf of language, swimming. Ralph Honner and four or five others were on a beach, 'enjoying the sun', as hordes of German tourists on Crete do now, when a German aircraft came low over the beach, making straight for them. 'We sat there, trusting to luck, our hearts in our mouths', Honner wrote to Marjory. The plane turned, went out to sea, and made another pass over these naked and tanned Australians. Did the pilot think the men on the beach were Cretans? 'The locals don't swim', Honner dryly remarked. Later, the plane crashed and it was discovered that it had been photographing the defensive positions around the airfield, perhaps the crew were concentrating too closely on their work to be bothered to shoot a group of idle swimmers. Or perhaps it seemed too heartless to shoot up a few blokes just going for a swim.

Bernard Freyberg had divided the island into four sectors: Heraklion, Retimo, Suda Bay and Maleme. It was almost as if the defence of these regions acted almost independently of each other, so undeveloped were the roads and communications between the towns on the island. Suda Bay was one of two ports for Crete and it lies adjacent to the town of Canea; the other three defended sites were close to airfields; the airfield at Maleme was the key. As the Dardanelles campaign had amply demonstrated, invasion of a defended place by troops coming from the sea is one of the most difficult of all military tasks. Prevent the Germans from taking the airfields and the ports and the island could be held. The defensive dispositions were obvious and sensible. All that was lacking was a sufficient number of troops (Freyberg had approximately 50 000 men at his disposal) and guns, transport and ammunition. And aircraft.

The German invasion of Crete began on 20 May 1941 with numbers of troops parachuting onto the island. But what stupidity was that? A parachute is not a fast-moving thing; its slow and gentle approach made the soldier hang lazily as if a sitting duck. Or better yet, shoot the large silk canopy bearing him. Some of those who were not shot out of the sky landed in the midst of the defenders. One group of German paratroopers had the bad luck to drift in among a New Zealand Maori battalion, who set upon them ferociously with their fists. Despite the fate of the parachutists, the overwhelming weight of German numbers would always prevail and when, within a couple of days, Maleme airport was lost the enemy could now bring its soldiers to the island in great numbers. In hindsight, Freyberg should have put almost all of his troops at the airfields and better planned their defence. By 23 May he was reporting that he would have difficulty in repulsing the attack. On 26 May Freyberg advised that 'in my opinion the limit of endurance has been reached by the troops under my command here at Suda Bay', and that the position was 'hopeless'. The next day Wavell signalled that Crete was to be evacuated. All over within seven days.

It was only in the Retimo sector that the defenders enjoyed any real success. Under Lieutenant Colonel Campbell, originally commander of the 2/1st Battalion, and who had fought success-fully in the desert, the Australians held up the Germans, retaining the airfield, and fighting with ferocity with two battalions (2/1st and 2/11th) and Greek troops. The troops at Retimo were quite unaware how the rest of the battle was going because of an almost total absence of radios or any decent form of communications, and

Colonel Campbell may have been less aggressive had he realised that elsewhere the position was lost. Ralph Honner, a company commander with the 2/11th Battalion, showed the flair and tenacity of his leadership that he had demonstrated at Bardia, but his battalion was being asked to do things beyond its capacity. The losses were consequently high in both of Campbell's battalions and, although Honner's accounts of the battles to his wife make inspired reading, it was all much of a waste. Eventually on 30 May those at Retimo decided to lay down their arms. Campbell and most of his battalion surrendered and went into captivity. The 2/11th decided to scatter in the hope of being evacuated from the south.

And here the real tragedy of Crete unfolds. To evacuate 50 000 soldiers would prove difficult, and it could only be done from the southern part of the island for the Germans now held the north. On their commemorative journey in 1995, the veterans went to Sfakia by bus. Sfakia is a pleasant, but isolated, fishing village with a steep descent down to a narrow beach, and it was virtually the only beach in the south from which the rescue might be carried out. We in the veterans' party drove for what seemed hours through the mountains to reach Sfakia. To walk there, only at night because the enemy controlled the skies, must have been truly terrible. Rations were almost non-existent so the Australians and New Zealanders were retreating on no food and little sleep. Only 13 officers and 39 other ranks of the 2/11th Battalion reached Egypt; Ralph Honner was one of them. Those numbers and their experiences in retreat were repeated among all the battalions seeking to get away. The 2/7th's war diary reported that by 30 May the battalion was very weak: '. . . discomforts of facing the enemy are magnified a thousand-fold with his air force cruising around unhampered.' That battalion insisted on retreating in good order, in battalion strength, but for other soldiers the retreat became a rout and some of the soldiers a rabble.

The 2/7th had not been intended for Crete. It had arrived in Athens on 12 April, travelling to battle on a train cheered by crowds all along the route. On 19 April the battalion was ready to face the enemy and believed it was well prepared. Reinforcements had recently arrived from Australia, such as young Aboriginal soldier Reg Saunders, and it would be their first experience of battle. But that was put on hold until 20 April, then the battalion received orders to retire, to march back eight miles to transports to defend another pass. On 26 April they left mainland Greece at Kalamata on a Dutch passenger ship, the *Costa Rica*, bound for Alexandria; 2600 men jam-packed on the decks and below and were bombed to the point of sinking after the *Costa Rica* had just passed Suda Bay. Rescued by British destroyers, all 2600 men were dumped at Suda Bay. Such are the fortunes of war.

Thus did Reg Saunders find himself on Crete. Born in 1920 on an Aboriginal mission in western Victoria, Reg's mother had died at a young age and his father had brought up his two sons, Reg and his younger brother Harry, to be skilled bushmen, able to look after themselves—good men, hard workers, loyal and faithful. Reg was working with his dad, timber-getting in the bush, when he suddenly said, 'I'm going to the war.' That was in April 1940. A year later he had been retreating in Greece, now he was one of the 'doomed men' on Crete. In seven weeks in Greece and on Crete the 2/7th Battalion would be almost entirely destroyed as a fighting unit, collapsing from 33 officers and 726 men when it had reached Athens on 12 April to seven officers and 65 men when it was evacuated from Crete. But the 2/7th had been a proud battalion and had maintained good order even as it approached the beach at Sfakia. Lining up for the evacuation barges, Reg Saunders was near the head of the queue as the last barge pulled away from the shore. 'That's it,' said someone in charge, 'there'll be no more barges. We are now a surrendered army. You can wait for the Germans to come and round you up or you can strike off by yourselves, but in small groups, mind you.' Trained and bonded as a battalion, these men were now on their own. Good luck.

Reg Saunders was an inspirational man to meet, but it was unlikely he would tell you his story unbidden. When I knew him he was a member of the Council of the Australian War Memorial. He did not say much at meetings, but he was one of those you would seek out at lunch just for the privilege of talking to him. You were on Crete for eleven months, you would ask, perhaps the only black man on the island; how on earth did you avoid captivity? 'Well,' Reg would say, 'we'd hide by day in caves or in the olive groves by day, and only come out at night. I'm pretty invisible in the dark,' Reg would say with a throaty laugh. But just think of it, on the run for eleven months, longer than the entire Gallipoli campaign. Never a change of clothes, never a chance to relax and rest, never enough to eat. The village people would have fed them but these soldiers well knew that there would be reprisals if anyone was caught, or even suspected of, helping those on the run. It was better if they stole what they needed rather than put good people's lives in jeopardy. Reg Saunders witnessed from afar a summary execution in one of the villages. A couple of people tied to chairs, the village people forced to watch, shrieking their hatred of the Germans, a round of bullets and the bodies handed back for burial. You could not knowingly put people through that.

It was his bush skills, taught by a dad he was determined to see again, that came to Reg Saunders' aid. He was lightning quick, always a good sportsman, and practical. But it is hard for us to have any comprehension of what he and his mates endured as they fought for their lives all those months on Crete. Eventually they were told that a boat would come for them. They were to be at such and such a place at such a time. All 75 of them made it to the beach, individually alerted by agents of the British using a network that existed throughout Crete, despite the Germans. These Cretans were a fierce and determined people who never forgot. Ordered by the authorities in Athens to attend a wreath-laying ceremony of reconciliation between Germany and Greece many years later, those Cretans in positions of authority who needed to attend turned up, but when the German ambassador stepped forward to lay his wreath they all turned their backs on him. In memory of Reg Saunders, I suppose, and his mates and all of their own people who were murdered just for helping the soldiers who had come so far.

On the beach all those now being rescued were ordered to strip naked and to leave their clothes where they fell. They were covered in lice, you see, had been for months. Just one of their many sufferings. Deposited, eventually, at Bardia, the war was far from over for Reg Saunders and his mates. It was now 7 May 1942 and they had a lot of catching up to do on how this war had changed as they had evaded the Germans roaming all over the island of Crete.

8. THE VICTOR TRUMPER OF AUSTRALIAN POLITICS

Bob Menzies returned to Australia, appropriately enough on Empire Day, 24 May 1941; four months, to the day, since he had left Sydney. The prime minister had left Britain on 3 May and then visited Canada, the United States of America and New Zealand—he was in no hurry, it would seem, to make Australian landfall. Indeed, he wrote in his diary of a feeling 'of sick repugnance and apprehension' as he neared Australia. The last words of his meticulously kept trip diary were: 'the hour approaches'. Menzies had endured a terrible flight from Auckland in appalling weather—'a nightmare journey across the Tasman'—and was in poor shape when his plane landed at the Rose Bay flying boat base. He virtually ignored Acting Prime Minister Arthur Fadden, who was there to greet him, but commandeered Fadden's official car, forcing Fadden to share a car back to central Sydney. Fadden, a down-to-earth Australian and a marvellous story-teller, with mates from all sides of politics, said that Menzies 'seemed about as happy as a sailor on a horse.'

People had been warning Menzies that the knives were out, and this was certainly troubling and depressing him. Is it enough to say that politics is a strange game, that ambition drives politicians to make trouble, particularly if they perceive a vacuum or a weakness at the top. Menzies had a tenuous grasp on power, always relying upon the votes of the two independents. The sudden death of one of his supporters and the government whip, John Lloyd Price, the member for Boothby in Adelaide, on 23 April 1941 meant that a by-election could further, possibly fatally, undermine the Menzies government. At first Menzies wondered if the Labor Party, in the interests of national unity and stability, would refrain from contesting the by-election, but this proved to be another of the prime minister's 'forlorn hopes'.

Labor had always insisted that Australia needed a strong and ongoing political debate if the country was to wage war successfully. It needed an opposition strong enough to push the government hard, to ensure those on the Treasury benches governed well and in the interests of all Australians. No one was better placed than Menzies to understand Labor's position and it was a little disingenuous of the prime minister to plead for an end to politics in support of the national cause. He had just seen at first hand the dangers of a 'one-man government' and come home worried by the inability of the British War Cabinet to say 'boo' to Churchill. Menzies believed there were other occasions when he thought that he was the only one standing up to Churchill, questioning him, challenging him, all, of course, in the interests of good government and good decisions. In his diary Menzies boasted that he had told Churchill that he needed chiefs of staff 'who will tell him he is talking nonsense'. The remark was passed off in good humour, it would seem, as Menzies went on: 'W. explodes. But it draws him and he reveals his real opinion of the chiefs of staff in terms I could not have equalled! He knows they are Yes-men, and does not love them for it.'

Labor, without the benefit of this insight into the British situation, was saying, nevertheless, that the last thing Australia needed as the world crisis deepened was a bunch of political yes-men in the Australian War Cabinet or on the Advisory War Council. Labor would contest Boothby, to push the government; and they would push hard in parliament too. Good governments require strong oppositions.

Coincidentally the Boothby by-election was held on 24 May, the day Menzies flew back into Sydney. You would think he might have been delighted to see his wife, to shake hands with his cabinet colleagues, to suck in the warmth of the Sydney public's welcome, but his attention must have been partly on the election results from Boothby as they came in. In the event, it was a good result for Labor, whose candidate picked up some 10 000 more first-preference votes than at the general election nine months earlier, but even so Menzies could breathe easily as his candidate, Dr Archibald Grenfell Price, had retained the seat for the United Australia Party. But, said Menzies a little later in parliament, it was 'diabolical that anyone should have to return to Australia and play party politics.'

Perhaps it was an Australian thing to yearn for the bigger, brighter world out there. Academics did it; the real world for them was in Oxford or Cambridge. Lawyers and doctors did it; a spell at the Inns of Court or a great London hospital could lift a career out of the ruck. But was it wise for a politician to tell his people that he had found a bigger world where his talents were better appreciated and where he could make more of a mark? There is a wistfulness, to put it no stronger, in what Menzies was saying that left his hearers in little doubt that he would prefer to be in London and not in this provincial backwater. And in time of war? That was odd, distinctly odd.

A welcome home had been organised at the Sydney Town Hall on 26 May, and Menzies would be feted with a motorcade in Melbourne when he reached his home city and there would be another public meeting at the Kew Town Hall in the heart of his electorate of Kooyong. At the Sydney rally Menzies tried to smoothe the feathers he may have ruffled at Rose Bay but, unfortunately, he adopted such a patronising tone when speaking of Fadden that the harm might only have been magnified. Perhaps Menzies could not quite get the measure of Fadden, a compromise Country Party leader when the rural rump was unable to choose between seemingly better men: Earle Page and John McEwen. Fadden came across as a bit of a yokel and Menzies, after all, had been mingling with the leaders of British society for months. Down-to-earth Australians seemed a bit raw now, don't you know? In his speech Menzies thanked Fadden for holding the fort but he immediately drew on his close friendship with Churchill—'Big-noting' it. 'Every now and then in London,' Menzies said, 'that great fighting leader, Mr Winston Churchill, would put down a newspaper or a cable and look at me across the table and say, "You know, my friend, this fellow Fadden of yours seems to be a pretty good one," and it always gave me the greatest pleasure in the world to be able to confirm that. I thank him publicly as I thank all my colleagues in the Cabinet.' That remark, alone, might have cost Menzies the leadership. It was so insincere and, as a story, barely credible.

Better, surprisingly, and more believable, was the way Menzies spoke of John Curtin, the leader of the opposition. 'It is something that the cynics have never quite been able to understand that the Prime Minister and the Leader of the Opposition should be genuine and wholehearted personal friends,' Menzies said. And Menzies thanked Curtin for his support and steadiness during the time that the prime minister had been overseas. These two, Fadden and Curtin, had led the country in Menzies' absence. As his speech in Sydney developed, Menzies stressed the value of a united approach in a time of crisis. Churchill, he explained, enjoyed the loyalty of the entire parliament and also the entire people. Perhaps Menzies was trying to draw Fadden and Curtin into partnership with him so that Menzies, too, might enjoy the loyalty of the entire parliament and people. Menzies expressed his 'utter astonishment', after what he had seen in Britain, that men of the calibre of Curtin, Forde, Evatt and Beasley—the Labor members of the Advisory War Council—'should be compelled to stand off and become the critics of an effort to which they might easily be powerful contributors.' It was a strong speech, appealing for national unity and great hard work, but it also reads as the speech of a man who recognises that he may be on borrowed time.

The unravelling of the Menzies prime ministership is more about personalities than it is about policy or principles. Cabinet and parliamentarians, particularly on his own side, seemed to grow sick of Menzies just as he was seeking to enthuse the public with his call for an 'all-in' war effort. The newspapers were now publishing the casualty lists from the Greece and Cretan campaigns, which were depressing, and there was a feeling in the federal parliament that Menzies had not done enough to prevent the twin disasters. It would be too much to claim that Greece and Crete cost Menzies the prime ministership, but the two campaigns certainly played a part in the developing idea that he was not the strong leader that Australia needed in time of war. As the *Age* put it, people were beginning to see Menzies in a better perspective: '. . . as the Victor Trumper of Australian politics with almost all talents except captaincy.'

With hindsight, of course, we know that Menzies handed over the leadership of the country to the junior partner in the coalition government, Arthur Fadden, leader of the Country Party. This is the only occasion in Australian political history when the junior coalition partner provided the leader. At other times when the Country Party leader has become prime minister, it has been due to the death or demise of the existing prime minister, and was done only to give the senior coalition partner the time needed to choose a new leader. So the first extraordinary thing about the change of Australian political leadership in 1941 is that the party with only 14 of 74 seats in the House of Representatives provided the national leader. The second extraordinary thing was that the change in leadership came without a severe or drawn-out crisis. The whole matter seemed to revolve around a feeling that Menzies was simply not a robust, or understanding, war leader. It was also as if Menzies was simply tired of it all.

The sniping from colleagues, the continual accusations of arrogance and snobbery, the inability, as he believed it, to connect with the people. Menzies spoke so frequently about London, and worried so obviously about Churchill, his colleagues believed that was where his heart truly lay. In early July he cabled both the Canadian and South African prime ministers with his idea that there should be a dominions prime minister on permanent watch in London. Only such a person, he seemed to believe, could rein Churchill in. With Russia in the war on the Allies' side, consequent of the German invasion, the war had become even more complex, and Menzies believed that Churchill simply could not cope alone. And if you wander the corridors of Parliament House in Canberra too often, bemoaning the fate that keeps you tied down in this backwater, even your own friends may soon desert you. Menzies' parents and his closest friends knew that something was desperately wrong and urged him to fight. Menzies announced with great fanfare that he would tour Australia in the first week of August to 'talk about the war' with ordinary Australians; that he would leave, though he did not say this, the poisonous atmosphere in Canberra behind him, to make contact with his people, just as he had made such good contact with the troops in North Africa.

Menzies started the tour in Adelaide on 8 August with a rousing speech; two days later he cancelled the tour and called a special War Cabinet meeting for 11 August in Melbourne instead. It was the growing crisis with Japan that had alarmed him, and once again he proposed, and cabinet accepted, that he go to London to give voice there to the mounting crisis in the Pacific. Menzies cabled to High Commissioner Stanley Bruce: 'I am more effective in London then here where at present a hail-fellow-well-met technique is preferred to information or reason.' This was on 13 August; Menzies had only been back in the country for less than three months after a four-month absence, and now he would be off again. This was simply not reasonable. The *Age*, perhaps his only remaining supporter among the Australian newspapers, recognised that Menzies would have to be given a 'pair' again if he was to absent himself from parliament (that is, effectively, seek Labor approval for the cabinet decision). This was, the paper reported, 'confidently anticipated'. Deputy Labor Leader Frank Forde said that cabinet's decision to send the prime minister back to London 'is actuated more by political expediency than by international considerations.' So Labor would not agree to the trip and Menzies felt trapped: he could not go to London and there were too many in his party whom he could not trust. Resignation seemed the only way out. On 26 August, when Labor formally rejected an offer for an all-party government, Menzies told his party room that he would resign the prime ministership. On 28 August the joint parties met to choose a new leader and Arthur Fadden was the only nomination. So the leader of the Country Party, the junior party in the coalition, would become the prime minister. It was bizarre. To his private secretary, Menzies said: 'I've been done . . . I'll lie down and bleed awhile.'

Arthur Fadden was 47 when he came to the prime ministership; eight months older than the man he replaced. Born in Ingham, north Queensland, the oldest of ten children, the son of a police-man, Fadden left school at 15 to begin work as a 'billy-boy' on the Queensland cane fields. Soon his flair for figures won him advance-ment and before too long he was town clerk on the Mackay Town Council. He married in 1916, studied accountancy part time, 'the poor man's university', and then set up his own business in Townsville. Later he was a member of the Queensland Parliament before being elected to the federal parliament in 1936. In March 1940 he became a minister without portfolio in the Menzies govern-ment, and after the Canberra air disaster became minister for Air and Civil Aviation. In October 1940 he became acting leader of the Country Party and was confirmed in the position only in March 1941, when he was already acting prime minister. A man with a rich experience of life, he could not claim an extensive experience in politics when he became prime minister in his own right at the end of August 1941. Journalists, though, regarded Fadden with affec-tion, as the 'epitome of mateship'; he liked a drink and a yarn. Perhaps part of the reason for Menzies' downfall was that, acting in the job for four months, Fadden had impressed everyone as 'a good bloke'. No one had ever said that of Bob Menzies.

Spare a thought for those organising the official opening of the Australian War Memorial in November 1941. The project, a tribute by the nation to the men and women who had served Australia in the Great War, had been long in the making. In exhibi-tion galleries were paintings, photographs, dioramas, models and, supremely, the objects used by those who had fought: a duckboard on which thousands of Australians had walked on their way to the fighting on the Somme; a water bottle from Gallipoli, evidence of the farthest penetration of the Australians. When staff at the memorial began planning for the opening ceremony Bob Menzies was prime minister and invitations were prepared in the name of the board of management and his 'ministers of state'. An appropri-ate seating plan was drawn up. And then redrawn to take account of the fact that Arthur Fadden was now prime minister and Bob

Menzies was minister for Defence Coordination. But the Fadden ministry lasted only 40 days and then all the plans had to be done a third time with former ministers relegated to the less important seats, the new ministers in the front row, and John Curtin, the new prime minister, speaking next after Governor-General Lord Gowrie.

It was never likely that the Fadden ministry would last. There was too much bitterness within the ranks of the United Australia Party and, to a lesser extent, within the Country Party. While Fadden became prime minister and treasurer, all the other minis-ters—Menzies excepted, obviously—retained their portfolios. All eyes turned, though, to the two independents. Arthur Coles, who had briefly joined the United Australia Party, only to flee in disgust when Menzies fell on his sword, was keenly looking to see if Labor would challenge this new administration. Alexander Wilson, a Mallee wheat farmer with a close interest in the plight of the small farmer, had already voted with Labor on a number of issues in the federal parliament and was being assiduously cultivated by Bert Evatt. Labor, it soon became clear, had decided that the party was ready for government. The opposition would strike at the first opportunity and would seek to defeat the new government's Budget. Rejection of the Budget on the floor of the House of Representatives would mean that the Fadden government could not govern and Fadden's resignation would follow. Observers in parliament could sense a change in the air. Labor, united and confi-dent, the government, squabbling and dispirited. Alex Wilson said he would prefer either a national government or else an election to give one of the parties a workable majority. As a third alternative he would be prepared to support Labor.

The Budget debate commenced in earnest on 1 October 1941. From the outset it was obvious the debate was not really about the Budget. As Bert Evatt said, 'a government led by the honourable member for Fremantle [Mr Curtin] would wage war more energet-ically and more efficiently than the present administration is doing.' That was the real issue. The debate staggered into a third day, Friday 3 October. By mid-afternoon Arthur Coles stood at his place in the House of Representatives to speak. Members might have expected Wilson, more sympathetic to Labor, to speak first; there was great interest that Coles was speaking, and great tension on the Treasury benches. Coles began by stating the obvious: the debate on the Budget was a motion on whether or not the government retained the confidence of the House. He said that the House of Representatives was now unworkable and that Australia needed unity and stability. Yet, he said, the government parties had, literally, fallen apart, stating: 'I desire to see responsible and stable government at this crucial time,' and then he sat down. The die was cast. For the first and only time in that building an Australian government would fall by reason of a vote on the floor of the House itself. Later in the afternoon Alex Wilson spoke, but this was really an anti-climax. He would not support the government either, he said, and he asked that the people be invited to make their own choice. But a second wartime election in just a year and in deepening crisis? It did not seem sensible. Shortly after 4 p.m. Curtin's amendment to the Budget was put to the House and passed 36 votes to 33. The government was defeated. Arthur Fadden soon gave in his resignation to the governor-general and recommended that John Curtin be invited to form a government. That same night Lord Gowrie asked Curtin to form a ministry; the new government would be sworn in on 7 October 1941.

There were those in the Labor Party who had been muttering throughout 1941, but more particularly since Menzies' return from London, that Curtin simply was not ruthless enough. The United Australia Party had handed him the sword yet he seemed disinclined to plunge it into the government's back. But you could see it from Curtin's point of view: Australia was in strife on the battlefield, and in increasing danger from Japan; the British Empire was in mortal peril. Political instability and turmoil was most certainly not in the national interest. And might a man not be allowed an element of self-doubt at this terrible time for his people? Am I the man to lead, Curtin must have thought; can I find the words to call the people to arms as our very survival is at risk; have I the strength and the courage the times demand? Even before he became the nation's leader, John Curtin was experiencing the loneliness of command. It would now be with him until the day he died.

Born in 1885 in Creswick, Victoria, nine years older than Menzies and Fadden, John Curtin was the eldest of four children of a policeman father, turned publican. There was never much money in the house; the family eventually settled in Brunswick, and 'Jack' left school early for work. But he was a voracious reader, settling in, night after night, at the Melbourne Public Library, widely and expansively educating himself. It was the union movement that provided his path out of poverty and isolation. Starting at the bottom, by 1914 Curtin was federal president of the Timber Workers' Union and stood for election to the federal parliament for the Melbourne seat of Balaclava. He lost. There is some evidence that Curtin now sought to enlist in the AIF but was rejected because of his poor eyesight. In 1914, too, he proposed marriage to Elsie Needham, a young Tasmanian whom he had met through his union work. He won. There is some evidence that Curtin now sought to enlist in the AIF but was rejected because of his poor eyesight. In 1916 he became an organiser of the Australian Trades Union Anti-Conscription Congress when Prime Minister Hughes, desperate for reinforcements after the terrible Australian losses on the Somme, decided to force young Australians to fight abroad. Curtin won that battle, too, or at least he was on the winning side: 'No' to conscription.

In 1917 John Curtin moved to Perth to be editor of the *Westralian Worker*, a job with an income that would allow him to marry. He and Elsie married in Perth on 21 April, living a quiet life of some obscurity and achievement. His paper prospered, Curtin had the time to read widely and the pleasure of discussing ideas with 'university men'. In 1923 he and his wife moved into a modest cottage in the seaside suburb of Cottesloe, home to Curtin, his wife, a daughter and a son, and his mother-in-law. This would be his family home for the rest of his life. Looked at now, it is a small house in a quiet street. Neither grand nor elegant, the house showed the simplicity of Jack Curtin's search for contentment. It was said that as long as he had an armchair and a pile of books he was happy. But the house was near to the railway station, and this was important as he never drove a motor car. And near enough to the beach, too, a good surf beach, and Curtin had always been a keen sportsman and swimmer. The good Australian life, you might say, if somewhat on the quiet side.

Curtin first stood for the federal seat of Fremantle in 1925, unsuccessfully. He won the seat in 1928 and again in 1929, when

Scullin took Labor to power for the first time since 1917. As one of the party's best speakers and thinkers, Curtin was disappointed not to be elected a minister. Unhappy on the backbench, he began drinking again—he had a life-long battle with alcohol. He lost his seat at the 1931 election, a victim of the economic Depression that had destroyed the Scullin government. Curtin returned to federal parliament in 1934 and, to his great surprise, was elected leader. He promised that his drinking days were over. Electing Curtin leader was an inspired but not an obvious choice. He was without ministerial experience and had only limited parliamentary experience. He was from Australia's most remote state, and he was largely unknown to people in eastern Australia. But John Curtin had a wonderful capacity to concentrate on what was important. He saw the coming war clearly, and concentrated his reading and thinking on defence and foreign policy issues. He was heavily influenced by Douglas Wynter's sober analysis of Australia's strategic dilemma. After the 1940 election, his second loss as opposition leader at which he only narrowly retained his seat, Curtin suggested an Advisory War Council and, as the leading member of the council, he immediately established himself as one of Australia's key war leaders. It would be fair to claim that John Curtin came to the prime ministership better acquainted with the issues facing the country than any other opposition leader taking over the reins of government.

What qualities did the new man bring to office? An acute intelligence and decades of reading, writing and thinking. A quiet but passionate determination that Australia would not go under as the war intensified. The respect and admiration of almost every member of federal parliament, and an eloquence and passion in speaking that would soon impress itself on all Australians. Menzies had spoken longingly of a parliament and people entirely loyal to the prime minister, and Curtin achieved just such a dominance through the exercise of personal qualities and capacities that emerged now that he was the leader of his people. It would be wrong to suggest that Curtin's strength of character surprised people who knew him, but if Menzies had all the qualities except leadership, then it soon became clear that leadership was the area in which John Curtin excelled. 'Breathes there an Australian with soul so dead' that he would be unmoved by Curtin's appeal to the nation, a Melburnian wrote: 'I have listened to every Australian leader of note for half a century, and, in my opinion, this sincere, rugged orator has never been excelled. Fortunate, indeed, are we to have such a forceful, though unassuming, leader.'

As might have been expected there was considerable news-paper interest in the new man and his family. His son, also John, aged 20, was in the Royal Australian Air Force; his daughter, aged 23, worked in the railway department in Perth. His wife, at home in Perth as the votes were being counted in the House of Repre-sentatives, was preparing for a modest family celebration and had taken a phone call from her husband with the news of his eleva-tion. She would celebrate her fifty-first birthday the next day. She had no idea when she would next see her husband and had made no plans to travel to Canberra.

Curtin himself spoke modestly of his victory: 'No matter what happened in parliament, all parties representative of all the people of Australia are united by one common purpose—to see the war through until victory is won.' He had no greater obligations, he said, though he had greater responsibilities, than any other man or woman in Australia today. For all of them shared the duty of serving the country in what was the greatest crisis that had ever confronted the nation. When the war came, he said, there was in existence a government that had been elected by the people, and he saw no reason why the government's difficulties should be added to by anything he could say or do, and so he had sought to support the government as best he could. Although he did not say it, it was obviously important to John Curtin that he came to the national leadership without blood on his hands. From the begin-ning he presented himself to his people as a prime minister for all Australians with but one idea in mind: the survival of his country in war and its ultimate victory.

Curtin spoke of victory in these first days in office but he did not speak of survival, for survival implied that the country was at risk. Coming to office in early October 1941, just two months before Pearl Harbor, Curtin could not speak openly to his people about the risk from Japan, but war with Japan was certainly what Curtin was preparing himself for as national leader. There was no talk of a quick trip to London to see the situation for himself. What might have seemed plausible in August for Menzies now seemed almost absurd in October. Australia, it seemed, would soon be fighting a war on its own doorstep.

The war, of course, dominated the first Curtin ministry; so central was it to everything that his government stood for and could achieve that John Curtin was not only prime minister but also minister for Defence Coordination—soon, simply minister for Defence. The political direction of the war would be his. There were three service ministers: Army, Navy and Air Force; respectively Frank Forde, also deputy prime minister, Norman Makin and Arthur Drakeford. Each of these men would remain in their service portfolios until the war was won.

Forde, a Queenslander born in 1890, missed election to the leadership in 1934, which Curtin won by just one vote. He was, therefore, highly respected by his colleagues, regarded as intelligent, widely read, and a good speaker. He was just 27 years of age when he was elected to the Queensland Parliament in 1917; in 1922 he had transferred to the federal parliament as member for the sprawling seat of Capricornia. In 1930 he became minister for Trade and Customs in the Scullin government. As deputy to Curtin from 1934, Forde was loyal, hard-working and effective. He was never one for the limelight.

Closer to Curtin personally was his treasurer, Ben Chifley. Born in Bathurst, New South Wales, in 1885, the same year as Curtin, Chifley had a curious upbringing: working on his grandfather's farm from the age of five, rarely seeing his mother or his two brothers, and attending school for only a couple of days a week. When he was 14, Chifley finally received regular schooling. But like Curtin, reading was a lifetime passion for Chifley, and he was a prodigious reader of history, economics and literature. By 1914 Ben Chifley was a first-class engine driver on the New South Wales railways, and there is a great deal to like about a man who, when he was prime minister, confessed that real power lay in the 14 railway carriages behind you for which you alone were responsible. And there was also much to like in a future prime minister whose personal telephone number at Parliament House in Canberra was one off the local butcher's. Those who misdialled may not have recognised his voice, but he would dutifully take down the meat order and pass it on to the bemused butcher. Chifley became treasurer in Curtin's government, the third man in seniority behind Curtin and Forde. He quickly made the Treasury 'one of the creative forces in the Australian war effort', and with enormous skill ensured the country would emerge from the war without the burden of an enormous foreign debt, as had happened in 1918. Chifley will rarely be glimpsed in this account of Australia at war, until he becomes Australia's fifth wartime prime minister, but his friendship with John Curtin and utter dependability and reliability made a real difference to the man who now carried the immense burden of Australia at war.

H.V. 'Bert' Evatt was the fourth most senior member of Curtin's team, as attorney general and minister for External Affairs, although few would have thought of Evatt as the perfect team player. Immensely gifted and nine years younger than Curtin and Chifley, Evatt enjoyed the education that they could only have dreamed about. Distinguished at school, Evatt shone at university with 'a swag of medals and awards'. Bert finished his university degrees in 1918, the year his second brother died as a result of the war—the shock of the loss of two of her children probably killed his mother as well. Evatt had every reason to hate war.

Evatt's reputation is sadly tarnished by his most unsuccessful period as leader of the opposition in Australia in the 1950s. For all the years before, however, his life appears a glittering success. Stand before his portrait, painted by Arnold Shore, at the National Portrait Gallery in Canberra and you will see the younger and successful Evatt. Painted in 1935, five years after he had become the youngest justice ever on the High Court of Australia, the portrait shows an attractive, energetic, relaxed man shrewdly assessing the world about him. As a young man Evatt was an active sportsman; as he matured his interests broadened into art, literature and history. He had an encyclopaedic knowledge and a remarkable memory for sporting statistics. Elected to parliament in 1940 after stepping down from the High Court—the first and only justice ever to do so, a progression in the opposite direction is more common—Evatt was impatient with Curtin's apparently leisurely approach to taking government from Menzies and Fadden. It was

Evatt who questioned Curtin's resolve; he who would have taken Labor into a national government. It was Evatt who worked hard to ensure that Alex Wilson, the independent, would be a supporter of an incoming Labor government. As a minister Bert Evatt was energetic, extremely ambitious and far-sighted. He needed Curtin, though, to rein in his somewhat excessive enthusiasm.

In addition to John Curtin there were 18 members of the cabinet: seven from New South Wales, five from Victoria, three from Queensland, and one each from South Australia, Western Australia and Tasmania. The cabinet was remarkably stable with very few changes throughout the remaining long years of the war. As members were sworn into office by Lord Gowrie on 7 October 1941 did they have any real understanding of the work and worry that would be theirs? There would be no victory celebrations, Curtin told his ministers, and no holidays; they were to hit the ground running. The new team faced the parliament for the first time on 8 October, and then secured an adjournment until 29 October to allow for the preparation of a new Budget. Ministers worked long hours indeed, reading their way into their jobs; meanwhile on the other side of the House there was Bob Menzies, a journalist reported:

> . . . the strangest sight of the week . . . Only six weeks ago the Prime Minister of Australia, with a battery of high pressure men around him to prevent unauthorised persons bursting in on him—lounging back [now] in a comfortable chair in the party room, wide open to the public gaze.

On 20 October Curtin took the people into his confidence with a prepared statement on 'ominous portents on the Pacific horizon'. A German victory over Russia, he reasoned, would leave Germany free to turn its attention to south-western Asia, as well as to North Africa. 'The war has been in progress for over two years now', Curtin wrote:

> during which time, except for odd raiders in our waters, we have been immune from attack, though our sailors, soldiers and airmen have been gallantly playing their part in theatres of operation overseas. There are now ominous

portents on the Pacific horizon which threaten to bring the conflict to our very doors.

Curtin spoke of the cooperation of the democratic powers in the Pacific, which he said was 'heartening', but of which he could not give details. Australians should know, though, that 'some time ago all necessary preliminary precautionary measures for the defence of the Commonwealth and its Territories were taken by the Services'.

War on our doorstep. It was a sobering realisation, for we had always gone away for war—to Europe, to the Middle East, to South Africa—as that great monument to Australia at war, the Australian War Memorial, showed. The official opening of the memorial in Canberra on 11 November 1941, 23 years to the day since the signing of the armistice to end the war 'to end all wars', was one of Prime Minister Curtin's first official functions. The first speaker at the ceremony after the two minutes' silence at 11 a.m. was Governor-General Lord Gowrie. The people at the War Memorial had drafted a speech for Gowrie, which he had not used. It had been filled with flowery sentiments thought appropriate for the occasion. Instead the governor-general was far more direct. He told the country via ABC Radio that the Great War had been 'responsible for the death of eight million able-bodied men . . . and for the wounding and maiming of many, many millions more. It caused,' this experienced and senior soldier claimed 'universal destruction, desolation and distress without bringing any compensating advantage to any one of the belligerents. It was a war which settled nothing; it was a war in which all concerned came out losers.' It ended, he said, with a 'temporary truce', and the world was now fighting 'to put an end once and for all to this diabolical menace to mankind.' He asked visitors to the memorial to reflect on the terrible cost of war and to say, with a firm and certain voice, 'never again, never again'.

Lord Gowrie had not yet taken the measure of his new prime minister, whom he was initially inclined to distrust. Soon, Curtin's charm, decisiveness and bold leadership would make Lord Gowrie a firm ally and friend. Gowrie was the one man to whom the prime minister could pour out his soul, his anxieties and doubts in the darkest days of the Pacific War. Curtin spoke after Gowrie, telling the audience of the excellence of the siting of the memorial, directly opposite Parliament House. 'The Parliament of a free people,' he said, 'cannot but be inspired and strengthened in the performance of its great duty by the ever-present opportunity to contemplate the story . . . of the deeds that helped to make the nation.'

Then came the laying of wreaths in memory of those who had died in the Great War. Sixty thousand Australians killed, many thousands 23 years later still mourning them. With countrymen again on active service it was a sombre moment. The governor-general and his wife were the first wreath-layers; they would lose their only surviving son to war in 1942. Then came the prime minister. And then members of the fledgling diplomatic corps that had begun to gather in Canberra. They proceeded in the wreath-laying in order of seniority, from the longest-serving diplomat in Canberra to the most recent arrival last. As it happened, the most senior foreign diplomat in Canberra was the head of the Japanese delegation, Tatsuo Kawai, who therefore followed directly behind Curtin. John Curtin would have known, with certainty, that the 'ominous portents' in the Pacific, of which he had spoken in October, were vastly more ominous now.

The Roll of Honour, a complete list of all our dead in all the wars, was not yet installed, but visitors on that opening day admired the cloisters where the roll, on bronze panels, would eventually be placed. Sixty thousand names for the Great War. But how many would be added from the current war? Who could tell? People moved through the cloisters with a sense of foreboding of the names of thousands of men still alive on active service, now at great risk. Death in war. Never easy to announce, either to the nation, generally, or to grieving individuals, but, sadly, just a part of the job for war leaders, clergymen and telegram messenger boys alike. It was work that John Curtin dreaded.

Curtin learned on 20 November 1941 that it was very likely that the light cruiser, *Sydney*, had been lost the day before in waters off Western Australia, and that there were no survivors from the crew of 645 officers and men. Curtin would be told within a matter of days that *Sydney* had been in contact with a German raider, *Kormoran*, had disabled and sunk the German ship but had apparently taken a direct hit itself and had exploded and sunk. The prime minister, naturally, was appalled to learn this and wondered how he could possibly break the news to the nation. He called on the governor-general on the night of 20 November to share his grief and to take counsel from him, possibly the first time these two men had opened themselves to each other. Curtin said that he could not bear to think of the impact of the news in the homes of the families of the men who had perished. The loneliness of command. For the tragedy had now become John Curtin's burden. It must have been a desolate conversation at Government House as the new prime minister came to an understanding of what would now be required of him with war ever closer to his nation's doorstep. The governor-general comforted him, John Curtin told a friend.

The nation learned of the loss of the *Sydney* on 1 December 1941; next of kin had been informed five days earlier. 'While regretting the loss of a fine ship and her gallant complement', the prime minister's statement concluded, 'the people of Australia will be proud that she and they upheld the traditions of the Royal Australian Navy and completed her glorious career in successful action against the enemy'.

9. THE GREY FUNNEL LINE

Tom Frame sat on the deck of HMAS *Sydney* signing copies of his book that the sailors, who had formed a long queue, wanted to buy. They were proud, it seemed, that one of their own, though an officer and an historian, had taken the trouble to write the story of the navy at Gallipoli. Helping sales, no doubt, was the fact that *Sydney* was then in the Sea of Marmara on its way to a mooring off Anzac Cove, in time for the 75th anniversary ceremonies of the landing, on 25 April 1990. How had the troops come to be at Gallipoli in the first place, Tom Frame had asked his naval shipmates in a short talk he gave before he started to sign the books. It was obvious, he told them, that the navy was crucial to the Gallipoli campaign in every one of its phases: the landing, the supply of troops throughout the campaign with everything they would need, the medical evacuation of casualties, the final evacuation of the entire force. Gallipoli was also a naval story, he told them. Tom Frame, naval officer, historian and later Anglican bishop to the Defence Force, was one of the first to tell the story of the Royal Australian Navy at Gallipoli. And that was in 1990, so the book was certainly a long time coming. It is not hard to find the pride in the title of Tom Frame's book, *First In Last Out*, but even those modern-day sailors I observed on the deck of *Sydney* as we sailed to the place that saw the beginning of the legend of Australia at war seemed to understand that naval history remained a small and largely unknown part of Australian military history.

You would think that a navy would be the most important aspect of the defence of a nation that is an island continent, that the story of the island nation's navy would be central to the story of the nation itself. As Tom Frame never tired of telling people, this has not been the case; no more so than in the story of Australia in World War II. Partly it is a problem of chronology and narrative. Perhaps you can see the dilemma: to include the navy we have to abandon chronology and range across the entire six years of war, to leap ahead of where we are up to in this narrative. Let me give you an example. Shortly in this book I will tell you of the Australians in the siege at Tobruk. No one who served in that arid, dangerous, ugly place, facing the possibility of German attack and triumph, will minimise, in their account of the siege, the role of the navy. Ships of the British and Australian navies ran the gauntlet to ensure that supplies, even of water, came in as required; that is, every night. It is an inspiring story, but it is not one you often hear in the telling of the story, of the 'Rats of Tobruk', the 'Tobruk Ferry Service' by Australian destroyers *Voyager*, *Vendetta* and *Waterhen*, which made 139 runs between them in and out of Tobruk.

Other Australian ships played a role, too, although not as heavily engaged as these three, but the names of these ships, and all the others, are not household names even to those with a reasonable knowledge of the story of Australia at war. Perhaps it is because the navies of all the 'British' nations seem to be rolled into one force, as a kind of backdrop to all the action. Naval ships guard the convoys that transport soldiers and then they seem to drop out of the picture. But a moment's reflection will tell us that Australia is dependent for crucial aspects of daily life on what comes to us from overseas, and on what we ourselves can send overseas. Our navy must have an important role in keeping those sea lanes open during time of war. People did recognise this, indeed there was a national public holiday on 4 October 1913, the day on which the first elements of an Australian navy—a battle cruiser *Australia*, several other cruisers, destroyers and submarines—arrived in Australian waters. The national hysteria for the American Great White Fleet visiting Australian ports and cities in 1908 is also an indication of the importance Australians placed on a strong navy. But during the First World War the story of the navy centred on HMAS *Sydney* chasing the German raider *Emden* in the Indian Ocean and the dramatic message, '*Emden* beached and done for'. And on the Australian submarine *AE2*, off the Dardanelles and then sailing through the Narrows into the Sea of Marmara. But that was about it. Not a story that captured popular imagination. So let us examine the crucial role of the navy in World War II.

The Australian navy suffered severe cuts during the Depression years, reduced to a force of five ships and 3200 personnel. Yet by the time war broke out in 1939 the navy had the largest number of permanent personnel of the three services and a substantial force to which had recently been added three modern cruisers, *Sydney*, *Hobart* and *Perth*. Only *Hobart* would see the end of the war; she was in Tokyo Bay for the formal Japanese surrender in September 1945. Even in these three ships there might be a story of significance. The explanation for the rapid rebuilding of the navy from about 1935 onwards lies in a recognition of the threat to Australian shipping, overseas cargoes, and Australian ports, towns and cities from enemy naval action. Certainly people accepted with equanimity and confidence that Singapore was the first line of Australia's defences, but even so they understood that a rogue raider, such as *Emden* in the earlier war, might easily evade Singapore and menace Australian shipping or cities if a new war were to break out. Hence the need for a navy as a vital part of Australian defence.

Only a permanent force would do. Any Australian factory hand or farm labourer might learn to handle a rifle and the elements of drill in a few weeks or months, but even the naive thinkers could see that the operation of complex warships required higher level skills than that. The Australian navy's peak wartime strength of 337 ships—though many of these were quite small— and 39 650 personnel made it the fourth largest navy in the world, so there was no lack of political will for the navy or popular support for it. Yet it was still not a force that entered in any great degree in the people's understanding of the story of Australia in the Second World War.

The story of the navy is not only the story of men at war, it is also a story of some romance that captures the imagination and focuses on the individuality of the ships and their crew. Each ship is different, with a separate personality, and sailors bond very closely with the ships in which they sailed. Consider *Waterhen*, briefly, that 'old chook' as she was referred to by her crew. On 28 June 1941 *Waterhen* left Alexandria on what would be her last run to Tobruk. The ship and her crew had been at this hazardous work since mid-May so the sailors on board were in no doubt as to the danger they faced. On her most recent run to Tobruk, a few days earlier, *Waterhen* and her companions had come under attack from a force of German dive bombers estimated to be at least 48 aircraft strong. It had been a terrifying experience, ducking and weaving to avoid the bombs and torpedoes, and here they were at it again. Now, early in the night of 29 June, *Waterhen* again came under prolonged German attack from the air and was fatally crippled and holed by two very near misses. The troops on board, being taken as reinforcements to Tobruk, together with the ship's company were hastily evacuated to another destroyer, and *Waterhen* was taken under tow while the German attacks continued. But the ship could not be saved. In the early morning of 30 June *Waterhen* 'rolled over and sank'. She was the first ship of the Royal Australian Navy to be lost in the war. They mourned her, those who had served aboard this defiant 'old chook'. Sailors came to regard their own ship, no matter how feeble, as special.

I cannot give you an account of every ship of the RAN in the Second World War, but perhaps we could look in some detail at the life stories of those three Leander class ships that were the focus of the rebirth of the Australian navy in the late 1930s when war seemed, once more, inevitable. Originally ordered in 1933 and intended for the British Royal Navy, these ships were taken over by Australia from 1935 onwards and renamed *Sydney*, *Hobart* and *Perth*. They were substantial vessels with a crew of around 40 officers and 600 ratings, were approximately 170 metres in length:

'The two funnelled profile and symmetrical arrangement of armament gave the ships a reputation as handsome vessels.'

Sydney, bought from the British in 1934 and commissioned at Portsmouth on 24 September 1935, was a light cruiser that arrived in Australia on 2 August 1936. Upon the outbreak of war in 1939, *Sydney* carried out patrol and escort duties in Australian waters until departing for the Mediterranean in April 1940. Her commander from November 1939, Captain John Collins, was in the original intake in 1913 at the RAN College as a cadet midshipman. Born in Tasmania in 1899, the youngest son of a merchant navy doctor who died before his son was born, Collins served in the Grand Fleet from 1917 on HMS *Canada*. In the inter-war years he served alternately in Britain and Australia; such was the integration between the two navies, to advance in the navy in Australia a chap had to be known and trusted in London. Collins, who commanded *Sydney* until May 1941, after which he was posted to Singapore, would become the first Australian to be chief of naval staff, appointed in February 1948.

Italy declared war and joined Germany against the Empire on 10 June 1940, and on 21 June *Sydney* experienced action for the first time when, in company with French and British ships, she bombarded Italian positions at Bardia on the North African coast. On 28 June the squadron was in action against three Italian destroyers, sinking one. The squadron was also present at the action off Calabria on 9 July. Air attacks were common. *Sydney*'s greatest triumph, however, was the sinking of the Italian light cruiser *Bartolomeo Colleoni*, on 19 July 1940, and the wounding of an Italian sister ship. Keeping strict radio silence, *Sydney* completely surprised the two warships; indeed the first news they had of the presence of the *Sydney* was when the Australian cruiser commenced firing. *Bartolomeo Colleoni* was ultimately torpedoed and sunk. Admiral Cunningham, Commander-in-Chief British Mediterranean Fleet, praised *Sydney*'s captain: '. . . who by his quick appreciation of the situation, offensive spirit and resolute handling of HMAS *Sydney*, achieved a victory over a superior force, which had important strategical effects.'

The Australian cruiser returned to Alexandria to a triumphant greeting from the fleet; Cunningham had called on the fleet at anchor in the harbour to 'give her a rousing cheer'. Captain Hector Waller, whom we will soon meet, then on HMAS *Stuart*, greeted *Sydney*'s arrival at Alexandria with a typical Australian signal, 'Whacko *Sydney*'.

Sydney continued in the Mediterranean theatre with considerable success until departing for Australia on 12 January 1941. She arrived in Sydney Harbour late on 9 February 1941, anchoring at Watson's Bay. The next morning she made a triumphal progress up the harbour to her berth, in a kind of re-creation of her welcome at Alexandria. As Australian soldiers had then only recently gone into action for the first time at Bardia, *Sydney* was returning home in triumph as the first sign of Australian spirit and success in the war. An estimated 200 000 people turned out to witness her ship's company march through the streets of the city after which she was named. With a brief refit the ship left Sydney on 27 February for Fremantle, whence she carried out patrol and escort duties in the Indian Ocean. In late June she departed again for Sydney and operated in the Pacific, visiting New Caledonia and Fiji.

Sydney returned to Western Australia in September 1941, under the command, since May, of Captain John Burnett—another of that 1913 intake of cadet midshipmen. Twice, *Sydney* escorted the troop transport *Zealandia*, taking Australian soldiers to Malaya in anticipation of the Japanese entering the war. At about 4 p.m. on 19 November, while returning to Fremantle from the second of these escort voyages, *Sydney* sighted and challenged what appeared to be a merchant ship, at a range of some 20 kilometres distant. Was it complacency in the glow of seemingly unending success for *Sydney* or merely human error that caused Burnett to sail so close to this ship, which was pretending to be a Dutch merchant ship, *Straat Malakka*? *Sydney*'s opponent was actually the disguised German auxiliary cruiser, *Kormoran*, already successful in the Indian Ocean against merchant shipping and soon to claim her biggest prize. At about 5.30 p.m. *Sydney* called on the other ship to make her secret call sign known, and it was then that *Kormoran* opened fire at a range of only about 1500 metres and with devastating effect. *Sydney*'s guns returned a short but effective fire, which fatally damaged *Kormoran*. But *Sydney* was also fatally stricken. *Kormoran*'s crew saw *Sydney* sail off over the horizon and then could see a glow which they believed to be *Sydney*, until it was extinguished around midnight. No one will ever know the story of the last hours of this warship. It was only on 1 December that Australians, who had taken such pride in her exploits, learned that *Sydney* had sunk with no survivors from her ship's company of 645 officers and crew. Only a few small pieces of wreckage were ever found.

Hobart, the second of the Leander class cruisers to come to Australia in the late 1930s, had a happier history than either of her two sister ships. Launched by the British in 1934 and known as HMAS *Hobart* from 1938 onwards after being commissioned into the Royal Australian Navy, she put to sea from Sydney the day war broke out. She escorted the first convoy of Australian troops to the Middle East, from Colombo to Suez, and then operated from Aden in oppressive conditions. As a ship of the Empire, *Hobart* even landed Punjabi reinforcements in British Somaliland in July 1940, but returned to more normal duties—trade route protection and troop convoy defence—in Australian waters from December 1940. In July 1941 *Hobart* arrived in the Mediterranean to replace *Perth* and took part in action at Tobruk, off Libya, in Cyprus, not leaving the Mediterranean until December 1941, the last of the Australian cruisers to be sent to the war at home.

Assigned to the Allied command in waters off Java, *Hobart* continued to live dangerously, escorting convoys of evacuees and reinforcements in the face of overwhelming Japanese aerial superiority. On 15 February 1942 she escaped relatively unharmed from a total of 13 Japanese attacks involving 109 aircraft. She was one of the larger ships to survive the Battle of the Java Sea. *Hobart* passed through the Sunda Strait on the morning of 28 February 1942; her sister ship *Perth* would sink there that evening. *Hobart* was then involved in the Battle of the Coral Sea, and assisted the Americans at the Guadalcanal landings in August.

Hobart was badly damaged by torpedoes from a Japanese submarine in July 1943 in the New Hebrides [Vanuatu], with 13 officers and ratings losing their lives. The damage was so extensive her repairs took 17 months. Thus the ship was not in action again until December 1944, serving with the Australians at Tarakan, Labuan and Balikpapan in 1945. She also saw the Japanese surrender in September 1945. A successful ship on any measure, it was her ignominious fate to end her days, in 1962, at a wrecker's yard in Osaka, Japan. She had been the most enduring of the Australian cruisers specifically commissioned for the coming war, and hers was a cruel final fate.

Unlike her two sister ships, *Hobart* was not commanded by a man marked out early for leadership in the RAN, nor was he among the first cadet midshipmen at the naval college. Rather *Hobart*'s captain from 1939 to 1942 was one of those characters who arise from time to time to enliven history. Born in New Zealand in 1896, Harry Howden was in the merchant navy in Scotland when war broke out in 1914, so he enlisted in the Royal Navy. As an experienced sailor he went straight to war as a reserve midshipman with the Grand Fleet. His grandson recalls that 'Harry had a short temper, foul mouth in the extreme at times [though] he was a thoughtful and kindly person,' short of stature and certainly unorthodox. Nevertheless he won the affection of his crew. They loved 'Captain Harry', or 'Den' as he was sometimes called, because he was a first-class seaman and navigator with a capacity to predict what his opponents would do. *Hobart*, they said, was 'a lucky ship', the 'luckiest of them all', according to one who served on her. They credited Harry Howden with bringing them much of that luck.

Not so lucky was HMAS *Perth*, also built in England, like her sisters, but commissioned into the Royal Australian Navy on 29 June 1939. Serving first in the Caribbean and the Pacific, *Perth* did not reach Australia until 31 March 1940. Until November 1940 she was engaged on patrol and escort duties in Australian waters, then *Perth* served in the Mediterranean and was involved in the evacuations of Greece and Crete in April and May 1941, during the course of which she was badly damaged by bombing. Back in Australia the ship came under the command of Captain H.M.L. Waller and operated off eastern Australia on patrol and escort work.

Perth was Hector Waller's second Australian command and he, like John Collins, had seemed destined for a fine career in the navy almost from the moment he joined as a cadet midshipman in 1913, just two years after the birth of the RAN. Waller had been born in Benalla in 1900, in north-eastern Victoria, the youngest of ten children, the son of a storekeeper. It is hard to know what might have sent 'Hec' Waller to the infant navy; it cannot have been a boyhood enthusiasm for Australian naval traditions that caught his imagination because, of course, there were none when he joined in 1913. Nor, you would think, was it a love of the sea, remote to him as it was in his childhood at Benalla. It might have been an excitement for English naval traditions—Drake, Nelson and all that—but without the intimate records of his thoughts it is almost impossible to get inside the head of a man like Hec Waller.

Official records tell us that Hec Waller graduated from the RAN College in 1917 and served aboard HMS *Agincourt* in the last year of the Great War. In the inter-war years he had a series of specialised signals training and seagoing positions and, although his career moved at a slow-paced trajectory, he was marked out as a man to watch. He married and had two sons. His first Australian command during wartime was in HMAS *Stuart*, and he served with distinction aboard her as part of the Mediterranean's 'scrap-iron flotilla' fire ancient ships, so mocked by Joseph Goebbels. *Stuart* was there for the campaigns in Greece and on Crete, landing troops and evacuating them, always with a dominant German air force above her. She was also an important member of the Tobruk Ferry Service. Through all this action Hector Waller was emerging, in the words of a naval historian, 'as the outstanding officer of his generation'. What was it about Waller? Another of his British commanders in the Mediterranean described him as 'a unique and wonderful character', whereas John Collins was 'just one of nine very able Cruiser Captains'.

From 14 February 1942 *Perth* joined a naval force of Dutch, British and United States light and heavy cruisers and destroyers in waters to the north of Australia in search of Japanese troop transports and naval vessels. Formidable as this squadron sounds, it proved no match for the ships of the Imperial Japanese Navy, which were better armed and more cohesive in action. The Allied force was in disarray after the Battle of the Java Sea on 27 to 28 February 1942, and *Perth* and USS *Houston* eventually left the main group to sail through the Sunda Strait to some safety. It was there that they encountered the Japanese invasion force destined for western Java. The opposing commanders might have been as equally surprised to be engaged in action, but the two Allied ships were now in mortal danger.

Waller was a true leader on his bridge and engaged in aggressive offensive and defensive action, but at about midnight on 28 February he was told that *Perth* had little ammunition left and would soon have no fight left in her. Waller decided to attempt to force a passage through the Sunda Strait. He ordered full speed and turned his ship south for Toppers Island. *Perth*, within only a matter of minutes, was struck successively by a series of torpedoes, probably four, and sank just after midnight on 1 March 1942. When the second torpedo struck Waller gave the order to abandon ship but he remained on the bridge, where he was observed forlornly taking in the sight of the break-up of his ship. Of a ship's company of 686 personnel, only 218 returned to Australia after the war; 23 officers and 329 ratings died in this ship's last battle in the Sunda Strait and 105 died as prisoners of war. Captain Waller went down with his ship, a grievous loss to Australia.

The service of these three ships can tell us much about the Australian navy during the Second World War. Remember these were Australia's newest and best warships, essential you might have thought to the defence of the country, yet they might be found off British Somaliland, at Ceylon, off Greece, back on patrol and escort duty in Australian waters, ferrying troops and supplies to Tobruk, at Singapore, at Guadalcanal in the Pacific, indeed on all the oceans of the world. Australia's navy was a part of the Imperial navy and went as directed by the Admiralty in London, with the agreement of Canberra, of course. As the war came closer to Australia, the Australian government sought greater control over its fleet, which was not readily conceded.

The second thing we learn by looking at the service of these three Leander class ships is how a ship took its character and its fate, often, from the character and competence of its commander; more so, perhaps, than a battalion took its character and fate from its commanding officer, although I would not want to push that contrast too far. Who the 'old man' was really mattered in the navy; he was likely to be with a ship for years and could not be readily relieved as Australian land commanders were relieved in New Guinea, for example, on apparent whim. Somehow, Australia had managed to train commanders of high ability for its navy, men like Waller, Collins and Howden, and their excellence possibly depended on the permanence of their service. These were men who made their life's career in the navy, not specifically recruited to the task of war from the farms and offices of Australia when war arrived, as army officers often were. The naval commanders were older men with life experience in their job, certainly in contrast with air force commanders who had to be young, and in contrast also to many of the army's leaders.

They were men of the Empire; more thoroughly schooled in Royal Navy traditions than the leaders of the Australian army or air force, although they would not have made that distinction. Until 1948 Australia found its chief of naval staff in Britain and brought him to Australia, so that the rule from 1913 onwards seemed to be that 'no Australian need apply'. The top people in the Royal Australian Navy, even into the 1980s, spoke with an accent that was certainly not broad Australian, although not quite upper-class British either; perhaps an accent peculiar to the navy and a further indication of the separateness of this service. If even in the Second World War the Australian navy was not yet wholly an Australian institution, that partly derived from its leaders, who were British, throughout the war.

Admiral Sir Ragnar Colvin came to Australia in 1937 to assume leadership of the Royal Australian Navy. He was 55 years of age, born in London in 1882. He joined the British navy in 1896 as a cadet midshipman and saw action in the Battle of Jutland in the First World War. The navy was Ragnar Colvin's life—he knew no other. He was rear admiral in 1929, vice admiral in 1934 and knighted in 1937. He was, the official historian of the Australian navy in the Second World War believed, 'an outstanding administrator, of reliable judgement and quick decision ... tall, and of commanding presence, ... he upheld the navy's status in the affairs of the nation ... inspiring confidence both inside and outside the Service'. His health failed, however, and Sir Ragnor returned home in March 1941 before the war had come close to Australia.

Sir Guy Royle replaced him. A specialist in naval aviation, 55 years of age on his appointment—another British career naval officer who had also served in the First World War. Of course, he had all the right credentials for the job but even Douglas

MacArthur, the American supremo, made no secret of his preference for an Australian in the most senior Australian naval position
when Royle's appointment came up for renewal in 1943. Royle was
renewed and MacArthur marvelled that this British officer should
continue to send Australian matters to London for consideration,
as if, like Sir Charles Burnett in the Royal Australian Air Force, his
first loyalty was to 'home'. 'He came to Australia a sick man', the
official historian reported, 'temporarily mentally exhausted from a
period of considerable strain overseas, to shoulder increasing
burdens'. Yet he was the leader of Australia's navy, which was soon
to be at war with Japan.

Perhaps, though, it is wrong to emphasise too strongly the British
influence on the Australian navy. When Sir Ragnar Colvin came to
write an obituary covering the loss of three leading Australian naval
officers—Waller, Burnett and Getting—he could claim:

> No finer sailors ever trod the deck. To one who has known
> them and worked with them there is something out of the
> ordinary about these sailors of the RAN. Coming from the
> Australian Naval College they worked and trained for years
> on their own and with the Royal Navy but they were never
> mere copyists. They assimilated the knowledge and tradi-
> tions of the older service, but blended with it something
> peculiar to themselves and the result was unmistakable and
> unmistakably good.

The typical Australian naval officer of the Second World War
was a middle-class Protestant male, who more often than not had
received a private school education. The great majority had been
born in Australia but had completed their naval training in Britain.
They related well to the lower decks, but the navy was not a citizen
force as was the army and remained something peculiar unto itself.
That the Royal Australian Navy was more than a mere replica of
the Royal Navy was in part a tribute to the men who became its
officers, confident in a certain Australian way of command, but in
a greater part due to the men they commanded, who would not
depart too far or too readily from the characteristics of the homes
and people from whom they came.

To know the Australian navy during war we would have to know a great deal more about the sailors who comprised it. For the most part, sadly, they are anonymous as not nearly sufficient work has yet been done about the background, roles and achievements of the Australian sailor in the war. When we look at Australian soldiers at Tobruk or on the Kokoda Track we can study known and named individuals. In telling their story, we can know something of their mates. This is not yet possible for Australian sailors at war because the work has not yet been done, but in some of the stories we do know we might find the spirit that made this navy Australian.

One of those who deserves to be better known is Edward 'Teddy' Sheean. He would be, had he been awarded the Victoria Cross, as he richly deserved. If the sinking of *Sydney* remains a mystery, then the failure to properly acknowledge Teddy Sheean's bravery and self-sacrifice is equally mysterious. Perhaps it speaks of a lack of confidence in the navy itself or a belief, at the highest levels, that an Australian sailor was somehow permanently inferior to his British counterpart and that no Australian sailor could therefore really deserve a Victoria Cross.

Born in Tasmania in 1923 at Lower Barrington, a little out of Devonport in the north of the island, Teddy Sheean was the last of 14 children. His father was a labourer and Teddy was educated at the local Catholic school. He was 17 when he enlisted in the Royal Australian Naval Volunteer Reserve after working on farms in his home area. Five of Teddy's brothers had already gone off to the war, four of them to the army and one to the navy, by the time Teddy took himself to the recruitment office. Did that increase the pressure on Teddy to enlist, or, on the contrary, did it give him reason to think that his family had already done enough? The record does not allow us to know. Yet you would think he was probably determined to do what his older brothers had done.

Teddy Sheean trained first in Tasmania, then at Flinders in Victoria, and finally he was posted to Sydney in May 1942 before joining his first ship. Sheean was billeted on *Kuttabul*, a requisitioned harbour ferry being used to accommodate sailors. Teddy was on home leave when a midget Japanese submarine evaded the boom at the entrance to Sydney Harbour, and detection in the harbour itself, to sink *Kuttabul* on 31 May with the loss of 19 lives.

Sheean, a gunner, was sent to a new corvette, HMAS *Armidale*, which was first engaged on escort duties in Australian waters. Then on 29 November 1942 *Armidale* sailed for Japanese-occupied Timor in company with two other Australian warships to take off the Australian 2nd/2nd Independent Company, and some Portuguese civilians and Dutch troops. With a part of that mission successfully completed and one of the ships already on its way back to Australia, *Armidale* and HMAS *Kuru* came under repeated attacks from Japanese aircraft. In the early afternoon *Armidale* was still under attack from 13 aircraft and without air support of her own, though repeatedly asked for; she was more or less a sitting duck. Though the corvette manoeuvred frantically, she was struck by a torpedo and then by a bomb, and the order was given to abandon ship.

Now the Japanese turned their attention to the survivors in the water, machine-gunning as many as they could find. Teddy Sheean, having helped some of his mates into the *Armidale*'s life rafts, then went back to his gun on the sinking ship, strapped himself in and continued to fire at the enemy aircraft to protect those he saw at such risk. Although wounded in the chest and back, Sheean kept firing, shooting down one bomber and managing to keep enemy aircraft away from some of the remaining survivors. He was last seen still firing his gun as his ship went down. Some 49 of the ship's company of 149 survived the ordeal and many would have said, surely, that they owed their lives to Teddy Sheean. He was 18 years of age when he died, 27 days away from his nineteenth birthday. His five brothers survived the war. Who would say that Teddy Sheean did not deserve the Victoria Cross, but for such heroism, self-sacrifice and gallantry all that Teddy Sheean received was a posthumous 'mention in despatches'.

No member of the Royal Australian Navy has ever been awarded the Victoria Cross, and its two most highly decorated members in the Second World War, Hugh Syme and Leon Goldsworthy, were neither serving with the RAN nor even aboard ships when they received their awards. Their stories show the diversity of employment that the Australian navy provided in the war, in all theatres, in a wide variety of actions.

Hugh Syme was born in Melbourne in 1903, a grandson of

David Syme, the founder of Melbourne's *Age* newspaper. He joined the family business after university, and in September 1940 joined the Royal Australian Naval Volunteer Reserve and was sent to Britain for training. He would not return home until February 1943. Appointed to the Royal Navy's quaintly named Rendering Mines Safe section, Syme worked in as dangerous a job as it would be possible to imagine. A television series 'UXB' (unexploded bomb) showed men rendering bombs safe by hand, painstakingly removing the fuse that armed the bomb. First the team needed to find the bomb and assess its stability. Then they might need to stabilise it and tunnel around it, to find the fuse and to make a space big enough for one man to work, listening carefully all the time, pausing frequently to regain his composure and steadiness. Meanwhile another man slowly unscrewed and removed the fuse mechanism, making sure not to move the bomb, even to the slightest degree. Any jolt or shake and the bomb or mine might easily detonate. Even on television this was hair-raising stuff. What it must have been like in real life is simply impossible to imagine. But the work had to be done, this was a bomb that might still kill hundreds of people and destroy houses, wharves, port facilities, shipping, or whatever.

This was the work that Hugh Syme excelled in. Tunnelling to find the mine or bomb and carefully removing the fuse to make it safe required extraordinary aplomb and the strongest possible nerves. At Primrose Hill reservoir, near London, on one occasion, Syme tunnelled down to a mine only to find that the fuse was on the underside and that he would have to tunnel under the bomb to reach it. If he had failed, there was the real danger that the reservoir would be breached and the neighbourhood flooded. This was just one of his exploits. In and around London, this brave Australian naval reservist defused dozens of mines and bombs.

Hugh Syme received the George Medal in June 1941 for his coolness in dealing with ten unexploded mines and bombs; in June 1942 he received a bar to his George Medal for defusing the Primrose Hill mine; in March 1943 he received the George Cross for carrying out a further 19 mine recovery operations. He was back in Australia by then, perhaps the anxiety of it all a distant memory. Although he taught the Australian navy what he had learned in London, the RAN had little real work for him and Hugh Syme returned to civilian life at the end of 1944.

At that point Syme was Australia's most decorated sailor, but that title was taken from him in early 1945 by Leon Goldsworthy, known as 'Goldie' or 'Ficky'—the latter derived from 'Mr Fixit' because that is what he did: he fixed unexploded mines and bombs. Leon Goldsworthy was born at Broken Hill, New South Wales, in 1909, and educated at Kapunda High School, the Adelaide School of Mines, and the University of Adelaide. His extraordinary military career began in 1941 when he, like Hugh Syme, joined the RANVR. In April Goldsworthy was sent to Britain for training and joined bomb disposal. It is a career that paralleled Hugh Syme's, but whereas Syme was tall and dashing Goldsworthy had initially been refused entry to the navy because he was too short. Height, as he was to prove, was no great advantage in underwater mine recovery work, which was Goldsworthy's specialty. Awarded the George Medal in April 1944 for 'gallantry and undaunted devotion to duty in rendering enemy mines safe' on two occasions, he was then awarded the George Cross in September for the recovery of four German ground mines, three magnetic mines and one acoustic mine in June 1943 and April 1944. The Distinguished Service Cross came in January 1945 for 'gallantry and distinguished service in mine clearance', with particular reference to his stripping of the first German 'K' type mine in 50 feet of water at Cherbourg, when the harbour was being hurriedly cleared for the Allied invasion of Europe following the invasion of Normandy. Goldsworthy then returned to Australia and worked with American underwater experts.

For a man initially rejected by the navy as being physically unfit, Goldsworthy finished the war as the most highly decorated man in the RAN's history—the acknowledged underwater mine disposal expert in Europe, the conqueror of over 100 weapons in European waters and about 30 in the Pacific. His story is as remarkable as Syme's, but the service of these two gallant men was in no sense typical of the life of the Australian sailor, except perhaps in the breadth of that service. Rather, Teddy Sheean's life as a sailor was more typical. Sheean was in an Australian warship and, in trying to protect his mates from attack, he was in a tradition that started for Australia at Gallipoli: men who would be prepared to give up their own lives so that their mates might have a better chance of survival. But we know too little about him and about the men who died with him, and all the others of the Royal Australian Navy.

Battlefield travellers to Gallipoli, the Western Front or, increasingly, the Australian battlesites of the Second World War, have the terrain to examine and learn from, and the graves of the dead to inspect and to meditate upon. For the navy, it is not like that. We do not even know the final resting place of *Sydney* and, if we did, would we be any better off? The ship, now a war grave, lies too deep in the ocean for Australians to view it, and so many of Australia's sailors, killed in war, likewise lie in similar war graves that their families and other Australians could never visit.

At its peak in June 1945, 39 650 Australians served in the navy. As a result of hostilities, 1911 of them died; the overwhelming majority of them, 1551, were missing presumed dead, having gone down with their ships, including 144 officers. Australia lost some fine military leaders from the navy and, though ships have later been named for one or two of them, there is not the same recall of the story of the navy as there is for the men of Tobruk or Kokoda, for example. But possibly John Curtin, as a very inexperienced and new prime minister, endured no more grievous sense of loss during his whole period in office than when he was told of the loss of *Sydney*. Curtin was devastated by the news. The loss of *Sydney* is an Australian naval story that has endured. In the whole complex story of Australia in the Second World War, though, some of the other naval stories deserve more recognition too.

10. DEFENDING THE MIDDLE EAST TO THE LAST AUSTRALIAN STANDING

I t had been the devil's compact really. If the Allies were to fight in Greece then the 6th Australian Division would have to be detached from the desert warfare and sent to Greece. Weaken the campaign in the desert for the doubtful campaign in Greece and destroy the 6th Australian Division in the bargain. With Tobruk firmly in British hands, the chances of a bigger or better army reclaiming what the Italians had lost would be significantly reduced if the Italians, on the run and demoralised, could be booted out of Tripoli. Instead, when the best of the desert fighters went to Greece they left behind inexperienced, ill-trained and ill-equipped troops to hold what they had won; to fight further along the coast towards Tripoli, if they could.

Leslie Morshead was shocked by what he found when he arrived in February 1941 to take control of the 9th Australian Division, now defending the earlier gains. Too few weapons and a lack of ammunition, too few troops—one of his brigades was without one of its three battalions—and all of them untrained troops at that. Morshead was a curious commander, a martinet but loved. 'Ming the Merciless' the troops called him after a cartoon character; later they simply shortened it to Ming. Morshead, born in Ballarat in Victoria in 1889, had served in the First World War, leaving schoolteaching to enlist. He was at the landing at Gallipoli and in the Battle of Lone Pine, so here was a real soldier's soldier. Given command of the 33rd Battalion in 1916 in France, Morshead quickly won a fine reputation for himself and his battalion. Again the roll call with which his name is associated places him firmly at the centre of the Australian experience of the great war: Messines, Passchendaele, Villers-Bretonneux. Charles Bean described the 33rd Battalion as 'an especially fine unit', commanded by the young veteran from Gallipoli. So Morshead certainly knew what good soldiers looked like and the 9th Division he was to command fell way short of his mark.

The trouble was that the general did not have a year to train his soldiers, as Mackay with his 6th Division had enjoyed. Rommel had landed in North Africa on 12 February 1941, about the time that Morshead was taking the measure of his men, so there would be no time to teach these Australians how to fight. It was wrong, surely, to take undertrained troops to war, but what else could Morshead do? Rommel seemed hell-bent on moving quickly. So quickly did Rommel launch his initial assault that the German high command in Berlin, caught by surprise by what they regarded as his impetuosity, sent a more senior general, von Paulus, to try to calm him down—the chances were, they reasoned, that the defenders could simply be overrun. The 9th Australian Division would learn on the job, and that was far from ideal.

Like Leslie Morshead, Erwin Rommel had learned his soldiering in the earlier war. Born in Heidenheim in southern Germany in 1891, Rommel fought in Italy during the First World War with conspicuous success, the hallmarks of which were his 'boldness and independence'. With these characteristics so much a part of the way Rommel looked at war, it was as if the war in the desert was specifically arranged for his personality and previous experience. Catching Hitler's eye, Rommel would be promoted from colonel to field marshal within the space of three years. His great strength was not in strategy but in his striking personal leadership, which exhilarated his troops and struck fear into his enemies.

Facing Rommel, at the level above Australian divisional commander Leslie Morshead, were the British generals Sir Philip Neame and Sir Richard O'Connor. O'Connor had already shown himself against the Italians to be an innovative and aggressive commander. Now, however, he was simply an 'adviser' to General Sir Philip Neame—demoted, in effect. Neame should have proved himself an attractive and exciting personality to the Australians; he remains the only man in history to have been awarded the Victoria Cross—at Neuve Chapelle in France in 1914—and an Olympic Gold Medal—at Paris in 1924. The Gold Medal was in 'running deer', a version of shooting, held for the last time at Neame's Olympics. Born at Faversham in Sussex in 1888, Neame seems to have developed a special dislike for Australians. I do not know whether the origins of this dislike can be traced to some experience Neame had of them in the First World War, or to sporting rivalry at the Olympics, or to a class-based, generalised British dislike of 'colonials', but such was the intensity of his feelings that Neame did not seem the best man to be given the job of taking the Australians to war against Rommel.

Writing to Morshead on 31 March 1941, Neame complained of the ill-discipline of the Australian troops. It was a full catalogue of sins. The general wrote of 'Australian drunkenness', of 'disgraceful behaviour', of 'streets [that] were hardly safe or fit to move in'. 'I am at a loss for words to express my contempt for those who call themselves soldiers who behave thus', seemingly to suggest that most, if not all, of the Australians behaved in a depraved way. Neame told Morshead that 'your Division will never be a useful instrument of war unless and until you can enforce discipline'.

It is more than probable that Leslie Morshead well understood the General's last point and did not need to be reminded of it. Morshead had perfected his understanding of the importance of discipline at Lone Pine, possibly, and at Villers-Bretonneux. He knew what made a good soldier, and he deeply resented the tone of Neame's letter with its broad-brush attack on 'the Australians' when in all likelihood there were but a handful of offenders, and almost certainly not all of them were Australians. Morshead would have taken no satisfaction in discovering very soon after the fighting had started that Sir Philip Neame had shown himself incapable of conducting the type of desert warfare that Rommel's speed and agility demanded. And he would have regretted, too, almost certainly, hearing of the capture of General Sir Philip by Rommel's troops. Well, he would have regretted the capture of Richard O'Connor, anyway. Now Morshead, the Australian, was the only officer of general rank, at this stage of the fighting in the desert, to evade capture. Well done the Australians.

When Rommel attacked at El Agheila on 24 March 1941 he had already moved his troops—the Afrika Korps—750 kilometres from Tripoli, their port of disembarkation. The logistics of this are staggering. Tanks, guns, other equipment and, most crucially, food and water, carried far across a desert waste. Rommel was soon menacing Benghazi, where the Australians were, and from there he would target the port of Tobruk, and then, he hoped, he would move on to menace Egypt. The British were now at risk of being completely booted out of the Middle East, just as they were being evacuated from Greece. The crisis was real. This is precisely what Rommel had anticipated: a war of movement, at speed, against an enemy that would struggle not to be outpaced by him. Disaster falling upon disaster, with his opponents given no time to catch their breath or to gather their thoughts. You do not lose generals in the field unless the pace of one army is vastly outstripping the speed of the other. Now this first phase of the second part of the Desert War had become a race for Tobruk. If the British (read the Australians), could hang on to Tobruk they might hold Rommel up; in holding Tobruk they could be assured, at least, of necessary supplies of ammunition, food and water. Without Tobruk the Allies ran the risk of becoming a rabble dashing for the protection of the Egyptian border.

Leslie Morshead had inspected the Italian defences at Tobruk—the structures, that is, the fortified posts, the anti-tank ditch, the perimeter, or the red line as it was known—in January 1941. He had worked out how he might make a stand there, if ever it came to that. And by late April 1941 it had most certainly come to that. The Australians had poured into the former Italian defences and had made them stronger where they could. They were prepared to make a stand. Morshead had told them simply that there would be no retreat from Tobruk. The Allies, he said, could not afford to surrender the position; if they surrendered, the whole campaign might be lost. Yet Morshead's men, fresh from the fighting retreat from Benghazi, their first taste of war, were exhausted and still ill-equipped. Yet 'there is to be no surrender and no retreat', Morshead said, and that was that.

Leslie Morshead's defence of Tobruk depended upon three separate strategies. First, and in this how clearly do we hear the resonances of the Australians on the Western Front in 1918, Morshead insisted that no man's land would never be neutral territory. Constant patrolling and constant incursions across it were demanded above all else. A battalion might have almost a third of its strength out in no man's land at any one time—during the night, of course—harassing and intimidating the enemy. There was a clear purpose behind this strategy: Morshead was determined to prevent the Germans from bringing up their artillery to pound the Australians on the perimeter when the battle finally started. He had seen this too often in France in the earlier war—artillery that kept men underground while attacking troops rushed forward. He had learned the danger of that in France and he would keep the enemy's artillery as far away as he possibly could.

Morshead's second strategy related to the attack. Though tanks were a relatively new and largely unsuccessful weapon in the First World War, Morshead had studied the way they could now provide cover for advancing infantry in an attack. The tanks would move forward, sucking up the defenders to oppose them, while the enemy's infantry followed almost unopposed. Morshead directed the troops on the perimeter to allow the German tanks to pass over them and beyond the perimeter line. Then the troops would turn their fire on the advancing German infantry and sweep them from the field with machine-gun and rifle fire. Morshead reasoned that if the full weight of their defensive effort was brought to bear on the advancing infantry, the German troops would suffer heavy losses and would have to fall back. This is indeed what happened. Only then would the defenders turn their attention to the German tanks, now isolated and without support. It was a clever tactic and it worked.

The third of Morshead's strategies for the defence of Tobruk was the continual improvement of their defences. In other words, he kept his troops employed at all times, either fighting or else repairing and strengthening whatever they had to keep the Germans out of Tobruk. Eventually the defence of Tobruk would consist of the perimeter, the red line, and two further defensive lines: the blue line and the green line. Morshead was making Tobruk a very difficult objective for the Germans.

In this way the Australians held up Rommel's advance by turning their defence into a siege. Morshead would have the Germans immobile in front of Tobruk for months, denied the speed on which their commander's plan depended, making enough time for the development of better plans for the defence of Egypt. In this way the siege at Tobruk was crucial in the eventual defeat of Rommel in the desert. Victory, as we will also see in Papua New Guinea later in the war, was built up through a series of events which, at the time, might have looked like setbacks or reverses. Mock them as they did, the Germans came to a standstill before the 'Rats of Tobruk', and you would like to think that Philip Neame was allowed to read something of the success of the Australians at Tobruk in his prisoner-of-war camp in Italy. Ill-disciplined some of these Australians might have been, waiting for the battle to begin, but once in combat they had shown themselves to be very skilled defenders. You would hope, too, that Philip Neame might have been able to look, at some time in the future, at the war diary of one or more of the Australian battalions taking part in the siege at Tobruk.

Each Australian army unit was required to keep a war diary, a daily record of events, to assist with planning and as an invaluable tool subsequently in understanding what had been done and with what degree of success. They would be essential tools, too, for military historians, as might be expected. Kept in a somewhat perfunctory fashion until a reform in 1917, for World War II the war diaries record where a battalion was and what it was doing as a matter of routine. They rarely make engrossing reading; there is no unfolding narrative and the text is peppered with jargon that is nearly impenetrable to anyone with little military knowledge. But Philip Neame would have understood a war diary. Here, in any of the diaries of the Australian battalions at Tobruk, Neame would have found the daily record of work, of patrolling, of building up the defences, of repelling attacks on the ground, of enduring attacks from the air; in a word, he would have found a daily record of 'exemplary discipline'. Battlefront discipline, in fact, day in and day out for a siege which the Australians endured for eight months, or, to put it in context, for nearly the entire length of the Gallipoli campaign.

It is impossible to provide the complexity and the detail of the story of Tobruk here, but let us imagine Neame looking at the war diary of Australia's 2/23rd Battalion: 'Albury's Own' it was dubbed. Its name should not be taken to mean that every man within that battalion came from the border city in southern New South Wales, although a substantial proportion of the men did. Like all Australian battalions, its soldiers came from many parts of the country, but were trained at Bonegilla in north-eastern Victoria, and sailed for war in December 1940. Of its first members killed in battle at Tobruk, one was a schoolteacher from Hawthorn and another was a lithographic printer from Northcote, both Melbourne suburbs. Still, 'Albury's Own' it was.

The war diary records, in subdued prose, the 2/23rd's early encounters with the enemy when the battalion was ordered to take out of action enemy artillery that was simply too close to the perimeter. At company strength to execute the raid, a party of about 100 men suffered 80 per cent casualties, including 24 men who did not return, some of them becoming prisoners. The official historian wrote of the 'exemplary discipline' of these men, but it was just an ordinary sort of raid really that would attract only a couple of paragraphs in the official history. The sort of thing that soldiers on the perimeter were doing all the time. To the men involved it was war; dangerous, exhilarating, but necessary work that sadly led to significant casualties. That was happening on the perimeter every day; a part of Morshead's strategy of softening up the enemy and denying him launching pads for his own attacks.

The war diary goes on to record the 2/23rd's active patrolling and observation 2000–3000 yards outside the perimeter, as ordered by Morshead, and the daily work of the battalion in improving its defences. The writing in the diary is formal, brief, jargon-filled, but it also reveals, to those who can read beneath the truncated army prose, an efficient, disciplined and successful unit at work.

Better, though, is the battalion's daily newsletter. Many Australian battalions going to war, or returning from war for that matter, have had some sort of shipboard newsletter. Usually quite humbly produced, the newsletters kept soldiers up to date with the news and diverted their attention from the unknown ahead. There is a large collection of these newsletters at the Australian War Memorial, but they are, in truth, of limited general interest. The 2/23rd's shipboard newsletter was produced by one of its sergeants, Jim Mulcahy, who, unusually, kept the newsletter going after the battalion moved from training to active service. Mulcahy even managed to produce the newsletter under the siege conditions at Tobruk, although he lost his hand-printing press in the chaos of the retreat from Benghazi. In Tobruk, he typed out his newsletter, made 20 or so copies, and these were circulated by hand to the members of the battalion each day and were eagerly read by the troops to stay in touch. Not knowing what was going on was a part of life on the perimeter of Tobruk, where men were stretched out along the front, in small groups of 20 or so, completely oblivious to how their mates were going even just a few hundred metres away, but for Jim Mulcahy's newsletter. It was called *Mud and Blood*, after the battalion's colour patch: diamond-shaped, brown on top, red beneath. The same as the colour patch of the 'original' 23rd Battalion who fought in Gallipoli and France. And *Mud and Blood* was a lifeline to the men of Mulcahy's battalion.

How to write for men under fire; how to explain to them the importance of what they were doing? Jim Mulcahy was not shy:

Today you and I are not only part of history. We are history in the making. For years we have enjoyed, almost without effort, freedom, won for us by others who endured, treasures of art and letters not painted or written by ourselves, free speech and enfranchised thought earned by unknown heroes in forgotten days. Today, the guarding and safety of all these things depends on us. The heritage of the ages is in our keeping. We are not creatures of destiny, but destiny itself, for without us all that is decent and kindly and holy, will perish from this earth.

Stirring stuff, Jim, and thanks for that, but normally the newsletter reported on actions and raids made by sections of the battalion, passed on gossip and stories, baited targets such as the cooks and headquarters staff who came in for a terrible ribbing, and also passed on a summary of the nightly BBC News. No doubt the world news was somewhat censored, but *Mud and Blood* did not leave out the bad bits. What would men out on the perimeter have made of the news of the evacuation of Greece that Jim Mulcahy printed on 29 April 1941? If they had been with us, instead of over there in Greece, you can imagine men thinking, we might not be in this pickle now.

'Congratulations today to B Coy', starts a typical entry in *Mud and Blood*, 'for the excellent little job they did the other night, when a patrol under Lieut. Jess accounted for some 25 of the enemy, with only one minor casualty to ourselves.' Cheerful enough, but sadly Lieutenant Carl Jess, a clerk from Toorak, Melbourne, not yet 21 years of age, would die, shot through the stomach and legs on 17 May 1941, telling the stretcher-bearers not to bother taking him back but to take, instead, those who might have a chance of surviving. *Mud and Blood* was not seen for a couple of weeks in late May because, in the action that saw Carl Jess die, the 2/23rd Battalion was sent to reclaim ground captured by the Germans on 1 May. It was a desperate fight supported with tanks and artillery, assaulting German strong posts across three days for little advantage. The battalion suffered 163 casualties, including 20 killed, 47 wounded and recovered, and 96 missing. The battalion commander wrote a few days later:

> . . . expressing my appreciation: Muds and Bloods all, it was that spirit which has put the 23rd very much on the map, and made this unit already worthy of its gallant predecessor, the old 23rd. For the sake of our brother Mud and Bloods who have passed on, we will maintain and possibly intensify this spirit wherever we go, and come what may.

But they would not be going far—this was a siege; the Australians were the defenders. They would attack to keep their defence viable; they would not be attacking to break out.

If *Mud and Blood* was playing its part in sustaining morale and keeping the defenders up to speed, 50 miles further back towards Alexandria another battalion, the 2/14th, had found someone prepared to do a job like the one Jim Mulcahy was doing, but in his own way. The 2/14th was at Mersa Matruh, strung out defensively too, in case Rommel overran Tobruk and pushed on towards the Egyptian border. Working with the battalion was Albert Moore, Salvation Army welfare officer, but wondering what more he could do. On 29 March he had opened a 'Hop In' hut and there was a party on the first night. Albert had cut some tomato sandwiches and served hot tea and biscuits. That sort of thing was fine in a training camp or at a base camp where the battalion was all in one place, but here at Mersa Matruh, just like at Tobruk, the hut was a bit of a waste as the battalion was stretched out, in little knots of men, again barely able to communicate with one another. *Mud and Blood* was the 2/23rd's response to the isolation of the battalion; Albert Moore came up with a new plan of his own because he realised he was not doing the job that was needed, and this made him feel 'wretched, tired and disconsolate'. If the men could not come to him, he would have to go to them—he would establish a mobile canteen. A moving 'Hop In', if you like. Armed with a truck, Albert went to Alexandria to buy his supplies: a primus stove, a couple of urns, and lot's more you would imagine, Albert's diary is not too detailed.

On 3 May 1941 Albert Moore, welfare officer, started his first battalion coffee run. He was out along the lines from 7.45 p.m. to 10 p.m., 'and were the men thrilled. A hot cup of coffee and a slice of cake, and they were all loud in their praise'. And why not? The cold of the desert at night, the boredom, the monotony of their food and drink. And here comes Albert, cheerful, a hot drink for all, and a bit of news, real news of other blokes along the line, what was happening at Tobruk, what he knew of the world war and what else was happening around the place. 'Perspiration rolled off', Albert wrote, but he served at least 200 cups of coffee that first night. Three nights later Albert served 18 gallons of coffee and 16 pounds of cake—nearly 400 cups of coffee he thought, well over half the battalion served.

The battalion truck was no good, Albert soon realised, and by 16 May he was back in Alexandria to buy a station wagon that would be much better for the work. He found one for £300, knocked the price down by £10, and also bought a radio for £28, another £10 knocked off. 'The bus was lovely to drive', Albert reported to his diary. He named the station wagon, a Willys, 'Vikel', remembering his wife and son—Vi and Kelvin—back home in Melbourne. How could he forget them? He drove around the lines yarning with the men. 'My waking thoughts', he wrote at the end of May, are 'of my Boy. I pray he is well'. 'Still no news of my Boy', he wrote a couple of days later, 'how I would welcome good news of him'. But to the men he was cheerful and a most welcome Mr Moore, every night out on his rounds, with hot coffee, a bit of food, news—reliable news now with the radio—and good cheer. 'They came to depend on me', Albert told me, 'and I knew that if I missed even one night they would wonder what on earth had happened'. He was on his way to becoming one of the best-loved men of the AIF.

There was a brief gap in Albert Moore's diary when the 2/14th Battalion, along with most of the 7th Australian Division, were moved from Mersa Matruh for action in Syria—fighting the Vichy French, alongside the Free French, the British and the Indians. There were 18000 Australians in Syria and 9000 British, giving strength to a view that was also gaining support in Australia: the British would fight in the Middle East to the death . . . of the last Australian. With hindsight it is impossible to make sense of the decision to fight in Syria. We now know that Hitler was turning his attention to Russia and had no intention of moving on Syria and Iraq to threaten British oil supplies. Even without hindsight the decision to participate in what was an instalment of a French civil war is highly dubious; it attracted little discussion at the British War Cabinet and none at all in Australia. Yet the 7th Australian Division would provide the majority of the soldiers for the invasion of Syria, and the majority of the casualties. Just booted out of Greece, under extreme pressure in the desert, Wavell's force was in no position to take on another campaign. But Syria it was and the command was again given to 'Jumbo' Maitland Wilson, who had hardly covered himself in glory in Greece.

The invasion began along three routes on 8 June 1941. It was expected in London that once the French occupiers understood that an invasion was taking place they would quickly lose the will to fight and resistance would collapse within days. Men of the 2/14th Battalion were told to wear their slouch hats into battle rather than their steel helmets in the hope that the French, recognising the sight of their gallant allies from an earlier war, would welcome the Australians rather than fight against them. Forlorn hope; instead the Vichy French, with superiority in numbers, equipment, and with all the advantages flowing to those familiar with the terrain and defending against invasion, fought with skill and determination during a five-week campaign. Again, the terrain was terrible, except for the third and interior route towards Damascus across the cruel Syrian Desert. The coastal route was plagued by a 'jumble of steep rocky spurs and narrow valleys', and the central route passed along the Bekaa Valley between huge mountain ranges. The first objective for the 21st Brigade, of which the 2/14th was a part, would be Beirut, beyond which, in fact, little further fighting took place.

Even the first day showed Albert Moore that this was real warfare. He wrote in his diary: 'learnt during day that the Adjutant's brother, Cpl Buckler, is our first fatal casualty. I served this lad with tea last night. It is terrible.' Hugh Alan Buckler, born at Coffs Harbour in New South Wales, died of wounds on the first day of the fighting in Syria, four days before his twenty-fifth birthday. He would be one of 37 officers and 379 other Australians killed in this part of the war, along with 1200 wounded. There were 1600 casualties all up, near to two battalions killed or wounded.

Moore's one-person mobile canteen, useful in the desert, came into its own in Syria. As the 2/14th plodded along the roads of what Albert described as 'this picturesque country', he was there with them, serving coffee, biscuits and cakes—'much appreciated'. Though attractive—'what a holiday could be spent here in Peace time'—Albert wrote that the land did not compare with Port Melbourne or Dudley Flats, hardly then Melbourne's most salubrious suburbs, 'or even the smells of Footscray, all [of these] are sweet because its Aussie'. Albert Moore, like many of the men he was serving, was homesick in the midst of war.

The welfare officer was at times under fire as he went about his work. On one occasion a shell landed 12 feet from the 'bus': 'this broke one window pane of truck and put several dents in as well.' Worst of all, the shell 'put wireless [radio] out of action'. While sheltering behind a rock during another bombardment, a former Anglican choirboy from East St Kilda said to him, 'Mr Moore, this rock is a real "Rock of Ages" to us today.' And then there was a feature on the road to Jezzine known as the 'Mad Mile', because French artillery had the road completely covered and any movement on it attracted a burst of shells. Travel on this section of road was confined almost wholly to the night, though there is a painting in the Australian War Memorial by Bill Dargie showing trucks careering down the hill in full light with shells exploding around them, left, right and centre. Albert Moore was cooling his heels, unable to do his work for the men because he had been told it would be too dangerous to go on along the Mad Mile. He took cover for a while, but knew that he had a job to do. After much hard thinking Albert risked the Mad Mile in daylight: 'Set off after seeking God's protection. Tore down the grade. No shells.'

Military historians have always struggled to describe battle; perhaps it is indescribable. The official histories attempt to give a strategic picture and insert individual moments of battle where something of real significance is taking place. The official histor-ians name individuals as they can, and I have thought that 'mentioned in Bean' is as significant as 'mentioned in despatches'. In a sense, though, the apparent emphasis on individuals is misleading because the official historians are always after the bigger picture. Battalion historians try harder to bring individual battle stories to life, but increasingly writers have recognised that you would have to go to platoon level (about 30 men) or company level (about 100 men) to describe actual battle. Peter Dornan in *The Silent Men* wrote at section level, 11 men; but what a section, one of the most decorated in British and Australian military history: men of the 2/14th Battalion, including Bruce Kingsbury, Alan Avery, Teddy Bear and Harry Saunders, Reg Saunders' younger brother.

Dornan wrote how this section, as part of 7 Platoon, A Company, 2/14th Battalion, attacked Hill 1284 (its height in metres) outside Jezzine, halfway to Beirut, on 24 June. On top of the hill stood a small fort, the only way up to it was a steep bridle path. The section faced a 670-metre climb, across some exposed ground, and the fort was heavily defended with machine-gun emplacements. From down below, the fort looked impregnable. But there they were, 32 men climbing slowly, over a couple of hours, up the steep, craggy face of the mountain. Two hundred metres from the fort the men rested and tried to work out their line of attack. Sheltering behind boulders, they were fired upon whenever they came under observation. Three men set up the Bren gun to the left, the rest would crawl along a narrow ledge, unobserved they hoped, to within 40 metres of the fort. Others were in the fight, of course, and the troops watched in horror as members of 9 Section took the full brunt of rapid machine-gun fire. They realised, possibly for the first time, that for every one of them, battle is a personal thing. Down to the individual, his skill, his bravery, his luck; personal, but relying on his mates, too.

Soon, the French had worked out where these sheltering men were and grenades started to rain down on them. 'Shit, they're bloody real,' Harry Saunders yelled to his mates. Another realisation of battle: the bullets, the shells, the grenades, all of them real and all of them aimed at killing you. Was this what Bob Menzies meant when he had written in his diary at Tobruk of 'friendly boys wise now in terrible things'. Leaping from rock to rock, taking shelter where they could, soon the section was within ten metres of the fort. The firefight between defenders and attackers had been going for 20 minutes or more, but time had become irrelevant, and soon it was afternoon. The French were now using mortars; the number of Australian wounded mounted. At some point in the afternoon the lieutenant realised he would have to break off the attack; at least one-third of his platoon was dead or wounded and the French were coming out of the fort in numbers. By 3.30 p.m. the wounded of 9 Platoon were in the regimental aid post, on their way to the ambulances. The battle around Jezzine would last for another week.

By 11 July the Allied troops were outside Beirut, Damour had been taken, Damascus was in Allied hands. The French recognised that the position was hopeless and their supreme commander,

General Henri Dentz, signed an armistice on 12 July. From 8 June to 12 July, a grisly, bloody battle raged, with hundreds of incidents like the failed attack on the fort atop Hill 1284; that is what war there was like. Too much detail to account for. Australia gained a hero from the fighting in Lieutenant A.R. (Roden) Cutler, awarded a Victoria Cross for his efforts during the fighting at Merdjayoun. Australia gained more than that, however. The 7th Division, though with significant casualties, had learned about war the hard way; understood war and had been strengthened significantly, toughened for the battles ahead. That would be important.

The 2/14th Battalion stayed in the Beirut area for the next month and Albert Moore kept up his work for the troops and his diary. 'Oh for an early night', he wrote on 6 August 1941; 'home was never like this', a few nights later. And on 16 August: 'A record. Whole Battalion serviced.' Coffee, biscuits and cake, and the wireless for the BBC News each night. Albert Moore had discovered one of the great truths about men in uniform: they are permanently desperate for news. They had placed themselves and their futures in the hands of others; they were at the whim of decision-makers they may never have seen, used for aims of which they may never have been told. No one asked Barney Roberts if it was alright before they moved him to Greece, in the full knowledge that the enterprise was almost certainly unsustainable; they never told Barney Roberts that either. No one told him that his life was potentially being sacrificed or his freedom taken from him for the rest of the war in order to keep the Americans interested. Barney Roberts, a small cog in a vast machine.

The Australians at Tobruk never saw their generals. Tom Blamey never visited them, and that bloke, Auchinleck, who the heck was he? General Sir Claude Auchinleck was born in England in 1884, educated at Wellington College and Sandhurst, and served from 1904 in Egypt and the Middle East. He replaced Wavell in July 1941 as Commander-in-Chief Middle East. Almost as soon as General Auchinleck took the top job Tom Blamey was at him to have the Australians relieved at Tobruk. For the men out on the perimeter, each day brought fresh challenges—but they wanted news, to know what was happening. You never know, it might just be about them.

Winston Churchill knew all about a siege. He had been a war correspondent for the *Morning Post* during the South African (Boer) war and had written a truly awful book, *My Early Life*, first published in 1930, which included a chapter, 'The Relief of Lady-smith'. Churchill's book was a set text in English in my final school year and ribald schoolboys joked over that chapter title. But in the chapter itself Churchill told how a British force defeated the besieging Boers, freeing troops caught in the northern Natal town. 'The garrison [in the town]', he wrote, 'was in dire straits'. Relief was desperately sought and desperately needed. Churchill wrote of 'gaunt figures' waving hands of welcome to the relieving troops; of a 'long-beleaguered, almost starved out Ladysmith'.

Blamey's case for the relief of the Australians at Tobruk might have been stronger if he had actually seen for himself how things were going there. And no doubt a visit from the senior Australian general and Deputy Commander-in-Chief in the Middle East would have done wonders for the morale of the Australians who had been under siege now for some four months. Wandering the Gallipoli battlefields I have again and again asked myself how soldiers could possibly have kept on going. They'd think, of course, pre-eminently about the danger from the enemy, but also of the awful living conditions, the lack of food, its monotony, the lack of water, the lack of rest and amusement, the lack of everything, in fact, that makes life liveable. And probably those in command would think about the health of the troops. And turn to the official historian of Anzac, Charles Bean, for the answers. He is good on health, devoting a chapter of his second volume on Anzac to 'Sickness of the Army'. 'At the end of July', he wrote, 'the corps was losing fortnightly through sickness as many men as would be placed out of action in a general assault. Nor did this represent the total trouble, since many who stayed on duty were almost as ill as those that were sent away'. Bean discovered that the decline in the health of the Anzacs soon became obvious to observers; you did not need to be a doctor to tell that these men were ill: 'during June and July the strength of the troops visibly declined. The great frames which had impressed beholders in Egypt now stood out gauntly; faces became lined, cheeks sunken.' Even though commanders could see this for themselves, 'several

warnings were sent in by medical officers pointing out the increasing weakness of the men'. This was by June and July 1915, three or
four months from the beginning of the campaign.

It is uncanny to note that a similar timeframe prevailed at
Tobruk. The Australians were locked in behind the defensive
perimeter at Tobruk by late April 1941. By July Morshead's
medical staff were telling him of the deterioration in the health of
his troops, just as on Anzac 26 years earlier. Again, the extent
of illness became obvious to observers. People spoke of the loss of
weight among the men, of disease, of the consequences of poor diet
and insufficient food and water. Morshead reported this to Blamey;
in his turn, Blamey raised the matter with Auchinleck and recommended that the Australians be replaced. As at Ladysmith, they
had done enough. Churchill would understand.

But Tom Blamey also wanted the Australians out of Tobruk for
another reason. With the campaign in Syria won and the 7th
Australian Division returning to rest and training, Blamey now had
the opportunity, if he could release the 9th Division from Tobruk,
of combining the two Australian divisions in the Middle East to
form an Australian Corps. This had been a strong ambition for the
Australians on the Western Front, too, from 1917 onwards but was
not achieved until the middle of 1918. The formation of a corps
appealed to national sentiment, played well in Australia, gave
confidence to the men themselves, and increased the possibility of
Australian control over Australian troops. But the British resisted.
Auchinleck did not think that the mobile desert warfare required
troops to be organised at corps level and he had little sympathy for
the creation of a national force. It would be tiresome and would
merely provoke more bother, making it less likely that the
Australians would be good and do as they were told. More power
to Tom Blamey? Not on, really. Most people thought of him as a bit
too uppity already. Air Marshal Tedder, in charge of air force operations in the Middle East, wrote of Blamey as 'really rather an
unpleasant political soldier'. The health of the troops, or the ambi-
tions of Tom Blamey? Why should the Australians leave Tobruk;
they were doing rather a good job, don't you know?

Menzies, still prime minister when Blamey started to campaign
for the relief of the Australians at Tobruk, supported his senior

army commander and wrote to Churchill advancing the idea. At first Churchill seemed to be supportive, but after Auchinleck visited him in London the British prime minister was far less keen to allow the Australians to be replaced. The new Australian prime minister, Arthur Fadden, was even more anxious than Menzies that the Australians be relieved. Indeed he set a timetable for the relief. It would happen, he directed, before the Australian Parliament reassembled in Canberra in mid-September, with Fadden now at the despatch box as prime minister. Fadden knew how Menzies had been politically damaged by the collapse of the campaigns in Greece and on Crete. He wanted to announce, at the beginning of his prime ministership, that he had negotiated the rescue of the Australians from Tobruk. He certainly did not want to announce another debacle should Rommel prevail there and thousands of Australian soldiers be marched into captivity. So there was a third element in the campaign to relieve the Australians, a political element that might sound plausible in Canberra but quite implausible in London.

An element of German propaganda was the notion that the Australians were carrying a disproportionate burden of the fighting in the desert, and that claim annoyed London too. Planners there preferred not to think in terms of the place of origin of troops at their disposal. In offering troops to the cause of the Empire, they liked to believe, the dominions ought to have surrendered effective control of those forces and leave the disposition of the troops and the fighting of the war to those who knew best. To those in London, in fact. To Army Minister Percy Spender, Tom Blamey wrote that, reclaiming those Australian troops who had passed into British command was like 'prising open the jaws of an alligator'. Churchill produced figures for the information of his War Cabinet, attempting to show that, on the basis of casualties, the Australians were not, indeed, taking the major role. Properly read, Churchill's figures might have shown that Australian casualties accounted for two-thirds of the total casualties. At Tobruk, and in Syria. Those figures, too, might have been used to advance the case for the relief of Tobruk, but, out in the open, Blamey argued on health grounds only. By 3 September he advised Auchinleck that there was 'a considerable decline in the fighting value of the garrison'. 'If left for another two months', he continued, 'they would be unable to withstand a strong attack'.

Churchill had difficulty in believing that the Australians would, in the long run, stand up to him. As he explained to Auchinleck in early September, 'I am pretty sure the Australians will play the game'. Had the long presence of Bob Menzies in London given Churchill a false confidence? Menzies, after all, had even agreed to the Greek adventure, eventually. So Churchill cabled Fadden asking him to see reason and not to disturb existing arrangements. He also had a bit of advice for the incoming prime minister, telling him 'to weigh very carefully the immense responsibility which you would assume before history by depriving Australia of the glory of holding Tobruk till the victory was won'. Fadden would have none of it. Halfway into his 40-day government he was not yet thinking of his place in history. The Australians at Tobruk would be relieved, Fadden replied. Then Curtin struck and the Australian government changed once more. Churchill thought he might make more progress with the new man and asked Curtin to leave the two remaining Australian brigades in Tobruk 'as an act of comradeship in the present struggle'. These men have been under fire for six months, Curtin might have replied, and are well due for relief. But instead, feeling his way, Curtin used the language of diplomacy: we have considered your request 'but do not feel disposed to vary the previous government's decision which was apparently reached after the fullest review of all the considerations involved'.

It is important to note how poorly London viewed this assertion of the primacy of Australian interests now fought for by three separate Australian prime ministers. David Day, who has closely examined the Churchill–Menzies relationship, asserts that the argument over Tobruk 'seriously damaged Anglo–Australian relations and practically destroyed Australia's reputation in the eyes of Britain's political and military leaders for the duration of the war'. That may seem too strong, but Day assembles considerable evidence; 'everyone was furious', one observer wrote.

Churchill seemed to believe that the Australians somehow lacked courage by insisting on the withdrawal of their troops; that they had somehow panicked at the prospect of a continuing and drawn-out siege. He also resented, it should be said, the independence that Fadden had shown in insisting on the relief of the Australians. Blamey simply described himself as 'the most hated man in the Middle East'. It should not have come to this for the Australians had served extremely well at Tobruk. 'They had patrolled, attacked, dug, wired, stood to their guns and hit the enemy by day and by night', wrote Alex Hill, a military historian who had been at Tobruk as a soldier. Hill continued: 'The defence of that miserable Cyrenaican harbour and fortress from April until . . . October was one of the few gleams of light in a year darkened by withdrawals and disasters.'

11. A NEW WAR

Paul Hasluck was the official historian of the Australian home-front during the Second World War. Though he divided them chronologically, Hasluck called both of his books, *The Government and the People*; even so I do not think he meant his treatment to be even-handed. Paul Hasluck liked the government far more than he liked the people. Towards the end of his first volume Hasluck quotes with apparent approval Tom Blamey's description of the Australians at home as he found them in mid-November 1941: 'like a lot of gazelles grazing in a dell near the edge of a jungle.' Being back in Australia from the Middle East gave Blamey, he said, 'a most extraordinary feeling of what you might call helplessness'.

Blamey's gazelle image is good. Nevertheless the image gives an idea that Blamey found in Australians a woeful ignorance of the real situation, of flightiness, of people too readily scared, and of a pack flight from danger. One roar from a beast in the depths of the jungle, one sniff of danger in the air and the whole herd will take off in fright, wheeling in terror, waiting for something to show them their next move. Nothing solid there. The jungle image is good, too. A place of darkness and danger, full of the sounds and the smells of terror; unknown, unseen terror.

We have all experienced it. You go overseas for a few months and return brimful of the excitement about the time you have had, the sights and the adventures. People are warm in their welcomes, genuinely glad to see you back, and for a little while at least keen to hear about your adventures. But you have so much more to tell. Or your child is born, one of the most remarkable, magical moments in life. People are delighted for you, genuinely pleased, keen to hear all and then return to talk of work and your shared lives. You cannot explain how you have changed, cannot tell what love and intimacy you have experienced. Or you go to war. To Tobruk or Beirut, through the Brallos Pass perhaps, and you come home, if only briefly, even as a general, and people listen, some might even have said, yes it was something like that at Lone Pine, but they cannot share what you have experienced and they seem to you, well, indifferent.

That hurt. Why do we have these war correspondents, Ken Slessor and all the others, the photographers and the cameramen, even the painter, Ivor Hele, why do we have them if the people at home, for whom we are doing all this, cannot seem to understand what we have been through, what we have been doing. Those men crawling along a ledge in Syria, attacking for a second day a fort that was holding up our advance on Jezzine, that was magnificent. Australian soldiers at their best, yet people do not even seem to know where Syria is and what we were doing fighting the French there. Aren't the French our allies in this war, again? Do these people have any idea of what is going on?

But it was more than that. Ignorance or indifference to the war, or the sheer inability to imagine the real horror of it was one thing, and many Australians felt something of that when they came home from war in 1919. But the other thing that disturbed Tom Blamey was that while people listened to John Curtin's warnings about the ominous portents in the Pacific, they really did not understand. What can you do with these people, Tom Blamey seemed to be asking; they are in extreme danger yet they hardly know it, and when war comes to their shores will they have the courage and maturity to face it calmly, or will they panic? Do they have the spirit of the Blitz? Not much trust of the people there. Their sons might be great fighters, but those at home squabble, they strike, they play their games, they amuse themselves but do they know there is a war on? 'You are leading a carnival life,' Blamey said, 'and you are enjoying it.' He added that he was 'astounded at the complacency with which people in Australia view the war situation . . . if you do not take your part you'll find your homes overwhelmed as were [the homes of] the people in France and Belgium.'

But wait a minute. Blamey had reached Sydney by flying boat on the morning of 10 November 1941. His 'carnival spirit' comments were given to the press that evening before he boarded the train for Canberra for consultations with the new government. How could a man who had been away from Australia since June 1940—that is, for 18 months—sum up the mood of the people in just a few hours? Blamey's comments were too easy, a knee-jerk response, a means of puffing-up what the Australians in battle had been doing while wasters were back here having a good time. It was part of that type of thinking that had been so strong during the First World War: in war every man should be at the front, in the trenches; those who were not were wasters and cowards, somehow morally inferior. Like Bob Menzies, for one.

John Curtin was not having it. While conceding that General Blamey was entitled to an opinion on this and any other matter, Curtin rejected his view that there was a 'carnival spirit' in Australia. 'The playing of games is not detrimental to the war effort,' he said, 'games are refreshing and beneficial to the physical welfare of thousands doing war work. They are good also for the nation's morale.' The Church of England chimed in too, in a joint pastoral letter: 'buoyancy, pleasure-seeking and unwillingness to give up opportunities for sports, to some extent, may be excused. They are due partly to the national temperament, and partly to a desire to find justifiable relief from the strains and stress of life in times of war.'

What had these people been doing to make these 'strains and stress in times of war?' Well for one thing, they had been working. By late 1941, with the war more than two years old, unemployment seemed a distant memory. The struggle now was to find enough workers for all the jobs that needed doing. With so many men in the forces, with the munitions industry now working at a white-hot pace, with aircraft production growing, with a defence force at home and abroad to be fed and clothed, the call was out for more and more workers. And if men cannot be found for the jobs we will most certainly take women, employers were saying at last. In April and May 1941 the War Cabinet had discussed expanding the range of jobs available to women, particularly in the federal public service, because of the severe shortage of men. Women were also being recruited into the munitions industries, where they seemed to be specially suited. That was largely a new industry in Australia and the recruitment of women there did not raise significant concerns.

But in traditional 'male jobs' the arrival of women in the workforce did raise eyebrows and cause union resistance. In Melbourne, the Tramways Board in April 1941 had said that it would not employ women even though it was hard to find the men. By August the board had changed its mind, but threw a sop to the unions by giving preference to the wives of employees on active service. Within a day over 500 women had offered to work on the trams, but the union insisted women were 'physically and psychologically unsuited' for the work. One woman, whose husband was a driver, worried about a younger woman working with him as a 'connie' (conductor), so she rode the trams with them both to oversee her husband and to prevent romance blossoming. A silly story, really, beloved of newspapers, indicative of the social change taking place in the workforce, to blow over within weeks as women joined more and more workplaces. These would be the first-wave feminists, these women now entering the workforce in big numbers, whose daughters in the 1960s would think only of themselves as the pioneers.

At the outbreak of war women had also enrolled in paramilitary organisations of their own designing, to learn useful and important skills to stand them ready for national service, should they be needed. Journalists and cartoonists laughed at the ranks the women gave themselves. 'Why didn't you salute your senior officer', a man in a cartoon asks his uniformed companion; 'We're not speaking', she replies. But what the women were doing could not be trivialised or mocked except by those for whom social change under the pressure of war was just too hard. Women learned to fly; trained in wireless, telegraphy, other forms of communication; trained in first aid and specialised nursing; trained as drivers and mechanics, in a thousand jobs. Their organisations had offered their services to the defence forces and had, of course, been regularly and routinely knocked back. But, being women, they persevered.

Air Chief Marshal Sir Charles Burnett, finding himself in charge of the Australian air force when no Australian was thought to be up to the job, came to Australia in February 1940 to take up duty. He brought with him his daughters, Joan and Sybil-Jean ('Buntie'), who had both already served in the British women's air force and were surprised to find that there was no similar organisation in Australia in which they might serve. Bob Menzies had seen the women's air force in operation in Britain during the Blitz and could see no reason why such a service would not be a success in Australia. Due to a severe shortage of male wireless and teleprinter operators in the air force, in mid-1941 the government gave approval for the recruitment of 250 women into a Women's Auxiliary Australian Air Force (WAAAF). The women would be paid two-thirds of the equivalent male rate and would serve 'until they could be replaced by qualified men'. They never were. As the labour shortage increased the other services looked to women too—before the end of 1941 there was an Australian Women's Army Service and a small women's naval service. 'Take my chair', the army poster shouted, with an empty chair pulled out from a desk, 'I'm wanted at the battlefront'. Well, good luck to you, but before long the women would also be an integral and vital part of an army that would be growing strongly.

Beryl Bedggood had left school at the end of 1940 and enrolled in a science degree at the University of Melbourne to study chemistry, physics, zoology, botany and 'science French'. It was a heavy load but that alone did not explain Beryl's poor results at the end of her first year at university. Study was not what she wanted; instead Beryl wanted to be in the forces doing something for the war, doing something for her country. Her country was at war and she would play her part, simple as that. Beryl's father, now at RAAF headquarters at the St Kilda Road Barracks, perhaps heard that the chief of the air staff was trying hard to win agreement from the government for women in the air force. Perhaps Beryl heard, too, over the back fence, that Bob Menzies had seen and admired the women of Britain, now in uniform and doing important war work.

Many of the boys Beryl had known during her school days were deferring university to join up. Geoffrey Serle, who became an influential Australian historian in later life, was one of them; they had been to school dances together, played tennis together. Now he was in uniform, ready to go to the war. How could Beryl just sit back and watch? The war, in 1941, looked bad and here was the new prime minister talking of 'ominous portents' in the Pacific, just as Beryl was taking her first-year university exams. Australia itself might be at risk. Beryl by then had already enrolled in the WAAAF, turning up at Lane's Motors showrooms in Exhibition Street, Melbourne, so great was the shortage of space for the defence force, on her eighteenth birthday in September. Sign here and thanks, we will let you know in due course, but it might be a long wait. Expect Beryl to concentrate on her university work with all this going on?

Yet the wait was not as long as they had warned, for in the face of the new and overwhelming crisis the call was out for as many women as possible. Beryl marched in with the WAAAF on 4 February 1942 to a former girls' school in the Melbourne suburb of Malvern, the WAAAF's first property. By the time Beryl joined up the novelty of women 'playing soldiers' had worn off and Beryl was not annoyed, as the first intake had been, by pressmen and boys hanging over the fences watching the rookies learn their drill. She needed to learn her work quickly as the world war had taken a totally new direction. Beryl Bedggood and all those young people, were they Blamey's gazelles intent on pleasure, were they likely to take fright when the first hint of trouble loomed? Have a good look around, Tom Blamey, Australia was not like that.

On 2 December 1941 Australian intelligence reported that the Japanese consulate in Melbourne had received an instruction from Tokyo to immediately destroy records and papers, including cipher books. On 4 December the consulate replied that all had been done as instructed. The Australian War Cabinet met on Thursday 4 December 1941 in Melbourne and the defence chiefs presented their normal weekly reports. The meeting seemed normal enough but there was tension in the air. After War Cabinet John Curtin was yarning with a few journalists, as was this old newspaper editor's custom. Curtin liked the company of journalists, could talk their language; liked being able to speak his mind, but completely off the record, of course. 'Are you going back to Canberra tonight,' someone asked him. 'Of course,' Curtin replied. But then the head of the Defence Department, Frederick Shedden, arrived and spoke privately to the prime minister; Curtin corrected himself, no, he would be staying put. The War Cabinet quickly reassembled right then for about another half hour. It was apparent to the journalists that something dramatic was afoot. It was the Japanese, it just had to be.

The War Cabinet, in fact, had been informed that a Japanese naval convoy was on the move in the Pacific and that a Japanese expeditionary force had embarked in Indo-China. John Curtin was about to end his second month as prime minister. Soon he would be leading his people as no other Australian prime minister had ever been required to do. Soon he would be telling his people that their country was now at risk, in danger of attack. Soon he would see for himself if this was an immature and frightened mob or a people who could accept adversity and sacrifice for their country's sake.

In Melbourne Curtin stayed at the Victoria Palace, a temperance hotel in Little Collins Street. He had been staying there for years and the staff were devoted to him. How did he spend the long hours of that last weekend of peace in the Pacific? The waiting must have been horrible, pushing out all other thoughts from his mind, thoughts of perhaps spending some time with his family in Perth over Christmas. In his armchair with a pile of books, perhaps. Did Curtin map out in his mind what he would say to the people when he had to tell them that war had come to the Pacific, possibly to their shores? Did he play with the words he would need to use, rehearse the tone he would need to adopt? To reassure the people, to steady them. We know that John Curtin visited close friends in East Melbourne, briefly, and to those who knew him best he appeared 'restless, and terribly disturbed'. Did he sleep well on the Sunday night? You would like to think so for life was about to change forever. His press secretary, Don Rodgers, woke the prime minister just after 5.45 a.m. on Monday morning, 8 December 1941. The government's short-wave radio monitoring service had picked up the news that up to 200 Japanese aircraft had attacked the American Pacific fleet at its moorings at Pearl Harbor, Hawaii, and had also attacked a United States Air Force base in the Philippines. The destruction of the fleet and aircraft and the loss of life were substantial, the report suggested. The Pacific War, which would cost Curtin his life, had begun.

In fact the news was far worse than it had first been reported to Curtin. As well as the attack on the American fleet at Pearl Harbor there were simultaneous raids on Malaya, Singapore, the Philippines, Guam, Hong Kong, and Wake, Midway and Ocean islands. At Pearl Harbor 360 Japanese aircraft had sunk four of the eight American battleships riding at anchor, destroyed 120 aircraft and killed 2403 American servicemen. The Japanese lost 27 aircraft. They had not declared war, they had just attacked ruthlessly.

'The Japs are at us,' a cyclist yelled as he rushed through the streets in the centre of Melbourne as the morning peak-hour crowd surged from trains and trams to begin the week's work. Crowds moved to the newspaper offices, the *Herald* in Flinders Street, the *Argus* in Elizabeth Street, the *Age* in Collins Street, waiting for the special editions that would be rushed out. News was harder to come by then. The mood among the people in the cities around the country was remarkably similar: not surprised that the Pacific War had come; there had been sufficient warnings of that over the last month and longer. It had been part of the national psyche, too, and for a long time, this idea of an Asian war. But the crowds were stunned by the range of the enemy's attacks and by their apparent success. Angry and shocked, too, by the treachery and deception of the Japanese, who had made no formal announcement of war. Always suspicious of 'orientals', Australians quickly saw their new enemy as particularly devious and treacherous.

War Cabinet sat that day, of course, with the defence chiefs in attendance. The meeting started with a summary of what was

known about the attacks as the news was being pieced together
from a variety of sources. A cable from the Dominions Office in
London said what was known there of the situation in the Pacific;
there was also news from short-wave radio broadcasts from around
the Pacific and Asia. The Admiralty in London advised that hostilities should begin at once. The defence chiefs described what
measures they would suggest for immediate action, but even as the
acting head of the navy, Commodore J.W. Durnford, asked how the
Americans could have been so unprepared, after all it would have
taken ten days for the convoy to have sailed from Japan, it
appeared that the Australian services would need more time to
come up with an Australian plan of action. Most worrying for the
War Cabinet was the news from the chief of the general staff,
General Vernon Sturdee, that 'on paper' Australia had a nucleus of
seven militia divisions for home defence but not one could be put
in the field 'as a good fighting force'. The air force had few planes
available in Australia and the navy was elsewhere too. Of course,
the question of the return of the AIF from the Middle East
surfaced, but John Curtin said that the AIF would stay where it
was even though attacks on Australia might severely damage the
morale of the Australian soldiers on duty at what was now immediately seen as the 'other war'.

Later that day Frederick Shedden wrote to Curtin:

> I was very disappointed at the showing of the Chiefs of Staff
> at this morning's War Cabinet meeting. The information
> they had to present as for preparedness for this emergency
> was, I thought, scrappy and meagre . . . I think the Govern-
> ment must press it right home that *this is a new war*.

Day one of the Pacific War and already the question of focus,
priorities, and a uniquely Australian perception of the world war
was emerging. The Pacific War had become Our War. How
remote Syria and Crete and Tobruk and all the rest of it now
seemed.

That evening John Curtin broadcast to the people of Australia.
Who among his listeners would have cast their minds back to that
Father's Day in September two years earlier when Bob Menzies

began speaking to 'Fellow Australians' and had done his 'melancholy duty'. John Curtin addressed the 'Men and Women of Australia.' We are at war, he told the people, because our vital interests are imperilled. These was no waiting here for a lead from London, for a declaration of war by Winston Churchill on our behalf; the King in London had acted on the advice of his Australian ministers. This is our war, John Curtin was saying, and we now decide.

The prime minister did not spare his listeners an account of the full horror of what had unfolded in our region. As the Pacific Ocean was 'reddened with the blood of Japan's victims,' he said, Japanese diplomats were even then negotiating with the White House in Washington; Japan, Curtin declared, had 'struck like an assassin in the night.' The prime minister continued, not seeking to shield the people from the new reality:

> This is our darkest hour, for the nation itself is imperilled . . . the call is to you for your courage, your physical and mental ability, your inflexible determination that we as a free people shall survive. My appeal to you is in the name of Australia, for Australia is the stake in this contest.

'You have been listening to the Honourable John Curtin,' the ABC announcer said in his best BBC tones. There were no tears now in homes across the country as there had been at the remembrance of an earlier war when war had come again in 1939; now there was just a steely determination and a realistic understanding of the gravity of it all. So quickly now the world had changed, and that earlier war, Gallipoli and the Western Front, seemed from another age.

'In two speeches yesterday [8 December]', the Melbourne *Herald* reported, John Curtin 'sounded for Australia the authentic note of national leadership'. Curtin had told the people that there was 'a place and a part' for every single one of them in the war effort. Every man of fighting age and fitness had the duty of joining the fighting forces, Curtin had said, and every other person had the duty of working to enable the nation to support and equip the greatest possible number of fighting men. John Curtin did not say, could not say, that the nation had too few trained troops, too few planes and ships, too few weapons and too little ammunition for the defence that Australia so urgently needed. But he gave them leadership. The prime minister 'gave his fellow Australians a taste of inspiring leadership', the *Argus* reported, while the *Sydney Morning Herald* stated that John Curtin had developed 'qualities of real leadership'. It is a simple point, and probably an obvious one, but in the first hours of this national crisis the nation looked to one man; closely listened to what he had to say, applauded what he did say, and prepared to follow where he would lead. The unity of purpose was striking and, for those who could see it, the burden of leadership now falling on the prime minister was heavy.

There was a confidence and a calmness among the people; almost exactly the opposite of what Tom Blamey had predicted just a few weeks earlier. To some extent Curtin inspired that mood with his words and his own demeanour. A journalist reported him yarning with press men at the barracks in Melbourne, ranging widely across the topics that everyone else in Australia was discussing:

> Where another man might be theatrically dramatic on such an occasion, he is himself . . . it was the sort of meeting that increased one's confidence in the man . . . it was 6.15 when the interview finished. 'See you tomorrow, boys,' said John Curtin casually. Then he pulled on his soft black felt hat and went to his dinner.

But the nation's confidence also came from two other sources; sources that may lead us to think that there was an element of false confidence here. Australians belittled their enemy, indeed they did not take the Japanese seriously. 'Made in Japan' was stamped on the plates and saucers that you bought in the cheaper stores, it was stamped on other household goods and manufactured goods, and it was a statement that most Australians thought automatically guaranteed that the goods were second-rate, cheap, shoddy and imitative. My grandparents still laughed at Japanese goods in the 1950s, despite the experiences of the Pacific War. For them, what was good, sturdy and finished to a high quality was stamped 'Made in England'. I have some of that crockery in my cupboards still, a reassuring crest, possibly the words 'by appointment' and then 'Made in England'. If the Japanese could not even make a decent cup and saucer how were they going to make a war? The Japanese were physically small, everyone knew that, they were short-sighted, Australians believed, and definitely not sportsmen. How could you take them seriously?

And then there was Singapore: British, strong, invincible. How was it that Singapore had become such an article of faith for Australians? Wishful thinking, possibly. Generations of Australians had been taught respect for the powers of the British race, possibly against all evidence. Was it not the case that the British had nearly been defeated in South Africa before that war had even really started? Had not hundreds of thousands of Australians seen at first hand and many more had read about British incompetence and worse in the First World War? Of course, but in both examples the British had ultimately prevailed. Singapore was not just a heavily defended island; it was a symbol of British power and might. The Japanese pushing themselves against such aura and majesty, why it was near laughable. Master and servant, that was it. The British had been in charge for so long; had an empire which was the envy of the world; laughed at the foibles of Europeans; ruled over the subjugated races. The British and we played cricket, which none of the rest of the world could understand. Cricket, a powerful source of myth-making. Of such flimsy ideas are national myths created. War in the Pacific was inconvenient; it was treacherous of the Japanese to steal a march—unsporting, if you like—but the British Empire would prevail. Of that there could be no doubt.

Yet here was John Curtin writing in a New Year's message in the Melbourne *Herald* that we look to America. The passage in Curtin's article has been quoted so many times, but many have overlooked the context: 'Without any inhibition of any kind I make it quite clear that Australia looks to America, free of any pangs as to our traditional links or kinship with the United Kingdom.' Those words stood out in his text, which was headlined 'The Task Ahead', because of their novelty, because there would still have been many among his readers who believed that this was war as usual, Australia supporting Britain over there and Britain supporting us at Singapore and, vaguely, over here. No, Curtin was explaining to his readers that this was a new war. Indeed, that was his explicit message, and that is where his article begins: 'The war with Japan is not a phase of the struggle with the Axis powers but is a new war.' That was his message to his readers, this was a new war for Australia, an entirely new experience for Australians: 'We refuse to accept the dictum that the Pacific struggle must be treated as a subordinate segment of the general conflict', Curtin continued. And therefore, he came logically to his next paragraph —we look to America. We two nations, Australia and America, have interests, he was saying, that are now more closely aligned than, say, our interest in the liberation of France. That was now for others; this Pacific War is for us.

Curtin's message was published on 27 December 1941, and presented a sophisticated and penetrating understanding of what the new war meant for Australia. The remarkable thing is that Curtin, his advisers and the War Cabinet had come to see the Pacific War as a new war as early as 8 December 1941 and had been talking about it in those terms from then. It was crystal clear to Australia; not so clear, apparently, to our British and American allies. Australia, under Curtin, was thinking for itself.

If John Curtin had so quickly understood a new world order for Australia—though in reality he had been coming to this position since the late 1930s—many in Australia were not as quick to understand his meaning. They talk about the fog of war and living through it, that you can not expect people to truly understand the implications of events as they unfold. Take the loss of the two British battle cruisers, the *Prince of Wales* and the *Repulse*, on 10 December 1941. This was a terrible tragedy with the loss of 840 lives, including that of the British admiral, Tom Phillips. The battle cruisers were part of a fleet, Force Z, sent to Singapore to strengthen the island defences. There should have been an aircraft carrier, the *Indomitable*, accompanying the battle cruisers to Singapore but it had run aground in the West Indies. *Prince of Wales* and *Repulse* were, therefore, without air cover. So what, traditionalists, would have thought, ships go at each other with their guns, have been doing so since before Nelson's time. But no longer. The *Prince of Wales* and the *Repulse* were attacked by aircraft and sunk by aircraft launching bombs and torpedoes. To show just what this meant it is worth noting that there would be, within six months, a major naval battle between the Japanese and the Allies where the ships involved did not even sight one another.

Even Admiral Tom Phillips did not fully understood how vulnerable his ships were without air cover because he made an awful miscalculation. He had maintained radio silence as he went to investigate a possible Japanese landing at Kuantan in Malaya, thus preventing the possibility of the scrambling of British fighter support that might have saved his ships. To Australians, the loss of the two ships was a setback, but it is too much to have expected the people then to have understood the implications: that the loss of the ships had seriously weakened the British campaign in Malaya and the defence of Singapore, and that British military leadership, again, had made a fatal error. Leadership of a nation in war was about telling people as much of the news as was possible and putting it in a context that assisted understanding insofar as it was possible. But it could never have been the whole story. Explain the nature of modern naval warfare, and condemn the British admiral for a series of mistakes, in time of war—hardly.

By mid-January 1942, there were suggestions that the situation at Singapore might not be as Australians had always thought it to be. In October 1941 an item in a Japanese newspaper had suggested that Singapore might be vulnerable to attacks along the northern shores of the island. On 15 January 1942 Churchill also discovered, to his great amazement, that 'there were no permanent fortifications covering the landward side of the naval base and city', the northern shores. So, at this late stage, Churchill now gave urgent consideration to the evacuation of all the Allied troops at Singapore to prevent what could now be foreseen as widespread disaster: the humiliating surrender of thousands of men, and of their arms and equipment. Any evacuation of Singapore would have appalled Australians; indeed it would be difficult to exagger-ate the effect to national morale of such an apparent betrayal. Singapore, to repeat, was a significant part of the Australian national myth. Not to put up a fight there would signify, surely, throwing in the towel completely. So Curtin and the Australian War Cabinet convinced Churchill not to pull out but, instead, to increase the number of troops at Singapore, to bolster the defence. To cut and run, Curtin had cabled Churchill, 'would be regarded here and elsewhere as an inexcusable betrayal'. After the withdrawal of the Australians from Tobruk, Churchill was not much disposed to take notice of anything that was coming from Australia, but with an eye more steadily fixed on the reaction to an evacuation of Singapore in America, Churchill did as Curtin asked; the troops would stay and they would be reinforced. Included in the reinforcements were six Australian battalions, destined, fatally, straight for the prisoner-of-war camps.

At home, commentators observed growing 'anger and consternation' as the threat of defeat at Singapore began, slowly, to dawn on the public. The sounds of danger from the depths of Tom Blamey's imaginary jungle were now coming more loudly and the gazelles, if gazelles they ever were, were certainly becoming restive. By early February it was apparent even to the man in the street that the gravest crisis faced Australia; people began to ask for how long could Singapore hold out. Would it be like Tobruk? A siege of some months while the planners regrouped and created a new strategy. Yes, some months, surely they could hold out for a while.

'We intend to hold Singapore,' British general Arthur Percival boldly stated on 9 February 1942. Editorials in Australian newspapers eagerly took up this cry: the troops must fight doggedly for as long as possible. Even as the end came near it was predicted that the Allies could hold out for some few months more at least. And then it was all over.

On 15 February 1942, one of the most important dates in all of Australian history, the fortress at Singapore surrendered. Australia lost 1789 men killed in the Malayan campaign, 1306 wounded and 15 395 captured—the entire 8th Division, that is, alongside 16 000 British troops and 32 000 Indian troops. No one in Australia bothered to put a brave face on the defeat and the newspapers rushed to point the finger of blame. The *Bulletin*, a journal that had never forgiven Winston Churchill for the disaster of the Dardanelles, found fresh cause to complain: 'Mr Churchill might be the world's great spellbinder, but he has proved himself the world's worst campaign planner. The direction of strategy and the disposition of forces, weapons and munitions must, once and for all, be taken from his guilty and incapable hands.' The *Age* railed against 'tragedy after tragedy . . . blunder after blunder'. For the *Sydney Morning Herald*, 'there have been few more serious miscalculations in all British history'.

As night follows day, four days after Singapore fell bombs began to fall on Australian soil for the first time ever. You could say that most Australians expected that. If Singapore was our Maginot line, when that line was destroyed it was inevitable that the enemy's troops would flow through the breach and onto our own soil. The imagery of war, developed from the Western Front, was all that Australians had within themselves to try to understand these momentous events. The government tried to keep the scale of what had happened at Darwin from the people. John Curtin issued a statement that read: 'I have been advised by the Department of the Air that a number of bombs were dropped on Darwin this morning.' A war communiqué was also issued:

> Japanese bombers raided Darwin this morning. Preliminary reports from Darwin indicate that the attack was concentrated on the township. Shipping in the harbour was also bombed. There were some casualties and some damage to service installations, details of which are not yet known. The raid lasted about an hour.

Yet it was not the detail that interested Australians. It was the fact of the exact causal link between the fall of Singapore and an attack on Australia. This is what had always been spoken of; that Singapore was the sole guarantee of Australian safety and security from attack. With Singapore gone, the people reasoned, of course Australia would come under attack. So the government may as well have come clean about the severity of what had happened in Darwin.

At 9.37 a.m. on 19 February 1942 the RAAF operations room in Darwin received a report from a Catholic missionary on Bathurst Island, some 80 kilometres north of Darwin, that a large number of aircraft had passed over the island, but the commander at Darwin assumed that the aircraft must be American. Launched from four Japanese aircraft carriers in the Timor Sea, these 188 fighters and bombers had, therefore, unfettered access to the town, the harbour and the military bases inland from the town. There were ten United States Kittyhawks at Darwin that might have been deployed, and there were, of course, anti-aircraft gunners, who could have been better prepared. The Japanese aircraft arrived over Darwin just before 10 a.m., bombing and machine-gunning virtually at will for over half an hour. A further flight of 54 bombers returned about noon to pattern bomb the RAAF base. The devastation was dreadful. There were 243 people reported as killed in the attacks and around 350 injured, eight ships were sunk in Darwin Harbour, 23 aircraft destroyed, much of the city was in ruins, including the wharf and the RAAF base. The civilian population at the time had been around 2000 (the women and children had already been evacuated); there were some 14 000 soldiers in Darwin, and two RAAF squadrons comprising about 2000 officers and other ranks. Among those killed were 22 waterside workers and five female telephone operators. An Australian anti-aircraft gunner, fighting in Darwin during these attacks and denied the 1939–45 Star for most of the rest of his life because Darwin was not deemed to be an operational area, told me in 1993 that he could see the faces of some of the Japanese airmen as their planes dived to bomb and to strafe.

John Curtin had issued his statement on Darwin from St Vincent's Hospital in Sydney, to which he had been admitted on 17 February suffering from gastritis, a catch-all term that might imply gastroenteritis, vomiting and diarrhoea. It is possible, but you would think unlikely, that a prime minister with the facilities of the Lodge at his disposal and its staff would be hospitalised at this level of the illness. More likely, the gastritis for which John Curtin was hospitalised might have involved a gastric ulcer, a relatively common complaint then, now known to occur as the result of infection in a weakened system, but exacerbated, too, by worry.

People have written of the loneliness of command, and noted British military historian John Keegan has written of the 'mask of command'. By this he means that, while a general may appear to adopt a friendly and humane interest in his troops, in fact, as he holds the power of life and death over them, he must remain disengaged. Politicians, particularly in wartime, need the mask of command. They need to appear genuinely interested and engaged in the lives of their people while remaining somewhat aloof, enabling them to take the tough decisions that will expose their citizens to danger, to death, parents to grief and suffering, their sons to conditions of the utmost danger and difficulty. It will be a question we will continue to seek to have answered as we look closely at John Curtin as Australia's war leader. Was he able to put on the mask of command and distance himself from the people in whose name he was fighting this war? That he was in hospital two days after the fall of Singapore is an early indication of how the question might be answered.

Smith's Weekly, a somewhat raffish Sydney journal that styled itself as the digger's friend, asked this question of John Curtin as early as 3 January 1942. 'His is the responsibility', the paper observed, 'and it is a ghastly burden for him to shoulder. Every life lost makes him feel like a murderer. That may sound brutal to you, but to a man of his sensibility the horror of throwing youth into the battlefield is a nightmare every moment of the 24 hours the clock ticks off'. Say it is not so, John, write to the newspaper in disagreement for if it is as *Smith's Weekly* has written, what will be the pain and suffering that this war will cause you?

John Curtin, regardless of his sensibilities, had every reason to be worried. Imagine an Australian schoolboy with his war map pinned to his bedroom wall to follow the movements of Australia's troops. The AIF consisted of four divisions, remember. Look at how they stand in the early months of 1942. The 6th Division has been taken from the desert to Greece and Crete and has lost half of its strength there. The 7th Division has completed its campaign in Syria and is recovering in training and at rest in Palestine. The 8th Division has been lost, entirely, at Singapore, although as yet nothing is known of its fate. The 9th Division, recently rescued from Tobruk, is, like the 7th, at rest and in training in Egypt. Australia is under attack and of the seven militia divisions on paper not one could be put in the field 'as a good fighting force'. And there were those who could have wondered, a month and a half earlier, why the prime minister had written that Australia looks to America. Small countries in mortal danger, John Curtin well knew, needed allies.

12. SINGAPORE

L es Bolger was born in 1920 and lived in the Sydney suburb of Concord. There were four older brothers and an older sister. His father, Charles, was a Boer War veteran and then served with the 7th Light Horse in the First World War. Charles Bolger, who already had five children when he went to war in August 1915, was gassed while on active service, returned to Australia in March 1917 and died in 1921. Les had never really known his father. His mother died in 1939.

Les Bolger enlisted in the AIF in 1941, first joining the 2/6th Field Regiment (Artillery) and then the 2/15th Field Regiment. His oldest brother served in the Middle East, another joined the AIF but served out the war in Western Australia, the third brother served in the RAAF in New Guinea, while the second oldest brother had volunteered but was knocked back for bad feet. Was it in memory of their father that each son sought to serve his country in war? Les could not say nor did he think that their combined service was remarkable.

Les reached Malaya in January 1942 to join a regiment that had
been on duty there for several months already. He did not have long
to wait to go into action as he was south of Gemas at Segamat on
13 January 1942, part of Brigadier Maxwell's 27th Brigade as he
told me proudly, waiting for the Japanese who were already
sweeping all before them—even at this early stage things were not
going well for the Allies. The 27th Brigade's job was to help to hold
the line against the advancing Japanese from central Malaya, where
the Australians were in thick jungle across to the coast, with British
and Indian forces to just south of Malacca. Incredible though it
seemed, even to the soldiers themselves, it was obvious the
Japanese intended to push southwards down Malaya to threaten
Singapore itself. On 14 January 1942 the 27th Brigade was ready for
its first experience under fire: 'The reputation not only of the AIF
in Malaya, but of Australia, is in the hands of this unit', Brigadier
'Black Jack' Galleghan told them. The official historian blamed the
inability of the Australians (and other troops) to hold at Gemas on
the Japanese control of the air and on the inexperience of the
troops. The Australians pulled back to the Muar River, and then
were pushed further along the road to Singapore.

By February 1942 the 2/15th Field Regiment had set up its guns
in the western part of the north of Singapore island near the
Causeway, the vital crossing point from Malaya to Singapore. Les
was waiting for the arrival of the Japanese, looking out across the
Johore Strait. It had not been a very glorious war so far; he and his
mates had been barely able to make a stand. The defence of Singapore would be a tough encounter, the Australians now believed.
Yet only two months previously the British and the Australians had
been brimful with absurd overconfidence. The commander of the
2nd Battalion Argyll and Sutherland Highlanders had told Air
Chief Marshal Sir Robert Brooke-Popham, commanding both the
army and air force in the 'Far East', 'I do hope, sir, we are not
getting too strong in Malaya, because if so the Japanese will never
attempt a landing.' Now, after only a few weeks, the Japanese
controlled all Malaya and were threatening Singapore itself.

The enemy had used the jungle well in Malaya and had moved
with unexpected speed. But now they faced a body of water and
defenders well dug in with what they thought of as reasonable

defences. If nothing else, Les and the soldiers around him believed, the Japanese would suffer heavily in attempting to cross onto Singapore island. It would take them many weeks to do so, the troops all thought. It would be a tough fight, but bring it on. Les's father had fought at Gallipoli; the Anzacs there had initially attacked from the sea and believed that the defenders on the land enjoyed all the advantages. The knowledge of how hard it had been for the Anzacs to come from the sea, then, encouraged their sons now as the situation was now reversed. Whatever happened, they thought, they would give a good account of themselves, for the reputation of the AIF and Australia, just as their fathers had done at Gallipoli. That story was still in the forefront of their minds as they stood to their guns, waiting for the coming attempt at invasion.

Inexperience accounted for the confidence of the Australians; they were, in fact, dealing in dreams and myths. They had grown up believing in the invincibility of Singapore; there must be big guns behind them, naval guns, they reasoned, ready to pound the Japanese into the ground. That was myth. In reality the defenders had too few useful guns, the naval guns could be used, they were not 'all pointing out to sea', but they fired armour piercing shells, of little use against troops on the ground. The Australian gunners simply had too few guns, only about 30 along an eight-mile front; they also suffered from too fragile a communications system, with phone lines knocked out early in the fighting and flares hard to see at the guns' positions. If gunners cannot see or hear they cannot fight and that was the problem for the Australian gunners on Singapore, they were very much on their own.

Troop dispositions had done this; the gunners were not integrated with the defending battalions of infantry. The battle plan was simply wrong. It was found, for example, that on the night of 8/9 February, of the 2/15 Field Regiment's seven troops of gunners, only two fired heavily that night, and two fired hardly at all. Effectively the higher command, their own leaders, had silenced their guns. The regiment's war diary will tell you that, and the historians too. But I sat with Les Bolger as he told me that he and his mates had not done their job. It would be too much to say that he was ashamed but the hurt was certainly still there in the voice of this gentle, lovely old man. He found it hard, nearly 60 years later, to tell me what had happened. 'We had the guns all lined up,' he said, 'and we weren't allowed to fire them. I was very down-hearted,' he added. 'I felt that we had let down the Anzac tradition.' He felt that he had let down his dad, in fact; had shown himself not to be the soldier his dad had been. Les was not alone in thinking like that.

These were men who died over the next three years in the prisoner-of-war camps, to which nearly all these men on Singapore island were destined, who went to their graves believing they had failed and disgraced Australia. Who went to their graves believing that they must be despised in Australia, thought of as men of no account, because they had so meekly surrendered at Singapore. You think I am exaggerating? Then let us eavesdrop on the conversations of returning Australian prisoners, those who had survived the camps, the railway, slave labour in Japan, the dropping of the atomic bombs. They sat in little groups, mates together, as the warships and the hospital ships made the slow journey back to their homeland once the war had ended. We know that all of Australia was at a fever pitch of excitement to welcome these men back home. And yet as they sat there, on the British aircraft carrier *Speaker*, for example (I could give you many more instances), they were 'debating endlessly how we would be received in Australia'. They had let Australia down, they thought; worse, they had spent three and a half years helping the enemy, building his airfields, his railways, his ships, making his roads, loading and unloading his ships. Worse again, they had trashed the Anzac tradition, they thought, ruined Australia's reputation for producing the best soldiers the world had ever known. Would they be treated as criminals for what they had done, as pariahs? Instead of offering the hand of friendship, would Australians turn their backs on them? That they could possibly have thought like that shows how deeply a sense of shame had been etched into their souls by the horror of surrendering at Singapore and marching, en masse, into the prison camps, near 20 000 of these Australians. 'All hands', an Australian lieutenant wrote in his diary as his ship approached Sydney Harbour, 'are quietly excited about tomorrow—arrival in Sydney. Or are we?'

So, what had gone wrong? How had this defeat come about? In a sense it is all in the telling of the story. Individual historians will emphasise different aspects of what happened. The official historian, Lionel Wigmore, uses thousands and thousands of words to describe the fighting in Malaya, the relentless retreat in front of the Japanese. He shows that the 8th Division fought well and carried a heavy proportion of the fighting. He writes of the jungle, the confusion, the heroism of men like Charles Anderson, awarded the Victoria Cross in the fighting at the Muar River. Taking his narrative onto Singapore, Lionel Wigmore spends hundreds of pages describing the way the troops were deployed by those in command, and will also tell in minute detail how the Australians prepared for battle and how the Japanese effected their crossing and bore down upon Singapore island until surrender became inevitable. Wigmore's is a narrative that is long on description but seems to miss one crucial aspect of the story, yet in his notes he shows himself acutely aware of that part of the story: the failure of command in Malaya and on Singapore. It is just that he did not write about it in his history.

That is not the way of today's historians. How do we explain the loss of the *Prince of Wales* and the *Repulse*, that event in early December 1941 that tipped the balance in the battle for Singapore so firmly in favour of the Japanese? Alan Warren, a contemporary historian, goes straight to Admiral Tom Phillips, his personality, the mistakes he made and the mistake those who promoted him seem so obviously to have made. Those who promoted Phillips should have listened to the sounds of jaws dropping all around the Royal Navy when the promotion was announced. Tom Phillips, said the commander-in-chief in the Mediterranean, Vice-Admiral Sir Andrew Cunningham, 'hardly knows one end of a ship from another'. Vice-Admiral Sir James Somerville, in charge of British naval forces at Gibraltar, 'shuddered to think of the "Pocket Napoleon" going to the East. All the tricks to learn and no solid sea experience to fall back on.' Just the cruel and catty remarks of officers who resented the rapid promotion of another? For Tom Phillips had jumped two steps from rear-admiral to acting admiral when he was promoted to command the Far Eastern Squadron (Force Z). The military may not be unique in gossiping about the promotion of one of its number out of his turn, but military leaders do seem to display a special skill in voicing their resentments.

'Pocket Napoleon' implied no grudging admiration; rather it was a cruel jibe and referred to Phillips' stature, a tiny man, five-foot two-inches tall and weighing barely nine stone. He was described as 'decisive', 'opinionated', 'a hard taskmaster at times abrasive', all attributes that could be ascribed to Napoleon. But unlike Napoleon, Phillips was very far indeed from being a strategic or tactical genius. Aware of the Japanese naval and aerial presence in and above the waters through which he was sailing as he made his way back to Singapore in December 1941, Phillips failed to ask for air cover for his own ships. Instead he maintained radio silence, as we have seen, so that the few aircraft he could have called on to help remained idle on the ground. Why? Because Tom Phillips refused to believe that the most dangerous Japanese aircraft had sufficient range that could put them above him. British torpedo-armed aircraft could not have reached Phillips' fleet off Kuantan, so how dare the Japanese? Simple ignorance was the admiral's undoing, stubbornly held beliefs lost him his ships despite alternate views offered by the admiral's subordinates. When, just hours before the end of it all, Japanese aircraft appeared above him and a young officer observed that the planes seemed to be armed with torpedoes, Phillips rounded on him and said that there were no such aircraft about. They could not be there; they simply did not have the range. Well open your eyes, sir, except that you do not say such things to an admiral. It was Tom Phillips' mindset and his certainty in his own opinions that cost 840 lives and two ships, crucial to the defence of Singapore. At least Tom Phillips had the decency to go down with his flagship, making no effort whatsoever to be rescued. But stiff upper lip and all that, at least the boys went down singing.

The officer commanding No. 453 Squadron RAAF, Flight Lieutenant T.A. Vigors, born in County Tipperary, reported seeing the end of the *Prince of Wales* as the ship sunk on the horizon. There were hundreds of men in the water, he later reported, clinging to life rafts and wreckage, and they were 'waving, cheering and joking as if they were holiday-makers.' Others have suggested that the sailors were in fact shaking their fists in fury and rage at the late arrival of the fighter aircraft. Lionel Wigmore doesn't tell you that, preferring to leave the reader with the holiday-maker image. In any case the failure in giving the ships air cover was not the fault of the air force; Tom Phillips had simply failed to call them up.

And it goes on, this failure of command. Long before his surprising decision to abandon his troops on Singapore and so evade capture, hardly anyone had a good word to say for the Australian military commander, Gordon Bennett. He had fought bravely at Gallipoli and in France in World War I, but somehow in the inter-war years he had developed an obsessive hatred for permanent Australian army officers. It was almost an illness with him, a corrosive passion that seriously warped his personality. Bennett confidently expected—no, he simply assumed—that he would be given command of the AIF when war broke out in 1939, and he did little to hide his fury when Menzies gave the appointment to Tom Blamey. No wonder, therefore, that Blamey ignored Bennett when choosing the leaders for the Australian divisions as they were created. No one believed that Bennett could work harmoniously alongside more senior British generals because he was as scathing of the British military leadership as he had been of the Australians. It is a measure of how bare the cupboard was that Bennett was given command of the 8th Australian Division. It is worth making the point, too, that many of his immediate Australian subordinates in the division were second-rate, and older than the men first chosen for leadership in the Middle East who had performed so well. This 'new' war needed Australia's best soldiers but they were on duty elsewhere and the 8th picked up what was left. It was the Canberra air disaster that gave Gordon Bennett his chance; the 8th Division's Vernon Sturdee replaced Brudenall White as chief of the general staff and Bennett stepped in to lead the 8th, second choice even then.

Well at least Bennett has a good military brain, people would say, despite his unfortunate personality. Yet, responsible for the defence of north-west Jahore, Bennett's dispositions were 'fundamentally unsound', writes his biographer. 'Bennett's conduct of operations [on Singapore] was questionable . . . and his interest in the campaign seemed to wane towards the end.' It was Bennett's 'failure to move forward and see what was happening' at Krangi, north-west Singapore, where Les Bolger was, that allowed the Japanese to land there. Or as Les would have put it, we weren't allowed to fire our guns, and Les and his mates went into captivity feeling that they had failed Australia and trashed Anzac. Gordon Bennett himself, though, escaped Singapore, justifying his dash for freedom by saying that he had learned how to defeat the Japanese and he needed to pass on the knowledge back home. But in Australia no one bothered to ask him what he knew because they did not believe that he had anything important to say. The hatred for Gordon Bennett lingered and after the war there was an inquiry into his decision to flee Singapore. When, in the 1960s, they put his portrait on display at the Australian War Memorial, someone slashed the painting at the throat. No forgiveness there. Sadly, I did not think to ask Les Bolger if he had ever seen Gordon Bennett or what he thought of him. Les was such a kindly, Christian man, I doubt he would have told me. But the fault was not yours, Les, it was the men who led you.

Bennett particularly disliked Brigadier Harold Taylor, who led the 22nd Brigade. 'As the Japanese swept across Singapore island', wrote Taylor's biographer, Bennett 'made "disparaging remarks" about the way Taylor handled the defence of his sector and about the men' of his brigade. One of Bennett's last acts was to relieve the brigadier of his command but, unlike Bennett, Taylor remained on the island and marched into captivity with his men. 'Had words with Taylor', Bennett wrote in his diary in March 1941. 'He resents receiving orders and does his best to thwart me'; and thus they went to war together.

Lieutenant Colonel F.G. 'Black Jack' Galleghan assumed that he would be given command of the 27th Brigade when its commander fell ill before the brigade reached Singapore. Instead Bennett selected a medical doctor turned soldier, Duncan Maxwell: 'Big' Maxwell as he had been called in France in the earlier war to distinguish him from his brother, 'Little'. Maxwell was tall, six-foot-three tall, and had, Bennett believed, a good temperament and a good mind. But he was junior to several other battalion commanders available for promotion, including Galleghan. Already in Malaya when his brigade arrived, Maxwell went on board ship to meet his new charges: 'You needn't expect

me to congratulate you on the red flannel you're wearing,'
Galleghan said to him; thus they went to war together.

Most odium, however, is reserved for Arthur Percival, the
commander of the land forces in the campaign. It was Percival, after
all, who sat opposite the victorious Japanese commander, Tomoyuki
Yamashita, in the Ford factory at Singapore to sign the surrender
document. Looking for the 'guilty men', perhaps it was all Percival's
fault. The general's appearance did not inspire confidence: tall,
extremely thin, buck-toothed, and wearing those absurd 'Bombay
bloomers' and pith helmet that shout gin and tonic and effete.
Percival never looked as though he was really in charge. And effectively he wasn't. Archibald Wavell had been sent out to Singapore
after handing over to Auchinleck in the desert. Wavell's headmaster had written to Archibald's father many years earlier, 'There
is no need for your son to go into the Army; he really is quite intelligent'. Between them, though, Percival and Wavell had produced a
plan for the defence of Singapore island that was, in the words of
an Australian military thinker, 'maladroit'. Essentially, they spread
their troops too thinly along the north coast of the island, where
concentration might have produced a better result. Nor did the
generals hold the bulk of their troops in reserve, ready to swing
them into action when the assault commenced. Mobility was what
had won the Japanese the victory in Malaya, but Wavell and
Percival had no time for it as a principle at Singapore.

With water running out, supplies of all sorts low, the morale of
the troops so damaged that there was looting, ill-discipline and
unauthorised attempts at flight on the part of a minority, Percival
was told by London to cease resistance when it became clear
that the fighting was no longer viable. Wavell left Singapore
on 11 February; Percival asked for a ceasefire at 8.30 p.m. on
15 February. A total of 130 000 Australian, British and Indian
troops became prisoners of war; nearly ten thousand had already
died. The Japanese had 9824 battle casualties. Their army had
fought its way down through Malaya to Singapore, travelling and
fighting over more than 1000 kilometres in just 70 days at an
average rate of 15 kilometres a day. The Japanese, dismissed a
couple of months ago as short-sighted and somewhat ludicrous
soldiers, now seemed nearly invincible.

Despite the evident incompetence and name-calling that seemed to be such a feature of the fighting in Malaya and Singapore, more so than in the other campaigns we have so far examined, perhaps the search for the 'guilty men' should be re-directed from Singapore to London, and possibly to Canberra. Simply put, the problem was that Britain found itself fighting a two-hemisphere war with a one-hemisphere navy. Douglas Wynter, as we have seen, had been explaining before war had even broken out that Britain did not have the capacity to fight two wars at the same time. Force Z, Tom Phillips' ill-fated flotilla, needed not just two capital ships, but dozens of them. Alan Warren locates the disaster at Singapore in the Washington Naval Treaty of 1922, which required Britain to scrap a considerable part of her fleet. To meet the Japanese navy on equal terms after decommissioning so many ships, Britain would have needed to have sent the bulk of her capital ships to Singapore; with war in Europe and the Mediterranean, this was simply never going to happen.

Perhaps successive Australian governments should have recognised the inherent weakness in the Australian dependence on Singapore and at least have counselled the Australian people not to invest too heavily in the myth of Singapore's invulnerability. And perhaps the wartime Australian governments might have kept some of the better Australian military leaders at home just in case war did break out in the Australian region. Menzies was looking closely at Japan in September 1939 and was wary of committing too many Australians to Europe. What might an Iven Mackay or a Leslie Morshead have done at Singapore? Still, Australians would not have wanted leaders of this calibre locked up for the remainder of the war in the prison camps, which was now the fate of the surrendering troops.

Large numbers of Italian prisoners had been taken in the North African campaign so there was some precedent for what was happening on Singapore. Shocked though the Australian government was by what had taken place, ministers nevertheless believed that a number of steps would now be taken in relation to the prisoners. First and foremost among those expectations was the idea that the 'detaining power' would soon communicate the names and service numbers of all those in captivity and their location.

This would enable the Australian government to inform the families of those in captivity that their son or, in very small numbers, daughter, was alive and in a prisoner-of-war camp. That was a reasonable expectation, laid down by the third Geneva convention, drawn up in 1929, outlining the rights and responsibilities of those powers detaining prisoners of war. Unfortunately, the Japanese had not ratified the convention.

This was new territory for Australia, the news that up to 20 000 of its citizens were held as prisoners of war. Some Australians had been captured by the Germans on the Western Front, particularly at Fromelles in July 1916. There are pictures of these Australians being marched through French and Belgian towns in occupied territory, paraded as 'trophies of war'. Few Australians knew that some of the AIF had been taken prisoner and fewer still knew of the experiences of these prisoners. Some very few Australians had become prisoners of the Turks. Even though one of their number wrote a book, Guests of the Unspeakable, again very few Australians knew the story in any detail. But now one-fifth of Australia's overseas fighting force was in captivity and no Australian could ignore that.

Is he alive, parents would be worrying, or wondering did he fall on the field of battle? It would be a mercy to have at least that one question—alive or dead—answered. Time later for letters and news of conditions in the prisoner-of-war camps, how the men used their time, what the food was like, how to send food parcels and news to the men. All that in good time. That at least was the expectation—we'll hear, surely, soon enough.

At first the government busied itself letting families know the barest news, which was really no news at all. A telegram containing a spare message for anxious people: 'Regret to inform you that your son ——— is missing and believed to be a prisoner of war as result of enemy occupation of Singapore. If further information is received it will be immediately conveyed to you.' These telegrams began to go out in mid-March 1942, just a month after the fall of Singapore. 'How's your boy?' anxious friends and work colleagues would ask. Extended family members asked too. In the playgrounds in schools across Australia little children would ask a particular friend, 'Is your dad alright?' or 'Have you heard from your brother yet?' Everyone was asking; 'We think he might be a prisoner of war' was all that anyone could say by way of reply.

During these first months the Australian government was content to wait for the names of prisoners and the places in which they were being held. It would be a mighty job, ministerial letter-writers told those family members who were pushing government ministers for better answers and more news, to process these hundred thousand and more men. Give the Japanese some time to put everything in order and then, no doubt, we'll hear. Remember, first they have to house and feed them, probably find additional clothes for them, there will be medical problems and possibly many casualties to care for, transport to bigger holding camps would be an issue; we faced the same situation in the desert when all those Italians surrendered. The lists of names, with the locations of each individual nurse, soldier, sailor or airman will be coming soon. Then you will be able to write to your loved one, send extra supplies, remembrances of home. It is hard to have to wait, of course, but be patient.

Gordon Bennett, back home safe and sound, was able to give some good news: 'Evidence so far is,' he said, 'that Australians in Japanese hands have been treated quite well, and there does not seem to be any need for undue worry by relatives.' That was in March 1942. Meanwhile cables were flowing between London and Canberra, seeking to put help for the prisoners on an organised and efficient footing: it will be 'obvious that the Japanese scale of diet will be hopelessly insufficient for Australian soldiery', London cabled, so foods to be shipped should aim at providing those things that the Japanese might overlook. London would also need to arrange food-stuffs for the Indian troops in captivity, things like chillies, curry powder, dates, nuts, rice. It was important, London told Canberra, that the two types of supplies arrived at the same time at Singapore, for if the Indians thought themselves overlooked they might suspect that they had been seen as second-class soldiers.

Looking now at these files in the National Archives with the benefit of hindsight is exquisitely sad. The officials in the two capitals meant well and you sense a certainty that normal civilised behaviour would prevail. Indeed that was not even a question in the minds of the officials. Only slowly did it dawn on them that things were not as they should be. In April John Curtin informed London that he was worrying somewhat about the slow release of the names of the prisoners; might not a bit of payback be in order ('reciprocity' is the polite word Curtin used), to hurry the Japanese along. Withdraw privileges from the Japanese prisoners in our hands until the list of names arrives, that sort of thing. The parents must know soon if their boy is alive or dead. The high commissioner in London, Stanley Bruce, told Curtin that authorities there were also becoming alarmed about the lack of names but he doubted that 'reciprocity' would work because of the massive imbalance between the numbers of Allied prisoners and the numbers of Japanese prisoners. And so it went on. The plans for shipping appropriate foods soon dropped from the officials' agenda. In September 1942 London plaintively cabled: 'Have you received any lists by wireless?' Australia's reply was truly depressing as only eight names had so far been officially sent to Australia by the Japanese—the names of five airmen who were prisoners of war and the names of three others who had been killed in action. That was it, eight out of 20 000.

If the Australian prisoners had been permitted to write home in the first days of their captivity the news would not have been all that bad. Apart from informing the anxious family that the soldier or airman was indeed alive, the letter would have been able to report that within two days of the surrender the prisoners had been moved to Changi on the north-eastern tip of the island, formerly a British garrison with large and airy barracks buildings and a large number of bungalows. There was a substantial parade ground, well-cared-for lawns and garden beds, 'a pleasant suburban atmosphere to the area', as the official history had it. Changi, then, was all that you would expect of a British military establishment in the 'Far East'. At first the prisoners were allowed to roam the area freely, even allowed outside the barracks to the straits of Jahore and the beach to the east of the prison.

Within Changi itself, Allied officers retained responsibility for the discipline and activities of their men and the Australian officers ordered the making of vegetable gardens to augment the food supplies, the establishment of a poultry scheme, the organisation of sport and education. The Japanese seem to have been caught short when they first took responsibility for the prisoners, as if this problem had simply never occurred to them. But it was an island for God's sake, so how were the men going to escape? Soon, though, the Japanese realised they had a massive labour force on their hands and began to offer the troops access to work, in return for some benefits. For men whose main enemy at this time was boredom, the work parties soon became quite popular. They took men out of Changi to the wharves or warehouses, gave them additional rations and canteen goods, and offered, unwittingly, the opportunity for pilfering as well. But it would be work and the conditions of that work would kill the majority of the near 8000 Australians who died in the hands of the Japanese over the next three years.

The first of those to leave Singapore on work parties were sent to construct airfields along the coast of Burma from May 1942 onwards. Here the conditions of work were not too bad, although the trip from Singapore in desperately overcrowded ships had been horrendous. The equipment given to the prisoners for the work expected of them was primitive in the extreme and this was perhaps an early warning of what was to come. With the airfields completed the work parties were then moved to locations in Thailand and Burma to start work on a railway that would link the two countries. Through the jungle. Historians of the prisoners of war write of the railway as the turning point in the treatment of the prisoners by the Japanese. The railway was intended to supply food and equipment, weapons and ammunition to the Japanese troops in Burma, when it was realised that the sea route to Rangoon for the Japanese was too hazardous. There was an urgency, then, in the completion of the railway if the war in Burma was to be waged successfully. The Japanese soon came to regard the Burma–Thailand Railway as vital war work. Speed, primitive equipment, tragic targets and a railway literally carved from the jungle all combined to create conditions of labour and horror such as Australians have simply never endured before or since. With the railway completed in 1943 these workers were then moved to Japan itself to continue, in equally terrible conditions, to work in coal mines, in shipbuilding, and elsewhere as required. The men were half-starved, brutalised, degraded, beaten with a rare cruelty—treated, in sum, without any regard at all for their humanity. The prisoners had become non-people.

Les Bolger was a gentle, good man, quietly spoken, deeply religious, generous and cheerful. He remembered the railway for the remainder of his days, experiencing fearsome nightmares for years after his release from captivity. Remembered his mate, Bill Scarpella, a giant of man, doing the work of two men on the railway, protecting his mate Les from the anger of the guards because Les could not work nearly as hard as they demanded. Les remembered, too, as just one random incident, the moment when, in rage, one of the guards picked up a big shifting spanner to belt Les across the head—it would have killed him for a certainty. An Australian officer intervened, saving Les Bolger's life. At least I do not have a mother and father at home worrying for me, Les thought. Bill Scarpella did, though, in Melbourne, and Les had the courage after his release from captivity to go to Melbourne to tell Bill Scarpella's parents how their son had died: in the South China sea, drowned after being driven mad by drinking seawater in the extremity of his thirst. There were tears in Les Bolger's eyes, 56 years later, as he told me that.

The people who were waiting for news, any news, found it difficult to understand how it was that no one could say, 'He's alright. He's alive and working on the wharves in Singapore.' Just something as simple as that. They wrote letters trying to penetrate the meaning of what the defence officials had written to them: '————is missing and believed to be a prisoner of war as a result of the enemy occupation of Singapore.' They wrote to John Curtin, the prime minister, confident that he would side with them in their anxiety and grief; confident, too, that he would be able to do something for them. As I read these letters in the prime minister's correspondence in the National Archives I was struck by the ease with which people wrote to John Curtin, as if he was a friend whom they had known for years. They opened their hearts to him, many of these writers, telling him things that you would normally reserve for family or close friends, telling him, simply, of their lives. I looked further into the prime ministerial correspondence, beyond the issue of the prisoners of war. It was the same wherever I looked. People were writing to their prime minister with their worries and concerns as if he was one of them.

All kinds and manner of people write to ministers and prime ministers. Sincere people, deluded people, clear-thinking people, confused people. Almost every letter receives some type of reply. 'Ministerials' they are called within the bureaucracy, and these replies take up a lot of time. What I had found in John Curtin prime ministerial correspondence was something of a different order. Let me give you some examples. Mrs Wallace of Glenbrook in New South Wales told her prime minister that all her four boys were in the armed forces, one of them a prisoner in Thailand. She had received a couple of cards from him, had been writing regularly but had no idea if he was receiving her letters. 'I am alone', she told the prime minister, 'and greatly worried about my son in Japanese hands, who is my best boy'. Mrs Grace Harrison of South Melbourne, while conceding that the prime minister must be 'very busy', wrote that she had, what she called, 'a great worrie'. 'My son is missing in Malaya and I am a very sad mother. If only I knew what has become of him.' She concluded, '. . . please forgive me taking the liberty and may Our Lady of Good Council [her spelling] help you in a task that is very great'. As the prime minister struggled with the terrible news from Singapore and the awful wait for news about the Australian prisoners, other correspondents came to him with so many other troubles. The burden was oppressive.

Writers suggested that as John Curtin was himself so clearly suffering on account of the war, then he would best understand their own suffering. And the letter writers almost always wished the prime minister well: 'I realise what a tremendous burden you carry in these strenuous days', wrote Mrs J.A. Lyons of Fullerton, South Australia, 'wishing you all the best'. Mrs Elsie Salter of Epping in Sydney, wrote to Mrs Curtin, the prime minister's wife, noting that she too had a son in the forces: 'You will be able to help us through your husband.' You understand, you do understand, Australia seemed to be telling the Curtins. 'I have a baby daughter who was born two months after the fall of Singapore', if I could only just let my husband know her name, 'it would be very comforting to my husband'. All the prime minister had to do was to arrange it.

A totally and permanently incapacitated pensioner from World War I in Tasmania wanted an increase in the petrol ration for men like himself who could not get around easily, 'So I am asking you to see if you can do anything further for me'. A soldier has been away from home (Victoria) for three years and wanted a local posting: 'I was thinking of seeking an interview with you but have no doubt that you would be over-run with such requests, have put the case in writing.' A Mrs Crowther needed her soldier–son back to help her on the farm: 'I would not ask you only I need him so. If you would stand by me and help me I would be very thankful.' A soldier–son got himself into a spot of bother by mixing with older and dubious army types: 'You will remember I wrote about [it] a couple of months back.' Things had turned out well for the boy: 'Mr Curtin, the wife, the lad and myself are very grateful to you for the trouble you went to.' A dairy farmer only has his youngest daughter at home and needs his son back to help: 'I am writing to you to see if you could do me a favour.' Another simply wrote to tell John Curtin that he was doing a good job. 'I had written', he said when Curtin had entered office, 'at that precarious time for us all. I told you I had a feeling of contentment and security with you at the helm'.

But at what cost to the helmsman? There were literally thousands of Australians writing to the prime minister each year of the war, reminding him that they believed he alone would stand with them, look after them, solve their problems. It was as if he was the national father of them all. If in addition to the strains and burdens of national leadership in time of war, of fighting hard for a minor ally's quarter, of arguing for resources and troops in the face of the terrible situation Australia faced in 1942, and of the day-to-day management of a government at war, John Curtin felt the personal burden for the manifold and manifest sufferings of his people, if the mask of command simply could not protect him, then the strain, worry and the intensity of the pressure might well have led to the diseases and illnesses that had begun to emerge as early as February 1942. In the kaleidoscope that is war John Curtin could not simply separate his various problems into a variety of boxes. A thousand worries pushed themselves to the forefront of his thinking.

The loss of Singapore was a terrible shock to Australians, but a far greater cause for alarm for the military planners and the politicians was the loss of an entire army division, and many airmen and sailors besides. Some historians, with access now to Japanese archival collections, have argued that Australia was never at serious risk of invasion and that the Japanese high command had prudently ruled out such a difficult undertaking. What was all the fuss about, these historians seem to have been saying. Australians, they imply, were like that flock of gazelles at the edge of the jungle, too ready to take flight in panic and alarm.

In the first half of 1942, particularly, that was not the way the war was seen in Australia. The prime minister and ministers were talking about the possibility of war on Australian soil, preparing the people for attack if it came. That was their duty and responsibility. The people looked at the possibility of invasion realistically and counted up the forces within Australia to meet trouble when it came. They knew that Australia's most proficient soldiers were overseas, either fighting or in captivity, and they assumed that their government would want to do something about that.

13. CRISIS

There is a beautiful war cemetery in Perth attached to the Karrakatta general cemetery. Unlike the sprawling and vast civilian cemetery, parts of which are unkempt, the military cemetery is maintained to a very high standard. There are 125 Second World War dead buried there; the oldest of these service-men and women, surely, is Private Lemuel Pritchard: born in Sheffield, England, in December 1888, who died on 23 June 1945, 66 years of age, serving in the 10th Garrison Battalion. His family chose these words for his Commonwealth War Graves Commis-sion tombstone: 'God saw his tired eyes and closed them in peaceful sleep.'

To one side of the military cemetery, in a small but beautiful garden, is a Dutch war cemetery with the graves of 26 Dutch nationals. Two of the headstones are in sharp contrast to that of Lemuel Pritchard and all we know about him; they simply say 'an unknown Dutch child'. Visitors, and there would be few of them, would wander around and ask how it came to be, the death of these Dutch people in Australia, and how it is that several of the graves have no names attached. This is Australia, after all, with all records maintained and available. In fact, the cemetery speaks eloquently of the crisis and confusion that prevailed in Australia in the first months of 1942.

With Singapore taken the Japanese pressed on remorselessly, menacing both Timor and Java. It had been expected that the Dutch would make a strong showing on Java, a colonial possession for more than three centuries. Elements of the 7th Australian Division, under Brigadier Arthur Blackburn, and known therefore as 'Blackforce', had landed to assist in repelling the enemy. Dutch civilians, particularly women and children, were encouraged to leave the island for Australia, in the first instance. Most of them would have come by flying boat and made Australian landfall at Broome. In the rush to evacuate these people few records, such as passenger lists, were made; all the details would be sorted out later.

Broome, a place, until the war, that was best known as the headquarters of the Australian pearling industry and a place Australians invested with a peculiar sort of romanticism, had now become one of the busiest airports in the South-West Pacific. As many as 57 aircraft had arrived in Broome in one day, and in 14 days between 7000–8000 passengers had also arrived. (These figures seem absurdly low for a 'busy' airport today but show how uncommon air travel was then.) There were only three hotels in Broome to accommodate all these passengers, although private houses and even the local school had been pressed into service. There were moorings in Roebuck Bay for only three flying boats, the remainder of the aircraft would ride at anchor. Aircraft were refuelled by a single refuelling lighter, *Nicol Bay*, but refuelling was hardly a highly organised operation. Flying boat captains would come ashore to arrange refuelling with the *Nicol Bay*'s master, Captain Harold Mathieson, and then they would probably see something of the town at the same time. There was no great sense of urgency in Broome, never has been.

In the afternoon of 2 March 1942 townsfolk noticed a Japanese reconnaissance aircraft passing three times over the town and harbour. There were only three flying boats at the moorings then; four more arrived just before dusk, and nine others arrived at various times during the night. All captains were warned to arrange for the departure of their aircraft as soon as possible after first light because of the risk of attack from the Japanese. The crew of the *Nicol Bay* had worked through the night to refuel the flying boats but only one of the aircraft in the harbour had departed by 9.20 in the morning when Japanese aircraft did swoop over the town. Some would say this was Darwin all over again: a warning given but promptly ignored. But huge Catalina flying boats need plenty of water under them for take-off, and with the substantial rise and fall of the tide in Broome some have suggested that the flying boats, in fact, could not make an early morning departure because of the tide. The flying boats were, in effect, stranded. Passengers, too, were stranded on the flying boats overnight when their preference would have been for a bed in the town. Again it was the tide that made taking them ashore too difficult.

There were nine Japanese Zeros in the attack. Flying at 500 feet and entirely free of any counterattack—although members of the Broome Volunteer Defence Corps, Great War men, fired off their old .303 rifles at the Zeros with little obvious effect—for the Japanese this was like shooting fish in a barrel. Indeed the remarkable story of this raid is of the survival of so many aircrew and passengers when circumstances might have led to a massacre. The story is also of the heroism of the crew of the *Nicol Bay*. With 180 drums of petrol on board, the *Nicol Bay* was in awful danger but with extraordinary bravery Harold Mathieson continued sailing, trying to rescue survivors from the sea. It was possibly not a wise undertaking given the nature of his cargo. Others were taking out row boats into Roebuck Bay to rescue survivors and one Dutch serviceman was found swimming on his back, with a baby resting on his chest.

Within 15 minutes the raiders had wrecked every flying boat in the bay and had destroyed every aircraft on the land, including shooting down an aircraft that had managed to take-off, loaded with 33 crew and passengers, most of them wounded. Eventually there was only one survivor from this aircraft. In all, 24 aircraft were destroyed and about 70 people lost their lives, though without proper records the final casualty list remained a best guess. The bodies of the victims recovered from the sea were taken to

Perth for burial and their graves still serve to remind people of the sadness of war and the danger that Australia faced in early 1942. There was no Australian force in the air or on the ground that might have defended the evacuees from Java at Broome. But it was not only isolated Broome that was undefended, Australia as a whole was largely undefended territory. For the national government this was simply an unacceptable situation. The first duty and responsibility of every government everywhere is the safety and security of its own people. Yet there was no move within the Australian government for the return of the AIF from the Middle East to garrison Australia, either in November, before the outbreak of the Pacific War, or in December, with the new war going so badly for the Allies.

Winston Churchill first raised the question of a move of some of the Australian divisions from the Middle East with John Curtin in late 1941. Churchill had cabled that perhaps the 6th and 7th divisions might be used to bolster the defence of Malaya or of the Netherlands East Indies. The Australian Advisory War Council on 31 December 1941 recommended to the government that if there was a request to transfer an Australian division from the Middle East to the Far East the government should approve the request. But the Australian government was in no hurry for this, concerned first to settle the command and administrative arrangements for Australian forces in both theatres of war. The War Cabinet did approve the transfer of the Australian divisions on 5 January 1942, but remained confident still in the strength of the fortress at Singapore and, possibly, was still inclined to underestimate the Japanese soldier.

In early January Churchill asked John Curtin directly whether, in Curtin's assessment, Australia was at risk of a substantial Japanese invasion. The Australian prime minister naturally turned to his military advisers for help in shaping his reply and they told him that invasion would remain a risk until the situation was stabilised in Malaya or until the Allies gained the upper hand against the Japanese navy. Yet even in early January, as Curtin was discussing these matters in Canberra and Melbourne, it was impossible to foresee the speed with which the Japanese would sweep down the Malayan peninsula. But as the position in central Malaya deteriorated, clearly the risk to Australia intensified. In the minds of Australia's military planners it was very clear that the situation in Malaya and Singapore directly impacted on the safety and security of Australia. Churchill's question was a bit like asking the British, after the fall of France in 1940, if they believed there was now a greater likelihood of an invasion of Britain. That would seem a naive question to have asked. From an Australian perspective at that time and in those circumstances did Winston Churchill's question to John Curtin seem any less naive?

The Australian War Cabinet had been receiving a steady diet of terrible war news since 8 December 1941, as expectations and pre-war certainties collapsed before the seemingly unstoppable Japanese advance. By late January 1942 John Curtin believed that one of his most important responsibilities was to prepare the Australian people for the possibility of invasion. Australia lacked a highly trained and fully equipped army at home, and the means to move such an army through the vast interior; Australia lacked an air force able to harass an invading force, and a navy able to repel an invading army. This was an extraordinary situation for any government to face, and to speak of an atmosphere of panic in the government or among the people is to run the risk of forgetting or minimising the danger that confronted Australia. Was it panic or a concerned realism? It is not panic but prudence that suggests to a people that they might need to arm themselves as guerrilla bands to offer resistance to the enemy. It is not panic for governments, federal and state, to draw up plans for a scorched earth policy to be implemented should an invasion occur. For people understood, even before the expression gained currency in Australia in the 1960s, that it would be the 'tyranny of distance' that would be the strongest element in the defence of Australia.

Those historians who now say that no invasion was ever seriously contemplated by the Japanese base their arguments in part on the sheer difficulty that an invasion of Australia would entail. There is no doubt that the Japanese could have landed troops on Australian soil in early 1942. But the question that then immediately arises is how would the Japanese feed and supply these troops, re-equip them, move them around the vast tract of land that is Australia, provide them with the ammunition that they would need to continue warfare against Australians. Part of the answer would lie, of course, in the capacity of a Japanese invasion force to live off the land. Therefore it was only prudent that Australian governments would draw up plans to deny the Japanese what they might need. So the governments, federal and state, made plans to destroy foodstuffs and fuel supplies, to disable trucks, buses, railways and any other means of transport, even to move livestock from coastal Australia to the inland. Of course some of these plans, in hindsight, sound somewhat hysterical and exaggerated, but at the time they could easily appear to be prudent and logical.

Too many Australians were probably wasting too much time in digging air-raid shelters in the backyards of suburban homes, but in the major cities air-raid precautions were logical and necessary. Certainly the Japanese did have a limited capacity to overfly Australian cities, not just Broome and Darwin, but also Sydney and Melbourne, and they most certainly did. Was it prudent to leave all lights blazing, plate-glass windows unprepared, buildings unprotected? Even without an invasion force the Japanese had the capacity to cause a great deal of disruption and turmoil to significant elements of the Australian population. What answer should John Curtin have given Winston Churchill when the British prime minister had asked about the possibility of the enemy landing some troops on Australian soil? A breezy, 'She'll be right, mate?'

Before John Curtin had much opportunity to respond to Churchill's inquiry he was involved in a much more testing cable exchange with his British counterpart. It had become apparent, with the 7th Division hastily embarked from the Middle East, that its field of service would now not be Malaya, for Malaya had already been lost. Wavell's plan was that the 7th Division should bolster the defence of Sumatra and that the 6th Division would be placed in central Java, but continued reverses made these plans impractical. By mid-February Winston Churchill was looking at the Australians being diverted to Burma, which was, for the Japanese, a pathway to India. If Burma were to be lost to the Allies then the Japanese believed that they would be in a position to threaten British rule in India, the 'jewel in the crown'. With British prestige in tatters, the Empire itself might be at risk of disintegration. The Japanese had already taken parts of southern Burma to prevent airfields there being used by the Allies for the defence of Malaya. So on 14 December 1941 Japanese forces had occupied Victoria Point and its airfield, which, though in Burma, was closer to the equator than Bangkok. The battle for Burma had begun, or to put it another way, another British fighting withdrawal, this time to India, had commenced. The British would finally be pushed out of Burma by the end of May 1942.

With Singapore lost John Curtin was now focusing on gaining agreement, in London and Washington, for the idea that Australia must now be seen as the main base for the counterattack against the Japanese that would eventually take place. In Curtin's mind Australia had taken on strategic significance. As an Australian, and as his nation's leader, Curtin's first thoughts must always have been for the safety and security of his country, but he believed that he had a stronger reason to interest his great alliance co-leaders in the defence of Australia. Australia, he could explain to them, must remain inviolate in the interests of the greater strategy of the Pacific War. Australia would be the base from which the fight-back would begin. It must be said that Curtin would struggle to win over either Churchill or Roosevelt to his view of the strategic importance of his country. Frankly they did not believe Australia to be at great risk of substantial invasion and they tended to dismiss Curtin as something of a 'nervous Nellie'.

Vernon Sturdee, the chief of the general staff, produced an appreciation of the Australian military situation for John Curtin coincidentally on 15 February, the day that Singapore fell, so that it would have been impossible for the prime minister not to have read Sturdee's paper except in the light of the staggering events at Singapore. Sturdee fully supported the idea that Australia must be the main base of Allied operations in the Pacific and in Asia, and he was not at all confident of the possibility of retaining the ring around Australia to the north, at Java, Timor or even in Papua New Guinea. Sturdee also advised Curtin that it would take many months to bring the militia to the peak of readiness in terms of the training and equipment that would be needed to then see the militia as the main force in the defence of Australia. Yet Australia did have a highly trained and relatively well-equipped force at its disposal: the AIF. The return from overseas of 100 000 trained and war-experienced troops, with their equipment, would immeasurably improve the prospects for the defence of Australia, Sturdee argued. It would more than double the present security of the country, he wrote. Some said that Sturdee was prepared to resign if the government would not agree to the return of the AIF.

What role should logic and rationality play in warfare, and how do leaders determine what weight is given to competing interests? Australia's most senior non-operational soldier had advised his prime minister of what he thought was in Australia's best interests. Simply put, Sturdee's message to Curtin was: bring home the AIF, you really have no alternative. But Australia's prime minister had to make judgements based not only on rational military thinking but also on the alliance requirements of his Allied partners. Curtin might suggest to Winston Churchill the return of the AIF to Australia in its hour of greatest need, but he would know that Churchill would have to consider that request in the light of the wider world war that the Allies were fighting. Churchill needed to consider the situation in the North African desert, the problem of Burma, not to mention the war in Europe and so many other matters besides.

Of course Australia could insist on its troops coming home—we sent our troops to help you when we ourselves were not at war at home or at grave risk of invasion, Curtin might have said, but now the situation has changed we must have our troops home. But the AIF, mightily as Australians esteemed their soldiers, was too few in number alone to defeat the Japanese at home or to halt Rommel in the desert. Australia needed the assistance, friendship and support of the Americans, primarily, as Curtin had been quick to note, and the British. Small partners in grand alliances have a very difficult path to follow and Curtin was now required to weigh very carefully the risk of antagonising his alliance partners against the need to secure Australia in the eyes of all Australians. Yet what Australian prime minister could watch the invasion of even a part of his country, knowing, and his people knowing, that the nation's best and most experienced troops were thousands of miles away fighting another war? Vernon Sturdee's paper had immediately made the prime minister's life a great deal more complicated. Two days after reading it Curtin was in his hospital bed. Who would be surprised?

Curtin had cabled Churchill on 15 February and again on 17 February, stressing the importance of retaining Australia as the main base for allied activities and requesting the diversion of the 6th and 7th divisions to Australia and the return of the 9th. These cables should be read in the knowledge, which Curtin now had, that the entire 8th Division had been lost to Australia. Curtin's own envoys in London, Earle Page and Stanley Bruce, were the first to reply to his cables, softening up the prime minister, perhaps, for Churchill's knockout blow. The various British councils and cabinets have looked at your proposals, Page told Curtin, and they have also looked at the wider strategic implications, as they must. India and China are crucial in containing and engaging the Japanese, and Burma remains absolutely central to the security of both. The 7th Division, Page continued, is the only body of trained and experienced troops able to reach Rangoon soon enough to make a difference. You are going to be asked to allow the division to go to Rangoon, Page wrote, and he strongly recommended that the Australian government agree to the proposal. Bruce, the high commissioner, supported Page. Clearly the view from London was very different to the view from Australia.

On 14 February Bob Menzies wrote to John Curtin about the grave decisions that confronted the prime minister. Menzies knew all about the pressure that could be exerted on a small ally when the bigger power wanted its own way. Greece had been the undoing of the Menzies' prime ministership and yet Bob Menzies, almost a year later, might still have pondered how he had ever allowed himself to be pushed into supporting the Greek campaign. Even as he had been agonising over his decision, asking for more time, cabling his own government at home, even while all this was taking place Churchill had given instructions that the Australians be embarked for Greece—in advance of Menzies' approval. 'He'll come to his senses', Churchill had thought, and Menzies, of course, had, from Churchill's perspective. Now Menzies was warning Curtin that the place for Australia's troops was in Australia; keep them out of the Netherlands East Indies, Menzies was saying, although at the same time recognise the importance of adequate reinforcements for Burma. Perhaps Menzies might have taken Curtin through the steps in detail, from his perspective, of how the Australians came to be in Greece. 'Don't trust him', he might have warned Curtin of Churchill. But probably Menzies could not take a step that far.

The Advisory War Council meetings in Sydney on 18 and 19 February considered the issue that was now central to the government's understanding of the defence of Australia, the return of the 6th and 7th divisions. The non-government members on the council agreed among themselves that the government should accede to the British request to send the 7th Division to Burma, but at a War Cabinet meeting on the same day, the government stuck to its guns. At the War Council meeting the tension had been high. Percy Spender recalled that 'one minister—Beasley—got stuck into me, to use an Australian idiom.' Non-government members spoke of what the reaction in America would be if Burma was lost and the capacity of the Chinese to hurt the Japanese if they could be supplied through Burma. Government ministers on the council spoke of the importance the Australian people placed on having their own troops back home and of the effect on morale. The fact that the meeting caused raised voices and long and passionate argument shows just how complex this decision was and how conflicted it was. This was not normal political argument— I oppose because you propose—this was about the best way of defending Australia in alliance terms and there was no easy answer. In the midst of the meeting, Spender recalled, Beasley, minister for Supply and Development, left the room. He returned in a very agitated state. 'The Japs have bombed Darwin,' he told the meeting. 'That settles it.'

Up to a point, that is. The government recalled parliament for a 'secret session'—no 'strangers' present, no Hansard record kept—on 20 February and showed no sign that it would change its mind about the 7th Division, despite Earle Page from London continuing to urge the British line. Indeed in Page's next cable he told Curtin that Churchill would undertake to have the Americans send more troops to Australia—a division had already been promised—if Curtin would agree to the 7th going to Burma. It was the only available division, Churchill cabled Curtin, and the Australians alone could prevent the loss of Rangoon. Unknown to Curtin as he read these last urgent cables from Churchill and

Roosevelt, Churchill had already instructed the Admiralty to turn the troopships carrying the Australians north to Rangoon. He'll see sense, Churchill no doubt thought of Curtin, just as he had anticipated that Bob Menzies would see sense over Greece. They bluster a bit these Australians, those in London might have been thinking, but they'll eventually do as they are told. Though Churchill had cabled Curtin again, ten minutes after he had diverted the convoy to Rangoon, he did not think it necessary to let Curtin know that.

When the Australian War Cabinet met again on Saturday 21 February, members learned that the Japanese were only 40 miles from Rangoon. As a last-ditch effort for the defence of Singapore the Australian government had sent 1800 reinforcements, men who went immediately into captivity with the rest of the 8th Division. Men wasted. Just a few weeks later the Australian War Cabinet wondered whether they should allow another Australian division to be swallowed up in a campaign in Burma that was probably already lost? Yet was there sense in Australia standing up to the Americans, standing up to the British? This was as tough a problem as an Australian government had ever grappled with. The meeting went on and on, around and around the issue. Eventually, in the early hours of 22 February, Curtin sent what he thought would be his last telegram to Churchill on the subject: the government could see no reason to change its mind, 'our wishes in regard to the disposition of the AIF in the Pacific theatre have long been known to you'. That was the essence of Curtin's message, contained in its opening lines, yet it was a long cable, over 700 words, and tightly argued. It needed to be. It was probably one of the most important messages ever sent by an Australian prime minister. There were some matters, it said in effect, that only Australians were competent to judge.

There is a sense of relief and release when a tough decision is eventually made. A sense of wellbeing. So the return cable from London, after the Australian decision, could not, surely, be asking for further reconsideration. Indeed so. And the cable sent from London on the afternoon of 22 February contained some surprising news. The convoy was not where Curtin had thought it would be because Churchill had already diverted it to Rangoon. So would

John Curtin please reconsider his decision because some of the ships in the convoy could not now reach Australia without refuelling. In all the circumstances, wouldn't it just be so much easier if the Australians kept on sailing straight for Rangoon? Curtin recognised now that Churchill had been treating him as a rubber stamp, as he had treated Menzies over Greece, and Curtin let Churchill know, but in the language of diplomacy, that he was not best pleased. He informed Churchill that the unilateral decision of diverting the troops to Rangoon, which now forced the convoy to return to Colombo for refuelling, had simply placed the convoy at greater risk. It would, though, still most certainly be coming to Australia.

For the troops on board the troopships those few days must have been bizarre. Soldiers complain that they are never told anything and they would have been keenly discussing and gossiping about their likely destination from the moment they boarded the troopships. Dramatic changes of course might be expected to baffle any possible submarines but the ships were making entirely fundamental alterations to the route. 'I told you we are on our way home, or to the East Indies.' 'No, looks like we are headed north.' 'Hang on, we're headed back where we came from.' 'What on earth is going on; what is happening to this war?'

There is no doubt that John Curtin felt deeply the stress of these momentous decisions. Indeed, these were probably the worst days of his prime ministership. He had argued painfully with Winston Churchill, earlier over naval and military reinforcements for Singapore, then for the return of these two Australian divisions when Churchill most strongly believed that the Allied interests would be best served by striving to retain Burma. At the height of this controversy, and possibly ever thereafter, Churchill treated Curtin with near contempt. The decision to relieve the Australians at Tobruk had incensed the British prime minister. Not to mince words, Churchill thought the Australian action cowardly. So to stand up to Churchill again meant that Curtin risked alienating a world power closer to his own country than even the closest ally. Curtin received strong support from his Australian military leadership, but if things had turned out differently the large and catastrophic loss of the returning Australian soldiers might have been placed squarely on his shoulders. Suppose Japanese submarines had found the troopship convoy in the Indian Ocean as it was on its unguarded way back to Australia. Imagine the loss of life. Imagine the frenzy in Australia. And what were they doing out there unprotected? Why had John Curtin insisted on their return against all the weight of argument from London and Washington? The trashing of the one enduring Australian myth, the Anzac legend, might have been sheeted home solely to John Curtin. It was not the Australian way to cut and run, his critics would have been quick to point out.

But there was more to it even that that. In this decision-making we can see John Curtin experiencing the loneliness of command, but in it too we can witness how fragile was the mask of command as Curtin faced the fear of the possible loss of the convoy. Leaders must not look as if leadership worries them. Nor can they allow their emotions to interfere with what they must do. But John Curtin was not like that. He worried, deeply, for the lives of the men who were being pushed about, to and fro, at sea. They had told his neighbour in Canberra, Frank Green, clerk of the House of Representatives, that Curtin was not sleeping, so one night Green went over to the Lodge to see if he could do anything to help. He found the prime minister alone, pacing the gardens after midnight. Curtin confessed that he could not sleep. 'How can I sleep,' he asked Green, 'when I know that our men are out there on transports on the Indian Ocean, with all those Japanese submarines looking for them'. The parents, the wives and the friends of these Australians of the 7th Division might well have been worried too if they had known where their sons and husbands were. But they slept soundly in their beds, not knowing. John Curtin knew and he worried for all of them.

In all the gloom and bad news of early 1942, there was some good news. The first Americans to reach Australia arrived in Brisbane on 22 December 1941. There were 4600 of them and they quickly dispersed—1300 to Darwin, 1500 to Townsville and 700 to the Netherlands East Indies—leaving 1100 in Brisbane. Americans would be a permanent and influential presence in that city for the remaining years of the war and would make a big impact, too, on many other parts of Australia. The pace of the build-up of American troops amazed Australians so unused to big-scale activity, and they watched goggle-eyed as huge American camps were erected in just a few weeks to house thousands of soldiers. By June 1942 there were 88 000 Americans stationed in Australia, by early 1943 there were 250 000.

At first the arrival of the Americans was a giant secret that only those who saw it knew. A person I once talked to recalled that she, her brother and their mother lived together in a house on Dandenong Road, East St Kilda, a little to the south of the city of Melbourne. Their father was away at war, it was early 1942, and there were terrors and anxieties everywhere. Children like these were unsettled by the war, though their mother did her best. With blackout screens securely in place, and thus locked in from the outside world, the family was about to go to bed one night in January 1942 when they heard the steady tramp of thousands of feet outside. These were not Australian soldiers marching outside on their road, the children knew that; Australian boots had a harsh metallic sound. Were they Japanese? British or American? Who could say? But the children and their mother would not open the door and go outside to look, that might be too dangerous. So they went to bed, the mother and her youngsters, not knowing what the morning would bring. Not knowing if the Japanese had already landed in Melbourne.

They were American soldiers making their way to camp at the Caulfield racecourse, marching along Dandenong Road to get there. The story of this one family's fear and anxiety has the ring of authenticity. Yet when this family, and perhaps many others also along the route of the American march, looked in their newspaper the next morning to find out what was going on they discovered that absolutely nothing was reported about arriving and marching troops. No news at all. But huge camps sprang up in the parklands of Melbourne and Brisbane; at racecourses and sports grounds. Even the famous Melbourne Cricket Ground became an American camp. The American uniform became just as common on city streets as the Australian uniform. Yet, although there were Americans everywhere, the papers made no mention of this; they could not tell people what was taking place before their very eyes.

At last we can tell you, the papers announced with some relief on 19 March 1942: 'It is gratifying to be able to announce', John Curtin said, 'that there are very substantial American forces in Australia ... We will not be left quite alone ... The Australian government extends the warmest greetings to the American forces'. But, of course, people in the cities had already done the government's work of welcome. When an American naval squadron had briefly visited Sydney in March 1941 an estimated 500 000 people had lined the city streets to cheer them on. In the dark days of January and February 1942 how might Australians have celebrated the arrival of the Americans if circumstances had allowed it? But what was missed with ceremonial entries to the cities and grand parades on a lavish scale, the people made up for in the intensity of their personal welcome. In truth, Australia had a one-eyed view of America. Australians did not read American books—an imperial publishing agreement saw to that—and with no direct air link between Australia and the United States, few Australians read American newspapers and magazines. News of America came to Australians through British eyes. American novels came to Australia in British editions. The one view that Australians had of Americans that was near-instant and unfiltered was what came to them via the movie screens, the 'pictures' as people called them then. Australians watched movies in staggering numbers; in one year alone before the war there were 68 million admissions to the cinemas of Australia against 16 million admissions to sports grounds and racecourses. This from a population of just seven million people. What does he know of America, who knows the movies only?

Australians tended to idolise Americans as if every single one of them was a screen star, making for a welcome in the dark days on 1942 that was warm, generous and slightly unbalanced. People competed with one another to invite a 'Yank' home for a meal and women's magazines helpfully published recipes that would ensure the Americans felt right at home. So people were apparently struggling to make fish chowder, breaded veal cutlets, shoestring potatoes, parsnip fluff, browned tomato sauce and butterscotch ice-cream cake. It all sounded exotic and romantic, and did provide a bit of life and fun just as the war seemed at its most dangerous. Cinemas adopted the practice of playing both the

British national anthem and the American anthem at the beginning of screenings—the British 'God Save the King' was the Australian anthem as well. American flags were seen everywhere in the streets. It was easy already to see these men as the saviours of Australia. Glamorous, idolised, attractive in their uniforms where the Australian uniform now seemed so drab, there was a real danger that the achievements of the Australians would now be overlooked after two years of hard fighting so far from home.

Yet there was even greater excitement than the arrival of the American forces in store. 'The President of the United States ordered me to break through the Japanese lines,' said American General Douglas MacArthur, 'and proceed from Corregidor to Australia for the purpose, as I understand, of organising an American offensive against Japan, the primary purpose of which is the relief of the Philippines. I came through, and I shall return.' Where was this tall, immacutely groomed and handsome American general delivering these powerful and inspiring words? In the House of Representatives chamber in Canberra, perhaps; at a state banquet, possibly; or on the steps of Melbourne's Town Hall before a mighty and cheering crowd with a beaming John Curtin looking on? No—MacArthur had been tortuously making his way from Darwin to Adelaide, overland first to Alice Springs, then by train for the rest of the journey. Learning more about the vastness of the country and the poverty of its transport system, impatiently learning in all likelihood. MacArthur's train had stopped at Terowie, a small railway junction 200 kilometres north of Adelaide, where there was a small number of reporters on hand to interview the arriving general, and so he spoke to them. But not as a bloke standing in the dust of a small railway town. In his own mind's eye he was a man of destiny, personally sent by his president to rescue these poor people from an evil enemy. It is an incongruous scene, the general and the reporters in a town of a couple of hundred people, but MacArthur would seize any moment, any opportunity, for the grand, dramatic gesture. This man was a born showman, and if you had just suffered a belting in the Philippines, as MacArthur had, and if you had just left your troops to misery, as MacArthur had, well then, why not present yourself as on special orders from the president to win the war, and 'break through' the Japanese lines to do so.

John Curtin had no knowledge of Roosevelt's decision to send Douglas MacArthur to Australia before the general had actually arrived at Darwin. But he welcomed the news 'enthusiastically' when the then American commander Lieutenant General George Brett telephoned Curtin to let him know the president's wishes. It was quickly agreed, as Roosevelt wanted it, that Douglas MacArthur would be the Supreme Commander of the South-West Pacific Area.

MacArthur had arrived in Australia on 17 March 1942, a day the war changed profoundly for Australians. The Australian War Cabinet declared that MacArthur's leadership of the Allied forces in the area would be an inspiration to the Australian people and all the forces privileged to serve under his command. Everyone, it seemed, agreed on the significance of what the president's gift to Australia would mean. Douglas MacArthur was 62 years of age when he reached Australia, having been born on 26 January 1880—a happy augury for Australians, his birthday was their national day. MacArthur's father was a famous general and the third son seemed destined for the army from infancy. Douglas MacArthur had served in the First World War, leading troops into battle in France in the August offensives of 1918. He had then been long associated with the Philippines, first serving there in 1922, and retiring from the United States Army in 1937 to become a field marshal in the Philippines army. In 1941 MacArthur was recalled to the United States Army as a major general, later general, in charge of American and local forces in the Philippines. There had been criticisms of his conduct of the fighting in the Philippines from December 1941 on, especially for allowing his air forces to be caught on the ground by Japanese bombers.

Arriving in Melbourne on 21 March 1942, MacArthur received a hero's welcome. Indeed, he attracted the adulation in the newspapers and magazines more commonly reserved for visiting American pop stars in the 1950s and 1960s. MacArthur established his headquarters first in Melbourne, later in Brisbane, and every detail of his household arrangements attracted attention. His young wife and his four-year-old son, Arthur, with the Chinese nursemaid were constantly photographed, as was the general himself. MacArthur's words carried more weight than

Anzac Day 1930, Sydney. The returned men in the foreground; family and friends to the rear. (Hood Collection, State Library of New South Wales)

Throughout Australia, in the interwar years, almost every town and suburb dedicated a war memorial to the dead of the Great War. This ceremony takes place in Wellington, New South Wales, 1933. Some of the children in the crowd will, no doubt, fight in the next war. (Hood Collection, State Library of New South Wales)

A new recruit for the AIF receives his regimental number. The lower the number, state by state, the earlier the man had enlisted. So these numbers counted. (Australian War Memorial Negative Number 058841)

Volunteers moving to Ingleburn, New South Wales, November 1939. These were the men clamouring at the barracks gates when Bob Menzies announced war in September. (Hood Collection, State Library of New South Wales)

Recruits on their first day in camp, Melbourne Showgrounds, November 1939. (Australian War Memorial Negative Number 000177)

Training troops at Ingleburn, New South Wales, November 1939. (Hood Collection, State Library of New South Wales)

Troops resting during a meal break at Cootamundra, New South Wales. (Bicentennial Copying Collection, State Library of New South Wales)

Troops leaving Melbourne, August 1940; a photograph taken by the farewelling prime minister, Bob Menzies. (Australian War Memorial Negative Number 007445)

Departure of the 6th Australian Division, 9–10 January 1940. (Hood Collection, State Library of New South Wales)

Airmen leaving Sydney for training in the Empire Air Training Scheme, February 1941.
(Hood Collection, State Library of New South Wales)

Four members of the Royal Australian Air Force. (Hood Collection, State Library of New
South Wales)

Spruiking for business but Australia was really awash with war news, August 1940. (Hood Collection, State Library of New South Wales)

Petrol quickly became a scarce commodity in wartime Australia and this harvest is made possible with a gas-converted tractor, Parkes district, New South Wales. (Bicentennial Copying Collection, State Library of New South Wales)

Heavily camouflaged ambulance with the 56th Battalion at Cootamundra, New South Wales. (Bicentennial Copying Collection, State Library of New South Wales)

Albert Moore, Salvation Army welfare officer, about to leave for the war pictured with his wife, Violet and son, Kelvin. Albert Moore found the pain of departure almost too hard to bear. (Australian War Memorial Negative Number P000525.010)

About to begin digging air raid trenches at the public school, Cootamundra, New South Wales. (Bicentennial Copying Collection, State Library of New South Wales)

Tom Blamey and Bob Menzies reviewing troops in the desert. Menzies found it hard, realising that some of these men would never see their homes again. (Australian War Memorial Negative Number 005736)

Men of the 2/13th Battalion on patrol at Tobruk, September 1941. (Australian War Memorial Negative Number 020783)

Exhausted men returning to Alexandria after the fighting in Greece, June 1941. (Australian War Memorial Negative Number 007789)

Sailor from HMAS *Perth* being farewelled by his family. (Australian War Memorial Negative Number 001223)

A prime ministerial inspection of the crew of *Perth*, Alexandria, February 1941. *Perth* would be sunk in the Sunda Strait in March 1942; of its crew of 686 personnel only 218 would eventually return to Australia. (Australian War Memorial Negative Number 005773)

The patient does not appear to be enjoying the attention from his nation's prime minister and most senior soldier, February 1941. (Australian War Memorial Negative Number 005732)

1941—the year of three prime ministers (L-R) John Curtin, Arthur Fadden and Bob Menzies. (Australian War Memorial Negative Number 042826)

'Mr Prime Minister, we two, you and me will see this thing through together.' Douglas MacArthur, John Curtin and Tom Blamey in Canberra, March 1942. (Australian War Memorial Negative Number 042766)

Bernard Montgomery (and the famous slouch hat) with Leslie Morshead in the desert, August 1942. (Australian War Memorial Negative Number 041981)

Men of D Company 39th Battalion returning to Isurava at the beginning of the Kokoda Track; one of these men is a Gallipoli veteran. (Australian War Memorial Negative Number 013288)

Wounded in the attack on Shaggy Ridge, December 1943. (Australian War Memorial Negative Number 062293)

Men of the 2/48th Battalion at dawn, about to attack Japanese positions at Sattelberg. (Australian War Memorial Negative Number 016205)

Australians on their way to Buna, December 1942, wished good luck by their commander, Tom Blamey. (Australian War Memorial Negative Number 013819)

An Australian pilot and his Spitfire, November 1943. (Australian War Memorial Negative Number 060732)

John Curtin lands in England on his only prime ministerial visit, no doubt much
relieved to be back on the ground; Curtin had a morbid fear of flying.
(Australian War Memorial Negative Number SUK12095)

John Curtin visits No. 467 (Lancaster) Squadron, RAAF, at RAF Waddington in Lincolnshire, May
1944. (Australian War Memorial Negative Number SUK12192)

'Back the Attack', Sydney, 1943. (Hood Collection, State Library of New South Wales)

Win the War Week, Martin Place, Sydney, October 1940; there was a job for everyone. (Hood Collection, State Library of New South Wales)

Take Buna, MacArthur had
told General Robert
Eichelberger 'or do not
come back alive'. Behind
him, left, is the Australian
commander Tom Blamey.
(Australian War Memorial
Negative Number 014101)

Tom Blamey giving a press conference, September 1943. (Australian War Memorial Negative
Number 056893)

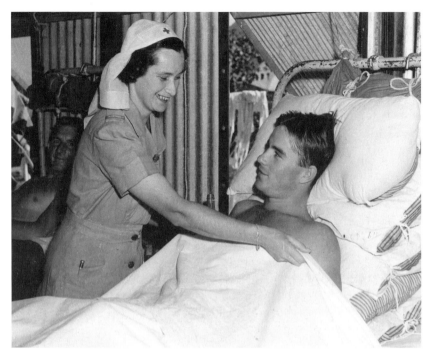

The nurse is from Hamilton, Victoria, and the soldier is from Petersham, Sydney; the hospital is in Darwin. (Hood Collection, State Library of New South Wales)

A Matilda tank leading Australian troops forward in the Finschhafen area, New Guinea, 1943. (Hood Collection, State Library of New South Wales)

Australian troops dug in at Gona. (Hood Collection, State Library of New South Wales)

In the Markham Valley, New Guinea, 1943. (Hood Collection, State Library of New South Wales)

'Diver' Derrick hoists the Australian flag at Sattelberg to claim the victory there; 3 December 1943. (Australian War Memorial Negative Number 016246)

A Japanese surrender, Cape Wom airstrip, New Guinea, 13 September 1945. (Australian War Memorial Negative Number 096234)

those of any person in Australia, John Curtin possibly excepted. Military historian David Horner wrote that 'few figures who have spent less than three years in this country have had such an impact on Australian life'. But his air commander, George Brett, described MacArthur as 'a brilliant, temperamental egotist; a handsome man, who can be as charming as anyone who ever lived, or harshly indifferent to the needs and desires of those around him. Everything about MacArthur was on a grand scale—his virtues and triumphs and shortcomings'. The war, MacArthur even then thought, might well prove to be a stepping stone to his great ambition—the presidency of the United States.

They were so important for each other, John Curtin and Douglas MacArthur. MacArthur gave Curtin credibility, an aura of authority, and made him appear to be a leader of equal ranking with MacArthur, now on a world stage. Every time a photograph appeared of the two of them in conference or in earnest conversation, Curtin was the beneficiary. What did Curtin give MacArthur? The American general desperately craved the world stage. He would have preferred to be in conference or conversation with Winston Churchill but that was never to happen, and in any case Churchill did not make public heroes of his generals, believing that the focus should always be on himself. Curtin gave MacArthur credibility; the prime minister might not be a real world leader, MacArthur might have thought, but he is the prime minister and I am his Commander-in-Chief. Together we will work mighty hard to keep some of the world's attention focused on the war against Japan, even if my president has bought Winston's 'beat Hitler first' line. And my prime minister is a mighty fighter for his country's interests and that will suit me. He can fire the bullets for sufficient resources and focus for my war; he and I together will ensure that our war will not be forgotten.

In agreeing to MacArthur being appointed supreme commander of the South-West Pacific Area with authority over all Allied, naval, land and air forces and placing the Australian forces under his command, the Australian government had surrendered 'a large measure of sovereignty'. But in reality the government had no alternative. Turn down President Roosevelt's offer? It was impossible. And the general had such a way with words, such an instinct for the most appropriate image that he would inspire Australians. Curtin had already touched their hearts with his courage, his humanity and his determination. MacArthur now would enthuse them, give them confidence, make them believe that the war, until now simply one defeat or reverse after another, could indeed be won.

MacArthur met John Curtin for the first time at Parliament House in Canberra. Welcomed on the steps of parliament by Deputy Prime Minister Frank Forde, who had also greeted the general in Melbourne and was already a warm admirer, MacArthur met Curtin in private, in the prime minister's office. After a brief conversation the general put his hand on Curtin's shoulder: 'Mr Prime Minister,' he said, 'we two, you and me, will see this thing through together'. It was a pact between them, perfectly orchestrated by the general, equal partners, though the general had seized the initiative and had shaped the words of the compact. At least now there were two sets of shoulders to take the burden of Australia at war. After this meeting with Douglas MacArthur, John Curtin might have felt just a little more at ease. Curtin might still pace the gardens of the Lodge at midnight with the worries of the war almost too heavy to bear, but at least, now, he could look another man in the face knowing that those worries were his problem too. The crisis had not passed, indeed there were long years ahead of them, but the first steps towards victory had been taken.

14. THEIR
FINEST
HOUR

Admiral Chester Nimitz, Commander-in-Chief Pacific Ocean areas, was not widely known to Australians during the Second World War, or after for that matter, but he deserved to be. Perhaps because his early career in the United States Navy was as a submariner, Nimitz might be classified as aggressive, certainly, but also silent and moving with some stealth. Chester Nimitz was a man of method and good sense, without theatrics— the exact opposite of his partner in command in the Pacific War, Douglas MacArthur. On 30 March 1942 the United States joint chiefs of staff had divided the Pacific War into two areas of responsibility. Nimitz received the Pacific Ocean zone, MacArthur the South-West Pacific area. Each man had ultimate responsibility for the air, land and naval forces under his command, but to this Nimitz added, more successfully than almost any other supreme commander, a fourth dimension—intelligence. Controlling his forces quietly from his headquarters in Hawaii, Nimitz listened closely and carefully to what Ultra—the generic name for enemy coded messages read since early in the war by the Allies—was telling him.

Nimitz used Ultra with great effect from the moment he assumed his command; and it would give him immediate results. Even so, as Chester Nimitz was taking command the Japanese continued to sweep all before them. By 20 February 1942 they had captured Timor and Bali; in the Battle of the Java Sea at the end of February, during six days of running battles, the Australians lost *Perth* and the Americans lost *Houston*. Survivors from both ships would swell the growing ranks of Japan's prisoners of war. A few days later the Australians lost *Yarra*, also in the Java Sea. On 7 March the Japanese occupied Rangoon, and might have swallowed up the entire 7th Australian Division, but for John Curtin's earlier intervention. On the same day the Japanese took the official Dutch surrender of Java, with more than 100 000 Allied troops entering captivity. At the same time Japanese forces started landing in New Guinea at Lae and Salamaua. On 9 April the Americans surrendered on the Philippines and on 4 May five Japanese invasion groups left their stronghold at Rabaul for assaults on several targets, including Port Moresby. The war map at home in Australia, on the kitchen or bedroom wall, was a sorry looking document indeed by early May 1942. The only question in any schoolboy's mind, as he shuffled the flags around the Australian region, was where next would the Japanese triumph.

He might have placed a flag on Sydney Harbour itself, an attractive target given the amount of Allied shipping at anchor there. If the Japanese could not invade Australia at least they could raise the crisis mentality among Australians to dangerous levels by an attack in the harbour itself, and do significant damage to Allied warships at the same time. The thirty-first of May 1942 was a Sunday, and a dark and overcast night in Sydney. The naval officer in charge at Sydney, Rear-Admiral Gerald Muirhead-Gould RN, knew that two Japanese seaplanes had already overflown Sydney, launched from submarinesand surely looking for something. Yet Muirhead-Gould took no special precautions that Sunday. Unknown to him, five large Japanese submarines were already in place off Sydney, three of them equipped with a 'midget' submarine resting on each deck; small, indeed, but certainly not made for the bathtub as the word 'midget' might imply. Each midget carried two crew, and the host submarine carried more than 100. That was the scale of the thing. In reality the midget was seen as a disposable means of delivering an attack, although it carried only two torpedoes. The control room of the midget was a mere two metres in diameter, and the submarine itself was unstable and difficult to control.

Shortly after sunset, and just a few miles east of the entrance to the harbour, the three midgets began their perilous journey. Sydney Harbour was protected by two nets designed to prevent such attacks as the Japanese were now attempting. The first midget, by navigational mistake, was caught in the second net at about 8.15 p.m.; observed by an alert watchman, James Cargill, he struggled for a couple of hours to have the navy take his observation seriously. At 10.35 p.m. the Japanese crew, firmly caught in the net and realising that there was no way out of their predicament, fired a demolition charge, destroying themselves and their submarine.

By now the harbour was aware of the danger and there was plenty of activity—searchlights and sirens, depth charges explosions and the rattle of machine-gun fire. Governor-Generl Lord Gowrie and his wife had a good view from their harbourside home, Admiralty House, and Lord Gowrie later reported to the King: 'small craft buzzing about dropping depth charges and searchlights moving all over the surface of the water'. The second midget apporached its target, USS *Chicago* near Garden Island. It released its two torpedoes, but one failed to explode and the other went under the ship and crashed into the sea wall exploding and destroying the former Sydney ferry, Kuttabul, which was being used as a naval depot ship, killing 19 Australian sailors. The navy hero, Teddy Sheean, might have been one of them, as we have seen, but he was on leave in Tasmania. The successful submarine evaded capture and its fate has never been satisfactorily accounted for. The third submarine was attacked and destroyed, and the bodies of its two crew were recovered and eventually given an appropriate military funeral. While Lord Gowrie wrote the episode up in a light-hearted fashion—the

King had endured very much worse in London, of course—Australians in general felt that the war had come just that much closer. Even so, after the Battle of the Coral Sea they were, in fact, breathing much more easily.

Australians still look to the Battle of the Coral Sea as a turning point in the Pacific War and continue to celebrate 'Coral Sea Week', although with less fervour today than in the 1950s and 1960s. But the celebration seems to miss the point of that engagement. True, the Battle of the Coral Sea stands in military history as the first naval battle in which the opposing ships did not even sight one another—aircraft now predominating—but the real point of the battle was that it gave the Americans necessary combat experience for the much more important Battle of Midway. Certainly on 8 May 1942 American and Australian naval forces in the Coral Sea were able to turn back the Japanese invasion force that had left Rabaul a few days earlier, but with little cost to the Japanese and with the loss to the Americans of the aircraft carrier *Lexington*. The crucial Allied naval victory, in fact, was at Midway, nearly a month later.

Chester Nimitz had studied the Ultra material carefully and had set his battle orders accordingly. The Japanese admiral, Yamamoto, designed Midway as a trap for the Americans, which he expected would see the destruction of much of their entire Pacific naval force. Had Yamamoto succeeded, Hawaii would have been left open to him, with unimaginable consequences for the Pacific War. In the manner of a feint, Yamamoto first sent part of his fleet to the northern Pacific, expecting some of the American ships to follow him. It was here that Nimitz's faith in Ultra proved crucial. Instead of dividing his force, Nimitz was out in strength at Midway, with three aircraft carriers, 233 aircraft, and an escort that included seven heavy cruisers. The Japanese were unaware that the American cruisers were in the region and, although American aircraft were despatched to the limit of their flying range, involving them in severe losses, the American airmen nevertheless caught the Japanese initially by surprise. Their persistence and bravery resulted in the loss of the three Japanese carriers. Cleverly, the Americans withdrew before the Japanese main force could inflict heavy losses in return. Midway tipped the balance of seapower in favour of the Allies, a balance that, in the days before Singapore and the American entry into the war, had heavily favoured the Japanese over the British.

Australians did not take to the streets to celebrate the Battle of Midway, as they might have if they could have read the strategic significance of the battle. But Midway played a major role in determining the next use of Australian military forces, the bulk of which had not been engaged in any fighting since Syria and the North African desert. For, thwarted at the Coral Sea instead of landing troops at Port Moresby to ensure the complete subjugation of Papua and New Guinea, with a view to further isolating Australia, the Japanese were now certainly looking for another way of achieving the same result. No one on the Allied side envisaged an overland assault on Port Moresby because it was assumed that the mighty Owen Stanley Range was impassable. Indeed Major General Basil Morris's forces—they had been at Port Moresby for almost a year now—had never really ventured much beyond the town of Port Moresby itself, believing it to be locked in by the mountains. Yet on 21 July 1942—a month and a half after Midway—General Horii's 18th Japanese Army, the South Seas Force, landed near Buna on the north coast of New Guinea. Within six days Horii's army was at Kokoda with the apparent intention of fighting overland to Port Moresby. Once again the Japanese had caught the military thinkers on the other side off-guard by daring to do the unthinkable. The defining battle for Australia in the Second World War was about to begin.

Basil Moorhouse Morris was one of those few Australians in the first years of Federation who had sought to make his entire career in the profession of arms. He was born in Melbourne in 1888, the ninth of eleven children, and named for the Anglican bishop of Melbourne, James Moorhouse, who in a severe Victorian drought had famously said: 'Don't pray for rain—dam it'. Basil did a year at university before joining the Royal Australian Artillery at the end of 1910. He served in France from 1916 onwards and was at the furthest point of the Australian advance, Bellicourt, when the war for the Australians ended in October 1918. Morris was more a supplies man than a military thinker. Seconded to the second AIF with the rank of brigadier, he was in Palestine by January 1940 to establish the Australian base at Jerusalem. But by June 1940 he was the Australian military liaison officer in Bombay, India, a posting that did little to advance his claims as a fighting soldier. It was as if Tom Blamey had seen enough of Basil Morris—if all the action was in the Middle East, it was hardly a mark of regard that he was posted so far away from the fighting. After Bombay Basil Morris was posted was to Port Moresby, another backwater, apparently, in which he could be hidden. That was in the middle of 1941. George Vasey, sent to Port Moresby in September 1942 to command the 6th Division and then the 7th, described Morris as 'a good scout—no brains but very honest and stout-hearted.' Tom Blamey, you would think, might have removed the 'good scout' from this description. Blamey said that Morris did not 'get down deep enough into things'.

Clearly a military presence in Papua, Australian territory, and New Guinea, held by Australia on trust under the peace settlement of 1919, needed beefing up. If the Japanese were to start a war in the Pacific, it was conceivable that Papua New Guinea (hereafter referred to as New Guinea in line with contemporary usage) might be involved. There was no need to waste the AIF on the territory, however, as Australian militia units—conscripted troops in the main which, therefore, could not be used outside Australia—could be sent to Papua New Guinea because this counted as Australian territory.

Perhaps it is a little late in this account of Australia in the Second World War to be introducing the militia—it was, indeed, the backbone of the Australian defence effort. Always had been, since Federation, except that wars were fought for Australia by an expeditionary force both times, raised separately from the militia— the Citizen Military Forces to use the correct title—as the militia was raised and trained for home defence. We called them 'chockos', the cadets at my school in the 1950s, short for 'chocolate soldiers'; pretty to look at, useless in fact, liable to melt in the heat. Unwisely I once used that term in my father's hearing, referring to our school cadets. He exploded, and I was given a quick account of the worth of the militia to Australia in the Second World War. It was a lesson that has always stayed with me. During the war the CMF was also referred to as chockos by others, and also 'koalas': not to be exported, not to be shot at, under government protection. In all the unfairness the myth-making of war seems to engender in Australia—for we all love dealing in myths about war—perhaps there is no greater unfairness than the way the militia seems to have been written out of the story of Australia at war. In the event, 250 000 Australians served in the militia during World War II, not counting the 200 000 Australians who had trained in the militia and had then transferred to the AIF.

We have already seen the savage reduction in the numbers of Australians training in the defence forces during the inter-war period, in part a response to the Treaty of Washington and world disarmament, and in part due to the Depression and the perception in Australia that defence should have a very low priority in government spending. When war came in September 1939 the Menzies government's first response had been to call up the militia for training. Drafts of 10 000 men at a time would be sent to the camps for 16 days of training, but this niggardly decision was soon overtaken by world events. From October 1939, 40 000 men at a time would go to camp for a month's training with a further three-month training planned for them in 1940. The government also decided to re-introduce compulsory training so that an element of the militia were conscripts. But after this initial burst of enthusiasm on the government's part, in response to the need to 'do something', the historian of the Australian army, Jeffrey Grey, reports that the militia soon lapsed back into 'lassitude' and was not taken seriously again until the second half of 1941. When Vernon Sturdee briefed the War Cabinet on 8 December 1941, immediately after Pearl Harbor, he reported, as we have seen, that while Australia had seven militia divisions, in fact not one of them could be put into the field as 'a good fighting force'.

Sturdee knew what he was on about. In July 1941 he had visited Port Moresby to see the state of preparedness there for himself and was appalled by what he found. The 49th Battalion, raised specifically for service at Port Moresby—Basil Morris's force—was, Sturdee wrote, 'quite the worst battalion in Australia'. But the trip to Port Moresby was important for another reason—it gave Sturdee a sense of the strategic importance of the town. When Curtin's government, in the anxieties of early 1942, floated the possibility of perhaps abandoning Papua's main town, Sturdee stood firm. Port Moresby, Sturdee pointed out, with New Caledonia, controlled entry into the Coral Sea. If Japan was to invade Australia, the capture of Port Moresby would be an essential first step for the enemy. For this reason, alone, Australia needed to retain Port Moresby. So the garrison stayed and would be reinforced. Indeed the reinforcements would come from Victoria (39th Militia Battalion) and New South Wales (53rd Militia Battalion), and these battalions would command a special place in Australian military history.

'Take your tennis racquets and prepare for the delights of the tropics', officers told the militia in Victoria as they tried to entice men into the new 39th Battalion; 'It will be an adventure'. Men believed them and the 39th filled. It was not so easy with the 53rd, perhaps they were more worldly wise in Sydney. So call-up notices found men required to attend the local drill hall, not knowing they would soon be destined for war. This was not the way to go about recruiting, to deceive the young and naive, nor to compel men who did not really understand what was going on, but it happened, for the only time so far in the Australian story.

Compelling men to join the militia, for service in Australia only, was the government's right, but in doing so the government created a two-tiered army, one part of which could not serve outside Australia. The decision created division within Australia and misunderstanding from Australia's allies. The two-tiered army might rank as Australia's worst decision of the war. And it is here that World War I exerts one of its strongest impacts on Australia in World War II. Billy Hughes, Labor prime minister from 1915 until he deserted Labor but retained the prime ministership in late 1916, happened to be within shouting distance of the Western Front when the Australians went into action at the Somme in July 1916. The losses were terrible for all the armies on the Somme and, for Australia with a only small number of men available, devastating. Hughes decided then and there that the Australian forces would have to be replaced by conscripts—there was, he believed, simply no other way to find enough replacements. On returning home, he plunged the country into turmoil by seeking to gain the people's agreement to conscription. He split the Labor Party. As we have seen, John Curtin campaigned strongly against conscription, and it became a tenet of Labor orthodoxy that conscripts could never be sent outside Australia to fight in any wars, no matter what the danger to the country. It had become an article of Labor faith that no Australian could be sent overseas to fight, against his will.

Chockos sheltering behind Labor ideology, that is how some of the AIF looked at the militia. And Australia's allies simply could not understand how a nation at risk, with too few soldiers anyway, could keep such large numbers of soldiers at home when the call was for men and more men. Certainly the militia could be sent, even press-ganged apparently, to New Guinea, for that was Australian territory, but they could not be sent elsewhere. Were the Australians serious about the war, their allies asked, or rather were they expecting us to do it all for them. It would have been very much wiser to have let the world know that the militia, the conscripts, were indeed overseas, about to challenge the all-conquering Japanese on Australia's doorstep, in the jungles of New Guinea. But Douglas MacArthur had stressed to Curtin and his ministers the importance of news censorship to keep the Japanese in the dark about the Allies' intentions. The effect of this was to deny the world the knowledge that Australian conscripts were fighting the enemy, and fighting bloody hard. Australians and the world knew of Gallipoli, almost from the moment the battle started; it was not like that for Kokoda. Hide that story and the myth of the chockos and the koalas would seriously detract from Australia's reputation of giving its all for its own deliverance. It was so important that the world should know but MacArthur and a too compliant government saw to it that it did not.

The preeminent Australian historian of Kokoda, Peter Brune, tells us that 'in the long, proud history of Australia at arms, there can be no more tragic and damning story than that of the raising, deployment, equipment and training of the 53rd Battalion'. The battalion came into existence on 1 November 1941. Think of the training of the 6th Australian Division before it was committed to battle in January 1941. Raised in November 1939 and briefly trained in Australia, the division spent nearly a full year in Palestine at general and specialised training. Short of equipment, certainly, but at least members of the division had access to basic weapons and extensive training in the handling of those weapons. It is reported, but it is barely credible, that a young Australian soldier, about to go into battle on the Kokoda Track, asked his officer how the rifle in his hands actually fired. Until now he had only ever worked with a wooden dummy replica.

Think of 'Jo' Gullett's description of a battalion at the peak of its powers. He wrote of a body of men so tightly drilled, so involved with each other and so dependent on each other, that they could act as one. He told how the bonds within the battalion took the place, if only temporarily, of the most intimate bonds a man might have formed with family and friends. Gullett wrote, too, of a battalion that would care for its own and of members who would be prepared to give their own lives so that the battalion might do its job and prosper. Only long weeks and months of training and working together could create a battalion, Gullett wrote. Pity then the men of the 53rd Battalion and the 39th, hastily thrown together, some of them resenting the way they were dragged to war unwillingly, trained for a couple of weeks only, or in a few cases for only a few days. The way Jo Gullett saw it, these were battalions in name only. If they did fight at all, it would be to their very great individual credit.

To create the 53rd Battalion, 18 existing militia battalions were required to detach 62 of their number for the new unit. You would most certainly choose the very best men to let go, now wouldn't you? Even so, the battalion was still short of men. Perhaps it is too much to use the term 'press-gang' but it was near enough to that. Boys of 18 years of age, some of them told to report to a drill hall with their gear, were then marched to Darling Harbour to the *Aquitania*, then the third biggest ship in the world, with no pre-embarkation leave and their wives, mothers or girlfriends, locked out of the wharves, though pleading desperately to say goodbye. For many of these conscripts, with no training at all, they needed to learn how to wear their uniforms, to drill and to fire a rifle, all on board ship, on their way to war. Looking back now, survivors of Victoria's 39th Battalion, also going to war on the *Aquitania*, watched in pity as some of the 53rd Battalion had to be literally dragged on board. Yanked out of the pubs, it seemed to some of them, and forced on board clearly against their will. The 39th had received about five weeks' training, that was something, though all of it had been open warfare training, as if they were going to fight in the desert. There was no preparation for the jungle they would soon be fighting in.

Both battalions left Sydney on 27 December 1941 and arrived in Port Moresby on 3 January 1942. The *Aquitania* ran aground in Port Moresby Harbour, or nearly so. Hundreds of men needed to get off the ship so it could be refloated, quickly, so the disembarkation was something of a shambles. Men of the 39th Battalion were marched off into the dark, expecting a camp to bed down in, expecting facilities for sleeping, eating, training and all the other things that soldiers need to do. Instead they were marched for hours, and when they were halted, they were told to fallout and go to sleep. Where? On the ground. Using their sausage bags—bags that held all their kit—as pillows, utterly unprotected from mosquitoes and all the rest of the trials of the tropics, and apparently on the edge of a jungle, these young soldiers fell into a deep sleep. Men of the AIF would never have put up with that sort of treatment but these men were too inexperienced to know any better. Apparently that was what it was like in the army.

There was a shake-up in the 7th Australian Division on its return to Australia: older men to be rested, proven leaders to be promoted. Arnold Potts, a West Australian, had commanded the 2/16th Battalion in the last part of its service in Syria and had earlier been decorated for his fighting in Syria. Arnold Potts returned to Australia from the Middle East a seasoned, experienced and senior soldier. Born in 1896 on the Isle of Man but growing up in Western Australia, it almost goes without saying that Potts learned his soldiering on the Western Front. He had been awarded the Military Cross for his fighting at Mouquet Farm on the Somme in July 1916, and had fought on successfully after that before being severely wounded at Vaire Wood, near Hamel, in August 1918. Potts retired from that war with a disability pension. Nevertheless, like so many other returning soldiers who were determined to live an independent life, Potts had turned to farming in south-west Western Australia after the war. In the spirit of the famous Roman general, Cincinnatus, he rejoined the AIF when war called again in April 1940; he was married then and had three children. In

April 1942 Arnold Potts was promoted to brigadier and was given command of the 7th Division's 21st Brigade in South Australia. His brigade comprised the 2/14th Battalion (Victorian), the 2/16th (West Australian) and the 2/27th (South Australian). It soon moved to southern Queensland and began training for jungle warfare. The brigade was, as Potts's biographer, Bill Edgar, writes: '. . . a very experienced group of units, battle-hardened, fit and confident.'

In early August 1942 Potts's brigade was again on the move. Its destination was kept a strict secret, except boxes on the wharf were addressed to 'King's Harbour Master, Port Moresby', which quite let the cat out of the bag. The men went from Brisbane by sea but their brigadier was ahead of them, flying into Port Moresby on 7 August 1942. His first call was on Basil Morris, still commanding the Australian forces in the territory and blissfully unaware, until Arnold Potts arrived, that the AIF was on its way to his patch. But Morris's own troops had been in action for a couple of weeks now. Horii's South Sea Force had already landed near Buna on 21 July and had immediately set off for the interior. Horii's men, too, were seasoned and experienced soldiers, 'battle-hardened, fit and confident', having fought previously in China and Manchuria. If there is no training for war better than combat itself then Horii's force was extremely well prepared.

It seemed unlikely that an enemy force would ever attempt the overland route across the mountains to Port Moresby, and Arnold Potts soon discovered on arrival that first-hand information about the track from Port Moresby to the village at Kokoda on the other side of the Owen Stanleys was virtually non-existent. Basil Morris did not have any maps; indeed, there were no decent maps or any of the other aids a brigade commander would normally expect to have on hand to make sense of his coming battlefield. Officially, then, Arnold Potts would be fighting blind. He would have no idea of the ground over which his men could be expected to fight. And Potts would soon discover that the troops fighting along the Kokoda Track were on a battlefield as bad as any the world had ever known.

From Buna to Port Moresby along the Kokoda Track is just on 240 kilometres; from Kokoda to Port Moresby it is just under 150 kilometres. While the Owen Stanleys themselves reach a height of over 4000 metres, the highest point of the track at the Gap is 2000 metres. Men walking the track would scale mountains and plunge into the steepest ravines. They would be engulfed in the deepest jungle so that even a few feet off the track the country was unknowable to them—the enemy could virtually be alongside the Australians without them knowing it. The jungle also provided a dense canopy, making the soldiers invisible to aircraft. In one sense this was a good thing, as those who had fought in Greece might have explained to those new to war, but it made the dropping of supplies from the air nearly impossible and always hazardous. And finally in this catalogue of woes, because it was the tropics the afternoon, every afternoon, would bring torrential rain. This meant, of course, surging rivers and streams that would have to be crossed. Mud, too, all along the track. And all of it in great heat.

Men of the 39th Battalion were already at Kokoda, indeed they had been there while Arnold Potts's brigade was putting the final touches on their jungle training in Queensland. Tom Blamey had told Basil Morris on 29 June 1942 that he must secure Kokoda, on the other side of the mountains, for use as an air base against a possible Japanese landing on the north coast of New Guinea. No one was thinking of an overland campaign, even at that stage. Sam Templeton was the man for the job, one of the best leaders in a well-led 39th Battalion, distinguishing it from its ill-led twin, the 53rd. Templeton had fought in the First World War but was refused entry into the second AIF on the grounds of flat feet, so he had to make do with the militia. Apparently flat feet didn't matter there. Age was not on Templeton's side either as he was at least 50 years old when he took B Company, 39th Battalion, out of Port Moresby and onto the jungle track to Kokoda. His men would follow 'Uncle Sam' anywhere and they made it to Kokoda, with who knows what privations and sufferings. At least they were not being shot at—yet.

How to supply these men? Basil Morris had no aircraft at his disposal so he would need to rely on native carriers and it was here that he made a really important contribution to the Australian fighting in New Guinea. Too easily, perhaps, dismissed as a light-weight, Morris in fact earned his stripes in the war by creating the

Australian New Guinea Administrative Unit (ANGAU). The civilian administration of the territory had been suspended on 14 February 1942, but, anticipating this, Morris had drawn up plans for a military unit to carry out the civilian administrative functions and augment them. For the remainder of the war ANGAU would maintain law and order among the civilian population, and would provide indigenous workers for the military forces—they recruited thousands without whom it is hard to see how the army might have operated. Still, as Peter Brune wrote, expectations for ANGAU were initially set far too high. As Templeton's B Company set off for Kokoda, Lieutenant Bert Kienzle, an old hand in the territory and now recruited to ANGAU, was ordered to begin the 'construction of road to Kokoda, to commence not later than 29 June. Road to be completed by 26 August 1942'. And that order 'must surely rank as one of the most ludicrous' ever given in the annals of military history, Peter Brune writes. It was an indication of how remote the understanding of those in Port Moresby was of the conditions on the route to Kokoda. Lack of any real knowledge and appreciation of the track would bedevil this campaign throughout, although those ultimately responsible for the fighting on the track had an absolute obligation to learn at first hand what the conditions were really like. You might not have gone to Tobruk, Tom Blamey, during any part of the siege there, but you simply had to walk the Kokoda Track, or some part of it at least, to understand what your troops had done there.

There would never be a road built on the Kokoda Track, that much was obvious to someone who walked even a small portion of its length. To walk the full length would take about eight days in the most gruelling conditions. As a native carrier would eat everything he could carry in 13 days, it was apparent that porterage alone could not supply the soldiers on the track; not to mention providing soldiers with their ammunition, medical supplies and all the other things soldiers need to fight a war. Ideally, supply dumps would be built up along the track through a combination of porterage and air drops, but this would take months to organise and implement; by mid-July the Australians realised that they did not have months on their side. Having landed near Buna and at Gona on 21 July the Japanese were immediately underway towards

Kokoda, too soon confronting elements of Templeton's company, which was easily pushed back to Kokoda village. Basil Morris ordered the rest of the 39th Battalion into action on 23 July.

The Japanese were a formidable enemy with a simple battle plan. They would push forward against their opposition with a scout and a small body of men to make contact with the Australians, and they were prepared for initial losses among the contact party in order to surround the Australians and overwhelm them. Sam Templeton, at the forefront of his company when he might have been of more value further back and in command, was an early victim to these tactics; his body was never recovered. Despite fighting magnificently, the 39th could not hold Kokoda and its airfield, and withdrew south along the track to Deniki on 27 July. The Australians were back in Kokoda the next day, however, when they discovered that the Japanese had not moved large numbers into the village. But this re-entry was short-lived and a counterattack by the Japanese consolidated the enemy's hold on Kokoda village. At this stage some 480 Australians were attempting to hold up as many as perhaps 10 000 Japanese troops; it was a grossly unequal fight and would remain so throughout the campaign. That fact, too, might have registered with Allied headquarters in Brisbane.

The airfield at Kokoda was crucial to the conduct of the campaign in allowing for supplies and reinforcements, and the Australians would not give up Kokoda easily. When the 39th Battalion's commander, Lieutenant Colonel Bill Owen, was killed at Deniki—foolishly, as he would not take his men's advice to keep low—he was replaced by Major Allan Cameron, who decided that Kokoda must once more be retaken. The battle for Kokoda raged from 8 to 12 August, but the unequal fight was made impossible when the 39th Battalion virtually ran out of ammunition. The battalion had fought with utmost bravery and determination, although in a series of almost disconnected actions at the company and platoon level. These were barely trained troops, remember, but there were enough old hands plucked from the 7th Division to lead the men expertly and to keep morale high by the evident success they were enjoying. Success, that is, in keeping the Japanese from advancing. It was this delay that marked success on the track, if not back at headquarters where all they wanted was to see the

Japanese overrun and booted out of Kokoda. Build a road along the track, boot the Japanese out; it was all equally unrealistic. However, the Australians doing the fighting knew they were frustrating the Japanese and holding them back in a way the enemy had never expected. 'They would never have got through,' one of the corporals of A Company, 39th Battalion, said. 'They would have had to kill every one of us—but you can't fight without ammunition.' Even in these first stages of the fighting the problem with supply was readily apparent.

By 13 August the Australians had fallen back as far as Isurava, in effect only a few kilometres from Kokoda, but to higher ground. Here was another place to make a stand. In Port Moresby on 1 August, Lieutenant General Sydney Rowell had arrived to take command of the Australian forces in New Guinea, replacing Basil Morris, who went off to command ANGAU. Rowell was one of the very first Duntroon cadets, beginning his course there in 1911. He was the first of the Duntroon graduates to make chief of the general staff, although that promotion was way off in the future the day he arrived in Port Moresby. He had been on Gallipoli, briefly, but ill-health had significantly interfered with his service in World War I. Rowell had fought alongside Blamey in the Middle East and in Greece just a year before, and had developed a realistic understanding of Blamey's strengths and weaknesses.

Rowell was a well-regarded leader, strong on planning. He believed that the decision to send militia units to New Guinea when the 7th Division was available was a 'cardinal error', and he would soon have that division with him in New Guinea and on the Kokoda Track. He spoke to his soldiers in a down-to-earth way that they readily understood, and Rowell could inspire loyalty and great effort. Addressing men of Potts's 21st Brigade as they were about to leave Port Moresby for the track, Rowell said to them:

> You're going to have a tough walk in . . . you'll need to be fit and you should be. But you'll have to walk hard so don't think you're in for an easy time. Yes, I know what you are thinking, 'That's alright for the old bastard, he hasn't got to do it himself'. That's as it may be but I know you'll do the job well.

The 21st Brigade would leave Port Moresby on 16 August 1942 but were not expected to be fighting on the track for a week or so yet.

At Isurava the 39th Battalion was only just holding on. The men were attempting to prepare their defences in view of an expected Japanese attack, using almost anything that was to hand to build up their positions, constantly alert for the first sounds of the resumption of the battle yet not able to see, for the thickness of the jungle, what was even immediately in front of them. Meanwhile, the Japanese were consolidating their forces and building up for a full-scale assault on the Australian positions; the prospect for the Australians was dire. There had been an attempt to resupply the Australians from the air, which had only been partially successful, and these men had been doing it extremely tough for more than a month now with little in the way of food, ammunition and medical supplies. All this discomfort and all of it in the knowledge that soon there would be much worse to come. High morale would be crucial in the coming days and, truly, it was a wonder that these ill-trained, half-starved, seemingly forgotten men were prepared to fight at all. It was at Isurava, on 16 August, that the 39th Battalion's next commanding officer arrived into these circumstances.

Ralph Honner had returned home to Perth from the disaster on Crete in May 1942. He had spent some time after Crete in Syria on garrison duties and had been given his first command there, the 19th Training Battalion. It was a promotion richly deserved, though certainly Honner was learning battalion-level command from the bottom up. Back in Perth there was some home leave and two growing boys to make friends with, but it was only seven days before Ralph Honner was back at Northam Camp, from whence he had started out to war two years before. On 1 August 1942 Honner received a telegram ordering him to Perth; he had been promoted to lieutenant colonel, he found, and was being sent to Port Moresby to take command of the 39th Australian Infantry Battalion. He was to leave almost immediately. How would you insert yourself into a battalion that had been fighting hard for a month, that was near to the end of its tether and was awaiting a major assault from an unseen enemy that might simply overwhelm it by sheer weight of numbers? You, whose only experience of the jungle was the draining walk from Port Moresby that you had just completed? Whose only knowledge of your new battalion was the barest detail of where it had come from and what it had been doing?

'This person', wrote the battalion's adjutant, Lieutenant Keith Lovett:

> walked up to a group of us . . . I saw he was an officer, and I said, 'Can I help you in any way?' He said, 'Yes, I'm Colonel Honner, I'm your new CO . . . I'd like you to take me around and introduce me to the company commanders and we'll settle down and start our business.'

There was no big-noting in any of this, but the men would have quickly learned where their commanding officer had already been, what he had already done. They would be impressed; 'He's fought a bit,' they would say. For Honner, though, the problems were immense. He had to learn jungle warfare in an extraordinary hurry; but more than that he had to learn about his battalion from scratch. Who were its leaders; what were its strengths; where were its weaknesses? He would have been told, pretty quickly, that these were boys, for the most part, with only a few weeks' training before being thrown into war. This was not an AIF battalion, bonded through hard training over many months. This battalion, and now its newest commanding officer, were learning on the job. And the Japanese might be at them, literally, at any moment. Australian history lacks drama, the doubters have been telling me for years, the story is all so bland. Yet this scene in a clearing at Isurava, in the heart of the Papuan jungle, before an all-conquering enemy, with boys to do a man's job, is, to me, almost Shakespearian in the intensity of its drama. It is a scene that tells us who the Australian people are and what it is that they might achieve. All of Ralph Honner's life was a preparation for this moment. This is your battalion, Ralph Honner, this is all you've got, and you must not fail.

Honner was appalled by what he saw: '. . . physically the pathetically young warriors of the 39th were in poor shape', he later wrote. B Company, Honner had been told, was a disgrace, simply not up to the job. Break them up and move the men to the other companies, the acting commanding officer, Allan Cameron, had said. How well would they be received in the other companies, Honner wondered; who would have them? And then Honner made one of his most inspired decisions. Rather than disband the disgraced company or move it out of the way, Honner put B Company at the apex of the mostly likely place of attack. I don't know who you are or how good any of you are, Honner was saying in effect, but we are all in this together and we'll do it together, with the same courage, the same determination, the same faith in victory. We are a battalion, he was telling them, a group of soldiers acting as one. We depend, each one of us, on all the others and every individual. We make no distinctions, we make no excuses. And B Company, as Ralph Honner knew it would, rose to meet his expectations. Dig in, Honner told them, deep weapons pits for the killing ground in front of you. Then he discovered that they did not have entrenching tools but were digging through the floor of the jungle with bully-beef tins and bayonets.

If the new commanding officer was shocked by the condition of the men, and the small number of them, this was information that he knew he must keep from the Japanese. If the enemy had suspected the weakened state of the Australians in front of them they would have 'annihilated us', Honner believed. So he had a patrol out, much as Iven Mackay had done at Tobruk, to prevent the enemy coming in too close to test the real strength of the Australians. The 39th Battalion was only just hanging on; the Japanese probed, looking for weak spots, they were met with machine-gun fire, with grenades and bayonets, 'then even fists and boots', Bill Edgar writes. Honner was buying time, and doing it most successfully. He knew that relief was coming, but painfully slowly along that terrible track.

The Japanese did not move forward in force until 26 August 1942, by which time the 39th and the 53rd battalions had been reinforced by two of the battalions in Arnold Potts's 21st Brigade, the 2/14th and the 2/16th battalions. But it was Honner's 39th Battalion patrol that took the brunt of the first main Japanese attack. Using tactics that had worked so well in Malaya, the Japanese attacked in force against the strength of the defenders, and used mountain artillery and mortars to good effect. Where stopped, they would attempt to outflank their enemy, with the idea of coming to the main force from behind, thus fatally cutting them off. A full account of the fighting at Isurava and along the track, which this book cannot attempt, would detail, as with a chess-board, the moves and countermoves that opposing commanders were making in dense jungle, which prevented too much observation of the other's manoeuvres. So the commanders on both sides needed to think continually and carefully about the placement of their troops, always probing, always pushing to see if they could find an opening.

What was the genius of Arnold Potts's command? It was in two parts. First, Potts would see for himself. He was indefatigable on the track—tireless—a 46-year-old man with enormous energy. Everywhere, encouraging, examining, planning. And the second part of his genius lay in knowing precisely when to withdraw and regroup. Potts soon came to know that he was vastly outnumbered, and he soon gained a great respect for the commanders and troops opposing him. He quickly perceived that it would be supply that would eventually defeat the Japanese. So he would delay them for as long as he could, then entice them on, slowly, further down the track where he would seek to hold them up again. Intelligence that the Japanese were as gaunt as his own troops was music to Arnold Potts's ears. They would, eventually, he believed, have to fall back to their sources of supply, and then he could hit them —hard, very hard.

Back in Port Moresby, and even more fatally in Brisbane, the most senior commanders could not understand what Potts was doing. He was withdrawing, damn it, always pulling back. Would the man not stop and fight? Those who had not walked the track still expected the Australians to break out and push the Japanese back beyond Kokoda. Underestimating the enemy's strength by perhaps 50 per cent or more and failing to appreciate the real nature of the fighting, anything less than the urgent recapture of Kokoda was seen as failure. Arnold Potts knew what he was about; Ralph Honner had instinctively reached the same conclusion in the first days of the fighting at Isurava. It was just that their sensible, winning strategy did not live up to the expectations of generals wanting victory.

On Christmas day 1941, the 2/14th Battalion had given Albert Moore a present of a sum of money, quite a lot of money for Albert, and he was very embarrassed. He wrote, the 'gift was given on condition that it must not go into general funds'. Then in late March 1942 Albert was back in Australia and on a train from Adelaide to Melbourne to be reunited with his family for the first time since Christmas 1939: 'This surely must rank among the greatest days of my life.' Albert Moore had brought his battered truck, Vikel—coffee urns and all—home with him from North Africa and Syria, and what a fund-raising coup this turned out to be. Parked outside the Salvation Army headquarters in Bourke Street, Melbourne, everyone soon knew the story of the Salvo and 2/14th Battalion's coffee run. When the battalion was on the move again, so was Albert Moore and Vikel. Shipped aboard the troop-ship to Port Moresby, Vikel, Moore believed, still had many miles left in her. When the battalion moved on 16 August out from Port Moresby to link up with Ralph Honner's men, Albert Moore was left behind. He was devastated and wrote: 'My heart was heavy. This is our first break and I am bewildered as to what I am to do.' You could drive a little way out of Port Moresby, they told him, that was as far as Douglas MacArthur ever got in his inspection of the track, but after that the road was impassable. There was no place for Vikel. 'My Black Sunday', is Albert's entry in his diary for this bleak day.

Within days, of course, Albert Moore had worked out the solution to his problem, 'I have in mind to try to set up a hut on the track', he wrote. He had worked out that he could not service the men in their lines, jungle warfare was not like that, but as there was now already a constant traffic along the track Albert would provide coffee and a smoke for all those wayfarers; the wounded coming back to Port Moresby, the terrified and exhausted going forward. How would he do this? Well, with help, he would lug the makings for the rest station up the track himself. He was on the track from 25 August 1942, just before the main fighting started, and you can see from his diary how he continued to walk up and down the track time and time again for the duration of the campaign. Not all the way to the battlefront, certainly, but up and down often enough for the reader of his diary to be near to tears, marvelling at this man's devotion to his men, and his determination. 'This place crammed with sick and wounded', he wrote on 30 August, just four days after the Japanese had begun their attack in force.

'Japs are breaking through our lines and position is becoming critical.'

'Arose early and got coffee etc. ready and from 8.30 a.m. a steady stream of wounded and sick came along, and were they delighted to see the Red Shield and the Salvos on the job. Men arrive here in state of utter exhaustion, and move on revived.'

'The news of the hut has been passed from man to man all along the track and officers and men are thrilled with our efforts . . . it is a marvellous job and we are filling a great need.'

Albert would pull back, too, as the troops pulled back. 'This was as near to hell as anything I could imagine', he wrote—and for Albert Moore hell was a real place—'and something I would never hope to see again'. Remember those men crawling along a ledge under a fort in Syria outside the town of Jezzine, under fire, trying to work out a way to put the French guns out of action? Well here they are again at Isurava, repelling four attacks in the afternoon, awaiting the fifth, now pinned down by heavy Japanese fire. Ordered to attack with their bayonets, Bruce Kingsbury grabbed a Bren gun and rushed at the enemy, firing from the hip. He caused dreadful casualties to the Japanese and probably prevented 2/14th's headquarters from being overrun. Kingsbury was shot by a Japanese sniper, but his bravery earned him the Victoria Cross, the only one awarded on the Kokoda Track. That was on 29 August 1942. On 30 August Albert Moore recorded in his diary: 'Dear old Butch Bassett has been killed.' He was one of this remarkable group of men; his brother, Stan, lived to fight on with 'Teddy' Bear, Alan Avery and all the rest of that remarkable platoon.

By the night of 10/11 September the Australians had been pushed back as far as Ioribaiwa, having come through Efogi and Nauro. The Americans in the air had been pounding Japanese bottlenecks along the route and had also been giving those bringing supplies to the Japanese at Buna on the coast a hard time. So by now the Japanese were running out of food and other supplies; literally, they were in danger of starving. To reach this point had required skilful and determined fighting on the part of the Australians, and brilliant leadership. They had slowed the Japanese advance and had coaxed them further along the track. If speed was the essence of the Japanese success in Malaya, this slow advance on the track was bringing the enemy undone. But the Australians had been fought near to exhaustion. Casualties were significant, sickness a daily part of life on the track, the discomfort unbelievable. But reinforcement by the 25th Brigade was on the way and, as they were now much closer to Port Moresby, they could also be resupplied more easily. The balance was tipping in favour of the Allies; there was in prospect a major victory, fought in appalling circumstances. By 17 September the Australians had pulled back to Imita Ridge and the Japanese, it was said, could see the lights of Port Moresby in the distance. But on 18 September the Japanese received word to start pulling back to Buna and Gona.

In Brisbane Douglas MacArthur was following the action on his map. Withdrawal, pull back, these words were all he ever seemed to hear from the Australians. MacArthur wanted victory; he wanted glory. One of his generals reported that MacArthur was 'obsessed by a plan he can't carry out, frustrated, dramatic to the extreme and even shell-shocked'. MacArthur seemed to believe that the Australians outnumbered the Japanese, whereas Arnold Potts thought that the ratio was seven to one in favour of the enemy. Nor, in retreat, though starving, were the Japanese a demoralised force. They would fight in their retreat with the same tenacity the Australians had shown in theirs. So instead of rushing the Japanese and provoking a major battle, as MacArthur wanted, the Australians seemed content to continue to probe and to harass the enemy.

MacArthur prevailed on John Curtin to have Tom Blamey sent to Port Moresby. With things going poorly in the Solomons, MacArthur began to fear his own recall. MacArthur knew that he had never had many friends in Washington and he needed a victory, and he wanted it now. The first to be sacked, surprisingly, was Syd Rowell in Port Moresby. Rowell was more than annoyed that Blamey had come up to Port Moresby, perhaps to steal his glory now that the Japanese were in retreat, and he detested Blamey anyway.

Blamey and Rowell had words. Removed to the army's unattached list for insubordination, only the future intervention of Bob Menzies would see Rowell's military career restarted.

The next to go was Arnold Potts on 22 October. Blamey telephoned: 'Change of climate for you, Potts. You go to Darwin, your successor, Dougherty, will meet you tomorrow and take over.' Officers in the brigade were incensed and many of them put in their own resignations to make a stand for Pottsy. But the army is not like that and Potts put them straight on that score. So one of Australia's best military leaders was dumped and it would be years before Australians understood what this man had done and how unfair his dismissal was.

Worse was to come. The place was Koitaki, at the very start of the track on the Port Moresby side, on 9 November 1942. The 21st Brigade was at rest; luxury was a wash, a bit of a feed, maybe some letters from home. But Old Tom Blamey was coming to see them, to thank them for a bloody good job, no doubt, to congratulate them, and maybe single out a few officers and men for special praise. Ah, they have to do it and it is all part of being in the army. Some blokes talked of Bob Menzies meeting up with troops in the desert after the first battles there; promised them the world and seemed genuine enough. They turned out, as spick and span as they could after all they had been through, and Tom Blamey started speaking. 'What now occurs', writes Peter Brune, 'is the greatest dressing down of all time'.

Those who have described this scene—Brune and then Blamey's biographer, David Horner, others too—have all relied on Blamey's personal assistant, Major Norman Carlyon, to describe what Tom Blamey did. Carlyon had great respect, affection even, for his boss. His account, therefore, can be believed. But even Carlyon cannot condone what happened at Koitaki. 'He told the men', Carlyon wrote:

> that they had been defeated, that he had been defeated, and Australia had been defeated. He said this was simply not good enough. Every soldier there had to remember that he was worth three Japanese. In future he expected no further retirements, but advance at all costs.

And then came the punchline, words which Carlyon described as 'particularly ill-chosen and unfair'. 'Remember,' the general told his troops, 'it is not the man with the gun that gets shot; it's the rabbit that is running away.'

One of the worst things in war, as I have observed from travelling to battlefields with Australian veterans from both world wars, is the grief and sadness still for mates who have died and are buried in the cemeteries so far from home but so close to the battlefields on which they fell. It was at Labuan, 50 years after the end of the Second World War, and I was walking among the rows and rows of graves in the substantial war cemetery there. I was walking with a marvellous man whom I had come to know on the trip. A dairy farmer from Victoria's Gippsland, a Scot originally, who had come to Australia as a child. 'Why me,' he asked as he stopped among the graves. 'Why did I live while all these men died, better men than me, and with families, many of them. Why me? I'll never understand it.' That was 50 years after the event. At Koitaki every man standing there listening to Tom Blamey had mates, close mates some of them, who had died in the fight. Bruce Kingsbury's mates stood there listening to Blamey, thinking of all that they had been through together, thinking of how Bruce had saved their lives only a few weeks before with his incredible bravery. Every one of those men listening to the general would have had a mate to remember and recall. And they still faced the trip to the mate's parents when they got home, to his wife possibly, to tell these grieving people how he had died, facing the enemy of course, doing his best, looking out for his mates. And Blamey was telling these gaunt survivors that they were cowards; rabbits who had run. So their mates who had died were rabbits too, shot down trying to run away. The men were murmuring in the ranks; the officers were trying to keep control of them. You tell me how it was that they didn't rush the box that Tom Blamey was standing on and knock the bugger to the ground. He wasn't worth it, they probably reasoned, as they looked at him with contempt and disgust.

Was Blamey just careless with his words, unaware of what he was saying? That is what his supporters try to suggest. But look at his track record. Turning up with his wife in Cairo, taking his son with him out of the fight in Greece, making no attempt ever to see

Tobruk for himself. And later that day at Koitaki, just in case they had missed what he was saying, Blamey rounded up the officers of the 21st Brigade for a separate and more private dressing-down. Then Ralph Honner, the hero of the 39th Battalion, who had turned boys into soldiers in a matter of days, and into extraordinary fighters, too, Blamey called for him when Honner was in Port Moresby after Isurava.

'Ah, Honner, just arrived up here have you?' They talked generalities, pleasantries, for a few minutes. Blamey never once asked Ralph Honner about the track or the fighting there. It's just war, I suppose, in its tumultuous evil, but the men of the Kokoda Track knew what they had done even if Tom Blamey did not have a clue. It was their finest hour, but certainly not his.

15. TO THE
STARS

How much of what we read as children influences the course of our later lives? Arthur 'Nat' Gould read every book and magazine article he could find on World War I flying aces—an ace is defined as a fighter pilot who had shot down at least five enemy aircraft in combat. You could say that Nat Gould was obsessed with flying and with the raw adventure of airmen in those primitive planes of the Great War. He found the stories thrilling, of another world; and you might say he lived at least a part of his life through these stories. Nat Gould eventually spent almost all of his adult working life with aircraft and was probably lucky to have found his great obsession so early in his life.

Like almost every other young man in Australia in the 1930s Nat Gould could see war coming and was 'quietly happy' about it. Born in 1920 at Roma in central Queensland, only moving to Brisbane for his last years at school, Nat Gould combed paddocks near to his home for cow manure to sell to neighbourhood gardeners. With each bag sold he was just a little further along the path to paying for the training hours that would allow him to fulfill his dream of a pilot's licence. Nat would hang around Archerfield aerodrome just to get a feel for things while slowly building up his bank account. It was the Depression, there were five children, he was certainly not going to ask his father for the money for flying lessons, but if there was a war, and he could be paid to fly, and perhaps emulate his heroes of the earlier war—well? Now that was something to dream about.

Nat Gould had his pilot's licence almost as soon as he turned 18 years of age. He had been out of school for a couple of years, earning money for himself, the lessons a lot easier to afford. In the dreadful shortage of trained pilots that the RAAF faced as war loomed, Nat Gould was precisely the type of boy that the air force was looking for. Trained to fly already, and dead keen. Nat remembers listening to Bob Menzies' 'melancholy duty' speech while lounging on the verandah of the family home; the rest of his family inside by the radio, taking in somewhat sadly the sombre moment for the country. But outside Nat Gould was quietly chuckling to himself. This was it, he remembers thinking, he could be a flying ace now just like his heroes. He also remembers, he had to 'pull on a long face when I talked to Mum about it'; no son could let his mother know just how keen he was to get to war.

Nat Gould was in the RAAF and on his way to Britain by mid-1940, and would serve with the Royal Air Force in England and Scotland, and in Russia, for the next couple of years. Flying Hurricanes out of Murmansk, this young Australian thought he had seen war at its worst. It was even something of a shock to be fighting alongside the Russians; 'Weren't they on the other side?' he remembers wondering. Nat Gould saw some terrible things, lost some close mates, but when the Pacific War began all he could think about was coming home. When he had enlisted it was all for 'King and Country', he said, but with the Japanese in the war it was all about 'Australia and Country'. 'Things were grim,' Nat Gould remembers, 'so we wanted to come home. We all put in for a posting home.'

By May 1942, among Australia's darkest days, Nat Gould was in Kingaroy in Queensland, posted to No. 75 RAAF Squadron, which by then had already served in Port Moresby. Indeed, the squadron was almost down to its last aircraft, and had lost many of its original pilots in what they referred to as the Battle of Moresby; 'not a very well-told story,' Nat Gould remarked. The New Guinea veterans looked on the new arrivals from Britain 'with suspicion. They thought we'd had too good a war, we had lovely messes over there and nice pubs down on the corner of the street, while they had been "slumming it up in Port Moresby".' The division, though, didn't last too long, there was too much to do and too much urgency about what they were doing for any sense of 'us and them' to last in 75 Squadron.

The first task for Nat Gould and his mates was to learn to fly the American P40 Kittyhawks, with which 75 Squadron and its sister 76 Squadron had been equipped. Gould had already flown Wirraways in training; in action he had flown Hurricanes and Spit-fires. 'I loved the Spitfires,' he said. 'It's hard to describe what it was like to fly one. It was absolutely beautiful.' Not so the Kitty-hawk: 'It was a big heavy aircraft, we described it as a bulldozer ... but it's pretty reliable, hefty and strong.' Just what they needed at Milne Bay, the next posting for 75 and 76 squadrons. 'That was one of the worst wars I've ever been to,' Nat Gould claimed. 'Russia was a picnic compared to Milne Bay.'

Milne Bay was the landing place for Japanese troops, from where they would march to Port Moresby. Along the way they hoped to link up with the troops landed on the north coast, who would make their way over the Kokoda Track to Port Moresby. It was to be their two-pronged attack, from the east and from the north. On the southern tip of the island, Milne Bay is a long and placid stretch of water, mostly swamp on the southern side of the bay but with plenty of good landing spots on the northern. Towering above the bay are high mountain ranges, but they would be no barrier, so the invaders thought, as the Japanese army had been a force no power or might had so far been able to stop in this gloriously victorious war. Opposing the incoming Japanese were Australian soldiers, both militia and AIF, with the support of the Australian air force. But it was more than support, as this battle involved the land forces and air forces working closely together, the victory won as much from the air as from the ground. Both the 75 and 76 RAAF squadrons were to play a crucial role in the victory at Milne Bay, and were to show the significant difference when soldiers and airmen worked together, even though the Japanese navy off Milne Bay was quite unchallenged at sea.

Cyril Clowes, born in Warwick, Queensland, in 1892, entered the Royal Military College, Duntroon, with his brother Norman in 1911. Both of these cadets would reach the rank of major general; Norman in the British army, Cyril in the Australian. Surely this was unusual. Cyril had landed at Gallipoli on 25 April 1915, was awarded a Military Cross for fighting in France in 1916, and was in the thick of the planning and fighting at Villers-Bretonneux in 1918 when the Australians really made a difference in that war. In the inter-war years, Cyril Clowes's career stalled, as did the careers of almost all the officers and men of the tiny Australian army.

Nicknamed 'Silent Cyril', Clowes served well in the debacle in Greece and was then brought home to Australia 'to sharpen the leadership of the home forces'. Silent Cyril flew to Port Moresby on 22 August 1942 to take command as a temporary major general of C Force (later 'Milne Force'). The Japanese began landing at Milne Bay four days later. Cyril Clowes did not have much time to study the land he would defend but he did have, his biographer claims, 'considerable advantages' in countering the Japanese landing. Most of the fighting would be within the range of his guns—that was his first advantage—then he had strong, indeed crucial, support from his two air force squadrons, and his soldiers, both militia and AIF, were disciplined, thoroughly trained and well-led. Cyril Clowes had some disadvantages too. Terrain and climate head the list, as always in the fighting in New Guinea. It was forever wet and so the mud reduced progress to a crawl, there were high mountains around the bay, and permanent, it seemed, low cloud. What maps there were of the ground over which the battle would be fought were few and totally inadequate. In this sense Cyril Clowes struggled to see; he could not discover his enemy's dispositions and intentions, and even his air force could not see too much of what was happening below because of the cloud. Adding to Cyril Clowes's difficulties was 'the continuous and gratuitous tactical interference by General MacArthur in Brisbane', desperate for victory and triumph somewhere.

At Milne Bay MacArthur would be given an unequivocal

victory. Clowes's 'rewards', his biographer—a soldier from the New Guinea campaign and later a historian and novelist—David Denholm, said, 'were meagre. MacArthur disparaged him and dismissed the efforts of his six battalions. Blamey added his own criticisms'. Silent Cyril, after success at Milne Bay, then saw the war out in various backwaters before retiring from the army in 1949. He had 'inflicted on the Japanese their first notable land defeat of the war', and had given MacArthur, Australia and the Allies their first victory against a seemingly unstoppable enemy. And for thanks he received sharp criticism and a series of unimpressive postings.

That was all in the future as far as Nat Gould was concerned. Milne Bay, he said, 'was bloody awful. Never stopped raining, the mountains came straight up from the strip [that] was just mud with steel planking on it.' To make matters worse, the Japanese controlled the land at the end of the take-off, so pilots were often under fire as they took off or came into land. And the conditions:

> Our living conditions were so squalid. We had six in a little bloody tent and a little bit of timber on the floor but mostly it was mud ... And the food! Baked beans, bully beef ... we couldn't even light a fire most of the time, it just rained and rained and rained ... the only time we ever got a cup of tea was when the Salvation Army came in.

Not Albert Moore this time, he was busy on the Kokoda Track, but others Albert would have known doing the same good work.

The Japanese began landing at Milne Bay on the night of 25/26 August 1942 and the air force's first job was to try to bomb the landing fleet. Kittyhawks are not heavy bombers, which might have been able to do the job, and Nat Gould and his fellow pilots operated with only two 500-pound bombs for each run at the enemy. They were ordered to attack troop transports, not the escorting naval vessels, to maximise the damage and limit the numbers of troops the Japanese could put ashore. The pilots did what they could but they were unable to prevent the Japanese coming ashore. That was a black mark against Cyril Clowes from those back in Brisbane, a lot of huff and puff from MacArthur, but the job now was to prevent the Japanese from making any advance, to push them back into the sea.

The Kittyhawks of the two Australian squadrons came into their own for this task, strafing the Japanese on the ground, keeping their heads down, keeping them bogged down, and preventing them from advancing and attacking in force. The pilots were in the air for as long as their ammunition would last, then it was back to the landing strip for more ammunition, refuelling, and a quick bite to eat for the pilot. Back in the air again, after manoeuvring the take-off carefully to mind the mountains on both sides, they wheeled and dived to the Japanese positions, shot blind, for the most part, into the canopy of dense jungle, but gave the enemy a terrible time of it. It was unrelenting work, daylight to dusk, in the air for as much time as possible. 'The physical demands,' said Nat Gould, 'I don't know how to describe it.'

The crucial battle was on the night of 30/31 August when, with about 2000 troops, the Japanese made a predictable but heavy assault on the airstrip. As the pilots could not fly at night—it was dangerous enough by day with the constant cloud and high mountains—night-time became battle-time. Clowes had solid artillery support, which held the Japanese back throughout the night, and the air force was put back in action at first light. Eventually the Japanese called off the attack and were in full retreat soon after as conditions were equally deplorable for the Japanese invaders, and because supply became a problem with the RAAF squadrons directing their attention to Japanese landing barges attempting to bring in additional ammunition and food. Trench foot—the scourge of soldiers in the mud of the Western Front in the earlier war—resurfaced in this vile jungle, along with malaria and dysentry. The Japanese, hungry, confused and without any air support of their own, faced either decimation or withdrawal. They chose withdrawal, taking the surviving troops off on the night of 4/5 September, having lost around 700 troops. There were 12 officers and 149 Australians killed in the fighting or missing; of these 11 were members of 75 and 76 squadrons.

Nat Gould was shipped out of Milne Bay by Christmas, he remembers, and then he had two weeks' leave in Brisbane. After that he was posted to Mildura, teaching boys who had just learned to fly how to be fighter pilots—and he was expected to do this job in just six weeks. They called Mildura the 'killer school', he said; four of the pilots died in crashes on the first day he arrived—'dreadful things went on'. This was not what Nat Gould's pre-war reading had prepared him for. The flying aces, whose wartime stories he had so eagerly read when he was growing up, were men involved in individual combat—it was almost medieval chivalry in the story of war, with aircraft substituting for horses. Duels in the sky, chase and capture, great skill and courage—the hallmarks of the flying ace. Nat Gould now had to accept that an air force was also a thing of numbers and machines, although there was still a place for the flying ace, he believed. Clive Caldwell, another instructor at Mildura, summed it up for the newcomers: 'Fly fast and shoot straight.'

In the story of the Royal Australian Air Force in the Pacific War there was still much scope for displays of individual bravery, courage and achievement. The only Australian airman to be awarded the Victoria Cross in the Pacific War, and the only Australian to receive the award as a member of an RAAF squadron under RAAF control, Bill Newton, exemplifies such bravery and initiative. His Victoria Cross, awarded for the courage he displayed during ten months of operational flying, cannot be pinned down to one single action, as is usually the case with this award. Born in Melbourne in 1919, Bill Newton was marked out early as a leader. A fine sportsman at school and after, 'an outstanding fast bowler', they said, who might one day play cricket for Victoria and perhaps even for Australia, and a member of his school's cadet corps, Newton enlisted in the RAAF in February 1940 and was commissioned as a pilot officer in June 1940. He did not serve overseas after graduation, working instead as a flying instructor throughout 1941. Only in April 1942, to his great satisfaction, was Newton finally posted to an operational squadron. He went to No. 22 Squadron based at Port Moresby, which was flying Boston light bombers—American twin-engined aircraft carrying three crew. From May 1942 until March 1943 Newton flew 52 operational sorties, 90 per cent of them, it has been estimated, flown through anti-aircraft fire. With a reputation for going 'straight at his objective', Newton had some close shaves.

The squadron was directed to target in particular Salamaua on New Guinea's north coast, slightly to the east of Lae, as a part of the Allies' eviction of the Japanese from New Guinea. The Japanese were heavily entrenched at Salamaua and were providing stubborn resistance to the ground forces. Bill Newton's squadron was assisting the troops on the ground with repeated bombing runs. On one of these sorties the starboard engine of Newton's Boston failed, but Newton kept on going to his target, completed his attack and then flew some 300 kilometres home, all on one engine. On 16 March 1943 Newton flew through 'intense and accurate shellfire' at Salamaua, and on his way to deliver his bombs his aircraft was repeatedly hit.

To make this type of assault once would have required courage, but to return again and again, knowing what was in store for him and his crew, required something more. On this trip 'his aircraft was crippled, with fuselage and wing sections torn, petrol tanks pierced, main planes and engines seriously damaged', but Newton managed to return to his base and make a successful landing. Two days later he was flying above Salamaua again, and had successfully bombed his target when his aircraft was hit and suddenly burst into flames. Newton managed to fly the plane out to sea, and brought the Boston down. He and a crew member, Flight Sergeant John Lyon, swam away from the wreckage and might have hoped to be rescued, but were both captured by the Japanese. Lyon was executed at Lae, Newton at Salamaua, decapitated by a Japanese commander using his ceremonial sword. There is an account of Bill Newton's execution from a Japanese observer that tells how clamly this brave Australian airman prepared himself to die. Bill Newton died two months before his 24th birthday.

In a bad breach of the tightening censorship provisions in Australia, newspapers in October 1943 published a picture of an Australian airman, they said, beheaded by the Japanese. It was Bill Newton, people said, but it was not; rather it was a picture of an Australian army sergeant executed at Aitape in New Guinea. It is still not clear how this story could have been printed in Australian newspapers at the time and naturally it caused considerable anxiety among families of aircrew and prisoners of war, and severe and apparently genuine grief to the government. In the New South

Wales Parliament a government member asked the premier, William McKell, to find out from the federal authorities:

> what public and national value publication of such gruesome narratives possesses; also whether the nerve-racking distress, pain and fear suffered by parents and relatives of Servicemen, particularly mothers of men fighting in New Guinea were taken into consideration before publication . . . was authorised.

John Curtin decided to minimise the damage that this unfortunate incident caused and stated that the government would tell the beheaded airman's next of kin all that was known about the death. While this would distress the grieving family it would remove the immediate doubt and anxiety from all other relatives of captured or missing airmen, although the publicity given the incident had alerted relatives to the certainty that atrocities were being committed by the Japanese. Curtin also said that the government would not reveal the name of the Australian who had suffered this atrocity; as he reasoned, 'this was a private and intimate matter associated with the deep grief of the next-of-kin.' He felt, however, that the family could be assured 'that there would be no bounds to the sympathy felt [for the family] which would be nation wide.' In an off-the-record briefing for the press, Curtin explained that these stories must not be released to the public in time of war because of the widespread anxiety caused to relatives and because 'it may provoke or lead to demands for reprisals on our part. Should this lead to counter-proposals, we are incapable of competing with a barbarous foe.'

In a message to state-based Australian censors the Australian chief publicity censor in June 1944 reported that atrocity stories, like this account of a beheading, were 'known to have a bad effect on the morale of Allied airmen. The fear of mistreatment by the enemy in case they are forced to land in enemy territory cannot but have a bad effect on the morale of the air forces.' This was more so than for soldiers, except during the first months of the spectacular Japanese success in the Pacific War, as aircrew were at considerable and constant risk of capture by the enemy. They

would be right to be wary of the Japanese, and pictures of behead-
ings were certainly not going to improve morale.

Of course, not everyone in the air force was a pilot. Beryl
Bedggood, at a large training base and flying school at Sale in
eastern Victoria from late 1942, was a weather observer. Her job
was to report on conditions locally and nationally to enable
weather forecasters to prepare briefings for the pilots. The work
required accurate observations and the use of increasingly complicated technology; it was exacting, unremitting work and at the
core of air force operations. There were about 2000 airmen at Sale
and around 200 airwomen; it was a big base. The women were
housed in a separate compound of huts with between 15 to 30
women per hut. The huts were spartan—unlined and unheated,
hot in summer and freezing in winter. Built for men, the toilets and
showers were open stalls with no allowance for privacy. All the
women were shift workers and allowance was not made for this
when space was allocated. Women who were trying to sleep had to
contend with women coming off a shift and wanting to let off a bit
of steam. The work was not only demanding physically and intel-
lectually, it was also emotionally draining.

The area around Sale was treacherous for fliers. Planes crashed
into the Gippsland Lakes; it had something like a Bermuda
Triangle reputation. There was no need for myth-making, though,
to explain the difficulty. A hazardous mist around the lakes
confused pilots into thinking they were much higher than their
instruments told them. It was discipline, tough discipline, Nat
Gould discovered, to abandon your own instincts and possible
observations in flying and rely only and always on your instruments. There was also another problem in that weather conditions
in Bass Strait could change quickly and imperceptibly. Aircrew
depended so much on the weather, and Beryl found it very
tough to accept the quite common loss of pilots and crew. Pilots
would come into the weather hut for a briefing before take-off
and would return to the weather hut for a debrief after they had
landed to give an account of the actual weather conditions they
had experienced. The weather observers and forecasters were
often the first, therefore, to know of a lost aircraft and crew when
a pilot simply failed to come back to them. But in war, death was

everywhere and people simply had to learn to cope, whether they were a weather forecaster in Sale or a frontline pilot in New Guinea. There was a sense of purpose about it all, though, but being Australian, everyone reserved the right to grumble and to complain about authority.

In the RAAF there was every reason to complain because from 1942 until the end of the war its senior leadership was simply dysfunctional. John Coates, the military historian and former chief of the Australian army, wrote of the 'chronic derangement of [the RAAF's] senior leadership'. That is a very tough call, and Coates went on to write that it was 'impossible to entirely separate the courage and excellence of its pilots and crews' from the madness at the top, claiming that 'a melancholy series of command blunders put the service at the mercy of badly considered, bizarre decisions'. It was hard enough that men like Bill Newton were putting their lives in extreme jeopardy for their country on their constant missions against the Japanese, but that they were doing it in an air force that was split with personality clashes and was clearly 'deranged' is appalling.

It was, in part at least, an alliance problem. Like the Australian army and the navy, Australia's air force had an overall leader, in this case the chief of the air staff. But because the RAAF worked so closely with the Americans, its own operational command was more closely linked to the Americans than to its own internal chain of command. In a formal decision, following disputes and an obvious breakdown in authority, John Curtin divided air force decision-making into two spheres: operational decisions and administrative decisions, putting a different man in charge of each. This might have worked if the two men in the top jobs worked together closely and harmoniously but there was a danger that the chief of the air staff, the head man in title and precedence, might be left out of the crucial command decisions; an intolerable situation, particularly if the chief was a man with even an average sense of his own importance. And herein lay the remainder of the problem. The two Australians in divided command, Air Vice Marshal George Jones, chief of the air staff, and Air Vice Marshal William (Bill) Bostock, operational commander of the RAAF, though fomerly close friends, soon learned to detest each other in their new roles and would never willingly allow the other man the advantage.

Bill Bostock, born in Sydney in 1892, went to sea as a wireless operator when he left school, enlisted in the AIF as a signaller in November 1914 and served at Gallipoli; later he joined the Anzac Mounted Division and later still served on the Western Front in the Royal Air Force. He experienced an amazing time of change and challenge. In 1921 Bill Bostock joined the infant Royal Australian Air Force, a tiny service, and endured the restricted training opportunities and limitations of the inter-war air force; nevertheless he forged ahead. He was a man marked out for leadership. Highly regarded by Chief of the Air Staff Charles Burnett, Bostock achieved rapid promotion during the Second World War, and Burnett and Bostock both believed that Bostock should replace Burnett when the Englishman retired from service in Australia. Indeed, Burnett told Bostock that he would be the next chief of the air staff; there was high expectation there. Instead Bostock became chief of staff to the American Allied Air Forces commander and George Jones became chief of the air staff.

Described as 'diligent but uninspiring' there is a suspicion that cabinet chose George Jones by mistake. The minister for Air, Arthur Drakeford, a former train driver and union official, deeply resented Charles Burnett's patrician disdain for Labor politicians and would not sanction Burnett's nominee, Bill Bostock, as his replacement. The minister's veto was as peeved and as petty as that. Drakeford, sensibly, wanted Dickie Williams, who had been languishing in London following Menzies' refusal to appoint him to the top job in 1940, but Curtin had taken against Williams. Once again the brightest and most able Australian air leader was overlooked. There was an impasse at the cabinet meeting and when advised to select the next most senior officer 'on the list', meaning the 'Air Force List of Senior Officers', Drakeford mistakenly produced an operational list that showed Jones as number four behind those cabinet had already rejected. By promoting George Jones into the top job, cabinet raised him three ranks and leap-frogged him over eight senior colleagues. There was amazement throughout the officer ranks and 'George Who?' from everyone else.

Four years younger than Bill Bostock, George Jones left school at 14 to become a motor mechanic. He served as a private at Gallipoli before joining the Australian Flying Corps in the desert as an air mechanic. He had a brilliant war; promoted to captain in the AFC and awarded the Distinguished Flying Cross. Jones, like Bostock, had joined the RAAF in 1921, and also rose through the ranks. He was with Minister for Air Jim Fairbairn in Ottawa in late 1939 for the drafting of the Empire Air Training Scheme agreement. It would be wrong to paint George Jones as a complete novice at leadership levels and, as he remained as chief of the air staff until 1952, nearly ten years in the position, he must have been giving some satisfaction. He was a good administrator, they said. Yet the air force historian, Alan Stephens, writes of the rivalry between George Jones and Bill Bostock as on an 'epic scale'. Bostock was embittered 'by this capricious turn of events', at Jones' appointment, and Jones fought 'doggedly' to receive his due as chief of the air force.

Did the rivalry between the two men make any real difference at the sharp end of the war? Air Commodore 'Garry' Garrisson, who for years attempted to write an account of the impact of the rivalry, would constantly astonish me with his anecdotal and well-remembered accounts of the divisions, arguments and pettiness right through and to the top of the air force. Garrisson wrote that Jones refused to delegate his authority over support functions needed for the conduct of operations, so that Bostock's supposed control of operations was in fact hampered by his inability to call on the support he needed. Garrisson also wrote of disputes between the two headquarters over 'appointment of officers, requirements for operational training, construction of airfields and camp sites, and the supply of ammunition, fuel, replacement aircraft and reserves of bombs'. These two 'leaders' were in permanent dispute over just about everything that an air force does. It was a terrible situation for which the polticians must take some of the blame; John Curtin and his ministers had a clear responsibility to fix this appalling problem.

John Coates writes of a 'grotesque incident' during the invasion of Tarakan in May 1945, where air power played a crucial role in the success of the Australians in the Borneo campaigns of that

year. The relatively light loss of Australian life was due in part to
the brilliance of Bill Bostock's organisation in planning and main-
taining air power that unremittingly assaulted the Japanese lines
and defences. At Tarakan MacArthur and his senior people
watched with some sort of awe as wave after wave of aircraft
attacked the Japanese and assisted, so crucially, in the successful
landing of the Australian troops. But there were no Australian
aircraft in this air assault; they were all American despite this being
a joint operation. George Jones had, unilaterally, sent a message to
the RAAF squadrons that were to be involved, instructing them
that as they had exceeded their monthly quota of flying hours the
squadrons were now grounded. Regardless of the importance of
the landings at Tarakan, a significant campaign in the last days of the
war, regardless that the Australian squadrons should have been in
support of troops landing to attack Japanese positions and take the
island, George Jones had ruled that Australia's air force would not
support Australian troops, simply as another way for George Jones
to get back at Bill Bostock. And you tell me why there was not
some authority in Australia to court martial these men, or make
them confront the consequences of their pig-headedness and
stupidity.

Such utter disregard for the wellbeing of the men and women
in their command might well have seen the collapse of morale in
Australia's air force. It was not as if you could keep this sort of
thing hidden. Perhaps it was the failure of leadership at the highest
level that was weighing on the minds of those involved in what was
called the 'Morotai Mutiny'. Eight senior officers, then based on
the island of Morotai, simultaneously submitted their resignations
from the air force in identically worded terms, in protest at the
work they and their aircrew had been given to do. These officers
believed that Australian lives were being lost on operations that
were contributing little or nothing to the ending of the war. It was
an embarrassment for the air force that one of those who submitted his resignation was Clive Caldwell, the RAAF's leading air ace.
The American air general, George C. Kenney, interviewed the
aggrieved officers and told George Jones, in forceful terms, that if
there was an attempt to court martial these men he would personally present himself as a witness for the defence. The matter was

then brushed aside. Yet it was largely the end of Clive Caldwell's career, leaving him embittered about the RAAF, which was a terrible shame.

Born in Sydney in 1910, Caldwell was in fact too old for the air force when war broke out in 1939 as there was an upper age limit of 28 for trainee flyers. But Caldwell, already married by this time, was passionate about joining the RAAF. Like Nat Gould, he was raised on a steady diet of the exploits of First World War air aces as a boy and knew one of these aces personally—Andrew King Cowper, Military Cross and two Bars, who had shot down 19 German aircraft on the Western Front. Caldwell had already learned to fly by the time he enlisted and, as a well-educated person and fine sportsman, he was just the type the air force was looking for. Amending his birth certicate to put his age down, Caldwell joined the RAAF and eventually made the Empire Air Training Scheme, graduating as a pilot in January 1941. Posted to the Desert Air Force, he served in Syria, Palestine and North Africa, and was credited with 20.5 'kills'—a remarkable tally that gave Caldwell the nickname 'Killer', which he detested but which stuck to him for the rest of his life. On one occasion in the desert Caldwell shot down five German aircraft in a single sortie, the rest of his squadron between them claiming six additional kills. Possibly young boys around Australia, plotting the war on their world maps, were now also devoted to reading stories of the Second World War air aces, and they would have put Killer Caldwell's saga at the top of their reading lists. By the time he came away from the Middle East Caldwell had a Distinguished Flying Cross and Bar.

With the Japanese in the war, Clive Caldwell was re-posted to Darwin to fly Spitfires and within eight months, in 1943, was credited with shooting down eight Japanese aircraft. George Odgers, an official historian of the RAAF, described an action involving Caldwell and three Australian squadrons against a flight of Japanese bombers with fighter escort. It is a thrilling account and shows how intimate, still, and intricate the work of these fighter pilots in combat was. Advised on 2 May 1943 that a force of enemy bombers was on course for Darwin, commanders ordered three Australian squadrons, Nos. 54, 452 and 457, into the air. There were at least 20 Japanese bombers and a large number of escorting fighters to oppose. As squadron leader Caldwell had 33 Spitfires at his disposal, but it took time to gain the height he would need to attack the fighters first and then the bombers. Caldwell decided he could not attack the Japanese until after the bombers had flown over Darwin, dropping their bombs. That, in itself, was a difficult decision but, for their own safety and success, Caldwell needed his aircraft in the best possible position for the attack. The bombers released over 100 bombs on Darwin, causing slight damage to two buildings and sadly killing a soldier. Only then was Caldwell in a position to go after the enemy aircraft.

The encounter became a series of 'dogfights', as George Odgers describes them, which 'took place at about 7000 feet, with aircraft turning figures-of-eight as pilots tried to get on each other's tails'. After the first wave of Australian Spitfires dispersed some of the Japanese aircraft a second wave dived into the formation of Japanese bombers, and more enemy fighter aircraft came in to deflect them, leading to more dogfights:

> Diving at a steep angle [Caldwell] attacked a [Japanese fighter] from a range of 350 yards. One of his cannons failed to fire and only ten shots came from the other causing the machine to slew. Caldwell missed the enemy and was immediately afterwards himself attacked by another two Japanese planes. He dived under these but another one came up behind him. This aircraft was seen by Pilot Officer Kenneth Fox who fired on it from it above and turned it away.

Ken Fox was then 23 years of age, had enlisted in 1940 and was an experienced pilot. Clive Caldwell was lucky to have him around. But that was life in fighter aircraft: individual brilliance and looking out, at the same time, for one's mates. Short and sharp, too, but intense while in combat.

This action over Darwin on 2 May 1943, a 'brief but furious' engagement in which six enemy aircraft were destroyed, four probably destroyed and a further eight damaged, was a common enough occurrence for fighter pilots. Waiting for action, then engagement, reports to write and then waiting for action all over again. Because of the height the Australians had to achieve to make their attack that day and the longer than usual extent of the battle, fuel became a problem for the Spitfires returning from combat on 2 May. Five aircraft made forced landings before reaching their airfields and three more were forced to land because of engine failure. Two Australians had been killed in the fight and eight Spitfires destroyed. Ken Fox, his engine hit by enemy fire, turned his aircraft upside down and then parachuted into the sea. Spotted floating in his rubber dinghy, Fox was later rescued.

Air power would, of course, end the Pacific War. Even as early as the beginning of 1944 it was apparent that the imbalance in the air would make the war unwinnable for Japan, which could now muster less than 1000 aircraft against the Allies' 3000. And the Japanese aircraft were becoming increasingly obsolete, whereas the Allies kept producing faster and more efficient models. One indication of the total dominance of the Allies in the air was the fact that from November 1944 to June 1945 there was a total of only nine recorded Japanese attacks against Allied targets in the South-West Pacific, involving only 17 enemy aircraft. Then came the terrible air bombardment of Japan itself. In one week in July 1945 no fewer than 10 460 air sorties had been sent against Japanese forces and the islands of Japan. The overall bombardment of Japan cost the Japanese 806 000, mainly civilian casualties of which 330 000 were fatal. Those thinking about the coming war in the 1930s had emphasised the terror that would rain on the civilian populations from the skies. The destruction of Japan was the exemplar of that.

There were 155 812 men and women who served with the RAAF in the Pacific War, 5233 of whom had become casualties. Nat Gould, just one of those airmen, had transferred to the Australian navy as a flier late in the war. As the war came to an end, like everyone else in the services, he had to look at his options. While most were itching for a quick return to civilian life, Nat Gould was not one of them: 'Not while there were all these aeroplanes to fly.' He would spend more than another 20 years in the services. Thinking back to his war years, Gould said that 'staying alive, getting through it all was my biggest achievement . . . it was 90 per cent luck, perhaps ten per cent skill.' He saw many of his 'pilot chums' killed, 'some [of them] very close friends.' It was the random nature of it all. After the war, he had a regular dream of being in a burning aircraft: 'Mum and Dad used to come and wake me up on one of my few days of leave. I'd be screaming.' The dreams continued, with less regularity, late into his life: 'Now and then I have this bloody awful dream. I'm in a strange aircraft, I don't recognise the cockpit, everything's all over the place. All these millions of dials and I don't know what they are and I can't find anything ... It's pitch-black night, I can't hear what they're telling me on the radio and I've got to take-off. I wake up absolutely sweating.' It's a long way from the boy dreaming of flying and reading all the books and magazines on air aces of the Great War. But by then Nat Gould had known his own war.

16. DESERT FOXES

On 22 December 1942, a few weeks after the infamous incident at Koitaki, another general had lined up another body of Australian troops to speak to them after battle. This was General Sir Harold Alexander, who was born in Ireland and had fought with Irish troops in the First World War. A senior commander in 1939, Alexander was in charge of the rearguard action at Dunkirk and is said to have been the last Allied soldier to have left France at the evacuation. Rapid promotion followed: lieutenant general in December 1940—the youngest at that rank in the British army—when he organised the British retreat from Burma to India; general in April 1942, as the Commander-in-Chief in North Africa; and Commander-in-Chief Middle East Command in August. Alexander faced Rommel's resurgent Afrika Korps. No original thinker, he was said to be a man of considerable personal courage, imperturbability, and able to make friends readily. With his experience, and some affability, he was a man the Australians could admire.

Before him on an airfield in Palestine stood the 9th Australian Division, 12 000 men. The parade stretched for more than a kilometre. Allied troops had just won a great victory in North Africa at El Alamein—Winston Churchill was to say, 'before Alamein we never had a victory; after Alamein we never had a defeat.' Would the general berate the Australians and speak of defeat and cowardice? Of course not; it was inconceivable, quite impossible. Instead Alexander only had words of praise and thanks for these Australians, so far from home, and worried, more likely, about the fate of their homeland than the blasted desert in which they had been living for far too long.

'Your reputation as fighters has always been famous,' Harold Alexander said:

> but I do not believe that you have ever fought with greater bravery or distinction than you did during the battles when you broke the German and the Italian armies in the Western Desert. [At Alamein] you have added fresh lustre to your already illustrious name.

The victory in the desert has been described as 'one of the most complete victories in military history' against one of the most astute generals the Germans had ever produced. When Alexander spoke to the Australians, Erwin Rommel had, some time since, been withdrawn from North Africa, a sick man. He would next command in France and would face the D-Day invasion.

Was Erwin Rommel the one 'good' Nazi, the only one of them that we could respect and admire? Goering, Goebbels, Himmler: hated and hateful men. But Erwin Rommel, the 'desert fox', cunning, quick, brave, unpredictable; an honourable opponent. 'How did it go in the desert, Father, how did Monty finally beat Rommel?', we would ask our Latin teacher, Father Craig, in 1957. He was ready to be sucked in every time, he would give up on Latin declensions and Caesar's conquest of Gaul and, with diagrams on the chalk board, he would outline the nature of the campaign and the brilliance of the opposing generals in the desert. For the desert campaign took war back to the chessboard of classical manoeuvre and countermanoeuvre, of the personalities of generals, of local heroism, of military thinking that really made a difference. It was a thrilling story for eleven- or twelve-year-old boys, much better than the Latin from which we had distracted our teacher. And it was hard to hate Rommel, really.

There was more to the story, of course, than those two magnificent generals, Erwin Rommel and Bernard Law Montgomery, and, typically for Australia in the mid-1950s, we never heard much of the Australian parts of the story. Perhaps we knew that there were Australians at El Alamein, but for us the story was all Monty and Rommel and the excitement of war. Perhaps we should have been told of the enormous war cemetery at El Alamein with 7240 Allied graves, including those of 1234 Australians. There are the names of a further 11 945 men on the walls of the cemetery building; names of the men whose bodies were never found or identified in the battles across the North African desert and the Mediterranean Sea between 1940 and 1943. Perhaps we should have been told, too, of the dark and imposing German mausoleum near El Alamein, honouring the dead of the Afrika Korps, or the Italian building—so like a church, filled with light—with a bewildering number of names on its walls. These places, the cemeteries, the memorials, the buildings at El Alamein, all tell us one thing—that war kills.

Battles, I have been telling battlefield tourists at Gallipoli and in France and Belgium for several years now, take place in some of the world's most beautiful places. Gallipoli itself can be stunning; the Somme river valley is a place of the utmost beauty. But although close to the sea, El Alamein is not a place of beauty. We landed in Cairo with our 'Australia Remembers' veterans in late April 1995 and drove to Alexandria. One of those in the party had been in the Royal Australian Navy and at an early hour he and I visit the harbour at Alexandria. He wants to live out in his imagination the arrival of HMAS *Sydney* at Alexandria after the victory over the Italian cruiser, the *Bartolomeo Colleoni*, when *Sydney* was given a rapturous welcome: 'a continuous roar [of voices] for about fifteen minutes' as she passed along the ships of the fleet to her station, close to the wharves. After our small tribute to *Sydney*, the veterans' party drive on to El Alamein for a ceremony the next day. The cemetery is a substantial but pitiful thing, impressive in size, but with none of the lawns and garden beds of Commonwealth war cemeteries elsewhere. For as far as you can see this is desert; the cemetery is made of the bare earth. There are a few attempts at shrubs, but the overwhelming impression is of men buried in the hard, unrelenting earth. You walk among the 7240 headstones—some of them, anyway—and you realise that each stone tells an individual story.

John Clyde Delaney was a labourer at Narrabri, west of Armidale, New South Wales, and 26 years of age when he enlisted at Victoria Barracks in Sydney on 5 June 1941. John, unmarried, joined the 2/13th Battalion; his father, Clyde, was his next of kin. John was killed on 24 October 1942 in the terrible fighting at the very beginning of Bernard Montgomery's final assault, at Tel el Eisa, just outside El Alamein. I went to the 2/13th's war diary to see if I could find how John Delaney had died. Just one death, I know, but we understand nothing about battle if we do not try to see it from the individual's perspective. War diaries can be a find or a disappointment; it all depends on the diligence of the junior officer usually ordered to write it up. On 24 October 1942 the 2/13th Battalion found itself in such strife that the war diarist knew he must tell the story as fully as he could. Part of the trouble was that the Germans had heavily mined the land over which the attacking troops advanced. Engineers attempted to clear a path through the minefields, but inevitably this funnelled the troops into narrow paths. Bernard Montgomery had told his commanders that either they fight their way through the minefields or he would find commanders who would.

The 2/13th Battalion were well prepared for the battle the men were about to enter. Using the technique John Monash had developed in France, the men studied a sand model of the terrain over which they would fight; in any case, these were seasoned and experienced soldiers, even if John Delaney had only been in the army for eighteen months. By 0247, on 24 October, the war diarist recorded, the minefield was 'gapped' and companies of the battalion proceeded forward. A Company was one of the first forward. They ran into withering fire. Captain Ross Sanderson, 30 years of age with a wife at Summer Hill, Sydney, A Company's commander, was killed almost immediately. Lieutenant Edward (Eric) Norrie, though seriously wounded, took charge and ordered the advance to resume. He, too, was killed. Eric Norrie's father had been at Gallipoli and in France as a distinguished leader, and remained in the army after the war. His son, 22 years of age when he was killed, would have known about war.

Now it was the turn of Lieutenant Charles O'Connor, born in 1914, now 28 years of age, to take control of the company. He, too, was already wounded. O'Connor called for volunteers to come with him to attempt to take out the strong post that was giving all the trouble and impeding the company's advance. Twelve men volunteered, but forget the parade-ground orderliness that the statement implies. Hear, instead, the ferocious noise of battle, machine-gun and rifle fire, shells overhead from tanks in front and behind, shells from anti-tank artillery. Fearful noise such as we can hardly imagine. Can O'Connor even make himself heard? Somehow he dragged together a party for the assault. He was again wounded, a serious wound to the head, the war diarist reports. Even so, his small party overran the crucial strong post and O'Connor 'personally inflicted several casualties on [the] enemy with [his] bayonet'. Charles O'Connor then staggered into B Company headquarters 'partially unconscious'. He died soon after. His wife, Daphne Anzac O'Connor, perhaps born a year later than her husband, in 1915, now also knew about war.

Somewhere in the midst of this action John Clyde Delaney also died; the war diary does not mention him by name. There was only one officer now left in A Company. The losses among the men had been so heavy that A Company was reorganised the next day into a composite unit with D Company; too few of its officers and men remained for existence in its own right. And this is the story of one company of 100 men or so across a few hours on a battlefield that was engaging thousands of men across a dozen or so days at the climax to the mighty battle for North Africa. The stakes were high; lose El Alamein and the path for the Germans would lie open to Cairo. Yet victory at El Alamein might smash the German army in North Africa decisively.

You stand before the grave of this one Australian soldier, John Delaney, in that barren, massive cemetery, and hope that in learning a little of his story you learn the story of them all. But you know you never can. No wonder my Latin teacher, all those years ago, broke the story down into a battle between Monty and Rommel, honourable men both of them. It was just so much easier than the messy complexity of real men dying on the battlefield, with wives and fathers and mothers left behind to grieve. But how had it come to this, in late 1942, still fighting to stave off defeat.

We earlier left the Australians at Tobruk when they were being withdrawn, exhausted men, after a long and debilitating siege. But the British were not in North Africa simply for a siege. Their objective was to boot the enemy out of North Africa entirely, so they needed to become an attacking force, not a defensive one. With considerable power, they were on the move again and by early January 1942 Erwin Rommel had been pushed back to El Agheila, even further back along the coast than Benghazi, where the Australian troops had earlier been. Once again, supply to the troops was a key part of battlefield success. Paradoxically, the closer the Germans were to their sources of supply, principally the port of Tripoli, the stronger they were, and the further the British were from the Egyptian border, and guaranteed supply, the weaker they became.

Rommel, now reinvigorated, started pushing the British back and by May 1942 was fighting a major battle at Gazala, between Derna and Tobruk. Rommel could be an authoritarian and arrogant commander, and he never left his subordinates to wonder what he was thinking. But he was also a frontline commander, in there with his troops, talking to them, seeing for himself, flexible in his thinking and quick to take advantage of his opportunities. In contrast the British generals fought from the rear and this war was no place for that. As a British general noted: 'The British High Command in Cairo and the Western Desert remained a well-meaning military democracy in which senior commanders continued to treat orders as a basis for discussion.' Against Rommel that would just not be good enough, and an impatient and ruthless Churchill in London began removing his senior commanders wholesale as he searched for a combination to thwart Rommel. The British lost decisively at Gazala and by mid-June were in full flight back to El Alamein, across the Egyptian border; the next realistic place to make a stand. There is a ridgeline, you see, where defences might be prepared, though to the battlefield traveller today, it is a ridgeline that is mighty hard to see.

The 9th Australian Division was not involved in the fighting to El Agheila or back to Gazala. After its rescue from Tobruk the division had enjoyed a modest period of rest and training in Palestine, and had then replaced the 7th Division in Syria in January 1941 (the 7th had returned to Australia). Leslie Morshead, 'Ming the Merciless', still commanding the 9th, was anxious that it spend as much time as possible in training in Syria to bring the division back to the highest standards, but he recognised that time might be short. The question of morale had to be considered carefully, too, as it was obvious the men's minds were firmly fixed on Australia as their country's situation in the Pacific War deteriorated. There is no doubt the 9th Division would have preferred to have been back home, particularly in the early months of 1942 when an invasion of Australia seemed likely, or at least possible. Morale fell even lower in June when the division learned that Rommel had captured Tobruk, which Morshead's men had worked so valiantly to defend. It was as if all their good work now counted for nothing and, with the enemy apparently gaining the upper hand, a return to Australia seemed much less likely. On 30 June 1942, the men of the division learned that they would be returning to the desert, this time to El Alamein. To do a tough thing once tests character; to go back and do it a second time requires courage and determination. It can only have been with heavy hearts that these Australians returned for their second round of desert warfare.

The Australians first went into action on 9/10 July 1942 at Tel el Eisa and its surrounding vital high ground, and were rewarded with success. That was good for morale but Morshead and his staff were worried. They could not find any plan in the skirmishes and battles that the British high command ordered. There seemed little coordinated thinking among the British, rather what seemed to be knee-jerk reactions in response to Rommel's continual probing and advance. There needed to be a plan. Morshead complained in his diary that there was 'no stability, [rather] a wealth of plans and appreciations! Fighting always in bits and pieces, and so defeats in detail'.

In London, Winston Churchill had come to much the same conclusion. He flew to Cairo on 3 August 1942, dressed in one of those ludicrous outfits, pith-helmet included, that the British seemed to think appropriate for the 'East'. But Churchill had more on his mind than clothes. Were his generals up to the job? He doubted it and he removed Auchinleck and appointed Harold Alexander to the top job, and made other widespread changes. Because of the death of his first choice, General Gott, whose aircraft crash-landed at Cairo under enemy attack, Churchill appointed Bernard Montgomery to the command of the 8th Army, which included the 9th Australian Division. Such are the chances of history.

Bernard Montgomery was not one of those British generals, like Phillip Neame or 'Jumbo' Wilson to name but two, who loathed Australians. In the vast collections of the Australian War Memorial there is one particular slouch hat with a difference; it is Montgomery's hat. Making his first visit to the Australians on 14 August 1942 after their victory at Tel el Eisa, and just after assuming his own command, Montgomery asked for a slouch hat: the symbol, everywhere, of Australia. He always wore the hat thereafter, adding, wherever he found the space, the badges of many of the other units in his 8th Army. Not all Australians of the 9th Division approved of this: Montgomery was reportedly described by members of 2/7th Field Regiment as 'a prize galah' who wore the hat 'jammed down on top of his head'. 'It looked like a bucket on his head', an officer wrote, 'and he didn't know how to wear it'. Probably the slouch hat offended some of the British, too, and later Montgomery exchanged it for the black beret that was to become his trademark. Yet after the war Montgomery donated the slouch hat to the War Memorial. Why, I asked the custodian of Montgomery's papers, Sir Denis Hamilton? 'Because he loved the Australians,' was the unashamed reply.

Bernard Montgomery, born in December 1887, was only two years of age when his father was appointed Anglican Bishop of Tasmania. At the time of his appointment the bishop had no idea where Tasmania was and rushed to his club to find an atlas. The family moved to Hobart in 1889 and would return to England in 1901, when Bernard was thirteen. The bishop soon discovered that his job required him to travel around his diocese extensively and he spent about six months of each year in the remoter parts of

Tasmania, including the wild west coast and the offshore islands. According to Montgomery's biographer, Nigel Hamilton, the bishop took to the bush in corduroys and hobnail boots, and wearing a broad-rimmed prospector's hat. Perhaps the young Monty took note. Bernard, understandably, picked up an Australian accent and was forced by his domineering mother to stand in front of the rest of the family and speak 'correct' English. Growing up in Tasmania left its mark on Montgomery. Though they may not of realised it as they muttered about the British 'galah', Montgomery's affection for the Australians in his command was partly due to his early life among them.

In 1907 the young Monty entered Sandhurst, destined for a life in the army; he took to it with relish. 'The profession of arms was a life-study,' he would later say, and he devoted himself to that profession with almost religious fervour, perhaps in that respect a true son of the bishop. Badly wounded in 1914, Montgomery served as a staff officer during the rest of the Great War but did not make a real mark; some believed that his detailed planning of battles made him overcautious. Others saw him as arrogant and abrasive, especially between the wars, and his promotion was accordingly slow. It was his work in France in 1940 that came to attention and from then on Montgomery's promotion was rapid: lieutenant general in July 1940, senior appointments thereafter. But he was second choice as commander of the 8th Army in August 1942, and some regarded the appointment as a poisoned chalice; the army seemed destined for defeat, Rommel was unstoppable, they said.

Monty's caravan is one of the more popular exhibits at the Imperial War Museum in London. It is a quaint little thing, barely room enough for one person. Above Montgomery's desk, though, is a large photograph of Erwin Rommel. Montgomery would study it for hours, it is said, working out what his opponent would do next. This speaks of an element of uncertainty in the general's mind yet his public image was of confidence, absolute certainty in his own plans and an eagerness to engage the enemy. Perhaps not much liked by his peers, Montgomery was immensely popular with the ordinary soldier. He was out among the troops, just as Rommel was, and could speak directly and easily with them. 'We'll hit 'em for six' was one of his favourite expressions, no doubt raising a cheer with the Australians of the 9th Division.

One of the first things that Montgomery ordered was the removal of the transport that could be used to take withdrawing troops from the battlefield. There will be no retreat, he said, and his actions showed that he meant it. But Monty knew that if Rommel attacked in August, as Montgomery was building up his supplies and retraining his army, then the Germans would have the advantage. Montgomery was sitting in his caravan wondering what Rommel would do but, much more importantly, he also had access to what the Germans were planning to do through Ultra, which had penetrated the German codes and could deliver to him the German cable traffic. Ultra told him that Rommel would attack at the end of August with a view to taking Alam Halfa ridge, inland from El Alamein. Should Rommel gain this ridge he would be in a position to cut off British supplies, and Montgomery would be in deep strife. Hence the order that there would be no retreat.

On 20 August the 2/23rd Battalion, part of the 26th Brigade and the 9th Division, celebrated the second anniversary of its formation in the desert, far away from Bonegilla and north-eastern Victoria where it had all started. That old philosopher, Jim Mulcahy, was still at his typewriter as the editor of the battalion's regular newsletter, *Mud and Blood in the Field*. Still spinning the yarns and passing on the battalion news, still giving a summary of the nightly BBC News, still passing on gossip, still attempting to enhance morale and deepen, if possible, the sense of camaraderie. 'Only by looking around at the many new faces', Jim Mulcahy wrote in his anniversary editorial:

and remarking upon the absence of many old friends are we aware of the eventful happenings that have taken place in the past year. Otherwise, life is much the same; the same job still ahead of us; the same story of effort and achievement behind us . . . One long year further away from our homes and loved ones, but, one must not forget, a year nearer to the time when our job will be successfully accomplished, and we will be able to return to them. How often in our dreams do we picture and anticipate that happy time?

Rommel had overstretched himself in the battle for Alam Halfa in late August—from Ultra, Montgomery knew his opponent was a sick man—and after furious fighting, greatly assisted by the British superiority in the air, Rommel withdrew. The line had held and Montgomery could breathe a little easier. Monty's was a 'model defensive battle', wrote pre-eminent contemporary Australian military thinker, John Coates, in reviewing the battle plans. But Montgomery wanted more than brilliant defence; his brief from Churchill was to attack, indeed to drive Rommel from the desert, and now he set about planning that offensive. The 9th Division was on Montgomery's right flank, by the sea, at El Alamein, and it was inevitable that the division would be heavily involved in the general's plans. Not involved in the fighting earlier, except for a diversionary attack by the 2/15th Battalion, the division was rested and refreshed and ready for the fight. There was, of course, the inevitable patrolling of the frontline, Morshead would never weary of that, and sentry duty, and the shelling from the enemy.

As you walk the ground now you are aware of how horrible it must have been to live in this place for months on end. Even digging in was a terrible task, the soil was so hard. Add to that the heat, the constant dust, the monotony of the food, the flies and you have yet another picture of the misery of battle. There were some improvements for these men over what they had experienced at Tobruk: for a start there was the possibility of leave—a few days in either Alexandria or Cairo—there was an issue of beer, too, from time to time, almost unheard of at Tobruk, and there were diversions like concert parties on very rare occasions. But it was the desert that was inescapable, and the heat. Once again you find yourself wondering how men could possibly have kept on going in conditions like this. What ideas and motivation encouraged them to put up with all this? Weren't they tempted to chuck in the towel? Was it the idea that they were fighting for their country? Well, their country was indeed fighting for its very existence, but that was back at home. The idea that they had to stick with their mates? There was probably plenty in that. Or, possibly, the idea that Rommel and his soldiers represented an infamy as bad as the world had ever known, an evil that just had to be destroyed. Did some of those in the 2/23rd Battalion remember what Jim Mulcahy had written in the newsletter when they were at Tobruk: 'Today you and I are not only part of history. We are history in the making . . . the heritage of the ages is in our keeping. We are not creatures of destiny, but destiny itself, for without us all that is decent and kindly and holy, will perish from this earth.' You would like to think the men remembered that sentiment, if not the exact words from the year before; you would like to believe that kind of thinking made all this present suffering endurable. Especially as you walk among the headstones in the vast cemetery.

After Rommel's withdrawal from the battle for Alam Halfa both sides continued strengthening their defences and preparing for the coming battle. The frontline stretched from the sea along some 65 kilometres to a deep valley, the Qattara Depression. Both sides were heavily mining the land in front of them—even today it is not possible to walk far into the battlefield for fear of unexploded mines—and erecting defences, wire and all the rest of the para-phernalia we would expect of battle. The balance was now at last swinging in favour of the Allies. It was unusual, to this point in the war, for the British to have superiority in the air; think of Greece and Crete and the havoc the Luftwaffe created there. Equally important was the control of the sea that the Allies now exercised. So much German shipping was now being sunk in the Mediter-ranean that Rommel's troops were beginning to suffer severe shortages of supplies. This would eventually contribute heavily to their defeat.

Rommel expected that Montgomery would attack and he anticipated that his opponent would choose the full moon period in the second half of October. Returning to Germany on sick leave on 22 September, Rommel had prepared well for the coming assault. He had had 500 000 mines laid across the whole of his front, and an urgent and important part of the battle would be the work of the British engineers in opening up gaps in the minefields that would make it possible for the infantry and the tanks to get through. The Germans correctly predicted the attack would commence on 23 October even though they did not have access to the British cable traffic as Montgomery had through Ultra. Correctly guessing the date aside, they were, in other ways deceived about Montgomery's plans.

Monty went to elaborate lengths to convince the Germans that the attack would commence in force in the south, by building up dummy tanks, dummy artillery, dummy transport lines. It worked. More important was the training that Montgomery had imposed on his army. Central to his doctrine was the idea that the troops should train specifically for the actions they would later be engaged in. The training was aligned to Montgomery's battle plan, and different units trained in different ways because they would be performing different jobs. As John Monash discovered before Montgomery, one great benefit of such detailed and specific training was the confidence it gave the troops. Soldiers going into battle like to know what they can expect to find in front of them and what they will be asked to do. They gain confidence, too, when they see their officers know there is a plan of battle and what role their unit has in the wider plan. Montgomery's brilliance lay in the way he conceived of the battle, and the way he communicated his battleplan to his soldiers through the most thorough training.

'The sky [was] literally one mass of flame', Jim Mulcahy wrote of the opening of the battle, heralded by a massive British artillery assault on the enemy; 'the noise something that no-one will ever forget.' The 2/23rd was in reserve for the first four days and watched its 'cobber' battalions in the 26th Brigade, the 2/24th and 2/48th go about their work. 'Our turn will come', Mulcahy predicted. And then the paper was suspended until a special Christmas issue for 1942. The 2/23rd, like all the 'cobber' battalions and brigades, was a bit too busy for typewriters and newsletters.

The guns began firing at 9.40 p.m. on 23 October 1942 and the infantry moved off precisely 20 minutes later. For all the sophistication of tanks and aircraft, Montgomery had decided that, as on the Western Front in the earlier war, it would be infantry that would make the most gains. Working with and behind the tanks was just too complicated for the troops, he believed, and soldiers on foot would assault the wire and face the enemy. Tanks played an important role, of course, and if there was a danger point in the assault it was when, on the first night, the armoured divisions failed to make any real progress. 'Either they would fight their way out of the minefield,' Montgomery had said, 'or he would find other commanders who would'. That, according to John Coates, was, psychologically at least, the turning point of the battle. The next night, 24/25 October, the 2/48th Battalion made a crucial dash for a low ridge, Trig 29, out from Tel el Eisa, and they were outstandingly successful. This was what Jim Mulcahy and his mates had watched from reserve and which had so delighted them.

Percy Gratwick was 38 years of age when he enlisted in the AIF, five days before Christmas in 1940. He had done it hard all his life. The fifth son of the family, Percy, was only nine when his father died. He left school in Perth in 1918, aged 16, and worked around the city for a while. Then in 1922 Percy went north, to the Pilbara, learned to become a drover, and eventually had his own team of mostly Aboriginal stockmen. 'He was his own man', writes Bill Gammage, his biographer, 'well used to looking after himself in that tough country'. I do not know what motivated Gratwick to join the Australians at war but certainly he was keen enough. He had tried to enlist but was knocked back because his nose had been badly damaged years before, so he paid good money to have it fixed and was accepted when he went to enlist a second time. Never married, Percy Gratwick sailed from Perth for the distant war on 5 July 1941.

Gratwick was briefly at Tobruk, but only at the end of the siege as the Australians were being withdrawn. Nevertheless, he wrote to a brother, 'I'm pleased and proud to be able to piss in the same pot with such a fine crowd'. Percy's first battle would be at El Alamein in October 1942. Did the country he found there remind him of the Pilbara? Perhaps he did feel somewhat at home. Like Jack Delaney in A Company 2/13th Battalion a couple of night's earlier, Percy Gratwick's platoon ran into a strongly defended German post in front of Trig 29, the slight elevation in flat, rocky landscape that was their objective. Pinned down, its leaders killed, Gratwick's platoon was now down to just seven men. The ground in front of Percy sloped down, then rose up again to the German positions, heavily defended with mortar and machine-gun posts. Percy Gratwick sized up the situation and jumped up alone, armed only with grenades and his rifle and bayonet. No one had told Percy what to do; no one had called for volunteers. Percy went first for the mortar post, throwing his grenades and putting it out of action. Then he charged the machine-gun posts, two of them, and, though badly wounded, as the war diary recorded, he went on 'using his bayonet with deadly effect'. The other six Australians now advanced, the remaining Germans pulled back, in awe, you would think, at what they had just seen, and the posts were taken. The 2/48th was on the way to its compelling victory and Percy Gratwick received the Victoria Cross, posthumously.

His headstone is there in the El Alamein cemetery, along with that of Jack Delaney and all the others. The difference though is that Gratwick's grave is decorated with the Victoria Cross, etched into the stone, to mark this remarkable man. Yet when Charles Bean was working on his plans for the Australian War Memorial they asked him if the national Roll of Honour, which would become one of the memorial's most moving and important features, would include any of the decorations that the war dead may have been awarded. No, Bean said firmly. Well, the Victoria Cross holders, they replied, they are put up, after all, on the head-stones in the battlefield cemeteries, they surely will be the one exception. No, said Bean again, more firmly. If the decorations were on the Roll of Honour, Bean said, people would come to the memorial and would say, these must be the brave men, these men with the decorations. And Charles Bean and Percy Gratwick knew that every man who went into battle was a brave man, a selfless man. While some found they were called upon for extraordinary bravery, and then found they had it within themselves to be remarkably brave, all those who fought needed their measure of bravery. And Bean knew, too, that while some of the remarkably brave acts in war were seen and reported by officers and that deco-rations might be awarded, other acts were known only to a small number of men and would forever remain hidden.

The 2/48th war diarist was firmly of Charles Bean's way of thinking; in battle the battalion could only operate as a team. The diarist gave attention to what Percy Gratwick had done, as was deserved, and wrote of his individual deeds in several sentences. But the cool prose continues once Percy Gratwick has fallen, going on immediately to describe the work of other men: 'Corporal "Ripper" King and Signaller Dick Ramsdale were seen feverishly bringing up ammunition reserves . . . their grim determination to do all they could to assist in the fight was inspiring . . . the team-work, co-operation and offensive eagerness of the whole battalion was most marked.' Leslie Arnold 'Ripper' King, aged 24 years, died of wounds on 2 November 1942, just like Percy Gratwick, who had died a few days before him; Dick Ramsdale seems to have survived.

The battle still had another ten days to rage; days and nights filled with ferocious fighting, of attack and counterattack. Montgomery was in constant touch with his commanders, continually revising and encouraging. Trig 29 became a focus for much of the next week because Rommel, back from Germany on 25 October but still a sick man, had been horrified by its loss and, at one stage, it seemed as if the whole of the Afrika Korps was counterattacking the 9th Division. But they held the 'high' ground and Montgomery then ordered the Australians northwards to cut the coast road and to come on the Germans from behind. It was an audacious, if not to say dangerous, move because of its complexity, but the Australians showed enormous persistence and determination in achieving it. With the bulk of the enemy opposing the Australians, Montgomery was then able to move his other troops, stationed away from the coast, against defended German positions. Eventually, after two days, the Germans there began to fall back. At 'the saucer', where the Australians found themselves after Trig 29—one of those battlefield features given a quick name to identify what might have only been observable to the troops themselves—Rommel personally took command in front of the Australians. As Morshead's 26th Brigade, of which Percy Gratwick's battalion had been a part, was nearing exhaustion, Morshead decided to relieve it in the course of the battle itself. A decision of 'high moral courage', John Coates wrote, and presumably one of great danger to that brigade and the relieving 24th Brigade. But it worked and was one of those actions that broke open Rommel's defences. When Father Craig, my Latin master, effortlessly and often described this battle in the desert between Rommel and Monty he left out, I think, the name of Ming the Merciless, Leslie Morshead. A pity, for Montgomery himself recognised the difference Morshead and his Australians had made.

Though Hitler ordered that there would be no retreat the logic of the battlefield took over. The Germans were in full retreat. The only criticism of Bernard Montgomery that is made in the Battle of El Alamein was that he was not determined enough in the pursuit. In truth, after twelve days of the most desperate fighting, there was not much capacity among his soldiers for further action. Congratulations fell on the Australians. Montgomery was quick to visit Morshead; other generals wrote full of praise.

The Australian newspapers covered the battle in great detail, as you would expect, for this was the first major defeat the Germans suffered in any theatre of the war. But the response in Australia was peculiarly low-key; there was no Gallipoli-like hype about the deeds of the 9th Division. In London Winston Churchill ordered that the church bells across the land be rung in celebration of the 8th Army's victory in Egypt. In Canberra John Curtin followed suit, calling for church bells to ring out across Australia— but 'in a spirit of thanksgiving rather than in actual celebration of victory,' he warned. It seemed as if Curtin was concerned not to let victory in North Africa take people's minds from the war that still had to be won in the Pacific. Curtin did, though, release to the newspapers the letter Lieutenant General N.M. Ritchie had written to Morshead, praising the Australians.

Did Curtin feel that he could not stand on a podium and tell his people what a victory their soldiers had won in the desert? Might the soldiers not have expected a bit of celebration at home for what they had achieved? A month later, in December, giving an overview of the war to the House of Representatives, Curtin did find room to describe the deeds of the 9th Division:

> After twelve days of bitter combat, the German forces who for once were swifter than their Italian comrades in reaching the available transport were in full flight . . . the Australian 9th Division played an outstanding part in this battle and Mr Churchill and President Roosevelt, in congratulatory messages to me, have both generously acknowledged the distinguished services rendered by the Australian troops.

Might not Curtin have sent Army Minister Forde to congratulate the men personally, or have gone himself? The trouble was,

Curtin wanted to bring the 9th Division home to join the 6th and 7th divisions, home to the Pacific War, and perhaps did not wish to draw too much attention to the division's military brilliance. Yet, Curtin told the parliament, at El Alamein the 9th Division had lost 2740 men, of whom 620 were killed in action or died of wounds. Men like Percy Gratwick and Jack Delaney. 'To these men who have fought in distant countries for the defence of their homeland, we pay the same tribute as we do to their comrades in arms who have defended their country in New Guinea and in other parts of the South-West Pacific Area.' Of course, in death all men are equal, whether death came in the appalling conditions of the desert or the stinking, steaming jungle, but it seemed as if John Curtin was distancing himself and Australia from that other war.

Barton Maughan wrote the official history volume devoted to Tobruk and El Alamein, a book of some 850 pages. Maughan knew the campaign well, knew what he was writing about, because he was an intelligence officer with the 2/13th Battalion throughout the desert campaign. Towards the end of his book Maughan described the visit of General Alexander to the 9th Division at rest in Palestine, three days before Christmas, 1942. The entire division was drawn up before Harold Alexander and Leslie Morshead; even the inspection of the troops took the generals a very long time. The men, Maughan remembered, 'listlessly resigned themselves to what might prove a long harangue'. But it was soon apparent that the Commander-in-Chief, Middle East had come to thank them and to praise them, well out of the ordinary requirements of duty.

'When great deed have been done,' Harold Alexander said, 'there is no harm in speaking of them. And great deeds had been done.' Maughan noticed an 'imperceptible stiffening of shoulders; heads were held perhaps a little higher'.

'Your reputation as fighters has always been famous', the general continued, 'but I do not believe you have ever fought with greater bravery or distinction than you did during the battles when you broke the German and Italian armies in the Western Desert.' Alexander, of course, also paid tribute to the dead and looked into a hard future which would see, he believed, the ultimate defeat of the enemy in all the theatres of war, but only after a long struggle. And then he said farewell to these Australians whom he knew were going home: 'There is one thought I shall cherish above all others—under my command fought the 9th Australian Division.'

Generous, warmhearted and sincere. Look on and weep, Tom Blamey.

17. ALL IN

In mid-July 1942, Douglas MacArthur moved his headquarters to Brisbane to be closer to the action. At the same time the Japanese landed at Buna, although nobody then could have imagined that the Japanese intended to make their attack on Port Moresby along the land route, across the Owen Stanley Range. So now John Curtin had another destination to consider alongside his regular trips from Canberra to Melbourne and occasionally to Perth. In mid-August, Curtin travelled to Brisbane for a conference with MacArthur, and he travelled in some style, the vice-regal rail coach being attached to the standard overnight Sydney to Brisbane service. Curtin did not have luxury on his mind, however; indeed he was about to become the most successful preacher of austerity Australia had ever known.

With hindsight you could say that an invasion of Australia had dwindled from a remote likelihood to a near impossibility with the naval victories in the Coral Sea and at Midway. But for MacArthur and Curtin the war was still supremely uncertain; there was even a sense of crisis about their meeting in Brisbane. For one thing, the Japanese had never yet been defeated on land. The enemy was pressing in on the Solomons and who knew what the landings on the north coast of New Guinea meant? Australia was definitely not out of the woods, both leaders believed. Yet for the Australian people the war lacked the drama and the focus that the nightly bombing of London had provided, for example. Shocking as the loss of Singapore had been, there was now a feeling in Australia that with the Yanks involved, she'll be right. To tell the truth at that moment about troop and equipment shortages, to detail the abysmal lack of aircraft and airmen, would have woken Australians to the reality of their situation but would have given great comfort to the enemy, too, and run the risk of panicking the Australian population. So the prime minister had to be forceful and circumspect at the same time; no easy task.

Curtin opened his secular campaign for a new austere lifestyle in a speech at the Brisbane City Hall on 19 August 1942, just after his conference with MacArthur. The key theme to Curtin's campaign was that there could be no real distinction between the battlefront and the homefront. Soldiers were living rough and doing it tough. People at home would not face the same dangers, but they could make do with a similar way of living. We are all in this together, Curtin was saying, and we cannot leave it just to the troops. 'I ask you,' Curtin said, 'to reconcile yourselves to a season of austerity, to make your habits of life conform to those of the fighting forces.' If the soldiers in North Africa were downing bully-beef and having only the occasional beer, then the rest of Australia, Curtin was saying, could also live like that. 'The civilian population,' he said:

> can learn to discipline itself; it can learn to go without. Every day you read about some man you knew dying fighting far distant from the places of entertainment, of even relaxation, fighting with all he knows for your defence. Let us think about them a little more and think about ourselves a little less.

Think about the man in the desert, perhaps, preparing himself for battle in conditions of unbelievable hardship and difficulty.

Curtin wanted all Australians to understand that the war united them all, regardless of whether they were in the factory or on the battlefield. He wanted an 'all-in' war effort.

It was, in fact, Bob Menzies who had first used that phrase. Speaking at an election rally in Melbourne in September 1940 Menzies had called for an 'all-in war effort . . . with great power and great responsibility in the Government, and each man doing his bit.' But it was John Curtin who made the expression his own. By 'all in' John Curtin meant that the nation was as one in the war: 'we cannot all be soldiers,' he said, 'or munitions workers . . . but we all must have a part.' Curtin had been speaking like this for quite some time, but by mid-1942 he must have decided that the people had not been listening and that his sermons would have to be intense and more direct. In late 1941, in his famous appeal to America, Curtin had written, 'the civilian way of life cannot be any less rigorous, can contribute no less than that which the fighting men have to follow'. In May 1942 he asked all Australians to see themselves 'in the second line of service to Australia,' immediately behind the frontline. 'Men are fighting for Australia today,' he said, 'those who are not fighting have no excuse for not working.' A month later, the prime minister raised the stakes again:

> A soldier who leaves his unit and his mates without author-
> ity is branded and dealt with as a deserter. A civilian who
> selfishly deserts his fellow Australians and his country is no
> less a traitor . . . There can be no distinctions between
> soldiers and civilians, everyone has a battle station.

In September 1942, on the third anniversary of the outbreak of the war, Curtin made a national broadcast, during which he gave a summary of all that had happened so far. It was a grim recital: the fall of France; the bombing of Britain; the failure to halt Germany anywhere—in Greece, on Crete, in the desert; the staggering success of Japan in land battles throughout Asia; the intensity, still, of the threat to Australia. People listening to the broadcast might have felt the full weight of the war on their shoulders, and that was Curtin's intention because all of that was but a preamble to his main message. Australians at home simply had to do more. 'Today

Port Moresby and Darwin are the Singapores of Australia,' Curtin said, and 'if these two places fall then, inevitably, we are faced with a bloody struggle on our own soil when we will be forced to fight grimly, city by city, village by village, until our fair land may become a blackened ruin.' These were dramatic words, intended to be so, drawing amused shrugs from some historians today who see Curtin exaggerating, dramatising, playing on the people's fear for no good reason. Curtin did not think so. 'Our fate is in the balance as I speak to you,' he said, as he turned his attention to the battle in the Solomons. The government, he told his listeners, would not allow anything to stand in the way of 'placing the nation on a full war footing,' and he was now announcing an austerity campaign 'which is opened as from tonight.'

Did Curtin really believe, as he said, that the nation was still at risk of invasion in September 1942, or was he just gilding the lily? 'The invasion myth', writes Peter Stanley a senior historian at the Australian War Memorial, 'has been useful to the reputation of key protagonists. Curtin has been portrayed as Australia's saviour'. But is that what John Curtin had in mind when he embarked on his secular crusade in the second half of 1942? The preacher with an eye cocked to history; the preacher determined to become the saviour? It is a view of John Curtin that simply does not survive detailed analysis of the record.

Curtin had four main hopes for his austerity campaign. First, he wanted people at home to curtail expenditure as much as possible, to save money and to divert their savings to the war loans in order to fund the war, substantially anyway, from current earnings so Australia would not come out of the war with an enormous debt. This is what had happened to Australia as a result of the First World War, and the substantial debt in the 1920s led, inexorably, to the extreme severity of the economic Depression of the 1930s, which was only just now, in late 1942, receding from the forefront of people's minds. Second, Curtin wanted to limit civilian consumption of goods, foodstuffs in particular, to divert those goods to the fighting forces. With so many men in uniform, Australia's capacity to feed and clothe itself was placed under some strain. Then the huge build-up of American troops in Australia had placed a further strain on supplies. All these soldiers had to be fed, clothed, housed and equipped, and Australia had a vital role in all of that. Third, Curtin had to increase productivity in Australia; simply put, workers had to work harder and strike less. This was a cultural change that Curtin wanted to impose on Australians. Given the poisonous labour relations that had prevailed in the 1920s and the assault on hard-won conditions that had happened during the years of high unemployment in the 1930s, John Curtin knew that he had a fight on his hands. Fourth, Curtin wanted to provoke a sense of equality of sacrifice between soldiers and civilians for what he saw as the sense of the thing. Curtin had grown up a committed and sincere socialist; his deep reading throughout his adult life had given his socialism a tinge—no, it was stronger than that—a sense of religious fervour. It was as if his personality and his lifelong learning and experience directed him to ask his people for equality of sacrifice. It was how, he thought, people should live anyway, almost regardless of war. Each with enough for his own needs and with a concern for the needs of others.

The immediate cause of the announcement of the formal austerity campaign arose from Curtin's fears for the safety and security of his country. Go back to that broadcast on the third anniversary of the outbreak of the war. Three long years of the horror and misery of war; three years without a victory to record, with little to cheer about. The Japanese still pressed hard on the outlying reaches of Australia. While Curtin was in Brisbane meeting Douglas MacArthur in an atmoshpere of some crisis, Billy Hughes, magically in view of his age and disabilities, was leading the main opposition party even though he was not the opposition leader, attacking the incompetence of the military leaders in allowing the Japanese to land in New Guinea. Hughes predicted dire consequences from these landings. From any perspective, the war in September 1942 looked far from benign; invasion far from a myth. John Curtin issued his ringing call for an all-in effort fully conscious that the war, for Australia, could still be lost.

Was this 'season of austerity', as Curtin called it, just the usual politician's ploy to be seen to be doing something—the 'alert but not alarmed' of the 1940s? Just a lot of words really, signifying little? Indeed not. Some stern measures had already been taken, of course, in relation to the immediate Japanese threat to Australia.

None of these measures was more revolutionary than the creation, in January 1942, of the Directorate (later Commission) of
Manpower. Unfortunate word that, 'Manpower'. Just shows that
the past is indeed another country; we would use it at our peril
today. Manpower was a word, however, with which all Australians
soon became familiar, a word to induce a certain level of fear and
apprehension. 'The Manpower,' someone would say, 'had a raid at
the pictures (movies) on Thursday, asking to see the papers of
everyone in the queue.' 'The Manpower sent her to Maribynong,'
someone else would utter, 'to the munitions factory there.' 'The
Manpower,' a third would say with worry in her voice, 'wants
15 people immediately to pick apples at Batlow.' The 'Manpower',
it seemed, was everywhere.

At first Manpower was merely a coordinating body to supply
labour, now the most wanted commodity in the Australian
economy, sending workers to those employers with the greatest
priority. Soon, though, Manpower had the authority to direct
people to work and to particular jobs. Through the registration of
the civilian population, the government was now in a position to
know the details of each of its citizen's lives. An unmarried
woman—young women now comprised overwhelmingly the
largest pool of unused labour—was required to register with
Manpower and could be told where to work, even if that was many
miles from her home. Women who had never dreamed of working
in factories might find themselves directed to do so. It was not
unusual for Manpower to 'raid' movie matinee queues to ask for
the papers of patrons with a view to discovering why these people
were not at work. Conscription of the workforce, at government-
controlled rates of pay and in government-prescribed work
conditions? Most certainly. Conscription of the civilian workforce,
certainly the biggest change ever in the working conditions of
Australians. All done in the name of the war and austerity.

It is not the place here to investigate the way Manpower
changed the lives of thousands of Australians—that is the job of
the social historian—but a good starting point for those interested
is the novel by Dymphna Cusack and Florence James, *Come In
Spinner*. More a social document than a novel, *Come In Spinner* is
set, in part, in a beauty saloon in one of Sydney's swanky hotels.

The employees of the salon are in daily fear of the arrival of Manpower officials with the right to relocate them to a remote factory away from all the fun and glamour. It was a real fear; hair-dressing was not a protected industry. The novel also touches on the effects of the 'American invasion' of Sydney, on the lives of ordinary working Australians in war, and on the difficulties of life that Australians accepted. While there is a tale of glamour and conspicuous consumption in the novel, the underlying background is of austerity and plenty of unremitting, grinding work. It is an account true to life in Australia during the war.

Before formally announcing the beginning of the austerity campaign, John Curtin's government had already introduced a significant level of hardship to the civilian population, including the rationing of various consumer goods. In part, rationing was designed to restrict spending; in part it was a response to a genuine shortage of goods and the acceptance of the principle of a fair share for all; and in part it was to divert goods to the fighting services. Tea was the first item to be rationed in Australia, in March 1942, but by an inefficient mechanism that would soon be reformed with the widespread introduction of more general rationing in the mid-year. Australians drank astonishing quantities of tea to accompany each meal, and also between meals and before bed—eight to ten cups a day would not be unusual. The rationing commission allowed each Australian 1.6 pounds of tea per week (about 43 grams)—enough for about three cups of tea a day. People noticed it.

The biggest change, though, was the introduction of clothes rationing, announced in May 1942 by John Dedman, minister for the War Organisation of Industry, to be implemented in mid-June. The warning order was designed to allow people to grow comfort-able with the idea of clothes rationing; in fact it led to an orgy of shopping with people stocking up, in some cases ridiculously over-stocking, before rationing came in. To control clothes rationing the newly formed Rationing Commission arranged for the delivery to each adult of a rationing book with a year's worth of clothing coupons. Each book contained 112 coupons and each item of clothing was given a coupon value. To buy a man's suit required 38 coupons; for a pair of socks the shopper needed four coupons. The ration books were delivered using the mechanisms in place for a general election. People attended the polling booth in their locality, were marked off the electoral roll and, instead of being given a ballot paper, were given a ration book. Now it was up to them to control their spending and balance their needs. Clearly the simple-minded person who blew the coupons in the first couple of months of the rationing year would live to rue the day if circumstances meant that, later on, additional clothes were needed. Clearly, too, the system favoured those with adequate wardrobes already. If you had been doing it tough in the Depression years and only now had a few extra pounds in the purse for the new clothes you had been dreaming about, well tough. Look with envy at your neighbour who had been in work throughout the lean years, with a well-stocked wardrobe and an adequate variety of clothes to choose from. Though Curtin's socialism might have desired it, rationing could never be conducted on a full need's basis. It was, to that extent, inherently unfair. 'The darning needle is a weapon of war these days,' John Curtin told the nation, 'use it on your old clothes.'

People accepted clothes rationing readily enough, as they had to, and Australia thrived on stories of 'making do'. Stockings were nearly unattainable but highly desired by young women who soon grew adept at painting their legs, together with as straight a seam-line as possible down the backs of their legs. It looked alright, possibly, and it was good for a laugh. More crafty people bought up big in the sheets and curtain departments of the department stores, for any fabric could be put to good use. Off on a date in curtains? Why not? In 1943 the government placed these goods on the ration, too. In 1943 and 1944 the government started to ration some foodstuffs. First was sugar because of a severe shortage in supply, then butter, largely to help provide butter for Britain, and finally meat in 1944. It will come as little surprise that the more rationing 'bit' into the community, the more there grew up a black-market, although the extent of this can be exaggerated. Certainly a Yank bringing gifts of stockings and chocolates to the girl he was dating was a fellow to be welcomed and retained. People muttered about the Yanks and 'our girls' but it was, after all, wartime, and Britons had muttered about the Australians in much the same way in the last war.

Of more impact than rationing was the shortage of goods in Australia, shortages that were unpredictable and infuriating. In the main part wartime shortages of food, of drink, of all types of consumer goods, were the result either of low production due to a lack of labour and materials or the severe reduction of shipping to Australia. The shortage of beer gained the most attention. The publican's cry, 'Beer's off,' was what every Australian drinker dreaded, and it might happen at any time and without warning. More so then than now, Australian men regarded a session in the pub after work as almost a bloke's right. Pubs closed at 6 p.m., so these were not long sessions at the pub, but a beer after work was part of the ritual of life. Men would comb the city streets looking for a pub where the beer was 'on', and when in Melbourne one Saturday something like 60 per cent of pubs were closed because there was no beer, police reported there were 'fewer calls to quell street brawls'. Bottled beer was virtually unobtainable for the long months of the war. If a black market did flourish in Australia, it was most certainly linked to the beer supply.

Shortages affected everything: beer, foodstuffs, clothing, household products, essential items, luxury goods. Shopping became hard and often frustrating. People needed imagination to think of an alternative and patience to go from shop to shop looking for what they needed. Seasonal variations in food required tolerance from those at home. At one time there might be an oversupply of tomatoes and everyone was eating tomatoes and wondering how to prepare them for storage. Later bananas might become plentiful and the diet would change.

People almost failed to notice the effect of the shortage of labour and materials on the building industry, and it is fair to say that for most of the years of the war very little home-building took place. Then the crisis suddenly became obvious to all. Towards the end of the war, people began to notice just how substandard much of the housing stock in Australia was. Nothing much had been done to patch up many houses during the Depression, and with domestic building almost at a stop from 1942 onwards the problem had reached alarming proportions by 1944. Thousands of Australians lived in foul, damp, crowded conditions or had moved in with relatives, giving rise to all the tension and discomfort of that solution. An Australia-wide survey of housing needs, published in September 1944, showed that Australia needed over 175 000 new homes for the growing population, and a further 82 000 homes to replace dwellings described as 'unfit for human habitation'. The report branded an additional 155 000 homes as 'substandard'. The Australian housing crisis would be one of the legacies that would endure for possibly another 20 years after the war.

When John Curtin began preaching austerity he was already talking to a community that was doing it pretty tough. Queues were a fact of life; shortages a part of everyday experience; work was demanded of all, often in repetitive and difficult tasks in shocking conditions. People were cold in the winter when the gas ran out or fuel supplies proved impossible to find; they were hungrier than they might otherwise have been; they travelled in cramped and crowded public transport with services cut back and private cars virtually unusable. Yet more sacrifices were called for. In October 1942 the government introduced the first of what were called 'raceless Saturdays'. The government did not interfere with football and cricket, at either the suburban or elite level, because these games obviously helped with fitness for the participants and were a recreation for the spectators. In any case, after five and a half days in the factory surely a couple of hours at a football match would not do too much damage to the war effort. Even John Curtin liked to go to the footy in Canberra, just for a break. But racing was an industry, taking men from more productive work and leaching money that might have otherwise gone to the national war loans. Part of the idea of the raceless Saturday was to permit racing only on three days a month rather than four so that those who 'lived by their wits' might be forced into more productive work. Perhaps the idea, too, was to show that Australians were taking the war seriously.

Much of the austerity campaign was, in fact, about perceptions. Australians thought of themselves as a hedonistic people where 'bludgers' were just a part of the scene and work was to be avoided wherever possible. The newspapers were quick to print criticisms from soldiers returning from abroad, finding the spirit of party and pleasure far too common. Australians, they said, were doing it easy,

though it they looked beneath the surface it might not have
seemed so easy. A country man on a brief visit to Sydney wrote of
what he saw: 'I expected to find Sydney toeing the hard and dreary
road. I was amazed to find it almost impossible to get a room—
hotels crowded out. Weekenders were still packing every train,
while every cafe was being rushed.' Money flowed freely, he
complained, pubs were full to bursting, 'it was the nearest thing I
could imagine to Christmas Eve 20 months ago'. Yet this really was
the surface of things; people did have money in their pockets for
the first time in years and if they could find a good time, if only
briefly, then why not? But for the vast majority of Australians the
war increasingly was work, worry, and when (will it all be over?).
The war was loneliness, dreariness and sacrifice. The season of
austerity would have been there, for most, even without the
preaching. Perhaps it was true that the government seemed determined to punish the majority of the people for the hedonism of the
few. The raft of petty restrictions and pinpricks that were introduced by zealous officials cannot have done much to help the war
effort but they showed a spirit which said, you will take this war
seriously, you really will.

Dedman was an unfortunate name, or, to put it more kindly, a
name easily misused by the critics of the man who presided over
the organisation of the nation for the war. Too easy for Dedman to
become 'dead hand', to easy for the name to slide into Dedmanism,
a term used to describe anything that was too fussy, too intrusive,
too silly. Like the prohibition on advertising in the lead-up to
Christmas 1942, a prohibition designed to rein in spending,
to discourage elaborate and expensive gift giving because 'there is
a war on'. Perhaps it might have been better for John Curtin to
have said directly to the people, 'look, cut back, now is not the
time for celebration and extravagance'. Instead John Dedman
became 'the man who killed Santa Claus', banning images of the
cheery old chap or the mention of his name in newspaper advertisements. Well, that was a waste of time: 'Children, come and see
your Old Friend in his Castle', invited a major Sydney department
store and did anyone not know what that meant? John Curtin did
ask people to exchange war savings stamps and certificates as
Christmas presents, but wasn't that just a little too dreary? Nor did

it help that John Dedman was a dour-looking former Scotsman who was said to have introduced his wartime austerity measures and nitpicking 'with all the bleakness of the kirk'.

Even more derision arose from the minister's redesign of men's clothing, all in the interests of saving cloth. Out went the double-breasted suit, and cuffs on trousers, and those extra buttons used forever, and perhaps foolishly, as decoration on suit jackets. The 'Victory Suit', personally modelled by John Dedman himself, which did nothing at all for its acceptance, was one of those clangers that governments will make when their sense of earnestness exceeds what the community will bear. Better accepted was the decision to Manpower domestic servants out of the homes of the well-off, or outlaw luxury items like 'evening wear' and 'dinner gowns', which, for those who needed them, were probably already in the wardrobe anyway. Was it necessary to ban the delivery of parcels, like the family's daily meat order, to any customer closer than a mile to the shop, and then, if delivery was allowed, no more than three times weekly? Was it necessary to weigh parcels from department stores so that no item less than four pounds or measuring less than three feet in length could be delivered to the home? Dedmanism attempted to regulate what might have been left to people's common sense and a cheerful acceptance that they were all in this together. For on almost all measures the people were coming through with flying colours.

If money is the measure of all things, then on that scale alone the people showed how generous they could be. Just as the recruiting campaigns dominated the First World War in Australia from mid-1915 onwards, so the loans campaigns were an important element of Australian life from 1942 onwards. The campaigns gave the prime minister the opportunity to appeal directly to the people and gave him the means of measuring the success of that appeal almost immediately. Television programs now live or die in Australia by the ratings and people meters have become the instant measure of these. From 1942 on, loans contributions were the people meters of the war.

John Curtin kicked off the first Liberty Loan in Sydney on 17 February 1942, supported by Arthur Fadden, leader of the opposition, and Billy Hughes. It was a powerful speech, broadcast live on

ABC Radio. Listeners would not have realised that Curtin was sick, and in pain, as he spoke. Nor would those in Martin Place, where the loan rally took place, have realised Curtin's condition, so vigorous was his presentation. But he was taken to hospital, suffering from gastritis, almost as soon as he finished. Curtin had asked the people to find £35 million for the new war loan; his recovery in hospital would have been speeded by the news that more than half that sum had been subscribed by the end of the first day. Within three weeks the loan was over-subscribed with a total of £48.3 million making its way into the government's coffers. There was a second Liberty Loan in June 1942; in September Curtin foreshadowed the Austerity Loan, aimed at raising £100 million. The war, Curtin told the people, was costing Australia £50 000 per hour, but that was perhaps too big a sum for people to comprehend. Put it this way, Curtin said, every two shillings saved would free a man to work for the war for an hour. Here was incentive indeed for the 'widow's mite'; you could imagine the less-well-off and children deftly defending each two bob against the temptation to spend.

The Austerity Loan opened in November 1942. The government wanted £100 million and 500 000 subscribers, making the loan by far the biggest yet attempted, particularly in terms of the number of subscribers the government was seeking. The Liberty Loans had attracted about 100 000 subscribers each. Australians had been living austerely for some months now if they had been following the prime minister's prescription so there should have been surplus money around. The loan was supported by public rallies, by the march of Australian troops through the major cities and by significant newspaper and radio advertising campaigns. City and suburban loans rallies, just like the recruiting rallies of earlier years, attracted speakers from all the political parties and community representatives as well. To make subscriptions easier, picture theatres (cinemas) throughout Australia became night offices for the loan, with volunteer staff drawn from the banks. The night offices meant that those who were working long hours during the day were still able to contribute.

One of the main tricks used during the Austerity Loan was the harnessing of Australia's competitive spirit and interstate rivalry.

A number of Sydney suburbs 'challenged' equivalent Melbourne suburbs to see which could raise the most money; the organisers showed a fine sense of social staus in pairing the individual suburbs. Thus St Peters in Sydney's inner-west confronted Port Melbourne (each had a target of £60 000), Randwick in the east attacked Melbourne's Caulfield (£425 000 apiece) and Kogarah in Sydney's south faced Preston in Melbourne's north-west (£160 000). After a sluggish start the Austerity Loan was a great success; it was over-subscribed by £4.2 million and attracted 420 000 suscribers. Significantly, launched in November and open for six weeks, the loan drew off a considerable amount of possible Christmas spending. The treasurer, Ben Chifley, said that the success of the loan showed how well the people had accepted the season of austerity that John Curtin had been preaching.

Thereafter loans campaigns became a regular feature of the war. In 1943 there were two further Liberty Loans in April and October of £100 million and £125 million respectively. Again there were rallies and marches, and advertisements; this time there were pennants and badges for groups and individuals to show they were doing their bit for their country. 'Strange things go into planes', one of the advertisements announced: 'there goes this year's holiday', 'there goes my new carpet', 'there goes my new cricket bat'. If a certain percentage of people living in the same street all subscribed to the war loan they were given the right to display a sign 'This is a war savings street'. Householders appointed a war savings street secretary who would attempt to sell more war savings certificates as the loan campaigns continued. The street signs were quite common in the 1950s and 1960s but it would be an absolute find to discover one today. A pattern developed where a government minister, usually the treasurer, at around the halfway point of the campaign, would announce that things were lagging, but within days of the loan's close officials would announce that there had been a last minute rush and the loan had been over-subscribed. The April 1943 loan netted 380 000 subscribers and these remained impressive figures.

Some of the appeals for the loans campaign seemed a bit tacky, after all this was a call for money: If you want to get your fathers, husbands and sons back, an air force officer in Martin Place said, 'you must give them good weapons to fight with and that means giving your money now'. It worked, of course, and organisers delighted in telling the individual stories that would encourage the others; like that of the woman spending her working hours peeling potatoes in a factory to feed the troops at the front. She had two sons at the war and she gave £400 to the Fourth Liberty Loan. 'What about you?' the advertisements asked.

The potato peeler reminds us that work was another measure of the success of John Curtin's austerity drive. Most people by now had two jobs, some had three. Except for those with small children at home, almost everyone was in the workforce. This might seem an obvious statement and unexceptionable today, but it was not the norm then. Before the war some women did work in shops, offices, and in domestic homes as servants, but many did not, living in their parents' homes until marriage gave them the responsibility for a home of their own. The war changed that. Women, as we have seen, entered the defence forces in increasing numbers, but they also took over jobs formerly done by men, working in the factories, on the farms, in all sorts and manner of jobs. From 1942 onwards, they could be forced to go to work by Manpower if they did not find a job for themselves, and they could be told where they would work. As well, a great majority of the workers, men and women, were also taking on unpaid, community jobs just because there was a war on. It would be difficult to measure the extent of this unpaid work but it was substantial. Women in canteens, making the lives of soldiers on leave and in training much more pleasant. Women in camouflage groups, parachute groups, knitting circles, a bewildering variety of jobs doing what needed to be done. Men in air-raid precautions groups, Volunteer Defence Corps (Australia's 'Dad's Army'), in community work groups, or looking out for the young families of the men at war, men building and renovating in their spare time to help out a family in need. So many jobs.

As an example of the work ethic Gavin Long, journalist and official war historian, writes about his visit to the Anzac buffet in Hyde Park, Sydney in early January 1944. He says there were about 3000 women enrolled to work there, and that there were three shifts, to allow for the women's different circumstances. Those in paid employment would take the night shift. There was a waiting list of women wanting to work at the buffet at nights and on weekends. Everything done for the soldiers at the buffet was free. The meals—three a day as well as morning and afternoon tea—were prepared cooked and served. There were also billiard tables at the canteen, a writing room, a chiropodist, baths and showers, and a dance floor. The women recalled how hard they had worked, and with what sense of joy when the 9th Australian Division returned after the fighting in the desert. The men were in transit on their way home, or off to further training in Queensland, and this was the opportunity for these women to celebrate their great victory at El Alamein. They fed thousands of them. A small drop in the ocean, really, as since opening the canteen early in the war these women had served 2.354 million meals to Australian and Allied soldiers by early 1944 when Gavin Long was there. All for nothing, all done by voluntary labour. They were working, the men and women of Australia.

A third job? What of the women at paid and community work who also had a family at home to care for? We have heard already of the potato peeler, now let us look, briefly, at the life of a woman in Melbourne who was working as an onion peeler. I cannot tell you how many women were working like this 'onion peeler'. When I read historians like Paul Hasluck slinging off at the slack and hedonistic homefront I think it is useful to recall this one woman; Australia seemed to be made up of people like her just as there were, also, a fair number of pleasure-seekers and good-time girls. She featured in an article published in the *Age* in May 1944. The article spoke of a factory in Fitzroy, the former MacRobertson's chocolate factory. Women there stood around tables in the factory peeling onions and preparing them for dehydration. Then the onions would be packed and sent to the forces to flavour the thousands of stews that were the staple of the soldiers' diet. This was essential war work, you can readily recognise that, but think about it, you and I could peel onions for a couple of hours, I suppose, even for a day, possibly, if our motivation was particularly strong, but in a factory, day in and day out, month after month, onions, thousands of them, millions of them possibly, how could anyone keep doing it? The women worked from 7.30 in the morning till five in the evening. I imagine there were three breaks during the course of the day. One of the workers in this factory lived in Murrumbeena, in Melbourne's south-east—a fair trip to Fitzroy and a change of transport to cope with as well. This anonymous war worker left home each morning at 5.30 and cycled two miles (3.5 kilometres) to the railway station. She got home again at 7 in the evening to begin her second job, the care of her family and her home. Her husband was at war and she was 46 years of age. She did this day in and day out in winter and in summer as her bit for the war, just peeling onions.

This woman would not have been celebrated as a war hero, she was just one of those doing her job and keeping her country going. But I do hope that she was listening to John Curtin in February 1944 when he addressed a 'few quiet words' to the war workers of Australia: 'I speak to the workers particularly,' he said, 'because without them, whether as members of the fighting forces or as industrial or rural workers, this nation could not have continued to wage war for more than four years.' Again Curtin was joining together those fighting the war and those working so hard at home to support them. It was his consistent theme. Why then was this woman, and the millions like her, not given a medal for what she had done for her country when the war was won? Why was she not warmly and insistently invited to march with the 'war workers in the fighting forces' on Anzac Day once the peace was won?

In Australia, it seems, we have adopted a very narrow list of those whom we thank for making the nation strong and successful in time of war and there were problems of fairness, even among those who had served in the armed forces, which had caused disquiet over many years. In 1994 the Australian government appointed a committee of inquiry into whether all those who should have received recognition for their war service from their country did, in fact, receive what was their due. One of those to appear before the committee (of which I was a member) was Peggy Williams from Sydney, representing those who had served in the Australian Women's Land Army. These women lived communally, for the most part, sometimes even in barracks, were under orders from their supervisors and gave their labour to rural Australia in the industries and areas of greatest need. Mrs

Williams convinced the committee that it was an injustice that this service had never gained any recognition whatsoever; that after the war the Land Army women had simply returned to their homes with not so much as a word of thanks. The government accepted our recommendation and instituted a Civilian Service Medal 1939–1945; that was in 1995, 50 years after the event. I met Peggy Williams at the ceremony instituting the medal. She and her friends were as delighted, I think, as it was possible to be. Honoured and proud. But what of the onion peeler, the potato peeler, or the women in the munitions factories, or in all the other thousands of jobs that Australian women threw themselves into because there was a war on?

Because they were not in formed, organised groups, they were not eligible for the Civilian Service Medal and they remain unrecognised by their country, but honoured, surely, by family and friends as mighty contributors to the cause of Australia in war. John Curtin knew that Australia's effort had to be an 'all-in' effort if the country was to survive; it is a shame that those who came after him lacked his inclusive vision.

18. THE
MERCHANT
NAVY

Alison Todd was born in 1930 and she was in her early seventies when I first met her. She had a story to tell me, she said, about her father. Alison, a former medical missionary and then a minister in the Presbyterian church, lived on her own in a neat house on Sydney's north shore. It was a simple story that Alison Todd had to tell, but good to hear at first hand. Even nearly 60 years later you could still see the emotion on Alison's face as she told her story—a story of love and loss; a story of the permanence of grief and of the sorrow caused by war.

William Angus Todd was born for the sea, to work in the merchant marine like his father before him. There are passenger ships at sea and warships, but the greatest number of ships on the world's oceans are those carrying goods for trade. Australia, an island continent, depends on the merchant fleet for much of what it is that people buy and sell. First and foremost, before it became a place of play and sport, Sydney's harbour was a working port. A hugely busy port with ships coming and going all day and all night.

It was the same in the other state capitals; each one had a frenetically busy working port, a bustling hub of the city: Fremantle, Port Adelaide and all the rest. Coastal steamers moving goods and foodstuffs around the country; bigger ships on the international trade. That was the world that Bill Todd was born into. An officer in the merchant marine, working for the Union Steamship Company of New Zealand.

Bill Todd was born in 1900, so he was 30 years of age when Alison, his first child, was born. There was a second child, David, four years younger than Alison. David can barely remember his father but Alison has a very clear memory of him. Four years an only child, there is a lot of bonding in that, particularly when a father who would be at sea for long periods and was welcomed with the greatest excitement when he finally came home. Late in 1941 Bill Todd transferred as first officer to MV *Hauraki*, a ship his father had brought out from England on her maiden voyage 20 years earlier. First Bill went to the Middle East on the *Hauraki*, returning in May 1942, with the Japanese now in the war. He was to leave in June from Melbourne, again for the Middle East, but in convoy because of the Japanese active in all the waters around Australia; it was better to travel in packs in the Indian Ocean, sometimes with naval protection. The *Hauraki* and the other ships in the convoy ran into a severe storm in the Great Australian Bight and Bill Todd's ship needed repairs at Fremantle. Thus she stayed behind and sailed alone to Colombo, leaving Fremantle on 7 July 1942. Japanese raiders captured the *Hauraki* on 19 July 1942 and Bill Todd and his shipmates became prisoners of war. Only the captain and 23 of his crew would survive captivity. Renamed the *Hoki Maru* by the Japanese, the ship resumed its merchant service, carrying Japanese goods until it was sunk by the American Navy in February 1944, two months before Bill Todd died.

For nearly a year there was no news of Bill Todd; no one could say what had become of him. Was he alive, drowned, was he a prisoner of war? Alison remembers the awful grief this terrible silence caused her mother. Then in June 1943 relief—a message from the government arrived to say that Bill Todd was indeed a prisoner of war. It had taken almost a year just to learn this; it was exquisite cruelty on the part of the Japanese, the 'detaining power', in the words of the conventions. Before the war Bill Todd had brought home quite a sophisticated short-wave radio from one of his trips to America. Knowing that he was a prisoner of war his family now tuned in every night to Radio Tokyo to listen as a select few of the prisoners broadcast simple messages to their families. It was propaganda for the Japanese, not a service of friendship, and the Australian government tried, at first, to discourage people from listening in. Fat chance. Families listened attentively in the hope that they might hear the voice of their loved one. On the day after her thirteenth birthday, Alison remembers clearly listening in as usual after dinner. Alison, her mother and brother heard that Bill Todd would speak to them the next night. He was apparently working in the Mitsubishi shipyards in Japan. The family was over the moon. 'We were ecstatic,' said Alison. Immediately the phone at home started to ring with friends, but predominately strangers, calling to let them know what they had also just heard: Bill Todd would be on the radio tomorrow night, you must not miss it. Alison told everyone at school that she would be hearing her father's voice that very night, she could hardly wait.

They were in the lounge room that evening: Alison, her mother, David—now nine years of age, 'Dad's sister and one of Mum's', the aunts, there to copy down every word. 'Could you recognise your father's voice?' I asked Alison. 'Oh, yes,' she replied instantly and without hesitation, transported back to that evening long ago when she heard her father speak to her for the last time. 'Hello, Natalie and Alison and David,' he started, 'hope you are listening.' Bill Todd told his family that he was in a camp with Australian, British and American soldiers, that they worked each day and received rations from the Japanese and the Red Cross. He had not received any letters from them yet, he said, but 'am hopeful each mail delivered.' Telling Alison and David to be good at school and to help their mother all they could, he concluded: 'You are always in my thoughts and fortunately I still have your photograph . . . [I] hope to be home soon, and so will close with fondest love to you all.'

Bill Todd did not say that he was being brutally treated and starved, as he most certainly was; nor did he say that the work was dangerous in the extreme because of the total indifference of the Japanese as to whether these prisoners lived or died. A survivor of the prison camps in Japan told me about working in the shipyards. His job was to carry heavy metal plates to the men building the ships. Balancing across thin planks of wood with a drop many metres to the ground below, this man was in terror for just about every moment of every working day. Bill Todd gave the impression he was well looked after; he wanted his family to think that his life wasn't too bad. This was a kindness, his last message to his family.

That familiar voice had been back in the lounge room, however briefly. A voice that had once been so much a part of that room and the house. And then that was it. They sat there, this little family and the two aunts, stunned. It had been such a fleeting embrace with this man around whom the whole family revolved, who was never out of their thoughts and for whom there was so much concern. As Alison told me this part of her story her eyes filled with tears and it was almost as if she was back in the room with the radio listening to her dad again. Loving him and missing him still. It was quiet then for a time while Alison recollected herself and lived with her sadness again; it was not a time for words.

On 3 October 1945, seven weeks after the war had ended, the family learned that Bill Todd would not be coming home. He died on 19 April 1944, eight months after he had broadcast to his family, at 44 years of age. Buried near the camp, his grave carefully marked, Bill Todd's remains were later reburied in the Yokohama War Cemetery, built by the Australian War Graves section after the war. Like almost all cemeteries in the care of the Commonwealth War Graves Commission, the Yokohama Cemetery contains the remains of the war dead from several Commonwealth nations—Britons, New Zealanders, Indians, Australians. There are 1555 burials and commemorations in the cemetery; the Australian section is at the front, near the Cross of Sacrifice. The cemetery is a place of beauty, enriched by the tranquillity and peace of the significant botanical garden on its adjoining border. A sad place, nevertheless, like all the war cemeteries.

Next to Bill Todd in the cemetery lies Hilton Keith Smith, 26 years of age when he died in February 1943, a gunner in the 2/15th Field Regiment, Royal Australian Artillery. Enlisting in

Paddington, Sydney in 1941, the records give us few other details of this soldier, except that like Bill Todd he was a prisoner of war, captured in Singapore. In the same unit as Les Bolger, in fact, whom we met on Singapore, ashamed that his unit had not fired their guns. Did Hilton Smith carry that shame to his grave too? We will never know. Hilton's father was his next of kin so we can assume that Hilton Smith was not married when he died. His name is on the national Roll of Honour at the Australian War Memorial in Canberra; he was a soldier. Bill Todd's name is not; he was in the merchant navy. Yet in death they lie in the same war cemetery, side by side.

'I have [them] on my conscience', Charles Bean wrote of the merchant seamen in February 1956. 'We have been committed by many promises.' The *Australian War Memorial Act 1952* seemingly unintentionally omitted the possibility of commemorating merchant seamen on the national Roll of Honour, though it had always been intended that they would be included. The co-founder of the memorial, John Treloar, argued that as merchant seamen were accepted for burial in Commonwealth War Graves cemeteries they should also be included in the national Roll of Honour. But Treloar died before he had a chance to push his case. The memorial returned to the question in 1967, prompted by an independent member of the House of Representatives, Captain Sam Benson, described as 'a [former] merchant seaman of marked gentleness and decency'. Benson wrote that he was 'absolutely astonished' by the omission of the merchant seamen from national commemoration: 'Australia must surely be the only country in the world where men who gave their lives in war are not remembered by way of memorial.'

Benson wrote that at the outbreak of the Second World War merchant seamen were declared 'protected industry personnel', which meant they were not free to resign from their jobs even if they wanted to. They served 'throughout the war under naval control and were routed to areas under naval orders'. Take Bill Todd's *Hauraki*, for example. In 1940 the *Hauraki* was requisitioned by the British Ministry of War Transport. The ship, under Captain A.W. Creese and crewed mostly by New Zealanders, though with Bill Todd as first mate, was placed on 'special service'. On her final voyage before being captured by the Japanese the *Hauraki* was on her way to the Middle East with a load of war supplies for the soldiers fighting there. Without the supplies the soldiers would not be fighting; it was fairly obvious really. Yet General Thomas Daly, a member of the War Memorial's council, debating the question of including merchant seamen on the Roll of Honour in 1967, explained that merchant seamen could not be regarded as 'service-men in the true sense of the word. They were paid higher wages by reason of danger money and penalty rates of one kind or another,' and could not be regarded as the equal of naval ratings 'who carried the heat and burden of war.' When someone on the council asked how many Australian merchant seamen had died on service during the war the answer came quickly: 'a hundred at the most.' The correct answer is more than five times that number.

As the chairman of the council, Edmund Herring noted, 'the Empire's effort depended on the merchant seamen tremendously. If Hitler could have stopped the ordinary sailor taking the ships across the Atlantic and through the North Sea to Murmansk we would have lost the war'. Even so, the council decided that the Australian War Memorial was not the place to commemorate the loss of life of these Australians and could not even agree to a plaque at the memorial letting the visitor know that the merchant seamen had served as well. Sam Benson was disgusted: 'Men of the Merchant Navy', he wrote, 'actually fought and fired guns in the front line, and suffered injuries and death.'

They called it the merchant navy in Britain because in wartime what had been the shipping industry before the war—individual companies with ships working to company direction —were, in war, subject to Ministry of War Transport control and Admiralty direction. This was essential if Britain was to stay in the war. Britain needed to import a huge quantity of foodstuffs, almost everything that the people ate, in fact; then there were the raw materials for war, and soldiers and airmen had to be shipped overseas and supplied. Only one fear ever, apparently, surfaced in Winston Churchill's mind during Britain's darkest days; not of what the Luftwaffe could do, but a fear that the U-boat campaign might knock Britain out of the war. As a former crew member of a German raider hunting British merchant ships in the icy waters of the Atlantic wrote: 'Every ounce of petroleum, every grain of wheat, every piece of war equipment that we could stop reaching the enemy would be much nearer to starving the British Empire into submission.' So the merchant navy was a vital part of Britain's war effort. Ships could be told where to go and what to carry, and the crew were not at liberty to do what they liked; they were subject to control. In wartime, then, the merchant navy did become a quasi-service and 'the fourth arm of the state'.

Yet in Australia when we write military history we are writing of battalions or brigades, squadrons or ship companies; we are writing about an organised force and often the individuals might almost completely disappear in the story. This battalion now moved up from reserve, that battalion moved behind the main force. Or a leader might move them: 'Monty now had the Australians come behind Rommel's troops', that type of thing. In writing about the merchant navy in Australia during the Second World War it is the individuals who come to the foreground, for the story of the merchant fleet is not a coherent or organised one. Individual ships move through Australian waters and the world's oceans, and individuals move between those ships and among the ships of the British Merchant Navy, too. It is hard to see a coherent 'fourth arm' in the Australian story, and it may be chiefly for this reason that military historians and Australian commemoration have virtually written out the merchant marine from the story of Australia at war. That is an injustice because in their stories individual merchant seamen show the same level of dedication, service, bravery and nobility in their service—and humour and mishap and misadventure—as the other three services. How then to tell something of the story of Australian merchant navy in the Second World War?

One of the best known stories of ships is that of the *Centaur*. On the afternoon of 15 May 1943 the naval office in Brisbane received a message from the United States destroyer, *Mugford*, reporting that she was 40 miles east of Cape Morton, just north of Brisbane, and was picking up survivors from the Australian hospital ship *Centaur*, which had sunk at 4 a.m. the day before. The survivors, therefore, had been in the water for nearly 36 hours. The *Mugford*'s report was the first news of the disaster and stunned those listening to it. The American crew worked as long as daylight lasted, eventually picking up 64 survivors from the 332 people onboard the *Centaur*. Of the ship's crew 29 were among the survivors, along with 34 army medical personnel, including one nurse, Sister Ellen (Nell) Savage. Lost were 45 of the ship's crew and 223 medical personnel, including 11 nurses, and one Torres Strait pilot.

Centaur was a merchant ship on the Western Australia to Singapore trade route before the war and then under Ministry of War Transport orders until released to the Australians for service as a hospital ship in January 1943. Having been refitted and registered as a hospital ship, *Centaur* made her maiden voyage in that capacity from Melbourne on 12 March 1943, arriving in Port Moresby on 13 April, and was back in Sydney on 8 May. She was on her second voyage to Port Moresby, taking medical personnel for service there, when she was struck without warning by a torpedo from a Japanese submarine. There was no excuse for the attack. It was a clear night and *Centaur* was brightly lit and clearly marked as a hospital ship. The rules of war would say that she should not be attacked; but were there any rules to war still in operation?

Sister Nell Savage was asleep when she heard and felt two massive explosions, and was 'practically thrown out of bed'. Calmly, she and her companion put on their life jackets and made their way to the deck; their commanding officer, Lieutenant Colonel Clement Manson, apparently said to them, 'That's right, girlies, jump for it now.' They jumped and within three minutes the ship had sunk without any chance for the crew to launch the lifeboats. Sister Savage was able to tell what happened next and, of course, all experienced much the same as she did, whether or not they survived. She was badly injured when sucked deep down by the sinking ship, suffering fractured ribs, nose and palate by hitting wreckage from the ship as she went down; she also suffered perforated ear drums and severe bruising. Nell Savage was then pushed to the surface, through an oil slick. Being a strong swimmer, she was able to make her way to a life raft. Though badly off herself, Nell Savage helped other survivors in the water during their 36-hour wait for rescue and for this was subsequently awarded the George Medal.

One of those from the *Centaur* to die was Robert Westwood, a 15-year-old cabin boy. Nell Savage had nursed the boy for a while on the life raft, trying to help him make it through, but the battle was lost. The loss of such a young life makes the disaster even sadder and I would like to tell you more about Robert but I cannot as the records about him are simply not there. I can tell you that the 11 nurses and 212 other military personnel who died have their names, of course, engraved on the Roll of Honour at the Australian War Memorial. But not the name of Robert Westwood, nor the names of his 44 crew mates of the merchant service, for they were not, in Tom Daly's words, 'servicemen in the true sense of the word'. And was Robert Westwood better paid, with danger money and penalty rates and all the rest of it, as Tom Daly had asserted in justifying keeping their names off the Roll of Honour? Better paid at 15 years of age? Hardly. Around £3 per month is about right, I believe.

It would seem that some 14 000 Australians served in the merchant marine during the Second World War, about 12 500 in Australian registered ships and the remainder in ships of other nations: British, mostly, but American as well and even Norwegian. We cannot be too sure for the records are imprecise. It was said that the merchant navy consisted, in the most part, of 'kids too young for the other services or men too old for them'. Take David Joseph, for example. He was born in Lower Plenty, outside Melbourne, on 13 February 1927. David attended a few schools but in truth he was not a scholar. His last school was the South Melbourne Technical School, which he left as soon as he could when he turned 14. After a bit of work around Port Melbourne David joined the merchant service in 1941, still 14, aboard the MV *Naracoopa* on the Melbourne to Tasmania run. He was constantly seasick for about the first six weeks but found his sea-legs after that. Dave Joseph, as his shipmates knew him, was a deckhand, a cabin boy, 'it meant [you did] anything.'

It was nothing special to be so young, Dave quickly found. Everyone in the service was a youngster, even the officers. It was nothing, he discovered, for the chief officer, next in seniority to the captain, to be as young as 21 or 22 years of age. They could not find crew, that was pretty obvious, and they were prepared to promote those with at least some experience. Bill Todd, first mate but in his forties, begins to sound like something of an exception. Dave was keen to go abroad, of course, all that he needed was a letter from his parents saying that they had no objection. In no time at all he was on a Norwegian ship bound for the Middle East. In the early years of the war the merchant ships were very lightly armed, if at all, but later in the war 'we were more heavily armed than a destroyer,' Dave Joseph said, though that sounds a little exaggerated. The ships were carrying foodstuffs, ammunition and weapons: 'Our job was to get these supplies to [the troops] no matter what conditions.' At this stage of the war, though ships were zigzagging to avoid enemy submarines, they rarely travelled in convoys, across the Indian Ocean anyway.

There was a bond among the merchant mariners that made for little distinction between nationality and race. 'When you went on board a merchant ship you were with a new crew every time . . . you simply boarded a ship this afternoon, by tomorrow morning you were all brothers.' On a typical merchant vessel there were about ten men on deck and about nine below deck with the ship's engines. There was a captain, of course, and a first, second and third mate. Below deck there was a chief engineer and second and third engineers. Dave called his captain 'skipper', and called the other officers 'chief'; you were rarely on first-name terms with the officers, he said. The ship's company also included a cook and a steward for the officers: 'That was the complete crew on an average ship.' On the completion of a voyage the crew was paid off and given two days' leave for every month they had been at sea. The leave was unpaid except that crew were given a subsistence allowance, of between 1/6 and two shillings per day. There was no accommodation allowance and even onboard ship the crew were entirely responsible for their own clothing and equipment; even bedding, though a mattress was provided. Leave over, merchant sailors were simply assigned to their next ship. They had no say in it, nor would they know where the ship might take them.

Dave Joseph was in about six Atlantic convoys and on one Russian convoy. The Russian trip, around Christmas time 1943, when Dave was 16, was clearly the worst voyage he ever made. There was about three feet of snow all over the deck every morning, which had to be shifted, and about six inches of ice attached to everything, which had to be knocked off using crowbars. Adding to the weight of the ship, the snow and the ice would eventually have sunk the vessel if left to accumulate. Touch the railing of the ship with your bare skin and your hand would stick to the metal. The Barents Sea was so cold at that time of year that if you fell into it, you would be unconscious within 30 seconds; within two minutes you'd be dead. Enemy submarines did sink ships in Dave Joseph's Russian convoy, but neither other merchant ships, which were forbidden to anyway, nor naval ships on escort duty bothered to stop to look for survivors. There was no point. Only about four Australians survived the Russian convoys, Dave Joseph believed, and 'I'm one of them'; but he did not know who the others were or how many Australians had served on the convoys, and we will never know now.

How could a young sailor know anything but fear in such awful circumstances? 'I've never deserted my post,' Dave said, 'but I've been very close; I've been that panic-stricken at times.' On leave in England and having a drink with a cousin, Dave Joseph suddenly had a severe panic attack, just thinking about what he had been through and what was in front of him. He turned white, his cousin told him. The next morning Dave was at the ministry office pleading to be put on a ship straightaway, that day. 'You've got plenty of leave', they told him, but Dave insisted. He knew that if he didn't sail immediately he would never be able to sail again; and that was impossible because he was bound to go to sea—he was in the merchant navy. And so this young Australian sailor was on board a ship again that very day.

Dave Joseph found himself in the invasion of Sicily, launched on 10 July 1943 with 180 000 Allied troops and 2590 ships. It was the second largest invasion fleet for Europe during the war, overshadowed only by Operation Overlord—D-Day. The Allies secured the port of Syracuse on the first day of the invasion and Dave Joseph's ship was to tie up at a wharf at Syracuse to unload necessary supplies. The ship, therefore, was 'subject to air attack 24 hours a day—every two or three hours day and night,' while they unloaded. Subsequently Dave was trained as a gunner by the Royal Navy as, increasingly, the merchant navy fleet was armed. It was while working as a 'second loader' to a gun on one of his ships that Dave Joseph suffered the disability that would see him out of the merchant navy. A 'nice Blighty one' (an injury that would see a man home), a soldier of the First World War might have said. It was nothing of the kind for Dave Joseph. It was the flashes from the gun, the constancy of them, and his closeness to the gun, Dave said, that caused his blindness—or near enough to blindness. So he was discharged, medically unfit, just after his eighteenth birthday, after four years at war.

Discharged to what? Well, to fend for himself. So rough were the conditions of service in the merchant navy that a sailor's pay even ceased if his ship was sunk. Not when he scrambled on board a rescue craft, or was back on dry land again. But the moment his ship was sunk. No ship, no pay. It was all rather brutal. But, as a kindness, rescued merchant mariners were given 28 days' leave to help them recover from trauma—unpaid leave, of course. Once discharged there was no pay for Dave Joseph, and no one to pay or help him with his medical expenses. He remembers sitting on a park bench in London, 18 years and three months old, listening to the sounds of jubilation all around him on VE Day; the war in Europe was over. Dave Joseph, who had served his country for four years, with his country hardly knowing it, was alone, near blind, and without, it seemed, a friend in the world.

The pay, Tom Daly, the pay? Well, by the end of the war, including bonuses, Dave Joseph was being paid about £20 per month. An able seaman in the Royal Australian Navy received about £4/10 per week (including deferred pay) or a little more than £18 per month. If he was married he received an additional 4/6 a day; he was, of course, 'victualled' at sea and ashore, clothed and accommodated while he was in the navy. All his medical expenses were met during his service and after (for war-related conditions), and he received a variety of repatriation benefits too. This is not an argument about whether one sailor should have received more than another, or whether governments should properly reward their citizens who do the awful business of war for them. It is to put the lie, though, to the idea that the merchant sailors were some sort of mercenaries and princes of the sea, doing their job for great financial reward while the humble sailor went about his job for nearly no pay at all. And a major general, by the way, received about £100 a month more than both of them in the same war.

It would be wrong to give the impression that all the action for the merchant navy was in the Battle of the Atlantic or in other northern European waters. Terrifyingly though, in the northern winter of 1943, the Germans were able to deploy over 400 U-boats to the battle, and certainly the battle reached a climax in early 1943, with March being the worst month, when U-boats were able to attack half of the North Atlantic convoys, sinking 22 per cent of Allied shipping. Thereafter, through tactical refinement, increased priority to the battle, with improved aircraft and better escort support, the battle swung in favour of the Allies. Churchill's one great fear for Britain's survival in the war receded from that point.

There was also danger in Australian waters too, not on the same scale as the North Atlantic, of course. Even so, enemy action accounted for the loss of 76 ships in Australian waters and at least 349 Australian merchant seamen lost their lives in these actions. Perhaps it is worth noting that the Royal Australian Navy lost 840 of its personnel, killed, missing or presumed dead in the war against Japan, and 900 in the war against Germany. The navy's strength during the war was just on 40 000 officers and ratings; there were something like 14 000 men in the merchant navy of whom some 500 were killed. The casualty rates are not greatly dissimilar.

Nor was some of the action that the merchant mariners experienced. Doug MacLeod was the radio officer on SS *Carola* and he wrote a progressive letter to his father across three weeks of enemy action, beginning on 17 June 1942. First he describes the loss of the *Macdhui*, a merchant ship hit on its way from Townsville to Port Moresby and spectacularly finished off in Port Moresby during bombing raids by the Japanese on the town and harbour. Three crew and one member of the military working party were killed in the first attack at Port Moresby and a number were wounded. The next day the Japanese returned to the badly damaged ship and the *Macdhui* again suffered direct hits, burning fiercely before finally sinking. As Doug MacLeod describes it to his father:

> I had the horrible experience of seeing a good ship blasted
> by three bombs and drift about the harbour burning like

hell and letting off terrific explosions and dense clouds of smoke. She finished up on a reef end slowly burned out and capsized with the Red Ensign still flying a couple of hours after she was hit.

During all of this the crew of the *Carola* were sitting on their ship waiting to discharge their 'very undesirable cargo' (44-gallon drums of aviation fuel), and could do nothing but watch the destruction of a sister merchant ship and fear for their own lives as the bombs fell around them.

MacLeod gave his father a dramatic personal account of being in an air raid:

I think I'll remember to-day's experiences of a full scale air-raid for some time. The alert sounded about 10.45 a.m. and they came over about twenty-five minutes later. Eighteen or twenty heavy bombers headed straight for us at about 25,000 feet. We could hear the drone of the engines, but they were almost overhead before we could see them. Their shape was plain enough, even at that height, shining like silver. We were the first target and all we could do was watch them shoot bombs at us. Our machine guns were manned, but naturally they were useless. The anti-aircraft batteries ashore started and I thought at first they were bomb explosions until I looked up and saw the puffs of white smoke around the bombers. The aiming was accurate, but they couldn't get high enough. Then the bombs started coming, we could hear them and some of us could see them when they were well up. The first one fell from fifteen to twenty yards a stern of us. The blast was terrific, and most demoralising. I don't mind admitting that I didn't feel too good, with the possibility of a few dozen more coming right on its tail. However, the next one fell approximately the same distance off our port bow and then, I suppose, about twenty or thirty between us and the [Macdhui]. Another lot fell between her and a Dutchman and the remainder just exploded across the harbour until a couple hit one of the heads, sending up a shower of rocks.

We estimate that between a hundred and a hundred and twenty bombs were dropped and the fun was all over in less than one minute. But, Gosh, what a minute!

Doug MacLeod wavered between bravado and realism in writing to his father, as might have been expected:

I wanted to see an air-raid and feel quite satisfied with yesterday's exhibition. I haven't any inclination whatever to see another one. Anybody who does is loco. Mind you, I'm not moaning about it, as I knew what to expect when we came here, but I don't think I realised that they would get so close. I didn't really give the matter any thought until they dropped a bomb twenty yards from me. That sort of woke me up to the fact that there was a war on and that at the moment I was in the middle of it.

The crew of the *Carola* successfully unloaded the aviation fuel and were all keen to head straight back to Townsville and Brisbane, but the navy had other ideas, forcing the ship to wait until a convoy and escort could be organised. They were under naval orders and could do nothing else but wait. Eventually the *Carola* sailed on 4 July 1942 to pick up a cargo of sugar in Townsville to unload in Sydney. Even in Australian waters the merchant seaman had adventures enough.

Alison Todd carries a memory of her father and his service to his country with her still. She was in Canberra, at the Australian War Memorial, when a tribute to the merchant navy was unveiled there in 1999. There are panels on either side of a large sculpture with the names of those merchant sailors who died in war. Bill Todd's name is there. Not quite on the Roll of Honour but better than total anonymity. Captain Sam Benson died in 1995, aged 86, and therefore did not live long enough to see even this modest recognition of the men for whom he had fought for so long. The British, though, have a substantial and moving merchant navy memorial at Tower Hill in London; they have always seen the merchant navy as the 'fourth arm' of the services and a lifeline to their country in war. The memorial contains the names of 24 000

British merchant mariners who died in the Second World War and the names of 50 Australians who died in the British service. Unveiled by the Queen in 1955 this memorial precedes even the modest Australian recognition by more than 40 years.

19. FIGHTING ON REGARDLESS

In Papua New Guinea at Koitaki we left Australian troops angry and disgusted at the dressing-down they had just been given by Tom Blamey. Their job was far from over, they knew that, and Douglas MacArthur still yearned for the kind of victory that would silence the doubters at home. Retreating back along the Kokoda Track the Japanese had reached the northern coast of the island, and dug in with great skill and efficiency. They were hard to dislodge. With Tom Blamey's words ringing in their ears the Australians were in no mood for caution and further criticism. They knew the Japanese were a fanatical and skilful foe; the coming battles would be to the death. Tom Blamey had given them reason to fight as if there was no tomorrow—they would show that old bastard, they really would.

Known as the 'bridgehead battles', these were truly horrible; there is no other word for what occurred at Gona, Buna and Sanananda from November 1942 to mid-January 1943. Although relatively flat, the terrain was terrible: high kunai grass, swampy ground, creeks and rivers, thick jungle cover. Added to this was the fact that the Japanese had prepared their defences brilliantly: well-concealed strong posts, well-sited guns, an 18-kilometre front with defence in depth. Attacking troops might be within just metres of an entrenched machine-gun position and not even realise it was there. Coconut logs, camouflage and vegetation that grew over almost instantly gave the appearance of permanence to what had been built just a week or so before. All the advantages were with the defenders; those attacking would have to be prepared to dig the Japanese out of their trenches and reinforced strong posts. Western Front experience, possibly looked upon as only remotely relevant in this steamy jungle, gave proof to the immensity of the task the attackers faced with its drawn-out trench stalemate.

Why not surround the Japanese and sit it out, in effect waiting to starve them out of the battle? With the sea at their backs and with no possibility of a sustained break-out they were not going anywhere. In any case, how many Japanese were there? Intelligence reports differed on this vital question. Some said a battalion, some thought double that number, say 2000 soldiers, others argued a much lower figure. With the Allies gaining superiority in the air, the Japanese could not land fresh troops easily, nor supplies for that matter. Supply problems had already defeated the Japanese on the track, so why not make that the solution again? Starve them out; leave them to their fate—MacArthur had none of it. He apparently thought the Japanese were still capable of reinforcing their troops and resupplying them. Now stationed at Port Moresby, MacArthur made his first-ever visit to Papua New Guinea on 2 October 1942, and this Commander-in-Chief wanted progress. The Americans had begun their assaults on the Japanese positions in mid-November but the going was too slow for Douglas MacArthur. No matter the strength of the Japanese defences and the terrible country over which the Americans and the Australians had to advance, there would be progress—the general would see to that.

General Robert Eichelberger, born in Urbana, Ohio, in March 1886, had made his career in the United States Army, graduating from the Military Academy in 1909. He had fought in Mexico and Panama, but not in Europe during the First World War. Fifty-six years of age in 1942, Eichelberger was older than every Australian commander in the field except Tom Blamey. On 30 November 1942 Bob Eichelberger was at Government House in Port Moresby, urgently summonsed by his Commander-in-Chief. He would have known that since the time the American 32nd Division had gone into battle two weeks earlier they had already lost 492 men in battle with nothing to show for it. MacArthur was 'striding up and down' the long verandah at Government House, portraying himself as every inch the leader in a funk. 'There were no preliminaries,' Eichelberger recalled, and certainly no pleasantries to lighten the mood of the meeting. 'Bob,' the American Caesar said in a grim voice, 'I'm putting you in command at Buna . . . and I want you to remove all officers who won't fight. Relieve regimental and battalion commanders; if necessary put sergeants in charge of battalions and corporals in charge of companies—anyone who will fight.' MacArthur then strode off down the verandah to let this piece of decisive leadership sink in. He returned to face Bob Eichelberger a second time: 'Bob, I want you to take Buna or not come back alive.'

That's how you pump up your generals for war, MacArthur might have thought as he strode off down the verandah again, but he would try a different approach, too. The next morning, before Bob Eichelberger flew to Buna, MacArthur put his arm around the general. 'If you capture Buna,' the coaxing general said now, 'I'll give you a Distinguished Service Cross and recommend you for a high British decoration. Also . . . I'll release your name for newspaper publication.' Death or glory, it was all quite straightforward, really.

George Vasey, born in March 1895 and known to his family as Alan, had fought at the Somme in 1916 and at Messines and Ypres in 1917. He ended that war assaulting the Hindenburg line in October 1918. George Vasey was therefore an experienced Western Front man even though he had only entered Duntroon in 1913—his class had been graduated early to get to war. Vasey commanded the Australian forces on Crete in 1941 after serving brilliantly through the short Greek campaign. From October 1942 he was commander of the 7th Australian Division, well aware that Tom Blamey and Douglas MacArthur demanded action—the Australians were to take Gona and then drive on through Sanananda to link up with the Americans at Buna. George Vasey was a popular general with the troops, a man whom Bob Eichelberger thought, even after many weeks in the jungle, still 'looked like a commander'. Decorated by his own country, Vasey would also earn the United States' Distinguished Service Cross in 1944, reflecting his importance in the fighting throughout 1943. There was some talk, much later in the war, that the Australian government was grooming George Vasey to take over from Tom Blamey. It never happened. In March 1945, flying again to New Guinea to take command of the 6th Australian Division, George Vasey's aircraft crashed into the sea off Cairns in north Queensland, killing all those on board. 'No soldier or general could have been so loved and worshipped by his men', a subordinate wrote. In late 1942, after a disheartening day at Sanananda where the Australians had lost too many men for too little gain, George Vasey had written that to send in infantry to attack perimeter localities studded with well-concealed pillboxes, was simply to repeat the costly mistakes of 1915–17. Vasey's Western Front experience told him that there had to be a better way.

It would not be the generals at the rear who would find that better way, nor generals told to fight and die, or to fight in any case. Ralph Honner, still in charge of the 39th Battalion, drew on his now considerable battle experience to develop plans that would save Australian lives and win, with his soldiers, a deserved victory. Honner was at Gona, on the western edge of the Japanese perimeter. Gona was a tiny, insignificant spot, a former mission station of no strategic importance, you would think. Too many lives would be lost at Gona, in remote jungle, for what? The Japanese were well entrenched there but they could not move forward and the sea was at their backs. When the Australians eventually overran the Japanese positions what they found in the trenches and strong posts sickened them. With no room at all to move, in fact imprisoned in their own fortifications, the Japanese had lived among their own dead, piling up the bodies as makeshift trench parapets. Unable to develop a latrine system, they also lived among their own waste. Yet they would not surrender and would fight to the death. It was horrid.

The fighting at Gona had started on 19/20 November, and the frontal assaults had achieved nothing except the loss of valuable Australian troops. Honner's brigadier, Ivan Dougherty, new to the job in the jungle, ordered that the brigade and the battalion attack again, across what had now been established as a highly successful killing field for the Japanese. Dougherty may have believed that the failure of the earlier attacks supported what he had heard about the Australians as being true after all. Back in Moresby they were muttering about these troops. Tom Blamey had needed to go and give them a dressing-down, apparently, telling them never to run from the enemy again; 'each one of you is worth three Japanese soldiers,' Blamey had said to them. Here they were at Gona and again they would not push forward. If Dougherty believed this scuttlebutt he also showed that he had no understanding, yet, of the enemy he was facing. So little did he understand his fanatical foe that he ordered an airdrop of leaflets calling on the Japanese to lay down their arms and surrender. Nothing came of this so Dougherty ordered yet another frontal assault against the entrenched positions.

An officer cannot ignore an order or disobey it. He might protest against the order, and Ralph Honner would later regret that his protest on this occasion had been too muted. 'I didn't want to have another company killed off', he wrote, 'and I didn't know how to get out of it'. What an appalling dilemma for a soldier: 'I didn't know how to get out of it.' Any officer, with the lives of his men at risk, would dread to receive an order that was inept or based on a poor appreciation of the true situation, an order that would almost certainly lead to failure and a severe loss of life. Military history is, of course, riddled with such orders, full of such dilemmas. Ralph Honner called the attack off even though his brigadier had ordered it, telling his brigadier that the lack of promised air support had rendered the attack impossible. Remember the Nek at Gallipoli when wave after wave of brave, young Australian soldiers raced to certain death because the officer on the spot would not contest or cancel the orders he had been given? To stand on that small patch of earth above the shimmering sea at the Nek, to see with your mind what these men must have seen in reality as the whistle sounded for their attack: the enemy's trenches only 25 metres away, bristling with rifles, the beginning splutter of machine guns on the higher ground and their flame. Every fibre of your being pleads with the officer to call it off, to save these young lives. But the story rushes to its inevitable climax with 400 of the 600 in the attack casualties. Not to weep for men in war seems almost inhumane. Well, Ralph Honner took a different path. In the meantime Ivan Dougherty was sacking two other battalion commanders whom he thought were not vigorous enough. Ralph Honner might have thought that there is some luck in war.

Ivan Dougherty, described as a 'warm and humane man', came to the command of 21st Brigade in October 1942. Although he had fought in Libya and in Greece, perhaps he was learning his craft in the early days of his brigade command or perhaps he truly believed what Blamey had said of his officers and the men at Koitaki. Dougherty would lead the 21st Brigade for the remainder of the war, principally in Papua New Guinea but also in Borneo in 1945. Gona was not his finest hour. Yet 'he consistently demonstrated a concern for his soldiers', wrote one military historian, 'and a refusal to risk their lives unnecessarily'. Perhaps Dougherty's best work at Gona was in not sacking Ralph Honner when he might well have done so for failing to make the attack that Dougherty had ordered for 7 December. Instead Dougherty gave Honner a day to come up with a better plan.

Honner's new plan for his 39th Battalion emerged from his detailed reconnaissance of the land over which he would fight. Honner had done this at Bardia, as we have seen, going so far forward to see for himself every detail of the land over which he would fight, when he might easily have been captured in doing so. Now at Gona he did it again. Honner's insistence on seeing what was in front of him may seem obvious but too much of the fighting at Gona and Buna was taking place without careful planning and detailed intelligence. Ivan Dougherty still wanted to press the attack where the earlier ones had failed, he wanted another frontal assault. Again, you have to ask why. Ralph Honner developed a much more sensible plan: he would launch his main attack from the jungle and scrub, allowing his soldiers the possibility of surprise, of coming on the Japanese unseen. Again, this seems so obvious and unremarkable that the truly remarkable thing is that

Honner had to convince Dougherty of the sense of what he proposed. When Honner explained later what it was that he had done differently he only added to the view that his battle plan was not radical or remarkable but just plain common sense: 'If in the last stretch [of the attack the enemy] has got an unbroken field of fire . . . he can mow you down. But if you've got a covered approach right into the heart of his defences he's gone.' Surely that is fundamental. Perhaps MacArthur's sense of urgency had robbed more senior officers than Ralph Honner of an understanding of the basics of battle.

Look at the evidence the Australians had to work with. The first assault on the Japanese positions at Gona had been made along the main track from the south, precisely where the Japanese had been expecting it. Not surprisingly, therefore, the Japanese set up strong defences on that track, defences of which, initially, the Australians had no idea. The first attack saw the loss of four officers and 32 men killed or wounded, and with illness rampant on both sides, losses like these would impact heavily on the chances of success. But still the Australians pushed on over subsequent days, assaulting these positions again with heavy losses. When Honner's 39th Battalion, with remnants of the 2/14th Battalion, attacked under the cover of scrub and jungle on 8/9 December they ultimately prevailed. First they drove a wedge through the middle of the Japanese defending forces and then gradually, and with great difficulty, they eliminated all elements of Japanese resistance. But it was slow and ghastly work, 'some of the bitterest fighting of the Papuan campaign', as John Coates described it. By nightfall on 8 December the 'game was up' for the Japanese, and sometime after midnight Japanese soldiers attempted a break-out to join troops fighting at Sanananda; these soldiers were simply never going to give up. Perhaps 100 of the Japanese trying to get out of Gona were killed during the night; perhaps a similar number did get away. In the light of day, the Australians were able to move about, and what they saw shocked and sickened them, 'a dirty, filthy mess', as one officer described it. The 21st Brigade lost 34 officers and 375 men as battle casualties at Gona; earlier the 25th Brigade had lost 17 officers and 187 men; with other actions in the area the total casualties for the Australians at

Gona were 57 officers and 677 other ranks. The Japanese appear to have suffered a similar number of casualties. All for a miserable strip of ground at a former mission station.

Still this campaign demanded more. The focus of the fighting moved eastwards along the coast to Sanananda, where the Japanese were again heavily entrenched. The numbers of troops now available for the fight became almost laughable, if it were not so sad. Even Ralph Honner had succumbed to the prevalent malaria and was away from his battalion for five days. When he returned on 27 December 1942 he learned that George Vasey had decided that the weakened troops could not dislodge the Japanese and they had been ordered to make Sanananda a holding operation, awaiting the anticipated victory at Buna. But as with Australian troops earlier, holding the enemy on a perimeter involved aggressive patrolling to keep the enemy alert and anxious.

Bob Eichelberger had taken command at Buna on 2 December 1942, committed by MacArthur to victory or death. There were two fronts at Buna: Urbana—nicely named after Bob Eichelberger's birthplace in Ohio—and Warren. The Americans were making little progress at either. Tom Blamey told MacArthur that the American troops were not up to Australian militia standards. What a grinding of teeth that statement must have produced; there was little love lost in this headquarters. To overwhelm well-entrenched troops an attacking force must have firepower, either from artillery or from the air. The Americans had neither. Again they might have sat it out, waiting for aircraft or artillery; waiting, too, for the Japanese, who were again confined to a fairly circumscribed area, to collapse through starvation and ill-health. But Douglas MacArthur wanted swift victories, although no one could now believe that Japanese commanders would bother reinforcing or resupplying these men. Reasonably fresh Australian troops were brought in from Milne Bay and they fought alongside the Americans on Warren front. Supported by light tanks which might break the impasse over firepower, the advance gathered some momentum and by 3 January the Americans and the Australians had overcome the Japanese at Buna.

Would Sanananda then fall, the final domino as the enemy's morale collapsed and the Japanese recognised the impossibility of their position? You would like to think so but these 'bridgehead battles', Gona, Buna and Sanananda—such an awfulness rarely seen, even in war—had a way to run yet. Stout Japanese resistance meant that, yet again, every metre of territory was contested, every strong post overcome only after considerable firepower could be deployed. Only on 22 January could Australian and American troops claim victory in the region. The Japanese had been reduced to eating roots and grass to keep alive; there was also a suggestion of cannibalism just to add to the true horror of these battles.

Again the losses at Sanananda were considerable, and indeed in the seven months of fighting since the Japanese had first landed at Buna in July 1942 the Australians had suffered 5698 battle casualties, including 1731 killed in action, 306 who died of wounds and 128 men who died of other causes. The Australians also had 15 575 cases of infectious diseases. On 23 January, when the 39th Battalion was ordered out of Sanananda and onto the airfield at Dobodura for the short flight back to Port Moresby, it mustered a strength of just seven officers and 25 other ranks from around 1000 originals. The battalion had basically ceased to exist. Yet it had become a true battalion in the course of its fighting on the Kokoda Track and at Gona and Sanananda. Requesting transport to Dobodura for his men who were so deplorably weakened, Ralph Honner was told to start the men walking and transport would be arranged to collect the stragglers. Honner and his battalion decided that there would be no stragglers and, somehow, they all made their own way to the airfield, 'marching' as a battalion would, but in threes with the two outside men holding up the man in the middle. Has there been any more touching sight in Australian military history than this remnant of a battalion proudly 'marching' to evacuation? An observer at Dobodura asked 'what is this mob,' as the men struggled past. 'This is not a mob,' the officer of the 39th bringing up the rear replied, 'this is the 39th Battalion.'

Jo Gullett had discovered what a true battalion was at Bardia and would have smiled had he heard that gallant story. But who can say what the sights, sounds and smells of the bridgehead battles, 'the bloodiest of the Pacific War', as John Coates has described them, did to the minds and souls of the men who fought them.

When I was describing for a radio audience the terrible plight of the 'man in the bath' who had lost his outer skin cover in a gas attack in France, I took a call from a listener off-air. She had been deeply moved by the story but in her turn she wanted to tell me her father's story. He had been a young medical doctor in Papua New Guinea in the second part of 1942. Perhaps he had seen some of the awful sights at Gona and smelt the fearful smell of death and excrement all wrapped in one. Perhaps he had seen what had happened to those Japanese soldiers who had walked into the sea, their defeat certain, holding hand grenades above their heads which they would detonate rather than be taken captive. Whatever this young doctor had seen at war deeply affected him: 'He had lost his psychological skin cover,' his daughter told me. It was a compelling phrase that she had used; terrible, truly terrible to lose your physical skin, but just as damaging, though unseen, was the loss of the psychological skin cover. Several times in the 1950s, and even later, this suburban doctor had tried to commit suicide, so badly had his war affected him. And the battles along the track, and at Gona and Buna, had deeply burned their way into the lives of this doctor's children as well. The attempted suicide of a much-loved father would cast awful shadows; truly for these people 'this war never ends'.

Yet Douglas MacArthur had his victory, although as the United States Army's official history put it: 'After six months of bitter fighting and some 8500 casualties, including 3000 dead [on the Allied side], the South West Pacific Area was exactly where it would have been the previous July had [the Americans and the Australians] been able to secure the beachhead before the Japanese got there.' Even so, the war in Papua New Guinea was far from over. Attention now moved further west along the coast, to the Huon Peninsula and beyond. If the Japanese were to be routed in the islands to the north they would also have to be eliminated on the mainland of New Guinea, removed from Lae and all the area to the west, and from Finschhafen, knocked off from Sattelberg, the mountain that dominated the entire region, fought out of the Ramu Valley and cleared from Shaggy Ridge. These were grinding, debilitating battles, involving three battle-hardened Australian infantry divisions, supported by American logistics, sea and air transport, and offensive air and naval support. The

Americans might have acknowledged that the Australians were doing most of the fighting on the ground except that, as John Coates has written, 'MacArthur's excessive vanity and ethnocentrism' prevented due acknowledgement.

For most of 1943, Australians read in their newspapers of battles in New Guinea that seemed to make little strategic sense except for the notion of beating the Japanese wherever they found him. The schoolboy following the Pacific War on his war map would now be pushing his many flags into a tiny area of a remote part of New Guinea, where once he had been dashing his flags up and down the coast of North Africa. For men in battle the remoteness of the location meant little except massive discomfort and grief. That these battles of 1943 were rarely mentioned when people were talking about Australia's military past must have annoyed the veterans but could not have really surprised them. Popular history needs drama, it needs heroes and stories. Gallipoli stood out for Australians at the time because, as nothing much was happening on the Western Front, the Anzacs suddenly had the limelight on the world stage and people at home basked in their fame.

There was no world stage in the Ramu and Markham valleys, or at Lae or Finschhafen, unfair though this is. The whole war map had become intensely interesting. In 1943 Hitler was in terrible trouble at Stalingrad, and his troops soon surrendered after the most extraordinary battles and terrible suffering for both soldiers and civilians. Montgomery's troops entered Tripoli after the Germans had abandoned it and the North African war was entering its final stages, and soon enough the 'Dambusters' made their famous raid on the Eder and Mohne dams in the Ruhr Valley with dramatic but little real, long-term impact, except a flag to show to highlight the story. Then the Allies would take Sicily in a significant defeat for the Axis powers, and a considerable number of prisoners of war were marched into captivity and the invasion of Italy began—the flags would now move up the Italian peninsula to Naples, Rome, Milan. As 1943 came to an end there was a real sense that an invasion of France was in prospect and the war could be taken to Germany itself.

Look at the Australian newspapers throughout 1943 and Europe dominates the headlines, is given the greater number of column inches, and attracts the best writing and pictures. Take the Melbourne *Argus* for 16 October 1943, for example. The main front-page story has a headline shouting, 'New Allied Landings in Italy', and the second story is 'Russians Cross Dnieper at Zaporozhe'. In just one half-column on the front page there is a story entitled 'Pacific's War's New Phase', but note, it is written out of New York. Too often stories from the New Guinea battlefront came from correspondents attached to Douglas MacArthur's headquarters, relying on army briefings for their information, not on what they saw themselves. For example, the *Argus* for 27 November 1943 leads with 'Germans Admit Loss of Gomel' (near the Ukrainian border), followed with 'Main Air Attack Switched to Frankfurt' and then the 'Closing in on Satelberg [sic]' story. This last one also comes from MacArthur's headquarters and reports that Australian troops are half a mile from the village and closing in. However, the few buildings of the Lutheran settlement there were hardly the objective; it was the mountain that the Australians had to win. With most of the correspondents remote from the action and with greater focus in the newspapers on the war in Europe, is it any wonder that the Australian battles of 1943 hardly became household names? Yet there was action enough if the newspaper reader or war map specialist could only find it.

'Diver' Derrick, they called him, though his parents had named him Thomas Currie. 'He was an extraordinary man', wrote biographer and war historian Bill Gammage. Gazing at the photograph of 'Diver' Derrick, which Gammage says became one of the best-known Australian images of the war, Gammage found a fit man, strong and stocky, a deep tan matching his brown hair, with a cocky grin. The photograph:

> suggests both the larrikin and the professional, both the man who stuck by his mates and the born leader . . . it does not reveal the man who collected butterflies, who wrote poetry and kept a war-time diary . . . it does not say that here is one of the finest fighting soldiers of the war.

Tom Derrick was born in Adelaide in 1914, the eldest of two boys and five girls; his father was a labourer, there was little money in the house. Going barefoot to school, often enough, Tom left school as soon as he could, at age 14, for a life with more adventure. But he ran into the Depression, as did so many of the men with whom he would serve in war. Like them, he found odd jobs, particularly around the Murray, living for long spells in a local 'susso' camp, where a little work and food was thrown the way of the unemployed. One week 'Diver', as he was now universally known, lived only on grapes. Then he got a job in a vineyard and stayed there for nine years. He married in 1939 and enlisted in July 1940; he was 26 years of age.

Derrick seems almost to have been made for war; he excelled in war's environment, but is that a terrible thing to say? His qualities of leadership, enterprise, bravery and determination, ingenuity and selflessness might equally have shone in other endeavours if only he had had the chance. Whatever, at Tobruk with the 2/48th Battalion Derrick was outstanding, described by an officer as 'resourceful, brave, aware, humane, forever bending over backwards for his men'. At Tel el Eisa in July 1942 he knocked out three machine-gun posts, and was promoted to sergeant before El Alamein, where he personally destroyed three more machine-gun post—those who saw him do this were certain he had earned a Victoria Cross. He was wounded at El Alamein and evacuated, but rejoined his battalion before it returned to Australia in February 1943.

The 2/48th was in action again at Lae in September. Every objective, every town and settlement was hotly contested by the Japanese, who were always well dug-in, never willing to surrender. The Australians were supported by British-built Matilda tanks, underpowered for the European war but useful in supporting infantry in the Pacific, but their successes were mostly a matter of gains won by the infantry. That was very much the pattern in the battle for Sattelberg, a Lutheran mission settlement where the village was only the first objective—it was the mountain that held the key. By 24 November Derrick's battalion was attacking Sattelberg mountain, overlooking Finschhafen. Derrick led an advance platoon and encountered 'an almost vertical slope of thick jungle' hiding Japanese machine guns, and then a patch of open ground leading to the crest. 'Even in peacetime the climb is barely possible', wrote Bill Gammage who spent several years in Papua

New Guinea and is an experienced and knowledgeable battlefield traveller. For a couple of hours the Australians tried desperately to clamber up the slope but each time they were thwarted by the Japanese on the higher ground with their intense machine-gun fire and grenades. The position seemed hopeless. With night falling, Derrick sought permission to have one last go. Leading from the front he personally destroyed the first machine-gun post impeding his company's advance. He moved a section of his company to the right flank, which then came under fire from six machine-gun posts. Derrick went forward again, throwing grenades into the weapons pits above him. The Japanese soldiers fled, leaving weapons and grenades behind, but three posts remained in action. Derrick assaulted these, 'throwing grenades at a range of six to eight metres'.

This extraordinary man cleared out ten machine-gun posts before nightfall stopped him. His men retained what he had gained throughout the night and the battalion moved on to take Sattelberg the next morning. In one of those moving photographs for Australia in the war, Diver Derrick, the man on whom it had all depended, is seen securing an Australian flag to the stump of a tree at Sattelberg, his slouch hat rightly prominent. This photograph should have become one of the iconic photos of the war, yet few Australians have ever seen it, or even know the name of the man in the photograph. Derrick's assault on the mountain 'was one of the most astonishing feats of the war', Gammage says. And this time Derrick was awarded the Victoria Cross that others thought he deserved earlier. He would die, as seems almost inevitable, less than two years later at Tarakan. Mortally wounded, he said to a mate, 'I've had it. That's that. Write to Beryl [his wife].' Diver Derrick was 31.

Still the grinding campaign pushed on. Winning Finschhafen and Sattelberg had given the Allies some control of the waters between New Guinea and New Britain, rendering the former Japanese strongpoint at Rabaul almost redundant. Now the Australians turned back inland to the Ramu and Markham valleys, intending to clear out the Japanese who might still have the capacity to cause trouble behind them. While the newspapers told their readers that Russian success at the Dnieper River had placed 750 000 German soldiers at risk, in these campaigns in the valleys and slopes of New Guinea we are talking of the engagement of soldiers in their hundreds, not thousands. Yet even so historians have managed to write whole books about these New Guinea campaigns, one of the most recent, *On Shaggy Ridge* by Phillip Bradley, certainly among the best. Shaggy Ridge, as a placename, reeks of Australia, so much so we prick up our ears on just hearing it. There must be a great Australian story there, we instinctively feel. In 1943 'shaggy' almost certainly referred to a 'ragged mass of hair' (although a 'shag' might just have begun to have a separate colloquial meaning, discovered in print by the *Australian National Dictionary* for the first time in 1944). But Shaggy Ridge took its name from the officer who was first ordered onto the ridge to keep the Japanese under observation—Jack 'Shaggy' Clampett. People noticed that Clampett's shaggy hair matched the terrain, and Shaggy Ridge it became. With a similar need for local identifiers, the Japanese named the ridge with their word for a folding screen, because the ridge in fact screened their right flank. You could write a history of war on the names the various armies have given to geographical features; Australians delighted in branding things in their own language.

I cannot tell you here about all the fighting in this region in late 1943 and 1944, you will have to go to more specialised books for that. But we can take up the story, briefly, of the 2/14th Battalion we first met in Libya, then on the track, then briefly at Gona, and now here in the valleys and mountains. Ralph Honner had been given its command after the disbandonment of the 39th Battalion, but he was badly wounded at a place called Wampun when—foolishly again—he had gone forward of his own troops looking for water and the enemy. He was shot through the hip and might easily have been captured or killed as he was so close to the enemy, but he was saved by enormous good luck. Ralph Honner earned that. Nevertheless, the war was more or less over for him.

Within days the 2/14th found itself on King's Hill, overlooking the Ramu Valley and adjacent to Japanese troops on a neighbouring hill linked to King's by a tenuous land bridge. The Japanese had the high ground and commanded the area; they had to be dislodged. The brigadier, Ivan Dougherty, appointed a new commanding officer of the 2/14th, Major Mert Lee, and gave him simple instructions: 'Throw the enemy off the ridge and do it now.' By a remarkable chance the platoon ordered to do this was the same platoon of the 2/14th who, at Jezzine in Syria, tried and failed to take a French-held fort on the heights above the Syrian town. This platoon must have had a head for heights for here they were at it again. Their situation was again diabolical.

The Japanese were 600 yards in front and above them. There were only three means of reaching them: across the land bridge, which would be suicidal as the Japanese could pick the attackers off one by one; or by scaling one of two routes—the first 1000 feet above the Uria River, a sheer drop below, and the second about the same distance above the Faria River, with just as sheer a drop to the water. The dangers of these latter two routes were from the enemy above, or, in missing your footing, a terrifying fall to the river below. But this section of the 24th was as experienced a group of Australian soldiers as could be found, and deeply bonded to one another. One of their number, Bruce Kingsbury, had already won the Victoria Cross on the track, posthumously, others too had been decorated. They were on their way to becoming, in the words of their historian, Peter Dornan, 'one of the most decorated in British and Australian military history'.

Why go on at all? Well, the Japanese on the heights with the command of all the land around them had the opportunity of holding up the Australian advance indefinitely and of holding up Australian supplies, so that any progress in this campaign depended on dislodging the Japanese from this high ground. Looking closely at the third option, the platoon commander, Noel Pallier, noticed that there was a slight gully running under the lip of the ridge that the Japanese occupied; it might give his men some protection and allow them to make their approach to the ridge unnoticed by its defenders above them.

This was as difficult a job as this platoon had ever been given and these experienced men were well aware of the danger that confronted them. There were only 29 of them and they shook hands with mates as they are about to go into action, thinking that few, if any of them, would come out unscathed. Two of their number, Johnny Cobble and 'Lofty' Back, were from out west in Queensland and were good mates. 'See you at the Winton races,'

Lofty said to Johnny, knowing his fate was sealed. Men don't make those remarks, tossed off as an Australian bushman would, unless the words take on an added significance. They should have been able to do that, go to the races at Winton, have a few beers together, enjoy a yarn, but here they were. A few hundred men doing as their officers told them in one of the remotest spots on earth, because it all fitted in somehow to the bigger picture. The bigger picture, that was a leap of faith. Get back to what we know: 'See you at the Winton races.' Good luck, cobber.

Those below looked on with a mixture of awe and horror as they watched 9 Platoon inch its way up and across the slope. Down below they fired their Bren gun and mortars anyway, knowing that they were out of range, but maybe it might distract the Japanese and keep their bloody heads down. In peacetime, Bill Gammage had said of Sattelberg, the climb was barely possible; here it seemed simply impossible, in peace or war. The gradient of the hill was so extreme that the grenades the Japanese began rolling down at them for the most part detonated well below the men struggling up the ridge. Suddenly the men of the platoon were near the top. Observers saw them fix bayonets, take out their own grenades and lob them into the Japanese positions. Standing up for the final rush, they slipped in the loosened earth but pushed themselves on, it seemed, beyond human endurance. Leaping into the Japanese positions, the Australians moved from one to the next, bayoneting and shooting all before them: '. . . for these defenders', writes Phillip Bradley, 'their foxholes became their graves'.

From below observers saw the silhouette of 'Teddy' Bear—such an incongruous name in this most appalling fight—'tossing enemy soldiers off his bayonet like sheafs of wheat'. At Chunuk Bair, almost the highest spot on the Gallipoli peninsula, Kemel Atatürk needed to urgently dislodge the New Zealanders who had just won the high ground. His soldiers attacked with a ferocity and violence rarely seen in war, fanatically pushing the New Zealanders back down the savage slope. It was the same on King's Hill, the same fury and passion with the same result. Those occupying the high ground had all the advantages but the attackers, coming from below, seemed to have all the passion. It was the scream that observers remembered, just as at Chunuk Bair, men screaming like madmen as they launched themselves at the enemy. And shouting orders—Lofty Back, ordering his men on, before being shot dead. Just like his mate Johnny Cobble.

Did every action in which the Australians fought in Papua New Guinea contain moments of sheer heroism such as at Sattelberg and on King's Hill? Of course, the answer is no. We linger on these stories, after all, because they do stand out in their difficulty and intensity. Some of these soldiers were, well, unique. Phillip Bradley described Teddy Bear as 'undoubtedly one of the finest soldiers his country ever put into the field, in any war'. And Diver Derrick deservedly received the Victoria Cross for fighting at Sattelberg. So these were extraordinary moments in the story of Australia at war. Yet there is something about the Australian fighting in Papua New Guinea that means that the story should be much more widely known by Australians now and in the future. Perhaps it was the fanaticism of the enemy that lifted these Australians to a higher level of intensity. Perhaps it was the hideous nature of the terrain.

Even today elite Australian athletes, like Brett Kirk and several team mates from the AFL's Sydney Swans, while walking the Kokoda Track speak in awe of the achievement of just making it from one end to the other. Reflect then on what it must have been like in battle. Others write of climbing the mountains along which the war, in part, was fought as 'barely possible' in peacetime, let alone in war. But perhaps, after all, the intensity of the fighting can be explained by what these Australians believed they were fighting for: the security of their country and the safety of their loved ones at home. When the New Guinea campaigns ended by about April 1944 the three Australian divisions, and those who had supported them, had every reason to feel pride in what they had achieved. Perhaps now Koitaki was behind them; they had taken Tom Blamey's words and flung them back in his face. The trouble was, too few Australians had any idea of the magnificence of what they had done.

20. 'TOO BUSY FOR BITTERNESS'

The Australian troops had been fighting for a long time in New Guinea and by April 1943 were well and truly looking forward to a rest. This would be followed by more training and, in all likelihood, more action. At home, people were distracted by the European war in the papers, which was much more accessible to the editors via reliable cable services. Much was also happening at home so in the kaleidoscope we must employ to make any sense of an event as vast and as long-running as the Second World War, even though we have limited ourselves here to Australia, it is probably appropriate to swing the wheels to focus now on the events at home. The future direction of Australia was under close scrutiny throughout most of 1943.

By the middle of the year John Curtin had clearly lost patience with the parliament that had been elected during wartime in 1940. Labor relied on the support of the two independents who had handed John Curtin power in 1941 and to that extent Curtin managed a 'hung' parliament. Speaking in parliament to a small numbers of members late at night on 24 June, Curtin said that the parliament 'had just about exhausted its resources for constructive legislation'; parliament should be sent, he said, 'to a higher tribunal.' Opposition Leader Arthur Fadden wholeheartedly agreed: 'The position of the Parliament has been unsatisfactory ever since it was elected, and for that fact the electors are entirely responsible.' With both sides saying that the voters should be asked to give a clear mandate one way or the other, the writing was on the wall. A federal election would be held on 21 August 1943.

'Look behind the Curtin', opposition posters and newspaper advertisements pleaded. Even though the posters were smaller in size than was usual—another Curtin wartime austerity measure: 'In the fourth year of the war . . . it was a little ridiculous to think that men should be taken from essential industries such as food production and the making of munitions and aircraft to paint election advertisement signs'—what would the voter find after looking behind the Curtin, in his opponents' view? It was all rather sinister: a dark and fearful figure, not unlike the popular image of an assassin, skulking in the shadows, a 'socialist' perhaps, more a Bolshevik? It was the politics of fear—the one constant, it seems, in Australian political campaigning from the conservative side. 'Too busy for bitterness', Labor countered, and for once there was more than a ring of truth in a campaign slogan.

Too busy indeed because the pressures on the wartime government were almost frightening in their intensity. War Cabinet remained the focus of the ministers' work, who were meeting for long hours, discussing the minute and the broader picture. But, the Advisory War Council was also in regular session and it took a lively interest in everything relating to Australia's role and position in the war. It is the detail that is astonishing when reading the records of both bodies, the direct oversight that ministers had of every aspect of the war. Yet there were a myriad of other things that demanded ministerial attention as well. Just to pluck out one problem almost at random: a report to government in August 1942 that dealt with the ongoing 'manpower crisis' in Australia. This problem would simply not go away and was one of the most difficult things the government juggled throughout the war years. Labour, the essential commodity, remained in critically short supply. The report indicated the economy needed an additional 139 000 men and 44 000 women immediately, and an extra 36 000 women also to replace the men being withdrawn from essential activities for the services. The report called for 'drastic action'.

The manpower regulations were strengthened yet again and there was another comb out of people not working at all or not working in essential industries. Any remaining domestic servants, for example, were to be redeployed and only women aged 45 or over would be allowed to look for work for themselves; everyone else would be directed to a job. The work might be to the auxiliary services, to the fighting services, to munitions factories, the Land Army, wherever. 'Report to the local National Service Office', the government told these people, 'and wait to find out where you will go'. 'Behind the fighting men in the front line,' said John Curtin:

> is a second line of men and women engaged in the production of supplies and equipment for the forces; behind these again are those engaged in producing, processing, transporting and commercially organising the innumerable items of supplies and essential services without which the nation's resistance would collapse.

It was the same message that Curtin gave time after time: we are all in this together, the nation must have an 'all-in' war effort.

Appointed general editor of the official Australian war history in March 1943, Gavin Long, an experienced journalist and war correspondent, made it his business to visit military establishments in Australia to find out for himself the mood of the fighting forces. Among the officers with whom he mingled Long found very little acceptance of Curtin's all-in line. 'The army', he wrote in August 1943, just one week before the election, 'thinks it—and the Air Force and Navy—is doing the hard work while the militia and the civilians are "bludging". All [whom] I have heard', Long wrote at another point in his diary, 'are caustic about strikers and well-paid munition workers generally'. These army officers seemed to believe they were putting in the hard yards and the civilian population was making the money while moaning about how hard they were working. All in it together, the army snorted, hardly.

Were the munitions workers well paid, way above the odds? In South Australia, when a munitions factory put out a call for help in February 1943, 450 women answered the appeal, said *Woman* magazine. So there was an attraction to work, or were these women simply following their patriotic instincts in one of the few ways open to them? The average wage at this factory was only £4/5/- a week (not much above the basic wage), less than that of a serviceman, let alone that of an officer. Equality of sacrifice is an impossible concept in wartime. There can be no comparison between the lot of the soldier or sailor in constant danger and that of the munitions worker, though admittedly at some risk, working hard and in often primitive conditions. Yet governments at war tend to speak of equality of sacrifice to encourage everyone to keep going and to do their best. Curtin's all-in phrase was better: 'We can't all be soldiers,' he would say, 'but we can all play a part.' But being human, even in war, there will always be someone looking enviously at someone else, wondering if they are better off than 'me'; it is what Australian elections are fought over so very often. Would the election of the seventeenth parliament be any different? 'Too busy for bitterness' might prove to be a dangerous slogan. Maybe you are too busy, the voters might think, but we are bitter— bitter that he's getting a better deal than I am.

It was that sour mood that caused some commentators to think that Labor might be in trouble in the election. The Labor Party's chances of winning a majority in the Senate 'are as remote as Mt Erebus [in Antarctica]', puffed the Sydney *Bulletin*. Frank Packer, owner of the Sydney *Daily Telegraph*, was even more confident about his side's chances in the election. Packer had arranged a victory dinner at a smart Sydney hotel in anticipation of Arthur Fadden leading the United Country Party–United Australia Party coalition back to the government benches. You would hope that in wartime the food would not be wasted, because Packer cancelled the celebration soon after the election results began to be posted. There was nothing for his side to cheer about that night. The government trounced the opposition, picking up an additional 14 seats (of 74) in the House of Representatives with a 49–23 seat split (and the two independents, who usually voted with Labor), converting a two-seat deficiency in the Senate to an eight-seat majority. Mt Erebus, it seemed, had moved a great deal closer.

Frank Packer was shocked. There was strong reason to believe that Labor might be in trouble. But it seems Gavin Long's army officers had either changed their minds at the last moment or were woefully out of touch with the mood of fellow voters. Labor presented itself to the electorate as the party that had turned around the nation's fortunes in war; presented John Curtin as the man who had saved Australia. The army officers to whom Gavin Long spoke found this idea 'laughable . . . that [Labor had] pulled the show together and saved Australia from the Japanese'. Instead, those Long questioned wondered why only Menzies was using the argument 'that it was because the AIF gained training and experience in the Middle East that it was able to beat the Japs in New Guinea'. There was an additional factor that also angered the military, Australia's 'two army' policy. Militia battalions, as we have seen, the chockos, fought with tenacity and great skill on the Kokoda Track and elsewhere in Papua New Guinea. People argued that it made no sense for Australia to have, in effect, two armies, and urged that the militia and the AIF now be merged into one force. If not, as the war moved further to the north, only a proportion of Australia's soldiers would be able to fight on because the militia was for home defence only and could not be used outside Australia and its territories. Curtin had seemed to be moving towards the idea of a unified force but then, in early 1943, in the face of strong opposition from within his own party, had backed down. In a compromise Curtin decided that the militia would be used in an expanded field of operations, but only as far north as the equator and not to any great distance east or west of Australia; the distinction between the two armies would remain. Opponents scoffed at the illogicality of this and the criticism hurt the prime minister badly. He worried, an observer reported, 'about some of his bad relationships within his own party', and Curtin apparently said that the strain of all this, and the intensity of leading the nation in war 'was taking a great toll on him, that he was really a dying man'. Equality of sacrifice indeed, some scorned, with a trained and fit army that could only be used on a limited basis. The voters will revolt, these people thought.

Billy Hughes could see the irony in the introduction of what really amounted to a limited form of conscription by the man who had worked so hard against Hughes's own proposal for conscription 27 years earlier. For Australians, even under Curtin's compromise, could now be directed to fight outside Australia and its territories— the very issue that had divided the nation so bitterly in 1916 and 1917. For hardliners, like parliamentary newcomer Arthur Calwell, who had won the seat of Melbourne in 1940, there could be no compromise on the issue. Conscription for overseas service was against Labor Party ideology, had been since 1916, and that was that. When this argument was raging most strongly within the Labor Party Curtin even thought of resigning; he knew that the issue was not nearly as clear-cut as Calwell made it and he agonised over what was in the best interests of Australia and his party. The inner conflict for Curtin must have been enormous and the fact that he was talking about himself as a 'dying man' as early as 1943 shows just how acute the pressure on him was. But there were critics outside the Labor Party, too, who regarded the compromise as humbug and who thought that Australian voters would see it as a sham.

Adding to that was the high and apparently increasing incidence of industrial turmoil in Australia—the second factor that informed observers thought might bring the Labor Party undone at the election. Gavin Long's army officers were able to readily dismiss many of the civilian population as 'bludgers', largely because of the prevalence of strikes in wartime Australia. To some, any strike at all during the war, when the nation fought for its life, was an act of treachery. To many others strikes simply added to the misery of wartime conditions. Good reasons, why the strikes were unpopular in wartime Australia. With labour in such short supply however, the bargaining position of workers had hardly ever bee· stronger, even as hours and conditions of work deteriorated und· the weight of the enormous need for production. Self-intere· prompted unionists to strike while the iron was hot, and it w red-hot during wartime, to maximise pay and seek to impr· conditions while workers had the whiphand. After all, 'th ground us into the dirt in the long years of the Depression.

Some of the strikes, at least, were bloody-minded and cl· not in the national interest. John Curtin spoke of 'lawless

naked and unashamed,' and particularly regretted strikes on the coalfields of New South Wales, which disrupted factories and war industries and meant that, for the householder, coal and gas rationing became a fact of life. Strikers were 'the antithesis of a true citizen,' Curtin said. 'I know I am using hard words,' he continued, 'but I am facing hard facts.' On the waterfront Curtin used military force to move essential supplies and, according to Gavin Long, after the prime minister had made this decision union leaders had phoned him encouraging him to 'stand firm'. Long continued: 'Union leaders of unquestioned honesty had told [Curtin] that large numbers of men in the waterfront unions were not waterside workers at all but had paid up to £20 for membership so that they could evade the call-up. That was the source of the trouble.' If this is true then Curtin might have felt somewhat easier in his own mind about breaking the strikes that were coming too frequently in 1943 and 1944. Even so, the personal cost for Curtin the strike-breaker was again high.

Despite the heavy knocks the prime minister had taken on these two important issues Curtin had reason to be confident that he had the people behind him. Strikes are universally unpopular, no more so than in wartime, with the twin issues of treachery and widespread misery from shortages of goods and services at the forefront of people's minds. A long-running transport strike or coal strike impacted on people immediately, and with thoughts about the soldiers in danger at the front and doing it tougher than anyone on the waterfront, for example, people looked to Curtin for leadership and applauded when they saw him standing firm. Curtin's political opponents in the election campaign probably made a major miscalculation in trying to focus on what was 'behind the Curtin'. They were trying to portray Curtin as a weak leader, buckling to party critics on the two army policy and to strikers on the coalfields and waterfront. To the people, though, the figure of the prime minister seemed to stand so tall that when they did take a close look they simply saw Curtin himself and nothing at all behind him; they were grateful for his leadership of the nation.

The people seemed to agree that Labor was doing the best job possible in winning the war and that a disunited opposition had

little to offer in that regard. True to his theme, 'too busy for bitterness', Curtin opened his party's election campaign not with a
rousing speech to a frenetic audience in one of the major cities, but
in a broadcast to the nation from a radio studio in Canberra. He
could be back at his desk in Parliament House within minutes of
his broadcast, he was telling Australians, back working for them on
all the issues that the war threw up. No time for an elaborate
election launch; this was a man who needed to be at his desk.

In his policy speech Curtin showed he was unashamedly proud
of his party's war effort and he drew effortless comparisons
between what Labor had done in prosecuting the war and what the
coalition team had done before him. Labor had been in office for
only 20 months, Curtin said, but in that time the number of men
in the fighting services had nearly doubled from 431 000 to
820 000. The number of women in the forces had grown from
3 600 to 40 000. When Arthur Fadden lost office there were
71 200 men engaged in munitions and aircraft manufacture; now
there were 144 000 men in those factories. More than one million
men and women were either in the forces or in war production
'compared to 554 000 when the Fadden Government left office.'

In terms of creating what the nation needed to wage war, its
infrastructure, Curtin said that the:

> achievements have been almost miraculous . . . aerodromes,
> landing grounds and flight strips have been built all over the
> Commonwealth. All-weather roads including two transcon-
> tinental roads, have been completed. Docks, shipping berths
> and harbour facilities have been installed to get troops and
> supplies to strategic points. Munitions plants, dehydration
> plants, flax mills, hospitals, camps and wireless stations have
> been put together in record-breaking time.

Almost miraculous. The government had harnessed women to
the war effort, Curtin claimed, with women now making up 30 per
cent of munitions workers and 13 per cent of rural workers. Something over 700 000 men and women each day were engaged in war
production. In directly addressing the strikes Curtin announced
that only 8000 man days per week were lost through strikes

compared to 21 000 man days per week under the Menzies government. Australia, Curtin claimed, had really thrown itself into the
fight for victory and his much boasted 'all-in' war effort was, in fact,
a reality. Doubled this and doubled that, Curtin was asking the
electorate to agree that it really was impressive what the
Australian people and government had done together.

The prime minister could not have gone into the detail of this
achievement then, but the extraordinary nature of Australia's
response to the Pacific War, in particular, was perhaps more easily
seen in rural Australia than in the cities. A remarkable aspect of
this, though, is that there is now virtually no evidence at all to
show what had happened in the bush in response to war. But at
Lake Bathurst near Goulburn in New South Wales you can still
inspect the massive fuel tanks the Department of Defence installed
in 1943 as emergency fuel dumps, specifically for the air force—
the five tanks could hold 666 000 gallons of fuel (3.02 million
litres), and this was only one of 32 new inland stores around the
country. The fuel dumps were secret of course, except to those
Lake Bathurst residents who provided board to the guards, but
people in the country knew that a lot was happening, just as the
prime minister was describing it in his broadcast. Take Tocumwal,
for example, a pleasant town, in the south-west of New South
Wales on the Murray River.

Tocumwal had become a major Royal Australian Air Force base
from 1942 onwards and from 1943 was the home of the RAAF's
No. 5 Officer Training Unit. When John Curtin was giving his
speech in July 1943 there were 4000 Australian airmen and women
living on the base at Tocumwal, presumably most of them listening
to him at the time. The size of the Tocumwal base was nearly half
the total number of permanent residents of Canberra, a city that
had been in development since the 1920s. Imagine the impact of
those numbers of air force people on the town and in the region.
Although conditions at the base were described as 'not particularly
good' to start with, it was a significant achievement to create such
a base in a relatively short period of time.

Just up the road from Tocumwal, at Narrandera, there was
another RAAF base also housing a training unit, not as big as
Tocumwal but significant nevertheless. And this was happening all

around Australia. While farmers lamented the decline in rural labour—John Curtin did not say in his policy speech that the number of workers on Australian farms had dropped from 416 000 in 1939 to 284 000 in 1943—farmers could at least see where some of their workers had gone: into the air force. Tocumwal later became the home of the heavy bomber training unit and towns-people became used to the sights and sounds of massive aircraft trundling around their skies. When John Curtin spoke of what had been achieved in building up Australia for the war his words would have found a ready response in Tocumwal, Narrandera and all the other places that had become home to Australian servicemen and women.

Curtin's election policy speech was hailed in most of the news-papers as that of a statesman, although Frank Packer paid the *Daily Telegraph*'s main man in Canberra, Don Whitington, to live it up in some style in a Sydney pub throughout the election campaign so Whitington could not travel with the prime minister. Whitington, Packer thought, was too strongly an admirer of John Curtin, and Packer wanted no starry-eyed, 'Curtin the statesman' style of commentary in his newspapers. It is touching, and a reminder of a different Australia, that Frank Forde, Curtin's loyal deputy and therefore deputy prime minister of Australia, at his home base in Rockhampton defending his own seat, could communicate best with his prime minister by telegram. 'Your speech last night came over very well', Forde wrote, 'and is a winning speech [stop] best wishes for successful campaign'.

Forde was by no means the only one sending best wishes to the prime minister as John Curtin did finally set off on the election trail. All types and manner of Australians wrote to their prime minister wishing him and his party success. If someone had been able to show a few of these letters, cards and telegrams to Frank Packer, perhaps his confidence in a Fadden victory might have waned a month or so earlier than it ultimately did so brutally on election night. From Wallumbilla, just outside of Roma in western Queensland, S.G. Griffin wrote:

Together with a number of other pastoralists in this locality, for the first time in our lives, we intend voting you, and your party, back into power . . . and trust that you will be returned with an overwhelming majority . . . you have kept the Japs out—please carry on.

Also from rural Australia, from Barmedman in the Riverina:

I want to impress on you that the Cockies [small farmers] are with you to a man and we pray for your return as prime minister. We go to the village every Saturday for stores and the general opinion is that you have done and are doing a great job . . . so chin up, cheerio, carry on.

And from Maryborough in central Victoria: 'I feel I must congratulate you from the bottom of my heart . . . I have never been more moved than by your sane, practical and inspiring policy speech.' Mrs J.H. Perry, on a property near Nevertire in the central west of New South Wales, wanted to 'sincerely thank you for all you have done for Australia', and she added a postscript: 'I have always voted for the United Country Party but will not now.'

People wrote to the prime minister as if he were almost a family member, or at least a close friend, as I have discussed already. 'Thank you', wrote Norma Davey of Bellevue Hill, Sydney, 'for keeping the Japanese away'. 'Wishing you all good luck', wrote Mrs Costello from Coburg, Melbourne, 'you will know the people of Brunswick and Coburg are with you in your fight . . . if there is anything I could do for you please let me know, hoping Mrs Curtin and yourself are well'. 'I would have sent this sooner', wrote Mrs Ford of Balgowlah, 'only my husband said not to worry you when you are having such an upsetting time in Parliament'. 'I am sorry I cannot get into the City Hall to meet you', wrote Mrs Michael Scully from Banyo, Brisbane, 'but I am pretty bad with arthritis . . . remember me very kindly to Mrs Curtin, best of luck'. You would think from this letter that perhaps Mrs Scully was known by the Curtins but the reply, following the usual somewhat personalised formula, gives no indication of that.

Some seemed to write out of a sense of duty: 'Beyond a shadow of a doubt you saved Australia from invasion and should have the admiration and gratitude of every Australian', wrote Mr Shearman from Mudgee, New South Wales. 'I feel it is the duty of every real citizen to write a letter of appreciation to you, after hearing your excellent, sincere policy speech, stating facts of the past and such stupendous facts', wrote Kay Manning of Stanmore, Sydney. Union officials and shopfloor stewards also wrote in large numbers and they were just as pleased with their prime minister, but it was the sincerity of the letters from ordinary Australians that indicates John Curtin's special bond with his people.

Heartwarming as the prime minister probably found these hundreds of letters they were at best only an imprecise indication of the mood of the people. Listening to army officers, Gavin Long, on the other hand, may well have concluded that the Curtin government was in real trouble. Opinion polls were in their infancy in Australia in 1943; indeed Keith Murdoch at the Herald and Weekly Times, the first to do so, had only begun investigating the use of opinion polls for that company's newspapers in July 1941, and commentators did not yet appear to take the polls very seriously. Curtin seemed popular but almost everyone was predicting a close vote. It might be well into next week, said the *Sydney Morning Herald* on election eve, before the final result is known. The *Daily Telegraph* suggested that a survey of the states revealed no swing to the government except, possibly, in South Australia. In Victoria, the *Telegraph* expected the opposition to gain three seats, and reported that there were long odds in Queensland of the government making any gains. In the event they were the two states that returned the status quo. The *Telegraph* should have been looking closer to home because in New South Wales Labor picked up five seats; and Labor gained four seats in South Australia, three in Western Australia and one in Tasmania.

In the absence of any real pre-election evidence it is hard to blame the commentators for thinking that the vote might be close when even a naturally pessimistic prime minister did think that he and his party might be heading for defeat. On 15 July 1943, on the second and last day of a premiers' conference in Melbourne, Curtin closed the proceedings and thanked the premiers for their support throughout his term in office without which, he said, 'I could not have carried on.' He called on them to give the same level of support to his successor, pointing out that 'whoever he may be, he will be an Australian, heading an Australian Government.' Was this pessimism a form of wishful thinking, almost a cry that the chalice be taken from him? After the election Don Whitington was freed by Frank Packer to write for the *Daily Telegraph* again and he claimed that he had 'never seen a man so happy and so confident' as when the prime minister had called the election. Might it not have been that when he entered the campaign John Curtin was dreaming of retirement and a vastly less stressful future with the chance for home pleasures—all those books—and some relaxation?

With the issues of the war pressing heavily on his government and on the people, Curtin decided that he needed to give the people some hope that Australia would be a better place when the war was at last won. This was not radical; indeed every British and Allied war leader since the outbreak of war was keen to talk of 'war aims' and for a better world afterwards. Indeed the democratic countries feared, even before the war began in 1939, that they may not be able to carry their people with them when declaring war. People were sick of war; they had seen too much of it and too much economic misery to be fired up again. Let's fight this war to the best of our abilities, the propagandists said, so that afterwards we can have a just society at home, and peace around the world. Although in Britain the war aims campaign faltered somewhat when the propagandists produced a poster proclaiming, 'YOUR resolution will bring US victory'. A classic distinction, unfortunately, between the cannon fodder and the class that would benefit from the victory. In Australia in 1939 Bob Menzies caught the dominant mood and decided that Australia's hopes for a just outcome from the war could be best advanced by a small unit with research and secretarial functions that he named the Reconstruction Division.

Curtin had been calling for an all-in war effort ever since he had become prime minister. He had asked for and received his people's loyal cooperation in fighting the war and significant sacrifice in putting up with all manner of sufferings and discomforts at home for the sake of the war effort. Clearly the prime minister could not have been thinking specifically of Melbourne's onion-peeling women when he spoke of the dehydration plants, along with the airfields and munitions factories, as part of the 'miraculous achievement' of Australia in the war, but he knew enough of the detail to know that on the farms and in the factories, as on the frontline, Australians had risen heroically to the crisis. Curtin now needed to give his people a vision for life after the war, as an incentive and as some sort of hope of a reward. First World War diggers had been promised jobs and prosperity and a world without war; many of them had endured the Depression years as members of the army of the unemployed and at the very bottom of the pile at that. John Curtin was determined to ensure that no such misery would be visited on Australians again when this war was over. They would have jobs, at a fair and decent wage, they would be housed in comfortable and affordable homes, they would be trained to better themselves in work and life, and they could look forward to a few of the luxuries they had glimpsed in the lives of the American troops in their midst.

In his last appeal to voters on 18 August, three days before what he described 'as the most momentous election in the history of Australia,' Curtin listed three tasks for the incoming government and told his listeners that only his capable and experienced government could carry out those tasks. The government, he said, 'will be responsible for the organisation and direction of Australia's part in the growing offensive action against Japan; will probably be responsible for participation in the peace conference . . . and will be responsible for the drafting of the plans for demobilisation and post-war reconstruction.' Curtin was looking, in other words, to the future. It was a simple program really. Australia would fight hard to bring the war to a swift conclusion; would work hard to ensure a just peace; and would plan with care to create a better Australia for all those who had already given so much to the war effort.

The Department of Post-War Reconstruction, created by John Curtin on 22 December 1942 with the treasurer, Ben Chifley, as its first minister, might have been the prime minister's Christmas present to his people, if only he had not been spending weeks reminding them that, in a time of austerity, there should only be war savings certificates under their Christmas trees. The department is testimony to the level of dissatisfaction that John Curtin and almost all the members of his party experienced with life in Australia in the 1920s and 1930s. There had to be a better way, they believed, of ensuring that everyone enjoyed a good and satisfying life. The opportunity to turn victory in the war to the advantage of all Australians should not be thrown away, they believed, by a lack of forethought and planning, even if the war was far from won.

Unemployment was the bugbear. Too few Australians had been in full-time, permanent work during the inter-war years, and even those in work had often experienced oppressive and demeaning conditions. Yet because of the war Australians enjoyed full or over-full employment. At last they knew what it was to have money in their pockets and they wanted that to keep going; they wanted to have the security of full employment and the freedom to make plans for a prosperous future. That, the people insisted, should be the norm for Australia: everyone in a job with some expectation of permanence and stability; that would be the foundation on which all post-war planning would rest; that was the reward Australians should expect for all the sacrifice, suffering and discomfort of war; that was now John Curtin's pledge to them. And he did this with the help of 'Nugget' Coombs.

Everyone called him Nugget, Herbert Cole Coombs, that is, but no one can quite tell you when he first became known, universally, by that name. Short, tough, possibly abrasive, 'nuggety', that's as close as we can get. Born at Kalamunda, near Perth, in 1906, the son of a country railway stationmaster, there was never much money and the family 'moved around a good deal. My mother was Irish, born in Ireland, the daughter of a very well-educated man, he was a scholar of Trinity College Dublin', who had come to Australia. There were six children in Nugget's close-knit family: 'I had an elder brother who died when he was about six, and I had four sisters all younger than me.' At school Coombs's first headmaster was ambitious for his pupils, and 'he bullied me and incited me and stimulated me so I got the 49th out of the 50 scholarships' awarded across the state to enable children without much hope otherwise to go on to secondary school. But for that scholarship, perhaps, Nugget Coombs's education might have ended then and there.

At secondary school Coombs was more interested in cricket and other games than his studies and he only began to blossom academically when he went to teachers' college. Perth Modern

School, then the teachers' college, it was a path identical to that followed by Ralph Honner, also from the country, although Honner was the son of a policeman. As Ralph Honner was born in August 1904 and Coombs in February 1906, there was only one class between them at school and college. They became firm friends, perhaps not surprisingly for how many others of the students at both these institutions were from the bush? Both of them scholarship boys, both of them doing it tough. It was a friendship that endured during the long lives of both men. And who can say which of the two gave more to his country in time of war? The inspiring officer in the frontline or the visionary public servant at home, first helping to direct the Australian economy at war, then planning for a better Australia after the war, to motivate all those war workers to keep on going.

Nugget Coombs was in the Treasury during the first years of the war, then ran Rationing and Reconstruction. He described himself as 'an activist and an interferer'; his hand could be seen in everything that post-war reconstruction was doing. Under Coombs, with departmental status and the protection of the treasurer, Reconstruction took a more active approach to its work from 1943 onwards. 'Post-War Reconstruction's domestic settlement,' said Nugget Coombs, 'was based upon the hypothesis . . . of full employment— that the government has an obligation to see that there is employment for each person.' Closely linked to the primary aim of full employment in a post-war world was the need to ensure the smooth implementation of demobilisation; of managing, in other words, the transition of men and women from the military to civilian life. At one level this transition had to be achieved, with varying degrees of success, at the personal level, with each individual looking to his or her own emotional, psychological, family and employment needs. At another level, though, reconstruction could assist with programs and policies, and with training opportunities particularly, to meet the needs of men and women out of the forces and hungering for more from life than they might have glimpsed pre-war.

One of the great successes of Post-War Reconstruction was the Commonwealth Reconstruction Training Scheme (CRTS), under which ex-service men and women were accepted for university, technical and rural training—those in the scheme had their fees paid for them, assistance with books and other expenses and were given a reasonable living allowance while they studied. For most Australians until the end of the Second World War university study was a remote, probably a nearly impossible, dream. University was a place for a small elite, destined for the professions. Now study became possible for those who had served their country, and men and women flocked to universities and technical colleges. Look at the leaders of the Australian Public Service in the 1960s and 1970s, almost everyone of them, to a man—there were no women—were CRTS graduates. Men who had served their country in war and whose country had rewarded them with the opportunity for study and advancement. We know their stories because they reached the very top; but the CRTS helped thousands of other Australians into better, more fulfilling, more rewarding jobs. Coombs's Post-War Reconstruction was at the heart of it—it was planned during the war and then the plans were put into action when the war was won.

If the government was to promote full employment after the war there needed to be national projects to soak up the excess labour of those released from the armed services. Post-War Reconstruction dreamed up some of the bigger schemes, the national schemes, that distinguished Australia in the years immediately after the war. The Snowy Mountains scheme, the most adventurous of them all, stands as an example of the boldness of the vision being developed. Post-War Reconstruction also recognised that the nation would have to address the housing crisis emerging as an issue by 1943. Then Coombs and his department identified the need to significantly boost Australia's manufacturing output, again in the interests of employment—the design and development of Australia's own car, the Holden, was an achievement of that aim. The munitions factories and aircraft production had shown the potential of manufacturing in Australia and the confidence that the people could do it. These people were now dreaming big dreams.

There was also a rural element to Post-War Reconstruction with an ambition of settling returning men on the land, but more sensibly and in a more planned way than had happened with the soldier–settlers after the First World War. Plans would be drawn up to ensure the land was suitable, that ex-servicemen were adequately trained for their new work, and that the new farmers were not saddled, from the outset, with crippling debt. And finally, although it might have seemed to conflict with the push for demobilisation and full employment, Post-War Reconstruction also began planning for an increased scheme of migration to Australia to build a bigger population in face of the fright the small nation experienced when directly menaced by a world war.

None of these plans, except for an undertaking about full employment into the future, would have been in the forefront of John Curtin's thinking when he campaigned during the 1943 election about the need for post-war reconstruction. But in that campaign Curtin was, at least, planting the seeds of a future Australia. As Coombs saw it, Curtin 'had never wholly shed the pacifist, anti-conscription convictions of his past. He had therefore a psychological need to justify to himself his total involvement in the war'. When, later, critics began to complain that Australia was less interested in winning the war than working for its own future after the war, Curtin might have linked post-war reconstruction with the war aims articulated earlier in Britain and America. Around the world there was a determination that societies would emerge from the war committed to peace, to security, to justice. This was, after all, the point of President Roosevelt's Four Freedoms—of speech, worship, from want, from fear—and the reason, from as early as 1942, for the emergence of the concept of the United Nations. John Curtin might have said that the idea of reconstruction in Australia was just a part of all of this.

John Curtin used the election campaign of 1943 to present to the people his vision for an Australia that would be richer, fairer, more inclusive. He had campaigned for austerity in 1942 with a preacher's zeal. Now he campaigned for a reconstructed Australia with equal zeal and determination, and the Australian people had responded to Curtin's vision by giving his party the biggest electoral victory in its history. If Curtin had fleetingly thought of release from the burdens of office as Australia's wartime prime minister, then the people had resoundingly said to him that he should be back at his desk again, to work punishingly hard. As he had said himself, 'too busy for bitterness'.

21. 'AUSTRALIA IS THERE FOR POLITICAL REASONS'

The third pilgrimage, they told me, was to Borneo. First North Africa, Greece, Crete, London and Paris. Then Port Moresby and other towns in Papua New Guinea. Third, Borneo. I looked puzzled but as historical adviser to the minister for Veterans' Affairs for 'Australia Remembers', an elaborate program of activities to commemorate the fiftieth anniversary of the end of the Second World War, I had no business questioning it. Of course we should take Australian veterans back to the places where they had served with distinction. To stand on the battlefield at El Alamein with the men who had fought there, or to lament with the men at Sfakia, the embarkation port on Crete, would be a rare privilege. To be with the veterans on Kokoda, even if only for a tiny part of the track, to stand in Bomana War Cemetery with them, would be inspirational. But Tarakan, Balikpapan and Labuan Island? Why? They were such obscure campaigns—the real war was elsewhere— and MacArthur, it seemed, had finally cut the Australians out of his command. The battlefields were a sop to an Australian sense of self-importance, weren't they, to the idea that we must be seen to be doing something? Why bother? And the places themselves in Borneo? They were hard to access, remote backwaters even in their own country today. It all seemed a bit, well, unnecessary. Unnecessary in war and even possibly unnecessary in commemoration. As David Honner has said, 'the decisions made by the Australian Government in early 1944 mark one of the great turning points. Australia is there for political reasons.'

John Curtin and Douglas MacArthur met for the last time in Canberra on 30 September 1944. Did they recall their first meeting at Parliament House in Canberra in the dark days of March 1942? Did they remember how MacArthur had placed his arm around the prime minister's shoulder and said to him: 'We two, you and me, will see this thing through together.' Neither man would have mentioned it but both would have been aware how much they and their world had changed since that first momentous meeting. Australia was no longer under threat of invasion, and that altered the strategic position for Australia and the intensity of concentration on the war by Australians. Since the election in 1943 Curtin had been spending almost as much time on post-war issues as he had been on the war itself. He had allowed himself a trip to Britain, where he emphasised the strength of his attachment to the concept of the Empire, and also to the United States. He would turn 60 in December as well, a time for reassessment for any man. In meeting with MacArthur in September 1944 there was no mood of reminiscence or leave-taking. But there might have been, for both men recognised that the war had changed for Australia because Australia no longer really mattered in strategic calculations.

Curtin was tired, there could be no doubt about that. He had fallen into the habit of watching Australian Rules football in Canberra on Saturday afternoons, taking along a 17-year-old office boy, Jim Maher, with whom he had got yarning in Parliament House when the young man brought documents to him from other ministers. Come to the football with me, Curtin seems to have told Maher, it will keep you out of trouble. So Curtin's car would pick up the young man at his boarding house and prime minister and office boy would talk their way through the football. Later Jim Maher recalled Curtin telling, 'me about how tired he was, that he was not sleeping well.' Going to the football with a young fellow was just as good as twelve hours of sleep, Curtin had told him.

Writing to one of his oldest friends just 11 days before he met MacArthur, Curtin reported that he was feeling 'flat, sad and overburdened', and that he was 'very tired after a few hours concentration'. MacArthur might have noticed how the burdens of office had flattened the prime minister, but perhaps not, for MacArthur concentrated too frequently on himself and his own image. In October, after their meeting, Curtin took time off for a holiday in Perth but was admitted to hospital in early November 1944. Although the people were not told of the seriousness of Curtin's condition, they might have worked things out for themselves when they heard he would not be returning to duty until January 1945. It was tiredness, his people said, he was overstrained; there was a general nervous exhaustion. It had to be that, after all a friend of Curtin's had found him in tears in Perth after he had received a cable telling him of a kamikaze attack on an Australian warship. But it was more, too. It was his heart; John Curtin was a seriously ill man.

Yet the issues piled up on the prime minister's desk, the most urgent of them the future strength of Australia's fighting forces, and their deployment. Australia's need for labour had intensified even more in the year since the federal election and with the AIF barely in action throughout much of 1944, there was a considerable public clamour for reductions in the number of men in uniform so they could restart their lives in the civilian workforce, where, it seemed, they were so desperately needed. Important as that was, the nation also needed a strong voice at the peace table, as Curtin had insisted during the 1943 election campaign. While he had not outlined the problem in so many words, what he might have told the people was that the Australian's military use to the Americans had diminished as the Americans own mighty war machine came to its peak strength. In 1942 and into 1943 the Australians had carried the bulk of the fighting on land in the Pacific War. At that stage they were seen to be experienced, determined and on the spot. By 1944 the Australians weren't as necessary to the Americans, who showed an absolute preference for using their own troops in those battles, such as the invasion of the Philippines, that attracted the world's attention, and under their own commanders. Crucial to Churchill's plans in 1940 and 1941, and central to MacArthur's mission in 1942, the AIF was now in danger of becoming somewhat irrelevant as the fighting moved further away from Australia's shores. Even though training on the Atherton Tableland for much of the year, the Australian public seemed to demand that the AIF either be in action, somewhere, or be demobilised. Government and people, both, had expected the Australians would join forces with the Americans in the campaign for the Philippines. They were surprised when this did not happen. Of all the problems that John Curtin faced by 1944, trying to assert a role for this small ally in an increasingly complex war and world was the most intractable. With an expectation that the war in Europe might be over by Christmas 1944, agreement to Australia's right to full participation in the peace process and general acceptance of Australia's concerns for Japan and the region, by the Americans and the British, might depend on a recognition that Australia had played a full role in the world war right to the very end—whenever that might be. The government had to ensure that Australia did not become the 'forgotten' or 'overlooked' ally.

In two world wars Australians had entered the fight in part to keep their own security requirements in the forefront of the thinking of their more powerful friends. We will help you, the Australians said in 1914 and again in 1939, and in return will you come to our aid should we ever need you? That was a part of the motivation but there was also, of course, an element of altruism. Concern for poor Belgium and the rights of the weak and helpless everywhere played a part in Australia's rush to war in 1914. A revulsion for fascism and a fear of Hitler's mad grab for world domination contributed to Australia's determination to be standing beside Britain in 1939. 'What has it got to do with us?' some asked on both occasions, but most Australians accepted that a blend of idealism and self-interest impelled them into the wars. That, and a love of adventure. Now Australia was nothing more than a marginal player, with the Russians and the Americans wielding the big battalions. Was it time for Australia's leaders to say 'enough of war?' Why should more Australian lives be put at risk when the number of soldiers Australia could deploy was dwarfed by the might of the armies of their allies?

The ends of wars are messy affairs, and while the AIF fought on valiantly in France in 1918 many Australians at home had almost turned away from the war after the second, hugely divisive, conscription campaign. Some historians have looked at the fighting in Borneo in 1945 and have labelled it 'the unnecessary war'. MacArthur spoke of the importance of the airfield at Tarakan, but when Tarakan was taken there was no rush at all to rebuild the airfield to render it operational. It played no part in the aerial campaign against the Japanese home islands and never would have. The airfield was a smokescreen. MacArthur also spoke of the importance of the oilfields at Balikpapan, but, again, there was no attempt to make these oilfields usable when Balik-papan was finally wrestled from Japanese control. Balikpapan's oil seemed another smokescreen. Some historians, then, have described the Borneo campaigns, Australia's last battles of the Second World War, as a means of keeping the Australians busy and out of the way while the Americans fought the real war. Australian lives, these historians asserted, should never have been wasted on those desolate patches of land in remote Borneo. These historians then accused John Curtin of not standing up to Douglas MacArthur when he ordered the Australians into action in such strategically negligible places.

This criticism does not pay sufficient attention to the alliance problems that Australia faced with the war apparently moving towards its end. Was it not the case that the Australian govern-ment was single-mindedly using its troops as a major weapon in its ongoing diplomatic struggle to ensure that its small but shrill voice be heard at the peace table? The Australians had been out of the action for most of the year. Would a latter-day Billy Hughes be able to eyeball an American president and claim a place at the table because of his nation's considerable commitment to winning the peace, consistent with its size? Perhaps that prime minister might have reminded the major powers of Australia's role in the desert, at Tobruk, at El Alamein; of Australia's nobility in accepting that alliance requirements dictated a presence—a losing presence—in Greece and on Crete; of Australia's forceful presence in New

Guinea and in saving Port Moresby. That prime minister might have asserted Australia's role in the Empire Air Training Scheme, providing aircrew that Britain desperately needed but was unable to find from its own resources. And might have spoken, too, of the Australians in Bomber Command, Coastal Command and other elements of the air war in Europe, and might have pointed with real sorrow to the casualty lists from 460 Squadron, equal to the worst of the losses of Australian battalions on the Western Front.

But sadly, while these places and actions meant a great deal to the men who fought there, and to the Australian people who watched them in battle from afar, the world had moved on. The eastern front and the inexorable advance of the Allies through Western Europe since the mighty landings at Normandy dominated people's thinking. This, it seemed, was where the real war was. Australia needed to demonstrate yet again its continuing relevance to the bigger picture and to show that Australian troops could still play a part. In agreeing to the operations in Borneo Australian leaders were displaying realpolitik such as, perhaps, they and their predecessors had not shown before. The campaigns in Borneo were not pleasant battles—there is no such thing—and victory came at a price—it always does—but Curtin and his advisers who were debating the Australian deployment might possibly have been operating in a more sophisticated way than their critics have allowed.

Australia's relative lack of clout certainly worried Curtin. In November and December 1943 at Cairo and Teheran, Churchill, Roosevelt and the combined chiefs of staff met to thrash out strategic directions and the future planning of the war. Obviously not involved in these meetings, the humiliating fact was that Australia could not even find out what had been decided there, even though the discussions would clearly affect Australian interests. The Cairo Declaration that emerged from the conferences stated the three powers present, the United Kingdom, the United States and China, had agreed upon future operations against Japan and had also discussed the future disposition of Japanese-held territories. These were matters of the greatest significance to Australia and yet Australia was left entirely in the dark about the nature of the discussions and about what decisions had been taken.

A small ally now felt even smaller. Australia feared that the Americans might have their eyes on New Guinea and the adjacent islands, long held to be within Australia's sphere of influence, in Australian eyes anyway. Somewhat ridiculously, in view of the relative weightings of the world powers involved, Australia, principally through Foreign Minister Bert Evatt, convened an Australia–New Zealand conference in Canberra in January 1944, as if to make up for the stinging snub that Cairo represented. The Anzac partners asserted their right to be consulted on the disposal of enemy territory in the Pacific, yet all the conference succeeded in doing was to antagonise the Americans.

It is a measure of how the world had changed, and Australia's place in it, that John Curtin had not left Australia since becoming prime minister in October 1941. With Britain almost completely alone in the first years of the European war Bob Menzies had been a welcome and energising visitor to London in 1941. But the Russian and American entry into the war had changed that. When he was in London, Menzies worried that Churchill was a one-man band, indeed, almost out of control. It was clear to Menzies that what was in Churchill's mind in 1940 and 1941 was at the centre of all war planning and discussion. This was now far from the case, and as Churchill needed to attend to the interests of his mighty alliance partners and fight for his country's corner, Australia's significance receded. There had been talk in 1941 that there might be a dominion's prime minister as a permanent presence at the War Cabinet in London; there had even been talk that Menzies might be found a seat in the House of Commons to contribute to the Empire's war on a daily basis. Perhaps this was idle daydreaming, even in 1941, but there was at least an air of plausibility about it, even if by the end of 1943 it was ludicrous to contemplate such a proposition. In no sense was the war any longer 'the Empire's war'; it was Russia's war and America's, even Britain now seemed a more modest power.

Nevertheless London wanted a meeting of dominion prime ministers, if only to assert the continued existence of the world-wide British diaspora. Curtin dragged the chain, partly because of his fear of flying—one of the few things he had in common with Bert Evatt. Finally Curtin agreed to visit London, and therefore

Washington, 'going only to avoid being a defaulter,' as he said. A better traveller might also have built into his travel plans visits to Australian troops in operational areas—remember Bob Menzies' visits to the Australians in North Africa? Such visits were not possible for Curtin in 1942, and even into 1943, but by 1944 where might Curtin have gone to inspect his troops? The Atherton Tablelands? MacArthur offered to lay on a special plane for Curtin when he learned of the prime minister's impending travel plans but a relieved Curtin accepted the suggestion of the head of the Australian Navy, since 1941, the British Admiral Sir Guy Royle, that the prime minister travel to America on an Australian warship. When that fell through, Curtin finally made his way to America on an American troopship, the USS *Lurline*, which left Sydney on 5 April 1944.

Included in the prime minister's party was his senior military adviser, Tom Blamey, along with Frederick Shedden, the head of the Defence Department. Shedden, an austere man naturally, might also have been described as a workaholic. He noted acerbically that Tom Blamey had carried on board cases of whisky, gin and wine on what was supposed to be a 'dry' ship. A week out from Sydney Shedden wrote in his diary that Blamey 'had obviously had too much to drink last night. He was very jolly and talkative and [Curtin] commented on it'. A briefing note prepared for President Roosevelt described Blamey as 'short, stubby, jolly, energetic and frank', and said that 'he was sometimes referred to as "Boozy Blamey"'.

Along with the prime minister's party on board the *Lurline* and returning American servicemen was a party of Australian war brides setting out for America to establish a new life in their adopted country. Ever since the Americans had begun pouring into Australia in early 1942 the newspapers had highlighted the increasingly close relations between American servicemen and Australian women. There is a pleasing irony in the anguish some Australians expressed for the 'over-paid, over-sexed and over-here' Americans, for this was precisely how many in England saw the Australians there from 1916 onwards. There was intense debate in Australia then about Australians marrying British women, and an early group of British war brides arriving at Australian ports were met by demonstrations at the wharves which, hopefully, did not include the women's future mothers-in-law. The Americans in Australia from 1942 onwards had money, manners and glamour. They also seemed to have taken charge of the feeble local supply of chocolates, stockings and alcohol, and they lavished gifts on their 'girls'. And why not? As with the Australians in Britain in the earlier war, these soldiers were far from home; they sought and deserved some fun and romance before they went off to the dreadful business of war.

By January 1945 some 1500 Australian women had already reached the United States as war brides or fiancées, and possibly 10 000 women in Australia waited to be reunited with their American husbands, or their families, at home in America. Elsie Curtin took a mother's interest in the women travelling to America on the *Lurline* with her. She later told a press conference that she was very worried about what the future held for these women with whom she had chatted because most of them seemed to have only the vaguest ideas about the life they would be making. Most expected to live in New York in a life of style, glamour and excitement, as if they were to live in the America of the movies. But Mrs Curtin found that instead they were destined for the 'back blocks'. 'If they are city girls,' she said, 'they will have a rude awakening.'

John Curtin, too, was in for a bit of a shock in America. He found that Franklin Roosevelt was not attracted one little bit to the notion of an Australian–New Zealand veto on the disposal of enemy territory in the Pacific. Roosevelt was a sick man, dangerously ill with hypertension, when Curtin met him, ironically, on Anzac Day 1944. The meeting was not at the White House but in the country, where Roosevelt was convalescing. Roosevelt only seemed to want to complain about the Australia–New Zealand agreement and eventually the two men agreed 'to forget the whole incident'. There were limits, obviously, in the freedom of movement of small players in the alliance and John Curtin could have been in no doubt where those limits were set. What else did president and prime minister discuss? As they were alone for their meeting we cannot know for certain but no doubt Curtin expressed his deep gratitude to the president for the American presence in Australia

and for Douglas MacArthur. If they discussed the future deployment of the Australian troops, and that seems unlikely, it would
have been with Curtin's then expectation that the Australians
would be with the Americans in their return to the Philippines.

Curtin left Washington on 28 April, comfortably travelling in
the Boeing flying-boat that had twice carried Winston Churchill
across the Atlantic. He was so terrified of flying, and so fearful of
conditions in London, that Curtin left his wife in Washington so
that she at least would be safe. Then he endured the flight to
Ireland strapped to his seat, with his hat 'pulled securely down over
his ears . . . grimly, fully-clothed and tight lipped'. It is a picture of
a terrified man, made worse by the fact that Tom Blamey took
advantage of the 'luxurious double bedded suite . . . [at the back
of the plane] and slept like a baby'.

John Curtin was not a well-travelled man, in international
terms anyway. In 1924, appointed by Prime Minister Bruce, Curtin
was a member of a three-person Australian delegation to an international labour conference to the League of Nations in Geneva.
He then took the opportunity of spending several weeks in Britain
in 1924 after Geneva, as his only experience of life at the 'heart of
the Empire'. That was his first and only overseas trip before his
prime ministerial visit in 1944. Now he flew from Ireland to
London escorted by six Mustangs of the Royal Air Force and might
have made a dramatic entrance to the Empire's capital, but Curtin
was little interested in making a splash. Instead he saw his mission
in London as one of enticing the British to a greater interest in the
Pacific War with a view to strengthening Australia's post-war
position. Even so, Curtin seemed to go out of his way to avoid
making the kind of personal impression that would enhance his
mission.

Of Bob Menzies, Churchill had formed the view that he was
one of those men with whom 'it was agreeable to dine', but he does
not appear to have placed John Curtin in that category. And
Curtin, apparently, reciprocated. Invited to Chequers, the British
prime minister's country house, Curtin declined: 'I do not care to
sit in an armchair and listen to one man,' he said. But he did go
to Chequers a fortnight later, and when Churchill asked him about
his appeal to America of late 1941 Curtin stood up for himself

without hesitation or qualification. He was forceful, too, in asserting Australia's post-war interests. At a well-attended press conference towards the end of his stay in London Curtin was asked whether Australia expected to have a say in dealing with Japan after the war and replied: 'As the Australian bushman would say, "My oath".' That was the issue that now dominated Curtin's thinking: Australia's role in the peace negotiations, whenever they might come.

Curtin left Britain on 29 May 1944, a week before the D-Day landings in Normandy, in which he showed little real interest. Nor, in Frederick Shedden's view, was Curtin much interested 'in the countryside, the historical places, nor the notable shopping centres'. We can excuse him the last, but it was not through lack of knowledge or lack of imagination that Curtin showed no interest in Britain's geography and history; Curtin was a widely read man with a keen interest in history. But as a prime minister in wartime with huge issues yet to be resolved he was also a man of intense focus and concentration. When he did allow himself time off he went to the cricket at Lord's for a match between service teams from England and Australia.

Keen though he was to be home, Curtin flew to Canada, again glumly strapped in and apparently terrified, to address the Canadian Parliament at Ottawa, and then travelled by train to New York, Washington and San Francisco. From there he steamed by ship to Australia. He was back in Australia, at Brisbane, on 26 June after an absence of 12 weeks. The prime minister might have made better use of his time away, or have been away for less time, had he flown to and from Australia. It is doubtful the long sea voyage was actually good for him, anyway, he was so anxious aboard ship. Reading Shedden's criticisms of the trip and of Curtin's near neurotic fears about being in the air or on the sea, it is hard to avoid the impression that John Curtin had, sadly, almost reached breaking point. Yet, as he fretted, there was still so much work to be done for Australia.

The first person to greet him on arrival at Brisbane was Douglas MacArthur, with yet another war issue for the prime minister to consider. At least Curtin had not come home full of dreams of imperial glory, as had Bob Menzies in 1941. Indeed he said that 'after seeing many places and many people, I have not seen any other people or any other country better than my own.' Although he was soon to be Australia's longest-serving wartime prime minister of either world war, he had seen surprisingly little of Australian troops or the war for that matter on these recent travels. If Australia and its people were better than anywhere else then he also probably believed that the Australians were better in action, too, than the soldiers of other countries. It would have been a surprise then for Curtin to learn that Douglas MacArthur had decided not to take the Australians with him to the Philippines for his crowning 'I have returned' moment. Probably MacArthur had always conceived of this moment of the war as purely an American episode, and perhaps he had intended for quite some time to throw the Australians the sop of the war in Borneo in recompense. Justifying Borneo action to his superiors in Washington MacArthur had written: 'The Australian troops have been out of action for more than a year and are prepared to carry out the plans that have been perfected . . . cancellation at this time and the postponement for many months of employment of Australian troops will produce grave repercussions with the Australian government and people.' Was MacArthur merely borrowing these words from John Curtin, who had written to him two months earlier, in February 1945: 'Elements of the 1st Australian Corps have been on the mainland for a period up to 18 months and have taken no part in the war since 1943 . . . there has been considerable public criticism of the inactivity of the Australian Land Forces.' Get them to war, Curtin was urging MacArthur. There has to be a reason for a prime minister to be so keen to have his troops in action. In Curtin's mind this was far from an 'unnecessary war'.

Diver Derrick's 2/48th Battalion had returned to Australia in February 1944 after the momentous days at Sattelberg and Finschhafen. In August Derrick went to an officer training unit and was commissioned lieutenant in November. We do not know how a man who had seen such action at El Alamein and in New Guinea coped with the settled life of training for more than a year while the war still raged and was still on everyone's lips. Was Derrick straining at the leash, or glad to be out of it? He took leave, back in Adelaide with his wife, but those words of Jo Gullett we heard before—'[a Battalion] involves not the weakening but the deferment of other bonds and interests; the acceptance that life and home are now with the battalion'—might have applied to Derrick just as they applied to so many other Australian soldiers. Derrick's link with his original battalion was so tight that he was sent back to the 2/48th as an officer, 'one of the few second AIF men promoted from the ranks who rejoined their old battalions'. Derrick would go into action again on 1 May 1945 at Tarakan, a tiny island on the north-eastern side of Borneo. A little more than a month later other Australians would land on Labuan and at points in Brunei Bay, on the north-western side of Borneo, and later still more Australians would land at Balikpapan, further south along the eastern coast of Borneo—three highly complex landings with perhaps more air and naval support than the Australians had ever enjoyed in battle. It was an ambitious use of the Australians.

On 30 April 1945 at Tarakan, Australians waded chest deep through the slimy, oily mud of a place that had an airfield and oil wells. The initial Australian objective was the airfield, then the elimination of all the Japanese on the island. The advance party was to clear obstacles from close inshore and on the beach to allow the main force ease of passage the next day. The Japanese were on Tarakan because of the oil, but that had been of little use to them once the Allies had gained control of the sea.

Tarakan is a dull, unattractive place, 24 kilometres long and 18 kilometres wide. Swampy at its shores, it rises, inland, into a tangle of hills and steep gullies covered with jungle. Another appalling battlesite for the Australians; hot, of course, and humid. Incongruously, they named the hills after their girls at home—Margy, Helen, Freda, Janet, Susie, for a few others perhaps after home and its people Ossie, Otway and Butch—instead of the usual prominent battlefield personalities, as at Gallipoli, nor with numbers, or local names. The profusion of names gives some idea of the nature of the fighting. Small local objectives held by parties of Japanese, who again would not surrender despite inducements. This would be a campaign lasting 50 days; about a third of the length of the entire Gallipoli campaign—to put it in perspective.

The Australians of the 26th Brigade, 9th Division, were very well prepared—they had rehearsed the landing on nearby Morotai—and well supported with artillery on Sadau Island, with a naval bombardment from two cruisers and six destroyers, and with aircraft in support. 'The beach appeared to be an inferno,' an observer commented, 'and was continually aflame from crimson flashes of bursting bombs and shells.' The Australians put 11 804 troops ashore. If their landing was an 'inferno', imagine the absolute inferno that must have been the Normandy beaches on D-Day nearly a year earlier. Some 21 days after the Tarakan landing, the night of 22/23 May, the 2/48th Battalion was attempting an assault on Freda, a hill perhaps ten kilometres from the airfield— slow going, ten kilometres in 21 days. The battalion was ordered to push the Japanese from the high ground on Freda which the Australians had been aggressively patrolling for the past several days, killing six to twelve Japanese each day for the loss of only seven of their own men in total. It had come to this, such small numbers on both sides, it was now almost personal. Although the Australians enjoyed significant support from aircraft carrying bombs and napalm, and from artillery and mortars, it was the infantry that did the close work. In the words of the official historian, Gavin Long, Derrick's platoon of the 2/48th Battalion 'moved from Ossie to Agnes to attack the Freda feature'. It all sounds slightly ludicrous, but the gentle names disguise the viciousness and brutality of it all.

The 2/48th made gains but the Japanese, committed to retaining the high ground of Freda as an essential defensive position, counterattacked at night. A machine gun began firing, Derrick, sleeping deeply just a few seconds earlier, sprang up to take control of his platoon but was hit in the stomach and thigh in a second round of firing. Though apparently fatally wounded Diver Derrick continued to bark orders for a few hours. When news of his death circulated in the battalion the next day it had a 'profound effect . . . He had become a legend and an inspiration to the whole unit,' a mate said, '[and at Freda] he fought as ever with utmost courage and devotion to duty.' Some thought that his courage and enterprise in that battle on Tarakan might have resulted in the award of another Victoria Cross. The possibility for this man was of a VC and two bars; that is, three times the highest bravery award: at El Alamein, at Sattelberg and now at Tarakan. Regardless, though, of the speculation about possible gallantry awards, surely Diver Derrick was one of the bravest Australian soldiers ever.

While the battle raged on Tarakan other troops of the 9th Australian Division were preparing to land on Labuan Island, at the head of Brunei Bay, the best harbour on the north-west coast of Borneo, therefore possibly the best site for an advanced fleet base. That was the theory, like the one that saw the Australians on Tarakan, capturing and repairing an airfield that would never be used offensively against the Japanese. Neither airfield nor naval base ever became operational during the course of the war, which, although no one among the Australians could have known it then, had only two more months yet to run. Unlike Tarakan, Labuan island is flat and gave its defenders few opportunities. On 10 June 1945 two battalions of Australians, with Matilda tanks, had landed and by 14 June the island was cleared, with the exception of a Japanese garrison in a rotten area of jungle and swamp known as the 'Pocket'. With tanks, artillery and the Australian cruiser *Shropshire* pounding the Japanese—in five days and nights they hurled 140 tons of shells into the Japanese positions—that wretched bit of land was finally captured on 21 June. Probably there had been 250 Japanese in the Pocket when the assault began; only six of them were taken prisoner and possibly 11 had escaped. All the rest were killed with the massive use of force and were pushed into mass graves by bulldozers.

Labuan later became the site of a substantial and beautiful Commonwealth War Graves Cemetery, containing the remains of 1788 servicemen and women, of whom 1726 are 'entirely unidentified'. There is also a colonnade or cloister at the edge of the cemetery, the Labuan Memorial, containing the names of 2294 men and women whose bodies were never recovered. The greatest number of those commemorated in both parts of the Labuan cemetery are Australians who were prisoners of war in the region in the hands of the Japanese. These Australians died at Sandakan, many of them, or on the brutal death marches to Ranau, into the hills and away from the coast, away from the advancing Australians who might have rescued them and to whom they might then have told their appalling story. That story of brutality, starvation and murder at Sandakan and Ranau renders Labuan, along with the horrific fighting there, a place of great sadness for anyone who is aware of its meaning.

One of those best placed to know that story, as the war veterans and war widows prepared to visit Labuan for 50th anniversary commemorations in 1995, was Joyce Braithwaite, married in 1941 to Wallace Blatch, 'Wal' or 'Wally' to everyone who knew him working in the bank at Barellan, between Temora and Griffith in New South Wales. It was the Australian disaster in Greece and on Crete that motivated Wally Blatch to enlist, even though he had only been married to Joyce for a year. He was only 21 when he joined the 2/15th Field Regiment, the same outfit Les Bolger was in, although I cannot say if they knew one another. Wal Blatch found a mate in Dick Braithwaite, a photo engraver from Brisbane, of whom they said never had a hair on his head out of place, even in battle. Wal and Dick soon became inseparable; war was like that. Wal was the stronger of the two and on their march to Ranau it became obvious that Dick Braithwaite just could not go on. He had reached the limits of exhaustion and starvation. Men who fell out along the way, whose mates could no longer carry them, were simply shot by the Japanese where they fell. This now seemed to be Dick Braithwaite's fate but a series of miracles somehow intervened. Dick Braithwaite fell off the track unobserved and made his way, eventually, to people who would take him to safety: he survived. But not Wally Blatch who died of acute enteritis on 1 June 1945 at 25 years of age. The chances of war.

His widow and I found Wal Blatch's place on the memorial panels together, and she placed flowers from her own garden in Canberra. I felt incredibly honoured that she had asked me to help her to find the place after the formal ceremonies had been completed, just to steady her, she said, just in case. How had she come to marry Dick Braithwaite after the war, I had asked her some time before. She had been preparing to nurse Wal when he came back, she said; she knew he'd be in a bad way and she had worked herself up to cope. But Dick came instead to tell her how Wal had lived and died as a prisoner, and she could see the hurt and the need in Dick, she just knew she would care for him. She was a small woman, Joyce Braithwaite, but if you want to know something about the strength that these Australians brought out of

the Second World War, think hard about her story. Dick Braithwaite died in 1986 and Joyce Braithwaite was a widow of Sandakan
a second time.

While these dreadful things were happening at Sandakan and
on the way to Ranau the 7th Australian Division was preparing for
its assault on Balikpapan, as it turned out, the last large-scale
Allied land operation of the Second World War. To commence on
1 July 1945 after 20 days of intense bombardment from the air and
sea, Balikpapan succeeded, again, because of the experience of the
Australian troops. But the firepower to which the Australians had
access was unlike anything these troops had experienced before.
Again they met a grimly determined enemy, well dug-in, with well-
sited guns. The Australians made good progress and it was all over
within the month, but again it was tough and dirty work, and
wouldn't the alternative, to isolate the Japanese and wait for them
to surrender, have been better?

The operations in Borneo, the last for the Australians in the
Second World War and using the three arms of the services
fighting in unison for the first time in the war, were successful and
revealed the value of training, experience and good leadership.
Australia, as historian David Horner argued, was the only one of
the Allied nations to increase its involvement and commitment to
the war after Germany's defeat. Australia was determined to have
an important say in the peace because if this war had shown
nothing else it had certainly shown how vulnerable Australia
might be in an unstable region. It was for the future security of the
nation that the Australian 9th and 7th divisions were fighting in
June and July 1945, although the men in the landing barges may
not have known that.

That security came at a cost. On Tarakan the Australians lost
225 officers and other ranks killed or died of wounds; on Labuan
and associated places around Brunei Bay they lost 114 killed or
died of wounds; and at Balikpapan they lost another 229 killed
or died of wounds. The number of wounded in the three
campaigns was approximately three times those numbers killed in
each of the operations. It was at Labuan Cemetery, as we walked
among the graves of these men, that a good man who had served
in these campaigns, a Gippsland dairy farmer in later life, suddenly

said, as if to himself, 'Why me? Why did I survive when these men, better men than me, with families, many of them, when I was single, why did these men die while I survived?'

It is the great imponderable of war. Les Bolger was not a strong man, nor even a strong swimmer, yet when his prisoner-of-war transport ship torpedoed by the Americans in the South China Sea he survived for days, while his mate Bill Scarpella, as strong as two men on the railway, died. Les Bolger survived while men of his unit, among 2000 other Australians, died at Sandakan and Ranau. There were only six survivors from Sandakan and Ranau, and one of the most chilling displays at the Australian War Memorial is a photo montage of the pay book photographs of every single one of those murdered at Sandakan and Ranau. Do you remember the story from earlier in this book of the boy looking into the photographer's studio at photographs of Australian soldiers. 'Every one of them is dead, you know,' another kid had said. It is the same with those pay book photographs, 'every one of them is dead'; Wal Blatch among them.

When Dick Braithwaite, rescued and now in hospital, managed to get out his story of men at the last extremity, brutalised and starved, he was told that the Australians would mount a rescue operation immediately. 'I can remember this so vividly,' he recalled. 'I just rolled on my side in the bunk, faced the wall and cried like a baby. And said, "you'll be too late".' They were.

22. 'A WAR CASUALTY IF EVER THERE WAS ONE'

B eryl Bedggood was not yet 22 years of age when the war ended on 15 August 1945, yet she had been in the Women's Auxiliary Australian Air Force for three and a half years, since February 1942. How the world had changed in that time. Could Beryl remember back to that Father's Day in 1939 when Bob Menzies had told her family and all the other Australians listening in that Australia was at war? Could she remember the person she had then been? A schoolgirl in love with sport, her home, her friends. By August 1945 she knew the cost of war, with good friends killed, had known for herself the devastation of aircrews not returning from a mission, for they were the first to hear the news at the weather hut where she worked at the air base at Sale if a crew had not returned. Beryl had known of orders and discipline, of mess and hard work, of sergeants you could cheerfully throttle, and of friends who would stick with you for life.

Beryl was out of the WAAAF by September 1945, engaged to be married to Ian Beaurepaire, originally a fitter/armourer in the air force who had remustered as a pilot. Born a year earlier than Beryl, by early 1945 he was just as keen as she was for an end to the war. 'Blast everything', he had written to her, 'and the RAAF particularly'. In mid-1945 Ian was in his Kittyhawk, a much loved aircraft, with the Australians in the Borneo campaign. Neither of them, Beryl or Ian, nor any other Australian, had any idea then that the last major campaign of the Second World War was about to occur. The European war had ended in May and there was celebration enough for that, but the experts told them that the Japanese would never give in—all the fighting since 1942 had proved that—and it might be years yet before Allied forces defeated the Japanese on the homeland itself.

Beryl Bedggood and Ian Beaurepaire were not alone in being heartily sick of the war. Increasingly Australians wanted their own lives back; they wanted family life again; parents reunited; sons, brothers, husbands no longer at risk; an end to living with anxiety every minute of every day. They wanted to find out what had happened to those thousands of Australians who were prisoners of war and of whom there were still only the most sketchy details. They were sick of rationing, of the shortage of everything, of crowded public transport, of raceless Saturdays, austerity, few holidays and too much work, far too much work. They wanted a few luxuries in their lives, a holiday probably, regular hours of work and a new home—how they dreamed of a place of their own and what they would make of it.

Beryl was sick of the barracks in which she lived; sick of the lack of privacy and comfort. She wanted to go into town to have lunch with her friends, to gossip and to shop, and not to have the minute-by-minute worry that Ian, in combat somewhere over Borneo, might randomly be listed as one of the casualties of war. She dreamed of motherhood and domesticity, of 'settling down', as she would have said. Yet the war had radicalised Beryl. No, it had not sent her to the political left—indeed her family thought that if marriage had not intervened she might have tried to find a place on Bob Menzies' staff as he went about the seemingly improbable task of rebuilding his political career through an entirely new political party, the Liberal Party, which, almost single-handedly, he had founded in 1944. But Beryl had seen too much of the lives of ordinary airwomen, seen too much discrimination in pay and the treatment of women to accept complacently that women were inferior, second class. From this war she would take an unshakeable feminism that would be the beacon for the rest of her life. Whether working for the Liberal Party—in what became a life-time committment—the Young Women's Christian Association, the National Women's Advisory Council, a host of hospitals, research institutes, children's film and television, whatever, it was the interests and causes of women that urged her on. The war and the WAAAF had done that.

Carried off the battlefield at Wampun in New Guinea in 1943, Ralph Honner was now a seriously injured battlefield casualty who would endure months in hospitals, a major operation, then long months of rehabilitation and recovery. They told him that if he was to walk again he would need a caliper for the rest of his life, but he would have none of that, although there was a walking stick for ever after and a pronounced limp. Ralph Honner left the army in late 1944 at 40 years of age. There were three children to provide for and a fourth on the way. Domesticity. How to go back to that life when so many thoughts of war might suddenly intrude without warning? Of lying on a beach on Crete as a German plane flew over at low altitude, hoping to be seen as a Cretan fisherman. Of taking a raw untrained group of boys—they had the effrontery to call it a battalion—at a moment of great peril in the battle for Australia and turning them into soldiers. Not just soldiers, but as good a unit as Australia had produced. Now he went to a life of public service ruling on war pensions for blokes he had served with and for thousands of others besides. There were higher honours, too: Australian ambassador to Ireland and a long life—he died aged 89—but the nation little noticed his passing in 1994, one of its better men.

Les Bolger, torpedoed by the Americans on board a Japanese ship in the South China Sea, a prisoner of war left by his captors to drown, rescued by the Americans four days later. He and his few surviving mates were the first Australian prisoners from the Pacific War to come home. They carried their story to Australia and they carried, too, on their shoulders the hopes and expectations of thousands of parents, wives, brothers, sisters and mates. It was, they soon found, an overwhelming responsibility. Les Bolger thought that his stomach must have shrunk in captivity because the sight and smell of normal Australian food, about which he had been dreaming for so long, made him violently ill. This was a man who had been systematically starved for more than two years. Custards and jellies were all he could cope with, baby food, he called it. More than 400 people wrote to him asking for news of a loved one. People called at his door or asked him out, hoping for a snippet that might tell them if a son or a husband was alive. Les Bolger left the army in May 1945. He joined the public service, like Ralph Honner, and found that the hours were long, the work almost too hard for him. There were terrible nightmares in that first year of readjustment—leaping from his bed screaming. Les married in 1949 but there were no children. Les told me that he and his wife would have loved to have had children but he thought it was the malnutrition of the prisoner of war camps that rendered that dream impossible. Les Bolger died on Australia Day 2002. There were often tears in his eyes when he told me his story a year or so before his death because Les Bolger could never forget.

Albert Moore had malaria in mid-1943, but that break from his work was short-lived, only a matter of days. There had been five weeks' leave earlier in the year, spent with his family in Melbourne, but apart from these periods of enforced rest Albert's devotion to the Australian troops in Papua New Guinea was ceaseless and untiring. 'We brewed', he wrote, 'hundreds of gallons of coffee each day'. Every day, that is, that Albert was in New Guinea. He worked for the troops, that was his job, that is what he did. On Friday 15 October 1943 Albert celebrated the third anniversary of his appointment to the Red Shield work, 'and what a lot had been crammed into three years', he wrote. Did he think back to that Christmas in Sydney in 1940 with his son, Kelvin, with the desperation of the separation from his family in Melbourne fresh in his memory; did he remember the disappointment in the desert when letters from home would not come; or that dash down the 'mad mile' in Syria, putting all his faith in his god; or his frustration when he found that he could not take his truck along the Kokoda Track? All that in three years. There would be almost another year's work for Albert Moore in New Guinea, among the troops in the forward areas, cordial and biscuits for them on the march, recreation huts to be opened with writing materials, musical instruments, record-players, coffee by the hundreds of gallons, concerts, almost anything to make life just slightly more bearable for the soldiers. After all that came what he had 'expected and dreaded for many moons': his recall to Melbourne.

It was Sunday 9 July 1944 when Albert Moore finally boarded a plane at Wau bound for home, then the train all the way down from Townsville. Albert finally reached Melbourne on 22 July 1944, a Saturday. Waiting for him at Spencer Street Station, where he had left nearly four years earlier, were his wife, Vi, and his son, Kelvin. There was a crowd of well-wishers too. No matter how heartfelt the welcome home you can be sure that Albert Moore was at the usual three Salvation services the next day. It was, after all, a Sunday.

For Ralph Honner, Les Bolger and Albert Moore these were endings to the war before the war itself was over. For Beryl Bedggood and Ian Beaurepaire there was now a heartfelt disdain for the war, for the military, and for all that authority and regulation. Everyone else, it seemed, was also heartily sick of war conditions, and orders and regulations, restrictions and shortages. That was a problem for John Curtin and his ministers: to keep the focus, to keep people working, to make sure that the war effort did not slacken. The government needed to balance intense enthusiasm for demobilisation against the need for troops for the coming campaigns and to fight a war weariness that seemed to be settling over the people. In 1945 victory in Europe edged closer and closer, and Curtin urged his people not to celebrate too enthusiastically; 'since when has it been customary to celebrate victory half-way through a contest?', a letter-writer to the Sydney Morning Herald asked in a way almost dismissive of the importance of the war in Europe. Yet when the war had started there had been only Britain. Now the war in Europe seemed such a remote contest. The emotional intensity that Australians had invested in the European war—tears at the fall of France, anguish at the nightly bombing of Britain—now seemed somewhat remote too. Australia and Britain had drifted apart in the last three years of war. Or had they? Perhaps the drift had really begun in the years after the First World

War. Remember Paul Royle writing from his RAF station in Britain to his family in Perth in 1939: 'There is nothing really worth fighting for, as far as you people are concerned . . . it is all so stupid and ridiculous.'

The news of the German surrender reached Australia just before midnight on 7 May 1945, and Acting Prime Minister Ben Chifley broadcast the news to the nation. Most people were in bed, of course, but some of them were enticed from their homes by the blaring of car horns and the shouts of people celebrating. There was a public holiday to mark the momentous occasion, but it was hardly a riotous event. The government closed all the hotels as someone with a long memory, it seemed, remembered the frantic scenes throughout the land in 1918 when the news of the armistice arrived—even in 1945 the First World War cast its long shadow over this war. In Sydney there was a strike of railwaymen, too, to deflate the occasion, and, as elsewhere, restaurants, cinemas, theatres, pubs and shops were all closed. At midnight police told people to go home, though goodness knows what they had been doing in trying to celebrate up until then. And a good thing, too, people said of the minor key celebrations. It was no time to be celebrating when Australians were still fighting and dying in the war against the Japanese. After all, the Borneo campaigns had not even yet begun. There was much yet for Australia to do.

People worried, too, for their prime minister. By late 1944 it had become apparent that John Curtin was a very sick man. Someone who had been following his health closely since he had become prime minister in October 1941 might have been able to list Curtin's known ailments; they included psoriasis, pneumonia, gastritis, high blood pressure, neuritis, a heart attack and, fatally, a lung complaint. Clearly not all of these matters affected the prime minister at the same time. That must have been the misery of his ill-health; as one thing cleared up another illness came along to trouble him. Nor is it easy to determine to what degree Curtin suffered from his various ailments. Psoriasis can be an awful and painful skin complaint, leading in its worst forms to arthritis; indeed it can be fatal. Psoriasis can have several causes, but a worried, anxious person might be more susceptible. Pneumonia, which Curtin experienced in 1941, was a vastly more common condition in the 1940s than it is today. Without access to penicillin doctors were limited to managing the condition with sulphur-based drugs, which were slow working and not highly effective. It was an older person's disease, possibly exacerbated for John Curtin by the winters in Canberra he necessarily had to endure. It would be a disease found more commonly in a tired and worried person.

In February 1942 Curtin was hospitalised, briefly, with gastritis, an inflammation of the stomach. In Washington in mid-1944 he was again hospitalised, this time with high blood pressure and neuritis, an inflammatory condition of the nerves, clearly linked to anxiety and worry. High blood pressure may have many causes but stress would be the one cause most doctors would look for. Returned from Britain and the United States, no doubt made more anxious by his morbid fear of flying, in November 1944, Curtin was again hospitalised, this time for two months, following a heart attack. His doctors cannot have been much surprised by this sad turn of events given the medical history they had been charting for at least three years. Curtin's fatal lung condition was almost certainly linked to his heart condition. Simply put, his heart was not now working at sufficient strength to remove the water from his lungs. He died on 5 July 1945 from slow, congestive cardiac failure. From November 1944 onwards, in all probability, unless he had completely removed himself from the causes of stress and anxiety, John Curtin was a marked man.

One of John Curtin's most recent biographers, David Day, concludes that the heart attack of late 1944 was 'the culmination of years of stress, heavy smoking, alcoholic binges and a simple but poor diet'. While I think there are many reasons to discount David Day's statement, it is still necessary to apportion weight to each of the factors he suggests. There are, moreover, elements within that statement that need further consideration. It is true that John Curtin smoked around 40 cigarettes a day. Possibly, it might be fair to say, Curtin used tobacco as a means of allowing himself to cope with the stresses and pressures of his life. The alcoholism and binge-drinking, to which Day refers, almost certainly ceased to be factors in Curtin's life ten years before his death. While heavy drinking may have done some damage to his body, he was never significantly overweight. It would hardly be useful to tell a man thinking of restricting his use of alcohol that even after ten years of abstinence the effects of heavy drinking might still prove fatal. You would think Curtin's victory over the bottle might have done him some good.

Curtin's diet can only be a matter for conjecture, although it might be reasonable to say that he was not a man who seemed to take a great interest in food. Still, living at the Lodge, Curtin had staff attentive to his dietary needs and requirements. The simple fact is that prime ministers are pampered and fussed over. Curtin did not have a butler, as later prime ministers did—Australia was not like that in those days—but it is inconceivable that a cup of tea did not appear at Curtin's elbow at regular intervals, with an enticing biscuit or slice; that staff did not coax him into eating regularly and well for they were supremely concerned to do their bit for a man who was clearly vital to the Australian war effort, and working hard for his country.

Striking off, or at least down-playing, the various causes of ill-health that David Day ascribed to John Curtin, that leads us to stress as the main component for John Curtin's awful health record as prime minister. Any leader in a world war would suffer stress. That is a given. But, remember the scene when the clerk of the House of Representatives, and neighbour, Frank Green, found John Curtin anxiously pacing the grounds of the Lodge after midnight. The 7th Australian Division was on the Indian Ocean on Curtin's direct orders, without escort, possibly prey to the Japanese submarines that were hunting the troop transports. 'How can I sleep,' Curtin had asked Green, 'when I know that our men are out there on transports on the Indian Ocean, with all those Japanese submarines looking for them.'

These were probably the worst days of Curtin's prime minister-ship. He had argued painfully with Winston Churchill, first over naval and military reinforcements for Singapore, then for the return of the two Australian divisions not yet involved in the Pacific War. At the height of this controversy, and possibly ever thereafter, Churchill treated Curtin with near contempt. The decision to evacuate the Australians from Tobruk incensed him; not to mince words, Churchill thought the Australian action cowardly. These momentous decisions that Curtin needed to make were taken in the full knowledge that Australia risked alienating a world power closer to his country than even the closest ally. Curtin received strong support from the Australian military leadership, but if things had turned out differently the large and catastrophic loss of Australian troops would have been placed squarely on his shoulders. The trashing of the one enduring Australian myth, the Anzac legend, bravely fighting on, whatever the odds, might also have been sheeted home solely to him.

The loneliness of command, they call it, and it strikes various leaders in different ways. The coolest of the Second World War leaders was undoubtedly George C. Marshall, chief of the United States Army from 1939 to 1945. Marshall never set foot on a battlefield, indeed he exercised his command only from the Pentagon in Washington. His routine was never disturbed even in the worst days of the war. Rising at 6.30 a.m. he exercised, arrived at work at 7.45, took lunch alone with his wife at home, left work at 5 p.m., exercised again, ate his dinner and retired at nine. Outside of office hours he answered the phone only to the president or the secretary of state for war. He believed that no one had an original idea after 5 p.m. When President Roosevelt once called him 'George', the frigidity of Marshall's reply meant that the president never took that liberty again.

The architect of D-Day, Dwight Eisenhower, had some three million troops at his disposal and the liberation of Europe as his responsibility. All nicely parcelled off into the lower levels down the chain of command, you would think. But for one dreadful moment it all came down to Eisenhower. The Normandy landings would only succeed if the Allies maintained the element of surprise. Rommel wanted to mass his forces precisely where Eisenhower would send his huge force, but Hitler had overruled him. As the Allied force grew to staggering proportions the chance of discovery was very real indeed and, if detected, Rommel would have reason to swing his troops into precisely the right place. And for these landings, whether at Gallipoli or Normandy, the weather had to be just right. Delayed already, 6 June was the last moment in the cycle of the moon that would allow for the invasion for a number of weeks. If delayed, Rommel would almost certainly discover the plan. Yet as day turned to evening on 6 June the weather deteriorated and forecasts suggested worse conditions to come. Then a weatherman gave Eisenhower the news that the weather might be improving. There was a break; it might be possible. The decision was Eisenhower's alone. 'OK, let's go,' he said, and at that moment Eisenhower was the most powerful soldier the world had ever known. Consigning huge numbers of men to terror, casualty and death and, ultimately, victory. But if the weather turned against him, to what?

A military leader treads a fine line between concern for his troops and getting the job done. We look at the generals of the First World War and marvel that they could seemingly so blithely contemplate and plan for casualty numbers such as the world had never known or can even now understand. We warm to Australia's Brigadier General 'Pompey' Elliott, mourning the loss of 5500 Australians at Fromelles in July 1916, looking, in the words of Charles Bean, 'like a man who had just lost his wife'. Most senior British officers would have looked at Elliott at that moment, if they had been close enough to the battlefront to see him, with something like contempt. Military plans and strategies cannot be allowed to unravel because of some misplaced sentimentality. That is a fact of war.

But what if these troops become known to a general, as individuals? Surely the stiff upper lip would waver a little then. And that is what a general must not allow to happen. It is said of Eisenhower that whenever he came across masses of American troops on the field of battle he would dive in among the boys asking if any of them hailed from Abilene in Kansas. He never found that soldier, but then Abilene, where Eisenhower grew up, was a crushingly small town. But when he found a Kansan Eisenhower's face would light up in a broad smile and the soldier and the general would exchange warm words. A neat, and possibly excluding, technique for having to deal at a personal level with too many. The appearance of warmth while preserving the necessary remoteness from men over whom the general had ultimate control, the power of life and death. The 'mask of command'.

Politicians, too, need to create the aura of engagement and involvement with their public while retaining for themselves a remoteness from the people as a form of protection. Politicians, too, need the mask of command. Remember the woman who told me of her doctor–father whom she had described as losing his 'psychological skin cover'. It was a compelling phrase, describing an attribute that will allow a soldier, a general, even a politician to survive in war. John Curtin, as prime minister, may have lost both his mask of command and his psychological skin cover, or may, at least, have been in danger of losing them. Stress is a given for all national leaders, particularly in time of war. But if that stress becomes personal it may well become debilitating, even fatal.

We have already seen how willingly the Australian people wrote to John Curtin, as if he were one of the family. As a national leader Curtin had projected himself as a father of his people in a way that others had not. Australians had taken Curtin into their homes and into their hearts; they felt they could unburden themselves to him. Maybe he couldn't solve their problems, they reasoned, but he would listen, and in the listening they would feel better.

There were hundreds of Australians writing to the prime minister each year reminding him that they believed he alone would stand with them, look after them, solve their problems. He was the national father of them all. If in addition to the strains and burdens of national leadership in time of war—of fighting hard for a minor ally's quarter; of striving to keep some focus on the Pacific War in the face of the 'Beat Hitler First' strategy; of arguing for resources and troops in the face of the terrible situation Australia faced in 1942; and of the day-to-day management of a government at war—if, in addition to all this, John Curtin felt a personal burden for the manifold and manifest sufferings of his people, if the mask of command simply could not protect him, if the people themselves had stripped away his psychological skin cover, then the strain, worry and intensity of the pressure on him might well have led to the diseases and illnesses to which John Curtin succumbed in the years of his prime ministership. Every single one of these illnesses, potentially at least, related to stress and anxiety. 'A war casualty if ever there was one', Australian historian and Curtin biographer Geoffrey Serle had written of the prime minister. It seems a fair conclusion.

The people seemed to think so. His death shocked Australians; his passing was genuinely mourned by all classes and persuasions of people, who recognised that he had given his all for the country he had loved so well. Bob Menzies, now opposition leader, said that while he had attacked Curtin politically, 'it was impossible and unthinkable to attack [Curtin's] probity, his honesty of purpose, the man himself.' A journalist sent out to sample the mood of the people found that 'through the tapestry of conversation in street and shop, cafe and office, bus and tram, the sombre thread of refer-ence to the dead leader was woven endlessly'. The reporter overheard one conversation and it seemed to sum up what many people were thinking: 'I always thought his real trouble was that he didn't have a shell hard enough for a politician. He couldn't shrug things off. He seemed to make everyone and everything his personal responsibility . . . Just couldn't ease up.'

The prime minister's body lay in state in King's Hall, Parlia-ment House, from 11 a.m. on 6 July until the memorial service at 2 p.m. After that the casket was taken on a gun carriage to the Canberra airport for the journey home to Perth. John Curtin had insisted that he be buried at Karrakatta Cemetery among his adopted people. The whole of Perth seemed to stop on 8 July, the day of the funeral, and there were 30 000 people at the cemetery for the burial. One of them was David Black, Curtin scholar and teacher, a small boy then, of course. David's grandmother, who lived in Nedlands, a reasonable walk from the cemetery, had never voted for Curtin or Labor in her life. But she and her grandson went to the cemetery because she thought it was the right thing to do. John Curtin, in his role as father of the nation, had crossed all political boundaries. So they placed him in Karrakatta Cemetery, wherein also lie the remains of Australian sailors, soldiers and airmen. They lie in the military cemetery; John Curtin is in the civilian cemetery.

President Roosevelt died on 12 April 1945 and was buried, as American presidents are, with a great deal more ceremony than was given to John Curtin, but the simplicity of Curtin's funeral was, largely, his own wish. His friend and Labor stalwart Joseph Benedict 'Ben' Chifley, who became Australia's fourth wartime prime minister, was sworn into office on 13 July 1945, but he did not even travel to Perth for the funeral. He was greatly distressed by Curtin's death and said to a friend, 'I simply couldn't go.' It seemed to the people's of both nations, the United States and Australia, a great pity that neither Roosevelt nor Curtin was to witness the surrender of Japan for which both had worked so hard.

Hardly anyone in Australia, perhaps not even the national leaders who had come together for John Curtin's memorial service in Canberra, could have anticipated the speed of the collapse of Japan. Harry Truman, so recently in office, faced perhaps the greatest dilemma ever encountered by a leader in war, without so much as a warning to him beforehand that the weapon he would be asked to use was even being developed. For within weeks of becoming president Truman had to decide whether to unleash the atomic bomb—a new weapon of such potential power that no one could really predict what it might do—or to fight on instead in a conventional way with the possible loss of hundreds of thousands of Allied and Japanese lives in the campaign for the Japanese homeland.

Truman, of course, chose the path of atomic weaponry. The first bomb in the American arsenal was dropped on Hiroshima on 6 August 1945 causing the almost complete destruction of that city and the loss of 64 000 lives instantly. The second bomb, three days later, at Nagasaki, caused less loss of life but complete destruction of the city. Used on a city like Tokyo, the losses could have run into millions of people and potentially brought about the end of Japanese civilisation as its people had known it for centuries.

The Emperor then broadcast to his people while Australian prisoners of war in Japan watched their guards assemble before the loud speakers in attitudes of the utmost respect—the Australian prisoners had no idea what was taking place. The guards listened with heads bowed; Australian prisoners observed, as if the speaker were a person of exalted significance. The broadcast was the first time in history that the Emperor of Japan had directly addressed his subjects, and his words had a profound impact. The listeners, these hardened and brutal guards of yesterday, were simply stunned, and it was as if they were now instantly different people. The Australians remember them drifting away from the broadcast with tears streaming down their faces. The Japanese dreams of conquest and domination were over. The years of stunning, swift victory, and of sacrifice, determination and loss were all ultimately for nothing.

At 9.30 on the morning of 15 August 1945 Prime Minister Chifley broadcast to the people of Australia. They had grown so used to Curtin's voice telling them momentous news that it was still something of a shock for Australians to realise that John Curtin was not with them on this memorable occasion. Bob Menzies had announced the war in 1939, addressing them as 'Fellow Australians'; John Curtin had always begun his broadcasts with 'Men and women of Australia.' Ben Chifley, his own man, now began with 'Fellow Citizens.' And then the most simple and joyous statement that could be made: 'The war is over.' The prime minister told his listeners that Japan had accepted the terms of surrender, and continued, 'at this moment, let us offer thanks to God.' Then he asked people to remember those who had given their lives for this 'glorious moment'; was he seeing then, in his own mind's eye, his former chief and friend who had sacrificed his own life for his nation in war. And as the prime minister spoke people in homes everywhere around the country were summoning up the names and the cherished memories of those they knew who had died in the war: husbands, brothers, sons, daughters. There were gentle tears aplenty even at this moment of joyous victory. Chifley spoke of these people in their homes and of their 'proud sorrow,' and of their thoughts for 'gallant loved ones who will not come back.'

Then the prime minister offered the thanks of the Australian people, and those of his government, to the fighting men of the United Nations, 'whose gallantry, sacrifice and devotion to duty have brought us the victory.' He thanked their leaders, 'especially do I mention General Douglas MacArthur,' for their 'skill, efficiency and great devotion.' He expressed the 'common regret' that president Roosevelt 'did not live to see this day,' and said that Australians 'will feel their happiness tinged with sorrow that another man, who gave his all, was not spared to be with us today. That man was John Curtin.'

Ben Chifley also recalled 'the great debt [we owe] to those men and women who performed miracles of production in secondary and primary industries so that the battle of supply could be won.' Nothing was spared, he said, 'so that the fighting men would not go short,' and Australia's effort in feeding and supplying the vast armies stood high in comparison with that of any other country; 'the Australian people may be justly proud of everything they have done,' the prime minister told them. It was a theme that John Curtin had returned to time after time during the war itself; that the war, for Australia, would be won on the farms and in the factories. That not everyone could be a soldier but every Australian could play a part in the victory. They had done that, loyally and generously, Ben Chifley was now telling them.

Then the prime minister turned to the men and women of the fighting services who would now come home: 'Our fighting men with battle honours thick upon them from every theatre of war. Australians,' Chifley said, 'stopped the Japanese in their drive south, just as they helped start the first march towards ultimate victory in North Africa.' It was a record, Chifley was telling his people, of which Australians could be mighty proud. Australian troops had stopped the Japanese at Milne Bay and on the Kokoda Track; Australians had contributed so significantly to the mighty victory at El Alamein that was the first real turning point in the war. 'Australians,' Chifley continued, 'fought in the battles of the air everywhere and Australian seamen covered every ocean.' Rejoice, he was telling his people, for all that has been done by determination and perseverance, generosity, skill and ingenuity, and great sacrifice. 'But they were coming home,' he concluded, 'to a peace which has [yet] to be won . . . the Australian Government which stood steadfast during the dread days of war, will give all that it has to working and planning to ensure that the peace will be a real thing.' Then he invited Australians to join in the thanksgiving services and, although he did not spell it out, in the celebration of the victory.

That day and the next day were instantly designated as national public holidays and 'peace delirium' broke out all over the country. In Sydney 'an entire city felt the burdens of six weary warladen years roll from its shoulders', while in Melbourne there was 'a battle against any show of dignity, of austerity and gloom'. There were 'conga lines' and 'hokey-pokey rings' and flags and torn paper everywhere. The police turned a blind eye to the two-up schools that flourished, and although the pubs were closed no one seemed to mind too much for everyone was too busy dancing and making as much noise as possible. Film footage, shot in Sydney on the day, has been replayed endlessly over the years featuring the 'dancing man', skipping joyously down Martin Place about to take off his hat, no doubt to throw it in the air. He is the image of joy and delight in victory.

I recall a letter I was once given to read in a war cemetery in France. It was written by the Methodist chaplain-general in the First World War, Albert Holden, and addressed to the parents of a young Australian soldier who had been killed in the last days of the fighting for Australia, on the second last day of September 1918. The chaplain described the cemetery at Roisel, a local French cemetery attached to the parish church into which a few war graves had been added. It was 11 November 1918 when the chaplain again visited the cemetery, and Albert Holden wrote of the sounds of joy that had broken out at 11 a.m. when the armistice was announced. The church bell pealed continuously, in the distance at the railyards drivers were sounding engine whistles in competition with each other to see who could make the most noise, villagers were singing, shouting and dancing around the small village square. 'And I stand here', the Australian clergyman wrote:

> before the grave of your son, whom I knew to be a gallant soldier and a good lad, feeling the sadness and grief that you must feel, even as these shouts and sounds of victory swirl all around me. And how do I know of your feelings of grief and sorrow. Because my boy, nineteen years of age, lies in the grave next to your lad, great friends in war together, lying side by side now in a war cemetery, their duty done.

Twenty-seven years later there were many in Australia who would have shared the emotions that Albert Holden experienced that day. A total of 30 445 Australians were killed on active service in the Second World War: 18 675 in the army, 9870 in the air force and 1900 in the navy. A total of 23 477 Australians were wounded or injured in action. Another 22 264 Australians became prisoners of war. The families of all these people had reason to grieve; reason, in many cases, still for anxiety and concern. For some, 15 August merely marked the beginning of perhaps the worst waiting period imaginable as people struggled to find out what had become of a loved one who had been a prisoner. It would take several weeks, in many cases, for people to find out. The family of Bill Todd, merchant seaman, waited until 3 October 1945, seven weeks after the war had ended, to learn that their husband and father would not be coming home. That he had died on 19 April 1944. We can try to imagine the hopes and expectations that 15 August aroused in the hearts of this family; we can try to imagine, too, the frustra-tion and impatience in seeking news across those long seven weeks. But I doubt that we can understand the anguish and sense of shock when word came, officially, that Bill Todd was dead.

People also had to come to terms with the dawning of the atomic age. Journalists interviewed the 'man in the street' about this new weapon, explaining that it had produced a blast 2000 times greater than any bomb previously used. A chemist from Vaucluse admitted that 'the consequences are frightening . . . we shouldn't feel so sure that it won't bounce back on us one day in another war.' Three Methodist clergymen in Sydney tried to encourage some debate about the ethical implications of the bomb, the use of which, they claimed, was a 'devastating blow' to the Allies' claim 'to the moral leadership of the world.' Largely, though, Australians seemed indifferent. Either shocked by the magnitude of what had happened and its implications, or unable to comprehend it. Nevertheless there was an edge to the peace cele-brations. To help people to understand the scope of this new weapon, the *Age* printed a map showing how great the devastation would have been if the bomb had fallen on Melbourne. The map showed the destruction of the entire city centre, as far away as South Yarra and Toorak to the south and Brunswick to the north. The shock waves would have been so extensive, the paper reported, that windows would have rattled in Echuca, on Victoria's northern border.

Tom Blamey was on Morotai when peace came. He had been in Canberra on 31 July in conference with Ben Chifley and other ministers, and had then been to see for himself what the Australians had done at Balikpapan. The British suggested includ-ing some Australians in their peace delegation but the Australian government was having none of that, instructing Blamey that, at the surrender ceremony, he was to sign on behalf of his government.

When Tom Blamey stepped forward to sign on 2 September 1945, on board USS *Missouri* in Tokyo Harbour, he had with him other senior Australian air force, navy and army officers. He alone, of all of them, had been in senior command since the Australian government first decided to recruit and despatch an expeditionary force to the European war. That thought must have given Tom Blamey a great sense of satisfaction. And he would also have derived particular satisfaction because he was signing on behalf of the Australian government, an independent party to the peace now, but a part of a force only, a participant merely in the Empire's war six years earlier.

Yet the British connection in Australia remained strong. Also on board *Missouri*, as an observer, was Lord Wakehurst, the governor of New South Wales, indeed that state's last 'imported' governor. Formerly a conservative member of the House of Commons for Sussex, Wakehurst had been governor in Sydney since 1937. He was on leave in 1945 and was touring some of the Australian battle areas when the war ended. The governor had his movie camera with him on *Missouri*—he was a keen amateur cameraman—but so overwhelming were the emotions for him that morning that his hand wobbled too much for the film to be of any use. It is a nice final image of the war, though. The Australian general signing the peace as the representative of his independent nation; the King's representative in New South Wales on hand to record proceedings. And the American Caesar, Douglas MacArthur, just behind Tom Blamey as he signed, keeping an eye on it all.

EPILOGUE

Bob Menzies became prime minister again in December 1949 in elections that saw a substantial swing away from Ben Chifley's Labor government. One of the first matters that Menzies wanted addressed was what he believed was the lack of proper recognition for Australia's Second World War military leaders, who Menzies thought Chifley had neglected. Knighthoods for the generals, that kind of thing. High on Menzies' list was the promotion of Tom Blamey to field marshal, Australia's first.

Oh no, old boy, they chuckled in London, the field marshal's baton is never held by a soldier from the dominions. Not done, don't you know? And what of Field Marshal Jan Christian Smuts of South Africa, Menzies countered? Well yes, but a field marshal can only be a chap on the army's active list, and of course old Tom retired soon after the war ended. Norman Carlyon, one of Tom Blamey's strongest supporters, reported all this some years later as an example of London putting the colonies down yet again. But might it not have been, rather, that there were very few in

London who wanted to see Blamey promoted? He was not popular there, had not been so during the war. As it was in Australia, too; there was no public clamour for any further recognition for the retired general. Menzies pushed hard. Tom Blamey was brought out of retirement, briefly, placed on the active list and promoted. What was it between Blamey and Menzies, people wondered.

Announced Field Marshal in the King's birthday honours list of June 1950, Blamey received his baton from Governor-General William McKell in September because by then Tom Blamey was too ill to go to London to be honoured by the King in person, as would have been expected. Instead Blamey received his baton sitting in a wheelchair in a sunroom at Melbourne's Heidelberg Repatriation Hospital. By then Tom Blamey was paralysed in both legs, too tired to talk much, but he was dressed in his field marshal's uniform, with seven rows of ribbons on his chest, and in attendance at the ceremony alongside the governor-general were Blamey's wife and son, other members of his family, the Victorian governor, the prime minister, other ministers and 18 of his wartime generals. One of the men Tom Blamey had sacked in Papua New Guinea in 1942, Syd Rowell, was now chief of the general staff and waiting in attendance on the field marshal ex officio, as it were. Blamey said that 'maybe it is to [the men with whom he had served in war] that this baton is due.' The men who had made him look good. Men like Syd Rowell, Arnold Potts, Ralph Honner and tens of thousands of others.

Tom Blamey died in May 1951; there was a statue, eventually, near Melbourne's Shrine of Remembrance, but he faded from the popular memory more quickly than might have been expected. Melbourne had its Monash University by 1962, honouring the name of Australia's greatest First World War general—not promoted field marshal—but for Blamey there was precious little recognition. Norman Carlyon produced a book in 1980 entitled *I Remember Blamey*, a strange title that seemed to imply that none of Carlyon's readers would remember. In that book, in its last chapter, Carlyon speaks of the crowds lining the route to the cemetery for the field marshal's funeral. Carlyon writes that he was startled by the number of people and their reverential attitude. 'I thought', he writes, 'what a contrast the scene was to that war-time day in George Street, Sydney, when I had ridden beside Blamey and heard the unmistakable hissing and booing of a crowd which had made its own hasty judgement of him'. What a note on which to end his book. That in wartime, a crowd of Australian people, watching with pride Australian soldiers as they marched to war, would boo and hiss the man who was leading them. This was not a drunken rabble misbehaving in herd instinct; these were Australians passing judgement on a man they thought did not deserve to be the leader of their boys.

Heritage 200 was one of those silly ideas that seem to surface when nations want to celebrate their own achievements. As a part of the 1988 celebrations for the bicentenary of British settlement at Sydney Cove, Heritage 200 would identify the 'people who made Australia great'—all 200 of them. Beryl Beaurepaire, once Bedggood, was co-chair of the project and therefore a prominent selector of the top 200 Australians, those who had made 'positive contributions to making Australia what it is today'. There were nine selectors altogether, including an historian, a trade unionist, a medical scientist, a distinguished former public servant, a sports commentator, a former parliamentarian; it was that kind of committee. Alan Coates, company director and a former Australian soldier was co-chair with Beryl. Born in 1923, Alan Coates had enlisted in 1942, was discharged in 1946 and had reached the rank of lieutenant.

Blamey's name came to the selectors at their meeting in November 1987. You would have thought the case for his inclusion in the top 200 was inescapable: served with distinction in the First World War, led Australia throughout the Second World War as an active commander in several theatres of war, honoured by the King and his people as Australia's only field marshal. Yet Blamey was not included: 'has anyone in this room served under the prick?' one of the selectors asked. 'I buried three men because of his arrogance . . . I'll never forgive him.' Beryl Beaurepaire remembers that the selector then threatened to resign from the committee if Blamey got up and would explain publicly why he had resigned. The committee released a short commentary on its selection proce-dures when the final list was promulgated. There would be debate about the inclusions and exclusions, the committee said, stating the obvious, but there were some inclusions about whom every Australian would agree, they said, for example, Flynn of the Inland and John Monash.

John Monash the automatic selection and Tom Blamey the pariah. That demands explanation. Monash was no saint in his private life, if judged by the harsh standards prevailing in the early twentieth century. And Charles Bean, well placed to observe the Australians at Gallipoli and in France, did not believe that Monash was the best person to command the Australian corps on its formation in 1918, and rated a number of Australian generals better leaders than Monash. Yet by 1987 Monash was an automatic inclusion among the small number of Australians 'who made Australia great'. Perhaps it was the enduring legacy of the Great War that promoted Monash to glory. Those who fought a second time would forever be in the shadow of those who had gone before them. Gallipoli is a word that resonates more powerfully with Australians now than it did 50 years ago. The First World War battlefields still draw Australians to them in a way that Second World War battlefields do not.

Perhaps there is a sense, still, that Australia had made a real difference in the Great War in a way that Australians could not in the Second World War. Australians fought well at El Alamein and stopped the Japanese at Milne Bay and on the Kokoda Track. Although there were Australians in the air on D-Day there were literally only a handful of them on the ground, and General Eisenhower that day had, what, some three million men at his disposal? You can make a strong and compelling argument that it was General Zhukov and the mighty Red Army that freed Europe from the scourge of Nazism with his numbers and his soldiers' implacable determination. And it was the weight of American numbers, on the battlefield and in factories, shipyards and laboratories that finally defeated the Japanese. The Australians were dwarfed in this company.

Yet the Australian story deserves to be told if for no other reason than it is our story. It is a story of heroism, ingenuity, determination, good leadership, generosity and success. It is a story of turning points, when the nation might have failed to reach the high standards Australians then expected, but did not fail. It is a story which involved just about every Australian alive during the war. It is a story, too, that aroused and still arouses strong passions.

The impact of the Second World War was momentous for Australia. So many men and women in uniform and in battle in all parts of the world; so many of the rest of the nation working flat out for the war effort. A national government that faced the most difficult circumstances any Australian government has ever faced. A government that managed to retain for Australia some independence and voice in a war that was so vast in its numbers, impacts and consequences. Yet there were Australians in every theatre of war trying their hardest to defeat the twin evils of Nazism and Japanese imperialism. Look at the Anzac Day march banner of No. 10 Squadron RAAF, on display for the 60th time in Melbourne on Anzac Day 2006. The banner lists the squadron's battle honours: Bay of Biscay, Gibraltar, Atlantic, Malta. The work of one Australian squadron that seemed perhaps remote from the Australian story of the war. The Australian story was vastly more complex, as the squadron's banner suggests. Australians were everywhere.

More than a decade ago the Australian War Memorial hosted an exhibition on loan from a museum in Prague. It was the memorial's decision to seek the exhibition and one of its staff selected the images for display in Canberra. They were the drawings and paintings of children in a concentration camp at Terezin, awaiting deportation to Auschwitz and death—the ordinary works of children such as parents and grandparents proudly paste on their walls and fridges. Few of the children drew scenes from the life they were then living, instead they called on the stories and fables they had been told in earlier, happier times. The drawings showed the children were surviving in a fantasy world to try to overcome the horror of the camp in which they lived. One little boy drew a very rudimentary kangaroo, perhaps dreaming of a country so far away that it could not, surely, know war and terror, the loss of parents, the brutality of a concentration camp.

What has this exhibition of the drawings of Holocaust children to do with the story of Australia at war, a critic asked. In Australia we tell our story, let the peoples of other nations deal with their own stories, he continued. But, though they might only have dimly perceived it, Australian servicemen and women had enlisted and fought to free those children from the concentration camp and to snatch them from a horrible death at Auschwitz. To liberate people in captivity everywhere and to prevent the domination of the world by evil men and evil ideologies; that was why Australian men and women gave themselves to the war, and were prepared to give their lives. This was the noble cause for which the Australians fought, and they did, indeed, fight for a better world.

'The strength of a nation is determined by the character of its people,' John Curtin had said in the dark days of 1942. The Australians who fought and lived through the Second World War had shown themselves to be generous, determined and able. They have every reason to look at their nation with pride and satisfaction.

INDEX